FEDERALISM

FEDERALISM

Robert P. Sutton

Major Issues in American History
Randall M. Miller, Series Editor

GREENWOOD PRESS
Westport, Connecticut • London

Library of Congress Cataloging-in-Publication Data

Sutton, Robert P.
  Federalism / Robert P. Sutton
    p.   cm.—(Major issues in American history, ISSN 1535-3192)
  Includes bibliographical references and index.
  ISBN 0-313-31531-0 (alk. paper)
    1. Federal government—United States—History.   2. Federal government—United
States—History—Sources.   I. Title.   II. Series.
JK311.S87   2002
320.473'049—dc21   2002016102

British Library Cataloguing in Publication Data is available.

Library of Congress Catalog Card Number: 2002016102
ISBN: 0-313-31531-0
ISSN: 1535-3192

First published in 2002

Greenwood Press, 88 Post Road West, Westport, CT 06881
An imprint of Greenwood Publishing Group, Inc.
www.greenwood.com

Printed in the United States of America

The paper used in this book complies with the
Permanent Paper Standard issued by the National
Information Standards Organization (Z39.48–1984).

10 9 8 7 6 5 4 3 2 1

*To
My Family*

Contents

Series Foreword

This series of books presents major issues in American history as they have developed since the republic's inception to their present incarnation. The issues range across the spectrum of American experience and encompass political, economic, social, and cultural concerns. By focusing on the "major issues" in American history, the series emphasizes the importance of an issues-centered approach to teaching and thinking about America's past. *Major Issues in American History* thus reframes historical inquiry in terms of themes and problems rather than as mere chronology. In so doing, the series addresses the current, pressing need among educators and policymakers for case studies charting the development of major issues over time, so as to make it possible to approach such issues intelligently in our time.

The series is premised on the belief that understanding America demands grasping the contentious nature of its past and applying that understanding to current issues in politics, law, government, society, and culture. If "America" was born, and remains, as an idea and an experiment, as so many thinkers and observers have argued, issues inevitably have shaped whatever that America was and is. In 1801, in his presidential inaugural, Thomas Jefferson reminded Americans that the great strength of the new nation resided in the broad consensus citizens shared as to the rightness and necessity of republican government and the Constitution. That consensus, Jefferson continued, made dissent possible and tolerable, and, we might add, encouraged dissent and debate about critical issues thereafter. Every generation of Americans has wrestled with such issues as defining and defending freedom(s), determining America's place in the world, waging war and making peace, receiving and assimilating new peoples, balancing church and state, forming a "more perfect union," and pursuing "happiness." American identity(ies) and interest(s) are not fixed. A nation of many peoples on the move across space and up and down the socioeconomic ladder cannot have it so. A nation charged with ensuring that, in Lincoln's words, "government of the people, by the people, and for the people shall not perish from the earth" cannot have it so. A nation whose heroes are not only soldiers and statesmen but also ex-slaves, women reformers, inventors, thinkers, and cowboys and Indians cannot have it so. Americans have never rested content locked into set molds in thinking and doing—not so long as dissent and difference are built into the character of a people that dates its birth to an American Revolution and annually celebrates that lineage. As such, Americans have been, and are, by heritage and habit an issues-oriented people.

We are also a political people. Issues as varied as race relations, labor organizing, women's place in the work force, the practice of religious beliefs, immigration, westward movement, and environmental protection have been, and remain, matters of public concern and debate and readily intrude into politics. A people committed to "rights" invariably argues for them, low voter turnout in recent elections notwithstanding. All the major issues in American history have involved political controversies as to their meaning and application. But the extent to which issues assume a political cast varies.

As the public interest spread to virtually every aspect of life during the twentieth century—into boardrooms, ballparks, and even bedrooms—the political compass enlarged with it. In time, every economic, social, and cultural issue of consequence in the United States has entered the public realm of debate and political engagement. Questions of rights—for example, to free speech, to freedom of religion, to equality before the law—and authority are political by nature. So, too, are questions about war and society, foreign policy, law and order, the delivery of public services, the control of the nation's borders, and access to and the uses of public land and resources. The books in *Major Issues in American History* take up just those issues. Thus, all the books in this series build political and public policy concerns into their basic framework.

The format for the series speaks directly to the issues-oriented character of the American people and the democratic polity and to the teaching of issues-centered history. The issues-centered approach to history views the past thematically. Such a history respects chronology but does not attempt to recite a single narrative or single historical chronology of "facts." Rather, issues-centered history is problem-solving history. It organizes historical inquiry around a series of questions central to understanding the character and functions of American life, culture, ideas, politics, and institutions. Such questions invariably derive from current concerns that demand historical perspective. Whether determining the role of women and minorities and shaping public policy, or considering the "proper" relationship between church and state, or thinking about U.S. military obligations in the global context, to name several persistent issues, the teacher and student—indeed, responsible citizens everywhere—must ask such questions as "how and why did the present circumstance and interests come to be as they are" and "what other choices as to policy and practice have there been" so as to measure the dimensions and point the direction of the issue. History matters in that regard.

Each book in the series focuses on a particular issue, with an eye to encouraging readers and users to consider how Americans at different times engaged the issue based on the particular values, interests, and political and social structures of the day. As such, each book is also necessarily events-based in that the key event that triggered public concern and debate about a major issue at a particular moment serves as the case study for the issue as it was understood and presented during that historical period. Each book offers a historical narrative overview of a major issue as it evolved; the narrative provides both the context for understanding the issue's place in the larger American experience and the touchstone for considering the ways Americans encountered and engaged the issue at different times. A timeline further establishes the chronology and place of the issue in American history. The core of each book is the series of between ten to fifteen case studies of watershed events that defined the issue, arranged chronologically to make it possible to track the development of the issue closely over time. Each case study stands as a separate chapter. Each case study opens with a historical overview of the event and a discussion of the significant contemporary opposing views of the issue as occasioned by the event. A selection of four to nine critical primary documents (printed whole or in excerpts and introduced with brief headnotes) from the period under review presents differing points of view on the issue. In some volumes, each chapter also includes an annotated research guide of print and nonprint sources to guide further research and reflection on the event and the issue. Each volume in the series concludes with a general bibliography that provides ready reference to the key works on the subject at issue.

Such an arrangement ensures that readers and users—students and teachers alike—will approach the major issues within a problem-solving framework. Indeed, the design of the series and each book in it demands that students and teachers understand that the crucial issues of American history have histories and that the significance of those issues might best be discovered and recovered by understanding how Americans at different times addressed them, shaped them, and bequeathed them to the next generation. Such a dialectic for each issue encourages a comparative perspective not only in seeing America's past but also, and perhaps even more so, in thinking about its present. Individually and collectively, the books in the *Major Issues in American History* thereby demonstrate anew William Faulkner's dictum that the past is never past.

Randall M. Miller
Series Editor

Preface

In 1776 American patriot leaders, in separating from English constitutional authority, created what they hoped was a viable substitute for the sovereignty of Parliament, a republic based on divided sovereignty, or federalism. In the Articles of Confederation they embarked on an unprecedented experiment. Always before, sovereignty (literally meaning "supreme power") had been seen as indivisible, the concept of two supreme powers in one body politic being incongruous. Unfortunately, the first experiment with federalism did not work. The structure of the Articles was lopsided. It gave so much power to the states and so little to Congress that within a decade the government collapsed. In 1787 at Philadelphia, fifty-five delegates from twelve states convened to try again. This time they invented a form of government whose basic operating constitutional principle was balanced federalism.

The delegates at the Constitutional Convention had just experienced historical lessons that spoke to them with ringing urgency. One, the most recent, was the hard reality that a government where the states were supreme in almost all areas was unworkable. The second lesson, twelve years of arguing with England over Parliament's sovereignty, convinced them that a supreme central power was equally unacceptable, indeed dangerous. So, in Philadelphia they crafted a constitution based on balanced and divided powers, giving some to the central government and reserving some to the states. But they never addressed the question of what would happen if a future conflict developed over one side abusing or expanding its legitimate power. This unanswered question is what this book is all about. It discusses the issues and controversies surrounding the history of federalism from 1787 and presents original documents that deal with watershed events of that story.

The narrative begins with a discussion of how federalism first came to be defined in the Articles of Confederation, the Philadelphia Constitutional Convention, and subsequent state ratification conventions. Then it examines the problems and issues associated with eight major crises over federalism between 1798 and 2000. These are presented chronologically, beginning with the first serious contest of congressional versus state power in the passing and enforcing of the Sedition Act, and ending with the recent controversy over federal intrusion into state criminal law regarding abortion in *Roe v. Wade*.

In a documentary history of such sweeping chronology I owe a special debt of gratitude to certain individuals without whose assistance this study could never have reached fruition. Randall Miller's thoughtful criticisms from the earliest rough drafts were absolutely crucial in helping me avoid costly mistakes of omission and commission. Sheila H. Nollen, Professor of Libraries at Western Illinois University and also a professional historian, showed me how to access Supreme Court decisions, congressional debates, and other public documents through the Internet. And Abigail Sutton Wondrasek and Rebecca M. Sutton, my daughters, both historians, were indispensable in their research of the Internet to locate nonprint items in cyberspace for each of the chapters.

Chronology of Events

1776–1777   The Articles of Confederation are drafted by the Continental Congress and submitted to the states for ratification on November 17, 1777.

1781   Articles are ratified and go into effect.

1786   In September Shays's Rebellion breaks out in Massachusetts and delegates from five states attend the Annapolis Convention.

1787   Constitutional Convention meets in Philadelphia from May until September and drafts the Constitution of the United States of America.

1788   Eleven state conventions ratify the Constitution. The first national elections are held in November.

1789   The new government under the Constitution begins in March.

1790   Alexander Hamilton, in his *Report on Public Credit*, recommends funding of the national debt at par and that the federal government assume the payment of all state debts. In his *Report on the Bank of the United States* he announces the creation of a national bank.

1791   Hamilton's reports, especially the second one, bring about
                the first debate over the legitimate use of federal power. In
                February, Hamilton argues for a "loose" construction of the
                Constitution to permit Congress to pass laws that are "nec-
                essary and proper." The opposition, led by James Madison
                and Thomas Jefferson, stands for "strict" construction, tak-
                ing the position that if any proposed statute is not author-
                ized by the Constitution, an amendment to the document is
                required to allow enactment of the federal law.

1798–1799   Congress passes the Sedition Act in July. Thomas Jefferson
                and James Madison secretly write the Virginia and Kentucky
                Resolutions.

1803   In February, John Marshall delivers the unanimous opinion
                for the Supreme Court in the landmark decision *Marbury v.
                Madison*, which establishes the principle of judicial review.

1810   In *Fletcher v. Peck*, the Supreme Court first applies judicial
                review to a state law.

1819   In *Dartmouth College v. Woodward*, the Supreme Court rules
                that a state's revocation of a college charter is an unconsti-
                tutional impairment of a contract. In *McCulloch v. Maryland*
                the Court declares that the "implied powers" of Congress
                are constitutional and puts all federal institutions beyond the
                authority of state law.

1820   The Missouri Compromise is adopted.

1821   In *Cohens v. Virginia*, the Supreme Court reasserts its earlier
                decision in *Martin v. Hunter's Lessee* (1816) that the Court has
                the power to review decisions of state courts.

1824   In *Gibbons v. Ogden*, the Supreme Court establishes the prin-
                ciple of broad construction of the Constitution and asserts
                federal control of interstate commerce.

1828   John Calhoun writes *The South Carolina Exposition*, introduc-
                ing his argument of state nullification of federal law, against
                the Tariff of Abominations.

1830   The Webster-Hayne Senate debates held.

1831   John Calhoun resigns as vice president.

1832   In November, South Carolina passes the Ordinance of Nul-
                lification. In December, President Andrew Jackson issues his
                Executive Proclamation condemning nullification as treason.

In *Worcester v. Georgia*, the Supreme Court sets aside state licensing statutes because they violate federal treaties with the Cherokee Nation. Jackson refuses to enforce the Court's ruling favoring the Cherokees.

1833   On January 21, Congress passes the Force Act. The Compromise Tariff is enacted on February 26. South Carolina repeals its nullification law in March—although at the same time it nullifies the Force Act.

1835   South Carolina adopts "Resolutions on Abolitionist Propaganda," which call upon the postmaster general to stop the circulation of "fanatical" abolitionist literature. President Jackson, in his annual message to Congress, denounces abolitionists as plotting to start a civil war.

1837   Chief Justice Roger B. Taney, in writing the opinion for the Supreme Court in *Charles River Bridge v. Warren Bridge*, holds that no monopoly or any other power can be implied in the charter of the Charles River Bridge Company, that corporations must be limited by the doctrine of *ultra vires* (acts beyond the powers of a corporation) and held to the explicit powers written in the charter, and that they have a social responsibility to the community.

1842   Justice Joseph Story, in *Prigg v. Pennsylvania*, declares the Pennsylvania "personal liberty" law abrogating the 1793 federal fugitive slave statute unconstitutional and argues that Congress's authority under the Constitution renders all such state laws invalid, but at the same time acknowledges that a state has no obligation to provide the police power to enforce federal laws.

1846   On August 8, the Wilmot Proviso, prohibiting slavery in any territory annexed from Mexico as a result of the Mexican-American War, is introduced in the House of Representatives.

1850   The debate over the slavery extension question culminates in a Senate debate on federal authority versus that of the states that eventually results in the Compromise of 1850. Congress, as a part of the Compromise, passes a more stringent Fugitive Slave Act expanding federal authority in recovering alleged fugitives.

1854   Congress passes the Kansas-Nebraska Act.

1857   In the *Dred Scott* case, the Supreme Court declares the Missouri Compromise unconstitutional and, in effect, says that Congress can do nothing to prohibit the movement of slavery into federal territories.

1859   In January, in *Ableman v. Booth*, the Supreme Court declares unconstitutional state "personal liberty" laws that had been enacted against the 1850 Fugitive Slave Act. In October, John Brown leads a raid on Harper's Ferry.

1860–1861   The secession crisis begins with Lincoln's election. By February 1861, seven states have seceded from the Union and formed the Confederate States of America at Montgomery, Alabama. Lincoln's refusal to compromise with secession and the fall of Ft. Sumter in April bring four more slave states into the Confederacy, and in June the Civil War begins.

1861   Congress enacts the first federal income tax of 3 percent on annual incomes above $800.

1862   Congress passes the first comprehensive tax law, which creates the Internal Revenue Bureau and sends a tax collector to every Union household.

1863   Lincoln issues the Emancipation Proclamation, following and confirming the preliminary Emancipation Proclamation of September 1862. Congress passes the National Bank Act, which eliminates the independent Treasury system and permits nationally chartered banks to issue bank notes supported by federal bonds. At the same time the act taxes state bank notes out of existence and creates a uniform national currency.

1864   Lincoln asks Congress for a constitutional ban on slavery.

1865   Civil War ends. The Thirteenth Amendment is ratified.

1865–1866   Southern states enact "black codes" severely limiting the civil rights of the ex-slaves.

1866   Congress begins Reconstruction by overriding President Andrew Johnson's veto of the second Freedmen's Bureau bill, essentially an attempt to enforce the Thirteenth Amendment in the South. Congress passes its first Civil Rights Act.

1867   Congress passes the First Reconstruction Act, providing for military rule in ten "unreconstructed" southern states.

1868   The Fourteenth Amendment is ratified.

1870   The Fifteenth Amendment is ratified.

1872   Congress passes the Amnesty Act, which pardons most of the ex-Confederates and prohibits only a few hundred from holding office.

1873   In the *Slaughterhouse Cases*, the Supreme Court declares that there are two kinds of citizenship, national and state, and that the Fourteenth Amendment does not give the federal government control over civil rights in the states.

1876   The Supreme Court, in *U.S. v. Cruikshank*, holds that the due process and equal protection clauses of the Fourteenth Amendment do not protect blacks from violence by whites.

1883   The Supreme Court, in the *Civil Rights Cases*, declares that the Fourteenth Amendment applies only when the states, as opposed to individuals, engage in acts of discrimination.

1887   Congress creates the Interstate Commerce Commission to provide for the first ongoing federal regulation of commerce among the states. It guarantees "reasonable and just" rates for railroads and prohibits rebates, rate discrimination, short and long hauls, and pooling.

1890   Congress passes the Sherman Antitrust Act.

1896   In *Plessy v. Ferguson*, the Supreme Court approves racial segregation by state law provided the different accommodations for the races are "separate but equal."

1920   The Nineteenth Amendment is ratified, giving women the right to vote in all elections.

1925   In *Gitlow v. New York*, the Supreme Court begins incorporating the First Amendment as a limitation on state constitutions.

1929   The stock market crashes in October.

1932   In *Powell v. Alabama* (the Scottsboro case), the Supreme Court incorporates the Sixth Amendment into the Fourteenth Amendment. President Herbert Hoover tries to save the banks by creating the Reconstruction Finance Corporation to provide loans to banks, insurance companies, and railroads. Congress appropriates $500 million for the corporation and gives it the authority to borrow up to $2 billion, a significant extension of federal fiscal authority before the New Deal.

1933   President Franklin D. Roosevelt lays the foundation of the
            New Deal during the "100 Days" by signing legislation cre-
            ating the Agricultural Adjustment Act (under which the fed-
            eral government establishes a system of price supports for
            specified farm products), the National Recovery Act (under
            which codes of fair competition are developed and workers
            are guaranteed the right to unionize and to collective bar-
            gaining), and the Tennessee Valley Authority (which creates
            a massive federal program of dam construction along the
            Tennessee River to generate electricity and control flooding).

1935   Senator Huey Long announces his "Share Our Wealth" plan
            as a radical alternative to the New Deal. The Supreme Court,
            in Schechter v. U.S., declares the National Industrial Recovery
            Act (NIRA) unconstitutional. Congress passes the Wagner
            Act, which reestablishes Section 7-a of the NIRA, which
            guarantees workers the right to unionize and to collective
            bargaining and creates the National Labor Relations Board
            (NLRB) to enforce fair labor practices. Congress also passes
            the Social Security Act.

1936   In January, the Supreme Court, in U.S. v. Butler, declares the
            AAA unconstitutional. In February, it unanimously decides,
            in Brown v. Mississippi, that confessions in a state murder
            trial obtained by whipping are violations of the Fifth
            Amendment.

1937   In February, Roosevelt submits his court-packing plan to
            Congress in the Judiciary Reorganization Bill. In April, the
            Supreme Court, in NLRB v. Jones & Laughlin Steel Corp., re-
            verses its opposition to the New Deal and declares the Wag-
            ner Act constitutional. In West Coast Hotel Co. v. Parrish, it
            upholds a state minimum wage law. In Stewart Machine Co.
            v. Davis, it approves the major provisions of the Social Se-
            curity Act.

1941   In U.S. v. Darby, the Supreme Court upholds the Fair Labor
            Standards Act. President Roosevelt issues Executive Order
            No. 8802, which prohibits racial discrimination in defense
            industries.

1942   In Wickard v. Filburn, the Supreme Court upholds the second
            AAA. A series of new federal agencies is created for the war.
            These include the War Production Board to oversee military
            production; the National War Labor Board to handle labor-
            management disputes; the War Manpower Commission to

organize labor supply for defense industries; the Office of Price Administration to regulate retail prices; the Office of War Information to build public support for the war; and the Manhattan Project to develop the atomic bomb.

1944   In *Smith v. Allwright*, the Supreme Court strikes down the "white primary."

1946   President Harry S. Truman creates the President's Committee on Civil Rights. The Supreme Court, in *Morgan v. Virginia*, prohibits segregation on interstate carriers.

1947   The Committee on Civil Rights issues its report, entitled *To Secure These Rights*. The Supreme Court, in *Louisiana ex rel. Francis v. Resweber*, first addresses the constitutionality of the death penalty.

1948   On February 2, President Truman delivers his Civil Rights Message to Congress and on July 26 issues Executive Order 9981, desegregating the armed forces. In *Shelley v. Kraemer*, the Supreme Court first shows its backing for the NAACP fight against *Plessy v. Ferguson* by declaring racially restricted covenants in the sale of real estate unconstitutional because they violate the equal protection clause of the Fourteenth Amendment.

1949   In *Wolf v. Colorado*, the Supreme Court rules that while the "exclusionary rule" does not apply to the states, the Fourteenth Amendment does apply.

1950   The Supreme Court, in *Sweatt v. Painter*, rules that the "separate but equal" standard of *Plessy v. Ferguson* is not attainable in state-supported law schools. It declares that forcing Herman Sweatt to attend an inferior law school for blacks in Texas violates his right to equal protection and mandates that he be admitted to the University of Texas Law School. In *McLaurin v. Oklahoma State Regents for Higher Education*, a companion case to *Sweatt v. Painter*, it decides that forcing a black graduate student to study, eat, and sit in separate facilities creates a "badge of inferiority" and is unconstitutional and that all-white graduate school education violates the equal protection clause of the Fourteenth Amendment.

1951   The Federal District Court in South Carolina rules against segregated public schools in that state.

1954   In *Brown v. Board of Education of Topeka* (Brown I), the Supreme Court unanimously declares that the "separate but equal" doctrine when applied to public education is a violation of the Fourteenth Amendment.

1955   In *Brown v. Board of Education of Topeka* (Brown II), the Supreme Court directs desegregation to proceed with "all deliberate speed." On December 1, in Montgomery, Alabama, Rosa Parks refuses to surrender her bus seat to a white man and is arrested. The Reverend Martin Luther King, Jr., leads a nonviolent boycott of the buses, bolstered by a Supreme Court decision in 1956 declaring Montgomery's segregation law on public transportation unconstitutional.

1956   "Massive resistance" of whites to the *Brown* decisions spreads throughout the South.

1957   At Little Rock, Arkansas, Governor Orval Faubus calls out the National Guard to prevent black students from attending the city's Central High School. President Dwight D. Eisenhower sends federal troops to maintain order and enforce the federal ruling on desegregation.

1958   In September, the Supreme Court, in *Cooper v. Aaron*, unanimously orders desegregation of the Little Rock schools to proceed forthwith and states that only the Court can conclusively interpret the Constitution.

1960   Black sit-in protests against public segregated facilities begin in Greensboro, North Carolina, and nonviolent civil disobedience spreads throughout the South.

1961   President John F. Kennedy forms the first federal Commission on the Status of Women. The Supreme Court, in *Mapp v. Ohio*, rules that the Fourth Amendment protects citizens from a "reckless search" by police.

1962   Governor George C. Wallace of Alabama attempts to stop desegregation of the state university. Governor Ross Barnett of Mississippi attempts to halt the admission of blacks to the state university, and President Kennedy orders federal marshals and troops to Mississippi to force compliance.

1963   Betty Friedan's *The Feminine Mystique* is published. On April 16, Martin Luther King writes "Letter from a Birmingham Jail." On June 11, President Kennedy delivers his Civil Rights Address on television. The Supreme Court, in *Gideon v. Wainwright*, rules that a person on trial for a felony is entitled to a lawyer.

1964   Congress, urged by President Lyndon Johnson, passes the Civil Rights Act. Congress enacts the National Wilderness Preservation System Act, which sets aside 9.1 million acres of wilderness as national forests. The Commission on the Status of Women publishes its report, *American Women*. The Supreme Court, in *Malloy v. Hogan*, compels the states to respect the Fifth Amendment's prohibition of self-incrimination. In *Escobedo v. Illinois*, it rules that a lawyer must be present during police interrogation.

1965   On March 15, President Lyndon B. Johnson addresses a joint session of Congress on civil rights. Congress passes the Voting Rights Act. The Supreme Court, in *Griswold v. Connecticut*, discovers the right of privacy in the penumbras of the Bill of Rights. President Johnson signs the Medicare and Medicare acts, as well as the Omnibus Housing Act to subsidize rents for poor families. Congress approves the establishment of the new cabinet-level Department of Housing and Urban Development (HUD), and the National Foundation on the Arts and the Humanities. Congress appropriates federal funds for colleges and universities for scholarships, loans, research equipment, and library acquisitions.

1966   President Johnson sends his "Message on the Civil Rights Bill" to Congress. The Supreme Court hands down the landmark decision *Miranda v. Arizona*, which guarantees citizens interrogated by police the Fifth Amendment's protection against self-incrimination.

1968   Congress passes the Fair Housing Act to build federally financed public housing. It also passes the Truth-in-Lending Act to protect consumers. Congress enacts laws to protect scenic rivers and expand the National Park system. Congress passes the second Civil Rights Act of the Johnson administration. The Supreme Court, in *Green v. County School Board of New Kent County*, declares that the "freedom of choice" plans that had permitted racially dual school systems to exist by state law are "discriminatory and unacceptable." In *United States v. O'Brien*, it upholds a federal law against the destruction of draft registration cards because the law does not infringe upon freedom of speech. Richard M. Nixon wins the presidential election in part on his promise to restore the balance between the states and the federal government.

1970   President Nixon reluctantly signs the Environmental Protection Act and the Clean Air Act. He approves the Occupational Safety and Health Administration (OSHA) to enforce federal standards of health and safety.

1971   The Supreme Court, in *Swann v. Charlotte-Mecklenburg Board of Education*, approves school busing to achieve desegregation. The Court, in *Reed v. Reed*, decides that gender discrimination violates the Fourteenth Amendment's equal protection clause. The Twenty-Sixth Amendment gives the vote to eighteen-year-old Americans. Congress passes a bill to establish a national daycare system for working parents, but it is vetoed by President Nixon. Nixon imposes wage and price controls.

1972   Congress adopts the Equal Rights Amendment and sends it to the states for ratification. The Supreme Court, in *Furman v. Georgia*, for the first time strikes down the death penalty as a violation of the Eighth Amendment. Federal executive agencies, following regulations of the Office of Federal Contract Compliance, require employers to provide written affirmative action plans to correct "underutilization" of minorities and women. Congress mandates that female college athletes have the same financial support as male athletes. Congress passes the Clean Water Act and the Pesticide Control Act. President Nixon, as part of his "New Federalism" to counter liberal policies that expanded the power of the federal government, has Congress pass a Revenue Sharing Act that distributes $30 billion over a five-year time period back to state and local governments to decide what problems should be dealt with and how to deal with them.

1973   In *Roe v. Wade*, the Supreme Court declares that the right of privacy includes a woman's right to have an abortion up to the last three months of her pregnancy. In *Frontiero v. Richardson*, it holds that job-related classifications based on sex are a violation of the Fifth Amendment's due process clause and are "inherently suspect."

1974   In *United States v. Nixon*, the Supreme Court unanimously orders President Nixon to release all of the White House tapes regarding Watergate. Nixon resigns. Congress passes the Freedom of Information Act over President Gerald Ford's veto. Congress passes the Fair Campaign Practices Act to demand accountability in campaign financing.

1975   In *People v. Brisedine*, the California Supreme Court claims that the state constitution protects its citizens from unwarranted searches.

1977   The Supreme Court, in *Macer v. Roe*, applies *Roe v. Wade* to
            two indigent women in Connecticut who requested an abor-
            tion under Medicaid. Congress agrees to establish a new
            cabinet-level department, the Department of Energy.

1978   The Supreme Court, in *Regents of the University of California
            v. Bakke*, strike down rigid racial quotas used to achieve ra-
            cial diversification in admissions to professional schools.

1979   The Supreme Court approves racially based set-aside pro-
            grams in *United Steelworkers v. Weber*.

1980   In *Harris v. McRae*, the Supreme Court upholds the consti-
            tutionality of the Hyde Amendments (1976, 1977, 1978,
            1979), which prohibit the use of federal Medicaid funds for
            abortions except when the life of the mother is endangered.

1981   President Ronald Reagan has Congress pass the Economic
            Recovery Tax Act, which gives a 25 percent income tax re-
            duction to all taxpayers.

1982   The Senate adopts the "right to life" amendments to the
            Constitution and passes the Human Life Statute. In 1980 the
            Equal Rights Amendment is given a two-year extension to
            be ratified, but by 1982 it falls three short of the thirty-eight
            states required for ratification. Congress renews the Voting
            Rights Act of 1965.

1986   Against the strong opposition of the state of California, Con-
            gress enacts the Immigration and Control Act, which im-
            poses new federal border security measures and mandates
            that employers of immigrants certify their workers as legal
            residents.

1989   In *Webster v. Reproductive Health Services*, the Supreme Court
            upholds state restrictions imposed on abortions. This deci-
            sion also upholds the right of states to add new restrictions
            on access to any abortion facility. Pennsylvania enacts the
            landmark Abortion Control Act requiring a waiting period
            before an abortion can be performed in the state and paren-
            tal permission for a minor to receive an abortion. President
            Reagan signs an executive order that withholds federal
            funds from clinics that counsel abortion. The Senate Com-
            mittee on the Judiciary holds televised hearings on the nom-
            ination of Robert H. Bork to the Supreme Court that focus
            on Bork's understanding of "original intent." The Court, in
            Texas v. Johnson, sets aside a state law prohibiting flag des-
            ecration because the law serves no legitimate governmental

interest and is a violation of the First Amendment's protection of "symbolic speech."

1991   The Supreme Court decides, in *UAW v. Johnson Controls*, that emphasizing biological differences between men and women in the workplace denies women "equal employment opportunity" and that a woman herself should decide under what conditions she wants to work.

1994   Speaker of the House of Representatives Newt Gingrich persuades Congress to support "The Contract with America," ten measures to revitalize the so-called conservative revolution: a balanced budget, tax cuts, term limits for congressmen, promotion of family values, a broader death penalty, and restrictions on welfare programs. When President Clinton threatens to veto the budget cutbacks, the Republican-controlled Congress refuses to yield and in effect twice shuts down the federal government.

1996   The Supreme Court, in *Seminole Tribe v. Florida*, blocks the right of states to sue in federal court for a violation of federal law. The Fifth Circuit Court of Appeals, in *Hopewood v. Texas*, rules against consideration of race to achieve a diverse student body in law schools. Voters in California pass Proposition 209 against affirmative action and eliminate racial and gender preferences in both college admissions and hiring for state jobs. President Clinton signs a sweeping welfare reform bill that reverses the social welfare policies of the Democratic Party. The new law stops the food stamp program and ends federal aid to poor children, turning the program over to the states.

1997   The Wisconsin Supreme Court, in the case of "Ms. M. W." (*State of Wisconsin v. Kruzicki*, 95–2480-W), rules that the fetus is not a person and that the courts and the law have no jurisdiction over it.

1999   In *Alden v. Maine*, the Supreme Court rules that individuals cannot bring suits in state courts for violation of a federal law. In *Florida Prepaid v. College Savings Bank and the U.S.*, it immunizes states from suits over federal patents and trademarks.

2000   On January 10, in *Dickerson v. U.S.*, the Supreme Court agrees to hear a case that would test the *Miranda* decision. In April, it hears oral arguments and decides in June that *Miranda* was a "constitutional decision" of the Court and declines to overrule it. In *Kimel v. Florida Board of Regents*, the Court rules that Congress has no power to compel states to obey the 1967 Age Discrimination in Employment Act and that state government employees cannot sue state employers in federal court.

2001   The Supreme Court's "federalism revolution," which since 1995 has placed new constraints on congressional laws and expanded the immunity of the states from federal power, results in two additional new decisions. In *Board of Trustees of the University of Alabama v. Garett*, the Court says that Congress has failed to show that discrimination against employees with disabilities is a matter of such constitutional importance as to justify federal intervention. In *Solid Waste Agency v. United States Army Corps of Engineers*, it holds that an Army Corps of Engineers regulation does not authorize the federal government to regulate the dredging of isolated ponds and wetlands.

1

Introduction

Federalism is the form of government in the United States where separate states are united under one central authority but with specific powers granted to both components in a written constitution. Patrick Henry coined the word in 1788 when, during the Virginia ratification convention debates over the proposed U.S. Constitution, he angrily asked, "Is this *federalism?*" But the idea had surfaced twelve years earlier in the Articles of Confederation as the solution to the challenge of creating a "national government" for the newly independent colonies. Unfortunately, that document gave too much power to the states and doomed this first experiment with federalism. In 1787 the Constitution replaced it with another, more balanced, version that has worked for over two centuries. During that time, however, the history of federalism has been incessantly disrupted by a constant debate between those who wanted to enlarge the central government and those who demanded that states' rights be strictly respected and even expanded.

Sometimes this debate has evoked eloquent language, as in Daniel Webster's 1830 peroration on the Union. Yet, at one point the passionate fight over federal powers regarding the protection of slavery tore the Union apart in a civil war. During Reconstruction after the war arguments over the use of federal power erupted in violence against newly enfranchised blacks and Republican governments in the South. In the late nineteenth century the federal government retreated from its temporary expansion of power in saving the Union and trying to remake the South. Whether in tolerating state-created racial segregation or striking down federal efforts to regulate the new industrial order, the federal courts limited federal authority in many areas of public life.

At the beginning of the twentieth century Progressive reformers wanted to enlarge the role of the federal government and solve glaring economic and social problems. With mixed success they sought federal legislation to regulate the workplace, protect labor unions, and promote "moral improvement." During the 1930s the New Deal redefined federalism and saved the economy by recognizing federal responsibility over many areas of public and private activity that previously had been unregulated or solely the purview of the states, including banking, the stock exchanges, and the workplace.

In the last half of the twentieth century federalism was the central issue in both black and women's civil rights. It was at the heart of a redefinition of criminal justice by the Warren Court. The liberal interpretation of it by this Court in turn became the target of a conservative attempt to diminish congressional power under the doctrine of "original intent" and to use the federal judiciary to return more authority to state and local governments.

At the beginning of the third millennium, the Supreme Court was bitterly divided over states' rights, with five justices generally seeking to curtail the application of federal laws and four justices insisting upon upholding Congress's power to apply the Bill of Rights to the states to prevent them from infringing on an individual's constitutional rights.

When America declared independence from Great Britain in July 1776, it changed the historical English definition of sovereignty. As Bernard Bailyn, Gordon S. Wood, and other historians have pointed out, the American patriots made a radical and abrupt departure from the British tradition by stating in the Declaration of Independence "that to secure these rights, governments are instituted among men, deriving their just powers from the consent of the governed" and thereby placed sovereignty in the people. This was inevitable because Americans, unlike the English, had never accepted the exercise of unlimited and undivided sovereignty, and so, in the words of Massachusetts patriot James Otis, sovereignty remained "in the whole body of the people." It took a tumultuous decade of war, constitution-making, and internal political wrangling before Americans recognized that sovereignty was inherent in "the people" rather than in their legislatures. In the British system it had resided in Parliament, but in the new state constitutions of the 1770s and 1780s Americans entrusted legislatures with "sovereignty"; now the Americans, recognizing sovereignty of the people, made the rulers subordinate to the ruled. The next step, according to Wood, had enormous and far-reaching implications in that, by removing sovereignty from any one part of government, indeed from government altogether, Americans made possible the idea of a government with separation of powers where no one branch, certainly not Congress, could ever exercise supreme power.

Constitution-making to define the powers of government began before the formal Declaration of Independence. Just five days after Richard Henry Lee introduced his resolution of independence to the Continental Congress on June 7, 1776, John Hancock, its president, appointed a committee to draft a constitution. Headed by John Dickinson of Pennsylvania, it formalized the powers that the Continental Congress had been exercising and presented the draft of the Articles of Confederation to the Committee of the Whole in July. Over the next sixteen months the delegates discussed, but did not seriously debate, the Dickinson draft because they spent most of their time organizing the war with England. Finally, in November 1777 they adopted the Articles and sent them to the states for the required unanimous ratification.

The framers of the Articles were extremely worried about creating a national government that would turn out to be another Parliament. And so they established a "confederacy" of sovereign states entering into a "league of mutual friendship." Article II made this fear of centralism explicit when it stated that "each state retains its sovereignty, freedom and independence, and every Power . . . which is not by this confederation expressly delegated to the United States, in Congress assembled." Those meager powers included conducting foreign relations, controlling naval affairs, regulating Indian trade, coining money, and settling disputes between states. More important, there were specific limitations on Congress. It could not impose taxes or duties, regulate interstate commerce, or interfere in the internal concerns of the states. It took a two-thirds majority, each state having one vote regardless of size, to pass "resolutions," which states were not bound to obey. When Congress adjourned, a "Council of State" served as a token executive department that could conduct naval and army operations, answer the mail, and resummon Congress. There was no national judiciary.

After the Revolutionary War the situation had become chaotic. By 1786 Congress itself was hounded from pillar to post by mobs of war veterans demanding land bounties promised during the war but never awarded. Congress moved from Philadelphia to Princeton, New Jersey, then to Annapolis, Maryland, and finally ended up in New York City. Unable to meet payrolls, it was also frequently unable to achieve a quorum. Under these gloomy circumstances Congress received a report from a convention of state "commissioners" who had met at Annapolis that September. It summarized the nation's deplorable condition and stressed that "important defects" existed in the Articles that could not be changed by the amendment process and that must be addressed by a special "Convention of Deputies." Congress responded by calling for a convention to meet the following May in Philadelphia to consider revisions to the Articles.

The delegates who came to Philadelphia were committed to strengthening the central government. But how could this be achieved? The majority of them, who after the convention during the ratification fight claimed the name Federalists, proposed a strong national government and were led James Madison, James Wilson, and George Washington. They believed that men were motivated by self-interest, that the noble republican experiment was dissolving into disorder, and that a strong central government was necessary to harness this passion and direct it to the common good. They also argued that a vigorous central government was essential to promote foreign policy and to develop trade, commerce, and manufacturing.

The other group, who called themselves Antifederalists in the ratification contest, were led by George Mason and Elbridge Gerry and still clung to the phobia of an abusive central power. They were, in the words of historian Cecelia Kenyon, "men of little faith." Saul Cornell and other historians have recently challenged this pejorative view. In a thoughtful analysis of the "dissenting tradition" in America between 1788 and 1828, Cornell saw them as spokesmen (although a diverse amalgam of planter aristocrats, frontier farmers, and local politicians) for the libertarian heritage in America and its concern for liberty and a commitment to individual rights. They were, above all, wrestling with the essential, enduring problem of federalism: how to preserve the autonomy of the states and prevent giving the central government too much coercive authority while at the same time strengthening the federal union in the common interest. To do this, they demanded a constitution with explicit limits on federal power.

From May until September, with the Federalists carrying every important vote, the delegates wrote a new constitution. In so doing they followed Madison's suggestions as outlined in a lengthy paper he wrote just before he came to Philadelphia called "Vices of the Political System of the United States." It reflected his extensive research on the history of governments (he hauled over 200 books to the convention) and concluded that America needed "such a modification of the sovereignty as will render it sufficiently neutral between the different interests and factions, to control one part of the society from invading the rights of another, and at the same time sufficiently controlled itself, from setting up an interest adverse to that of the whole Society." In other words, it needed a fundamental law that was based on what historian Harry N. Scheiber, in *American Law and the Constitutional Order*, has called a "compound principle," where the central government and state governments function simultaneously.

Accordingly, the Constitution permitted the states equal representation in the Senate, allowed them to control elections, and gave them authority over the health and safety of their citizens. But the states had significant prohibitions limiting their prerogatives: they could not interfere with contracts, impair interstate commerce, or coin money. Although Congress was given only "enumerated powers," the all-important "necessary and proper" clause invited a broad interpretation of its potential authority. Article I, Section 8 gave Congress the authority "to make all Laws which shall be necessary and proper for carrying into Execution" the powers vested by the Constitution in the federal government. And while the states had their own courts, the Constitution mandated the creation of a Supreme Court and a system of federal courts. There was no doubt that the new central government, compared to the Articles of Confederation, was intended to be the predominant partner in the federal system. In contrast to the Articles, Congress under the Constitution had the power to act directly on the people, without the intervening agency of a state. It could regulate interstate commerce, levy taxes, and raise armies. Its laws, not resolutions, were to be enforced by a president and the federal courts.

Although the Antifederalists lost the argument in Philadelphia, they continued the fight in the state ratification conventions. A fundamental problem with the new constitution in the eyes of the Antifederalists, as Stanley Elkins and Eric McKitrick pointed out in their 1993 study, *The Age of Federalism*, was legitimacy. The initial call for a convention had been only to revise the Articles, not to discard them out of hand and devise a totally new form of government. Illegally circumventing the Articles, the Federalists had created a consolidated central government that invaded state sovereignty. This invasion, the Antifederalists warned, would only lead to arbitrary, expanding national power. They firmly believed that the states were the only safe repositories of liberty and that the new central government would weaken if not ultimately destroy it. They condemned the structure of the Senate as unrepublican. Most of all, they decried the lack of a bill of rights.

The Federalists, better organized and more imaginative, had their selling points, best summarized in *The Federalist*, a series of essays written by James Madison, Alexander Hamilton, and John Jay for the New York ratification contest. Their main concern was to show how the Constitution contained checks on Congress. Legislation had to pass both houses. The president could veto bills. Hamilton pointed out that the Supreme Court could review and set aside congressional laws. And Madison, in a most ingenious essay, developed a "kinetic theory" of federalism. In the Tenth Federalist he wrote that the "energy of the people" in a government spread over so vast an area as the United States would provide a "geographic" check on the concentration of national power. With the promise to include a bill of rights as a first priority, the Federalists gradually prevailed. Beginning first with Delaware and Pennsylvania in December 1787 and ending with a narrow victory in New York in July 1788, the Constitution was ratified. With North Carolina and Rhode Island still out of the union, the new government held its first elections that November.

Madison, elected as a member of the House of Representatives from Virginia, was chair of the committee to prepare a bill of rights. Initially, he was somewhat hesitant to begin, fearing that if the amendment process were begun the Antifederalists might use it to weaken the powers given to the national government under the Constitution. He was also concerned about putting limitations on the new government. Lastly, he thought it unnecessary to have a national bill of rights in a government of delegated powers. But by June 1789, he recognized that public opinion was against him and that his own state as well as New York had called for another constitutional convention to write a new document that would include a bill of rights. On June 8 he delivered a speech on the floor of the House on why there must be a federal bill of rights. He argued that all power can be abused and that Congress's power was especially dangerous in this regard because of the "necessary and proper" clause. He added that some states had bills of rights, some of which were defective, and still others had none.

When it seemed that Madison intended to have Congress put the Bill of Rights into the body of the Constitution, Roger Sherman of Connecticut, on August 13, proposed adding its provisions separately, as amendments, and Madison acquiesced, despite his earlier misgivings about the amendment process and the Antifederalists. By the end of August, the House accepted seventeen of the nineteen amendments that Madison had proposed after his own winnowing of the various proposals for amendments from many others. The Senate reduced them to twelve, and in September Congress sent them to the states for ratification. Eventually, all the states except Connecticut and Georgia accepted ten of the articles, rejecting the first one (which provided a fixed formula for representation in Congress) and the second (which prohibited Congress from raising its own salary in the same session).

Historian Leonard Levy in *Essays on the Making of the Constitution*, has argued that in adopting the Bill of Rights Congress evinced no real passion for safeguarding personal liberties; rather, Congress was reacting to political pressures left over from the ratification fight, and the adoption of the Bill of Rights had a healing effect on these lingering divisions. Even so, the main legal innovation of the Bill of Rights was to limit the power of Congress, unlike the 1688 English Bill of Rights, which limited only the Crown, not Parliament. But the Bill of Rights initially applied only to congressional statutes and not to the rights of individuals under state laws; that would not come until the Bill of Rights was "incorporated" into state constitutions by the Supreme Court in the twentieth century.

Although the framers of the Bill of Rights might not have been worried about civil liberties at the time of its adoption, a serious crisis involving the First Amendment's guarantees of free speech and free press surfaced almost immediately. In 1798 Congress passed the Sedition Act and usurped what had been a legislative prerogative of the states. This law was the result of the appearance of political parties during the first decade under the Constitution, a development that the framers in Philadelphia had never anticipated. Permanent political parties, with ideology, newspapers, and national and state committees, came about because of a defect in the Constitution's version of separation of powers. In it, the president was the chief executive of the country and acted as an important check upon Congress with the veto. But there was no mechanism whereby the president and Congress could work together to govern. Political parties, one called Federalist, the other Republican, emerged over differences on economic policy, the powers of the national government, and foreign policy, and bridged the gap. As party politics matured, the president assumed two roles: chief executive of the nation and the leader of his party. As such, he had regular and direct communication with Congress and could initiate legislation.

But some Americans believed that political parties would destroy the new union, just as factionalism had helped to wreck the Articles. Washington, in his Farewell Address, said as much. These men, found almost exclusively in the Federalist Party, viewed any organized, sustained criticism of the government as dangerous. But Thomas Jefferson and James Madison, because of their disillusionment with Alexander Hamilton's economic policies, moved away from their fervent nationalism of the late 1780s and became part of the "loyal opposition." This was a new concept, heresy to many, which claimed that organized criticism of elected public officials played an important and legitimate role in helping voters choose between two clearly different programs.

By the summer of 1798 the tensions created by this rapidly developing two-party system became acute because of the "quasi-war" with France. The Federalists, then in control of Congress, used the growing public hostility to the openly pro-French Republicans to pass a law designed to suppress party opposition to their administration. By a straight party vote—Federalists for, Republicans against—they enacted the Sedition Act. This first federal common law of crimes set heavy fines and imprisonment for anyone who wrote, printed, or uttered "false, scandalous and malicious" statements against the government. As enforcement of the act showed, the federal judges, all supporters of the Federalist Party, used it as a meat ax against the Republicans. Twenty-five of them were charged with sedition, fifteen were indicted, and ten were convicted, fined, and sent to prison. In reaction, Thomas Jefferson and James Madison secretly wrote the Virginia and Kentucky Resolutions, in which they argued that the Constitution gave common law jurisdiction only to the states and that, consequently, the Sedition Act was unconstitutional. As a result, the states, Jefferson wrote, "being sovereign and independent, have the unquestionable right to judge of the infraction" and could nullify such a law. Surprisingly, the "reign of witches," as Jefferson called the times, came to an end when President John Adams, on his own and without consulting any member of his cabinet, ended the war with a peace mission to Paris in 1800.

Adams, just before he left office, appointed his secretary of state, John Marshall, the third Chief Justice of the Supreme Court. He also signed into law the Judiciary Act of 1801, a measure that created a total of sixty-six new federal judicial positions, which Adams filled with loyal Federalists. So began President Jefferson's "war on the judiciary" where he tried to use the power of Congress to change the federal court system through impeachment. But after the impeachment trial of Justice Samuel Chase for judicial malfeasance in the Senate in March 1805 ended in his acquittal, Marshall led the Court in a series of landmark decisions to establish a strong definition of federal power known as "judicial nationalism." In these cases the Court for the first time spoke with one voice, the "majority opinion," and clarified the vagueness contained in the Constitution's wording on the extent of federal power in the supremacy clause, which stated that the Constitution was the "supreme law of the land" to be enforced in a court of law, thereby opening the way for judicial review of congressional law by the Supreme Court. In so ruling, the Court also assumed an authority it did not have before and at the same time avoided political partisanship in those cases that established federal supremacy over the states.

In *Fletcher v. Peck* (1810) the Marshall Court ruled that a state could not impair a contract. In *McCulloch v. Maryland* (1819) it said that a state tax on a federal institution was unconstitutional because "the power to tax involves the power to destroy," and no state could destroy a federal institution. In *Cohens v. Virginia* (1821) it declared that the Constitution operated directly on the people through the federal courts and that the Supreme Court could overrule state court decisions if they violated the Constitution. In *Gibbons v. Ogden* (1823) the Court decided that the Constitution gave Congress exclusive control over interstate commerce. And in *Worcester v. Georgia* (1832) the Court set aside Georgia's licensing laws because they went against federal treaties and infringed on interstate commerce. In all these decisions one central idea predominated: Congress was superior to the states.

This definition of federalism led to the nullification crisis over congressional fiscal power. The South, with its unique staple-crop economy and heavy dependence upon imports, refused to accept the protective tariff of 1828—the "Tariff of Abominations." Against this law John Calhoun, then vice president, anonymously composed *The South Carolina Exposition and Protest* (1828). He argued that the federal government was strictly limited to those powers specified in the Constitution and that sovereignty resided in the people of the states. The Constitution, he said, was a compact among these sovereign states, and any state could prevent the enforcement of an unconstitutional congressional law. Basing his arguments on the ideas contained in the Virginia and Kentucky Resolutions, he claimed that states could decide the constitutionality of the tariff and, if necessary, nullify it. He maintained that it was an unfair and uneven tax, a tax on southern planters to benefit northern factory owners. As such, it should be nullified because it violated the Constitution's requirement in Article I, Section 8 that all duties "shall be uniform throughout the United States."

But the tariff was not repealed, and Calhoun, keeping his authorship of the *Exposition* secret, permitted other politicians to advance his ideas. In the winter of 1830 Senator Robert Y. Hayne of South Carolina used them to defend nullification and states' rights. He said that the North, in the "spirit of false philanthropy," was trying to destroy the South. Daniel Webster, in one of his most famous speeches, denounced nullification as a violation of the Constitution that would lead to "civil feuds . . . drenched . . . in fraternal blood!" The nation was not a compact of states, he said, but a union of the people, and "Liberty *and* Union, now and forever [were] one and inseparable."

Calhoun could not keep his authorship of the *Exposition* secret forever, and after President Andrew Jackson found out about it, the vice president resigned and returned to South Carolina, which in November 1832 passed the Ordinance of Nullification. But the president's tough response in his "December Proclamation" caused Calhoun to rethink his position. He returned to Washington as a senator and worked with Henry Clay to pass the Compromise Tariff of 1833. That law, which reduced the tariff to 20 percent over a ten-year period, in effect ended the nullification crisis. But Jackson demanded from Congress, and received, the Force Bill, which empowered the president to use military force in the future to collect federal import duties.

South Carolina did not concede federal authority to compel submission to federal law. Its legislature only repealed the nullification ordinance and, in an act of states' rights defiance that presaged the rabid fire-eater style of the sectional duel in the 1850s, nullified Jackson's Force Bill. Although South Carolina stood alone, since no other state endorsed nullification, the South never again dropped back into its old nationalistic way of thinking, and defending states' rights and resisting the federal government became watchwords for politicians in the region.

Equally important, before the nullification crisis federal issues had been considered rationally; now they would be viewed more and more emotionally because of the ever-growing fear that the South was becoming a helpless minority. And it was this inability of southerners to consider issues rationally that ultimately prevented compromise in the 1850s and led to secession in 1860–1861.

No sooner had the nullification crisis subsided than the issue of slavery forced new, more acute confrontations over the meaning of federalism. Specifically, the South insisted that Congress's power over slavery was limited; that it had no authority over the "peculiar institution" and could not prevent its expansion into the territories. Most northerners, citing the Northwest Ordinance of 1787, believed that while the "police powers" of the states shielded slavery from a federal abolition statute, Congress could keep it from spreading to the territories. In 1820, with the Missouri Compromise line, it did just that, and sealed off slavery from the area of the Louisiana Territory above 36°30′. Then in 1846 the Wilmot Proviso would have had Congress quarantine slavery by prohibiting it in the vast territories (California, Utah, and New Mexico) acquired in the war with Mexico. Again Calhoun, now the Jeremiah of the South, condemned the Proviso as a violation of the property rights in slaves protected by the Constitution. He called for a convention at Nashville to take action to protect these rights and, if necessary, to consider secession. Only the strenuous efforts of Senators Henry Clay, Daniel Webster, and Stephen Douglas preserved the Union in the Compromise of 1850.

But the Compromise created still more controversy over federalism and the extent of congressional power. Ironically, now the North condemned the expanded federal power of the Fugitive Slave Act of 1850, a critical part of the Compromise, and passed personal liberty laws to defy it. In 1859 the Supreme Court reinforced its ruling in *Prigg v. Pennsylvania* (1842), where Justice Joseph Story had declared unconstitutional Pennsylvania's law to hamper the return of runaway slaves. In *Ableman v. Booth*, it decided again in favor of the South by denying the right of a Wisconsin court to interfere with the Fugitive Slave Act. To allow it to do so, Chief Justice Roger B. Taney warned, "would subvert the very foundations of this Government." This ruling led to another ironic development when the Wisconsin legislature defended state sovereignty by adopting measures that echoed the language of the Virginia and Kentucky Resolutions. To many northerners, the use of federal power to protect slavery in *Booth* was but a frightening extension of the Court's ruling in another case two years before. In *Scott v. Sandford* it had vacated the 1820 Missouri Compromise line and ruled that Congress had no power to prevent the spread of slavery into the territories. So, as events proved, the Compromise of 1850 solved none of the tensions between North and South over federal power and slavery; it only bought time.

A decade later the Union dissolved over the issue. Abraham Lincoln's election in 1860 on the Republican Party pledge of "no further extension of slavery into the territories" caused seven states to secede from the Union and form the Confederacy. His refusal to compromise on any possible spread of slavery, when followed by a call for troops to put down the rebellion after the Confederacy fired on Fort Sumter in Charleston Harbor, persuaded four more slave states to join the new government, and the Civil War began. During the war Lincoln issued the Emancipation Proclamation, and Congress approved an amendment to free the slaves and forever end the debate over slavery after the end of the conflict. The Thirteenth Amendment, ratified on December 6, 1865, vastly expanded federal power and set the stage for Reconstruction. Its enabling clause, Section 2, read, "Congress shall have power to enforce this article by appropriate legislation."

During Reconstruction the antebellum fight over race reemerged, this time over the freed slaves and the role of Congress in dealing with their plight. In 1866, in defiance of the Thirteenth Amendment, southerners adopted "black codes," which Congress reacted to by passing the Freedmen's Bureau Act, the Civil Rights Act, and in 1867 the Reconstruction Act, which imposed martial law on the South. It also passed the Fourteenth and Fifteenth Amendments to assure blacks their civil rights, which by 1867 included suffrage. Southern resistance only intensified, often with the Ku Klux Klan and terrorism. As a last, desperate effort to enforce federal law in the South, Congress enacted the Ku Klux Klan Acts, called the Force Acts, between 1870 and 1875, and the Civil Rights Act of 1875.

But when it became obvious that the South would never accept Congress's version of Reconstruction, northern voters and businessmen became impatient with the struggle. Congress signaled a retreat in the Amnesty Act of 1872 and allowed southern whites to "redeem" their state governments. The Supreme Court, too, withdrew federal protection from the freed slave. In *U.S. v. Cruikshank* (1876), it decided that the Fourteenth Amendment did not allow federal law to be used to punish violent acts by individual whites against blacks. In the *Civil Rights Cases* (1883), it declared unconstitutional the provisions of the 1875 Civil Rights Act that prohibited racial discrimination, in effect inviting more repressive versions of the black codes. And in *Plessy v. Ferguson* (1896), the Court established the "separate but equal" doctrine, which gave constitutional sanction to state-mandated racial separation. With *Plessy* as a green light to southern whites, as C. Vann Woodward argued in *The Strange Career of Jim Crow*, they constructed a legal wall that totally separated the two races and relegated blacks to second-class citizenship.

In the two years following the 1929 collapse of the stock market, the nation's free-market economy all but imploded. First, the banks, tied to the stock market, began to shut down as frightened Americans withdrew their money in a panic. By the end of 1930, 1,350 banks had folded, and in 1931 alone 2,293 more closed their doors. Many people, their savings exhausted, found themselves both out of work and out of money. By 1932, 40 million people, one-third of the work force, were unemployed. Families, evicted from their homes, took to sleeping in shanty towns made of crates and boards, called Hoovervilles. Farmers saw markets for their crops and produce evaporate and farm prices decline 60 percent. In the early summer of 1932, 15,000 angry World War I veterans, desperate for help, marched on Washington, D.C., to get Congress to authorize bonuses due them for serving in the war. When they camped on vacant lots and occupied government buildings, President Herbert Hoover ordered the army to evict them. In July, General Douglas MacArthur, with Majors Dwight D. Eisenhower and George S. Patton at his side, moved in on the men and their families with tanks and bayonets.

In the 1932 presidential campaign, Hoover discounted the seriousness of all these developments and promised a full recovery if Americans would just remain calm, and urged businessmen to maintain employment. As the Great Depression deepened, however, he expanded federal authority to cope with the crisis. In 1932 he established the President's Organization on Unemployment Relief to assist private charities. He created the Reconstruction Finance Corporation (RFC) to lend millions of dollars to banks and their corporate debtors, mainly railroads and insurance companies. The RFC was able to reduce the number of bank failures from seventy a week to one every two weeks. He signed the Emergency Relief and Construction Act of 1932, which permitted the RFC to lend states up to $1.5 billion for public works that would pay for themselves and allowed another $300 million to go directly to states to help them deal with unemployment. Yet he refused to support any comprehensive, direct federal unemployment relief program, convinced that it would create a "federal dole" that would destroy the moral character of the recipients and result in a permanent class of public wards.

The Democratic candidate, Governor Franklin D. Roosevelt of New York, called for something much different. To him, the country was in a crisis as severe as if it had been attacked by another nation. He promised federal unemployment relief, federal farm legislation, and "bold and persistent experimentation to give a new deal to the forgotten man." Americans elected him president with 57 percent of the popular vote. In his inaugural address on March 4, 1933, he electrified the nation with the ringing assertion that "the only thing we have to fear is fear itself." He told Americans that he would ask Congress for "measures that a stricken nation in the midst of a stricken world may require." He threatened that if Congress did not comply he would seek "broad executive power to wage a war against the emergency as great as the power that would be given me if we were in fact invaded by a foreign foe."

Congress did act. During the "First Hundred Days" it passed a bewildering number of laws known as the First New Deal that took the federal government into areas theretofore left to the states. Two of them became focal points for both Roosevelt's critics and supporters: the Agricultural Adjustment Act (AAA) and the National Industrial Recovery Act (NIRA). These measures, for the first time, used Congress's fiscal and regulatory power to assure the farmer and worker a minimum standard of living. Congress created the Civilian Conservation Corps (CCC), which put over 2 million men between the ages of eighteen and twenty-five to work planting trees and building dams, fish ponds, and other conservation projects. It enacted the Public Works Administration (PWA) and provided direct cash grants of over $3 billion in matching funds to states to hire unemployed men to construct roads, public buildings, dams, and other projects, and in so doing established an important precedent for cooperation between the federal and state governments. Congress entered the area of housing by creating the Federal Housing Administration (FHA) to help homeowners finance repairs and make house construction possible through federal mortgages. Through the Home Owners Loan Corporation (HOLC), Congress made an additional $4 million available in federal mortgages. The Social Security Act of 1935 established a cooperative federal-state program of unemployment compensation, aid to dependent children for single-parent families, and an old-age insurance program for workers who paid taxes out of their wages that were matched by employers. Although the program was inherently conservative, since the workers and the employers paid for the old-age benefits, many Americans feared it as the beginning of socialism.

The New Deal expanded the role of government in labor issues. In the summer of 1935 Congress passed the National Labor Relations (Wagner) Act, which gave workers the right to unionize and to settle disputes with management through collective bargaining. It provided for federal supervision of union elections and for penalties for unfair labor practices. And after black leader A. Philip Randolph threatened to lead a march on Washington to protest the fact that New Deal programs engaged in racial discrimination, Roosevelt issued Executive Order No. 8802, which created the Fair Employment Practices Commission (FEPC) to curb racial discrimination in federal industries and jobs.

Debate over the New Deal erupted in Congress, in the newspapers, and on the radio. Conservative Democrats formed the American Liberty League and cried out that the New Deal subverted individualism and self-reliance. They asked for laws to cut taxes and abolish all federal relief programs. Critics from the left said the New Deal was inadequate. Senator Huey Long's "Share Our Wealth" scheme wanted Congress to seize all incomes over $1 million by taxation, confiscate all inheritances over $5 million, and then use the money to give every family a $5,000 homestead allowance and a $2,000 annual stipend. Dr. Francis Townsend put forth the "Old Age Revolving Pension" plan in which every retired person over the age of sixty would receive a $200 monthly pension, provided that he or she spent it within thirty days.

The Supreme Court, dominated by conservatives, reviewed the New Deal centerpieces, the AAA and the NIRA, and declared them unconstitutional. In *U.S. v. Butler* (1936), the Court in a 6 to 3 vote set aside the AAA because it said that a tax on agricultural producers was not for raising revenue but to force compliance with a federal program. It also ruled that the general welfare clause of the Preamble of the Constitution, which allowed Congress to enact laws to "promote the general welfare," did not allow Congress to do whatever it pleased. The Court invalidated the NIRA, in *Schechter Poultry Corp. v. United States* (1935), when it decided that the law was unconstitutional because the interstate commerce clause did not give Congress the right to regulate manufacturing. The Court battle over the New Deal reached a climax in 1937 when the president tried to add liberal justices to the bench. Then the Court, for reasons never fully explained, reacted almost immediately, reversed its earlier negative positions on federal regulation, and in *NLRB v. Jones & Laughlin Steel Corp.* gave judicial approval to the New Deal. It ruled by a 5 to 4 vote that federal regulation of industrial relations and activities "was necessary to protect interstate commerce from the paralyzing consequences of industrial warfare."

Ironically, in the last half of the twentieth century federalism became the center of a Supreme Court controversy over the very racial segregation it had sanctioned in *Plessy v. Ferguson*. By World War II racial separation was a salient feature of the American South. Yet new forces had begun to compel a reassessment of the idea that a democracy can have separate but equal facilities and institutions. First, the presence of military bases in the South, and race riots started by whites in these camps, focused public attention on a region, and a racial problem, until then isolated from national interest. Also, during the war, with expanding defense industries in that segregated region, the need for federal dollars to maintain these operations raised new issues of federal-state relations. As a result, the War Department issued an order that stopped segregation in military transportation and in recreational facilities. Roosevelt's 1941 Executive Order No. 8802 mandated that employers in defense industries hire "without discrimination because of race, creed, color or national origin." By war's end 1.5 million blacks had left the South to work in the industrial factories of the North and West. But they often had to live in segregated neighborhoods and attend segregated schools. Sometimes the situation became ugly, as in 1943 in Detroit, where a riot broke out and left five blacks and nine whites dead. The federal government, with its focus on the war, did nothing to stop the racial violence. Indeed, Secretary of War Henry L. Stimson claimed that militant black leaders were to blame for the trouble.

By 1945 many blacks were prepared to push politically and economically in a struggle for integration and full civil rights. Their efforts were aided by the emerging Cold War. Simply put, the conflict between the United States and the Soviet Union made segregation a dangerous liability for America. How could this nation, when it practiced racism, condemn the Soviet Union's denial of human rights under communism? How could the United States gain the allegiance of the nonwhite peoples of the Third World to democracy if American blacks were forced to live with segregation?

President Harry S. Truman recognized these compelling reasons to take a critical look at the situation. In December 1946, he established the President's Committee on Civil Rights, which the next year published *To Secure These Rights*. The report recommended the passing of federal laws against lynching and for desegregation. It called for congressional legislation to assure blacks voting rights and equal employment opportunity. It wanted a permanent Civil Rights Commission. Although Congress refused to support any of these recommendations, Truman, in 1948, by executive order forbade racial discrimination in the federal government and began racial desegregation of the armed forces.

While the executive branch began to attack segregation on its own, the Supreme Court started to hand down important desegregation decisions. Beginning with *Smith v. Allwright* (1944), it ended all-white primary elections as a violation of the Fifteenth Amendment. In *Morgan v. Virginia* (1946), it forbade segregation in interstate bus transportation. In *Shelley v. Kraemer* (1948), the attorney general filed a "friend of the court" brief on behalf of the National Association for the Advancement of Colored People (NAACP) to eliminate restricted covenants in the sale of real estate. The Legal Defense Fund of the NAACP, created in the 1930s, under Charles Houston won an important equalization case against separate black schools when a South Carolina district court, in *Briggs v. Elliot*, found segregated schools both unequal and inferior. And as a result of other lawsuits by the fund, black students gained admission to graduate and law schools at several southern state universities.

In 1950 Thurgood Marshall (who later became the first black Supreme Court justice) took over the fund and challenged the separate but equal doctrine of *Plessy v. Ferguson* in a series of cases against "separate but equal" in public education filed in Kansas, Virginia, Delaware, and the District of Columbia. Then, in 1954, he consolidated them into one brief before the Supreme Court in *Brown v. Board of Education* (Brown I). Under the new Chief Justice, Earl Warren, the Court unanimously declared the separate but equal doctrine a violation of the Fourteenth Amendment. Warren's opinion also tried to show how blacks in segregated educational facilities were harmed because of their race. The following year, in another *Brown v. Board of Education of Topeka* (Brown II), the Court put the principal responsibility for enforcing Brown I "with all deliberate speed" in the hands of local school boards working in cooperation with federal district judges.

But southern states resisted *Brown* by a variety of laws designed to keep their schools segregated. At the same time violence erupted. In 1956 in Clinton, Tennessee, a mob confronted twelve black students who were trying to attend a high school. In 1957 President Dwight D. Eisenhower had to call up the United States Army to keep the peace in Little Rock, Arkansas, when whites threatened violence rather than allow Central High School to be desegregated. The Supreme Court tried to stop what was called "massive resistance" to racial integration in *Cooper v. Aaron* (1958), but to no avail. In this ruling it unanimously ordered a more aggressive desegregation effort and stated that only the Court, not state legislatures, could interpret the Constitution.

Southerners continued to defy the law. Prince Edward County, Virginia, went to the extreme of closing all of its schools for six years and enrolling white students in segregated "private" academies. Television dramatized and heightened the growing conflict between federal power and states' rights. It showed Alabama governor George C. Wallace defiantly standing in the doorway of the state university to bar the admission of a black student. In 1962 Governor Ross Barnett of Mississippi intervened personally to prevent James Meredith from registering for classes at the segregated state university. President John F. Kennedy ordered federal marshals to escort Meredith to a campus dormitory. He then went on national television to condemn Barnett's open defiance of federal authority and announced that the University of Mississippi had been integrated and asked its students to follow the law. Instead, a mob invaded Ole Miss and went on a rampage of shooting and rock throwing. In 1963 Americans watched Sheriff "Bull" Connor of Birmingham, Alabama, turn dogs, fire hoses, and cattle prods on a peaceful civil rights demonstration of blacks and whites. Later that year a white racist murdered Medgar Evers, the black head of the Mississippi NAACP, in the driveway of his home. In September a bomb exploded in a black church in Birmingham during Sunday School and killed four young girls. Such intransigence convinced many Americans living outside the South that the government had to act.

Matters intensified. Along with Martin Luther King, Jr., and the Southern Christian Leadership Conference (SCLC), blacks fought segregation through a new tactic of nonviolent civil disobedience. They tested racial segregation by sit-ins at lunch counters and other public facilities. They formed the Student Nonviolent Coordinating Committee (SNCC), which demanded "Freedom Now" and stepped up "direct action" tactics against all forms of racial segregation and discrimination. A northern black organization, the Congress of Racial Equality (CORE), organized Freedom Rides beginning in May 1961 where busloads of blacks and whites traveled to the South intending to test whether or not federal authority would enforce the Supreme Court's desegregation orders. It did not, and, unprotected by either federal marshals or state police, the Freedom Riders were beaten and their buses burned.

Indeed, the federal government responded hesitantly to these shocking events. In 1957 Congress passed the Civil Rights Act, the first federal attempt to protect blacks since Reconstruction. The act created a civil rights commission and gave the Justice Department the power to sue to obtain black voting rights in the South, but the statute was ignored in the region. The following year the federal government extended its jurisdiction in a voting rights act that, likewise, was largely ineffective. Not until President Lyndon B. Johnson pushed a sweeping civil rights act through Congress in 1964 did the federal government move decisively to ensure that desegregation and black voting rights would be enforced and protected. The statute outlawed racial discrimination in employment, public facilities, and voting. It created the Equal Employment Opportunity Commission, which prohibited racial and sexual discrimination. It empowered federal agencies to refuse to finance state programs that discriminated against blacks. The next year Congress enacted another, stronger voting rights act and gave the attorney general the power to supervise voter registration where less than half of the black residents of voting age were registered—in Mississippi, for example, only 7 percent of the blacks over eighteen were registered. But progress toward racial integration was slow, and when the Court, in *Swann v. Charlotte-Mecklenburg Board of Education* (1971), ruled that busing could be used to create racially balanced school systems, it only brought more opposition, now from some northern communities.

During the 1960s, while racial desegregation moved at a snail's pace, another issue opened a conflict over the power of the federal government and the state—namely, sexual discrimination against women. In 1961 President John Kennedy established the Commission on the Status of Women, and two years later it issued *American Women*, which recommended the elimination by federal law of all obstacles to the full participation of women in society. To lobby Congress for implementation of the report, women formed the National Organization for Women (NOW). The 1964 Civil Rights Act outlawed sexual discrimination. Congress, in Title IX of the 1972 Educational Amendments to the Higher Education Act of 1965, required colleges and universities to give equal financial aid to female athletes. That same year it adopted the Equal

Rights Amendment (ERA), which prohibited any state from denying or abridging civil rights "on account of sex" (though the states, exercising their constitutional powers in the amending process, refused to ratify the ERA).

The Supreme Court, in two landmark cases, set aside state laws because they infringed upon a woman's right to privacy. In *Griswold v. Connecticut* (1965), it vacated Connecticut's 1879 law criminalizing the use of birth control because it violated the right of privacy in marriage. In *Roe v. Wade* (1973), the Court ruled that a Texas law criminalizing abortion violated a woman's right to privacy. Two years earlier it had unanimously held in *Reed v. Reed* that statutory gender discrimination was prohibited by the equal protection clause of the Fourteenth Amendment. Then, in *Frontiero v. Richardson* (1973), by an 8 to 1 vote in a case involving salary discrimination in the military, it cited *Reed* to declare that all job-related sexual classifications violated the due process clause of the Fifth Amendment. Gender classifications, it said, were like racial classifications and required a "compelling government interest."

The Warren Court (1953–1969) attacked states' rights in criminal justice. The move of the federal courts into an area previously the province of local authority was based on the doctrine of "incorporation." It held that the guarantees of the Bill of Rights limited not only the federal government but state and local governments as well through the due process clause of the Fourteenth Amendment. Incorporation appeared first in 1914 in *Weeks v. United States*, where the Court ruled that evidence secured without a search warrant was excluded from federal courts. In *Palko v. Connecticut* (1937) the Supreme Court found that some immunities in the Bill of Rights, such as protection against double jeopardy, were so basic that the states could not violate them. In *Wolf v. Colorado* (1949) it established the "exclusionary rule" and prohibited the use of evidence seized without a search warrant. And in *Mapp v. Ohio* (1961) it again applied the exclusionary rule by deciding that evidence from a reckless search of a private home was inadmissible in court. The Court incorporated the Fifth Amendment's protection against self-incrimination into state constitutions: in *Brown v. Mississippi* (1936), when the Court threw out confessions obtained by whipping, and then in *Malloy v. Hogan* (1964), when it held that states must comply with the Fifth Amendment's provision against self-incrimination. It decreed in *Gideon v. Wainwright* (1963) that under the Sixth Amendment a person charged with a felony who could not pay for a lawyer would be provided one by the state. The following year, in *Escobedo v. Illinois*, it ruled that anyone undergoing police interrogation had a right to remain silent until a lawyer was present. Then, in 1966, it handed down the controversial 5 to 4 opinion in *Miranda v. Arizona*. In this bitterly criticized decision the Court determined that the Fifth Amendment's privilege against self-incrimination required that criminal suspects be informed of their rights before an interrogation could begin, that they had the right to remain silent, and that any statement they made could be used against them in a trial.

However, a conservative reaction to these liberal Court decisions had been building steadily ever since *Roth v. United States* (1957), when the Court decided that pornography was not a criminal offense and was protected by the First Amendment unless, in Justice William Brennan's words, it was "utterly without redeeming social importance." The ruling ignited a political firestorm of criticism of the Court. After his election to the presidency in 1968, Richard M. Nixon used this growing resentment to build a conservative offensive against the Warren Court, whose activist rulings he thought were socially disruptive and morally wrong. In civil rights, he reversed the position of support that the federal government had taken under Kennedy and Johnson. In 1969 he had the Justice Department back an unsuccessful petition to the Supreme Court from the state of Mississippi to delay integration of its schools, and he openly disavowed the efficacy of court-ordered busing to achieve school desegregation.

This remarkable shift on civil rights was symbolic of Nixon's determination to end the era of judicial "legislating" by the Court. When Earl Warren resigned in 1969, Nixon appointed conservative Warren E. Burger to replace him. Then he filled other vacancies on the bench with conservative appointees such as Harry A. Blackmun, a Minnesota jurist, Lewis F. Powell, Jr., a conservative Virginia lawyer, and William H. Rehnquist, a doctrinaire conservative from Arizona. These appointments transformed the Court, and it no longer stood in the forefront of the fight for minority rights.

President Nixon broadened the conservative attack. In what has been called the New Federalism, he advocated significantly limiting the dependency of individuals on Washington and, instead, increasing the role of state and local governments in their lives. For example, in 1972 he proposed giving block grants of federal money directly to state and local governments and allowing them to decide how to earmark the funds for specific purposes. Congress responded by passing a revenue-sharing act that over a five-year period appropriated $30 billion. He advocated a "Family Assistance Plan" that insisted on "workfare" as a substitute for welfare. But Nixon was no knee-jerk conservative; he wanted to stress individual initiative and local authority as the best way to identify problems and develop ways to solve them.

During the 1980s, President Ronald Reagan continued Nixon's attack on the liberal decisions of the Warren Court and spoke out against affirmative action, abortion, and the banning of prayer in public schools. He added two more conservatives to the bench: Sandra Day O'Connor and Antonin Scalia. The president wanted conservative law professor Robert Bork confirmed, too. But the Senate rejected Bork's nomination after hearings revealed that he firmly believed that the Court must abandon "judicial activism" and render its decisions based on the "original intent" of the framers of the Constitution. When Chief Justice Burger resigned in 1986, Reagan elevated William H. Rehnquist to be the new Chief Justice. Rehnquist immediately led a judicial crusade against expanding federal power and women's rights. In Congress, conservative politicians moved against federal support of abortion rights. For example, in the House of Representatives, Henry Hyde of Illinois asked for laws that would terminate Medicaid funds for the procedure. President Reagan opposed federal subsidizing of child care and issued an executive order withholding federal funds from pro-abortion clinics. The Rehnquist Court, in *Webster v. Reproductive Health Services* (1989), returned control of access to abortions to the states. Attacks on abortion clinics and physicians increased, and some states passed anti-abortion statutes.

The Rehnquist Court became a bastion of the conservative assault on federal power. Deeply divided in almost every important case involving federalism by a 5 to 4 vote, the Court consistently circumscribed congressional power and expanded that of the states. It backed away from support of the exclusionary rule established in *Mapp v. Ohio* when, in *United States v. Lear* (1996), it decided that the rule did not apply if police had acted in good faith when they secured evidence without a warrant. In *Seminole Tribe v. Florida* (1996), the Court struck down the federal Indian Gaming Regulatory Act as abrogating the states' Eleventh Amendment immunity from being sued. In *Alden v. Maine* (1999), it held that states could not be sued by state employees for violating the Fair Labor Standards Act. In *Florida Prepaid v. College Savings Bank* (1999), it made states immune from suits over federal patents and trademarks. On January 11, 2000, the Court, again by a 5 to 4 margin in *Kimel v. Florida Board*, held that Congress did not have the authority to make states comply with the Age Discrimination in Employment Act. Other federal laws were struck down as an intrusion on states' rights: the Child Support Recovery Act, the Federal Arson Law, and the Brady Handgun Bill. In an article in the June 27, 1999, issue of the *New York Times* entitled "The Justices Decide Who's in Charge," Linda Greenhouse pointed out the seriousness of the new conservative direction of the Court, stating that it had dramatically "reconfigured the Federal-state balance of power" and given states "a broad sphere of immunity . . . from the reach of Federal law." She further noted that it had established a position of being unwilling "to credit Congress's own view not only of the way legislation should be written but even of the justification for Federal legislation at all." Clearly, the deep divisions that first appeared at the birth of the debate over federalism continue into the twenty-first century.

Over the last two centuries the history of federalism in America has evolved in stages, each with its distinguishing characteristics. The first, from the Revolution to the election of George Washington as president, saw the emerging dialog between the Nationalists and the Localists. The Nationalists became more and more convinced that a federal system with state sovereignty meant only worsening chaos. The Localists, on the other hand, seemed traumatized by the fight with Parliament that had led to independence and jealously defended state governments as the bastions of liberty. A compromise was worked out during the Constitutional Convention and the subsequent ratification fight in which the "compound principle" of divided sovereignty and simultaneous functioning of the federal and state governments laid the foundation of a new government for the United States.

With Washington's election in 1789 by the unanimous vote of the Electoral College, the new government got under way, and within a decade another version of the debate over federalism broke out. The opening salvo of this contest erupted in 1792 with Hamilton's economic recovery program. Defending his program, he argued that Congress could enact any statute it wished if it were "necessary and proper" and not against the Constitution. Jefferson opposed Hamilton and, with a "strict construction" interpretation of the Constitution, insisted that Congress could only pass laws allowed by the powers the document gave to it; all other powers resided in the states, and if Congress wanted to go beyond these specified powers, it had to have a constitutional amendment. The two political parties, the Federalists and the Republicans, formed over these contending views of federal power. During the "quasi-war" with France these differences led to the passing of the Sedition Act and the use of federal law and the federal courts by the Federalists to destroy their opponents. Only an eleventh-hour decision by President John Adams to end the war stopped the "reign of witches" and saved the First Amendment.

During the thirty-five years after Adams's peace mission resolved the dangerous political use of federal power, the Supreme Court under Chief Justice John Marshall put expanded congressional authority on a solid constitutional basis and vindicated Hamilton's interpretation of federalism. The Marshall Court's landmark decisions gave judicial sanction to the supremacy of congressional law and the federal government over the states. And between 1828 and 1833, President Andrew Jackson defended the supremacy of the Union against the threat of John C. Calhoun and the states' rights nullifiers, who claimed that a single state had the constitutional power to vacate a federal law within its borders. But other states' rights disciples appeared and advanced states' rights to protect the "property rights" of southern slaveowners. The debate eventually proved to be irreconcilable, and despite the Compromise of 1850 the country dissolved into civil war.

The war seemingly settled the argument between the Union people and the states' rights advocates once and for all. The Union won. Although the South was "reconstructed" for a time and readmitted to the Union, eventually, with racial segregation as a substitute for slavery in defining race relations, the subordination of the states to the federal government was no longer much contested.

It was not until the nation reeled under the calamity of the economic collapse of the Great Depression that still another stage of the federalism debate developed. Franklin D. Roosevelt's New Deal moved the federal government into areas where it had never ventured before and laid the foundation of the "welfare state" with its assumption of almost unlimited use of federal power. Republicans opposed the New Deal and evoked the pre–Civil War states' rights arguments against the intrusion of federal power, but to little avail. Even the moderately conservative Republican president Dwight D. Eisenhower made little headway in blocking the liberal ascendancy, and under Democratic presidents John F. Kennedy, and especially Lyndon B. Johnson, federal authority prevailed over states' rights in the new federal statutes and programs of the 1,000 days of the Kennedy administration and Johnson's Great Society. Under Chief Justice Earl Warren the Supreme Court supported the constitutionality of liberal federalism and asserted its own active mission to use the Constitution to protect individual rights against the threat of state law.

With the election of Richard Nixon in 1968, the conservative counterattack against liberalism took shape and the most recent stage of the history of federalism began. Nixon advanced a "New Federalism," more accurately perhaps the "New Antifederalism," that harkened back to the arguments of the 1780s when the Localists had used states' rights against the idea of a predominant national power. Nixon's ideological successor, Ronald Reagan, launched a "conservative revolution" in 1981 to roll back the liberal legislation of the Roosevelt, Truman, Kennedy, and Johnson administrations. In a real sense, conservatives hoped to dismantle much of the welfare state as it had developed by the 1980s. Backed by a Supreme Court dominated by conservative states' rights justices, Reagan successfully began returning to state and local control areas that had been steadily taken from them by the federal government since 1933. So much did the conservative "revolution" change public opinion and the political climate in Washington that by the end of the century liberal president William J. Clinton signed legislation to reform, and in fact reduce, the federal welfare program. And so the battle over federalism, present at the creation of the Republic continues into the twenty-first century between those who support federal power as a legitimate, even essential, means of improving the lives of Americans and those who, like the embattled Antifederalists two centuries ago, look to state and local government as the only secure authority to protect the liberties of all citizens.

BIBLIOGRAPHY OF SOURCES

Bailyn, Bernard. *Faces of Revolution: Personalities and Themes in the Struggle for American Independence.* New York: Alfred A. Knopf, 1990.

———. *Ideological Origins of the American Revolution.* Cambridge, MA: Belknap Press of Harvard University Press, 1967.

Cornell, Saul. *The Other Founders: Anti-Federalism and the Dissenting Tradition in America, 1788–1828.* Chapel Hill: University of North Carolina Press, 1999.

Elkins, Stanley, and Eric McKitrick. *The Age of Federalism.* New York: Oxford University Press, 1993.

Fairfield, Roy P., ed. *The Federalist Papers.* Garden City, NY: Doubleday & Company, 1961.

Kenyon, Cecelia M., ed. *The Antifederalists.* Indianapolis: Bobbs-Merrill, 1966.

Levy, Leonard W., ed. *Essays on the Making of the Constitution.* 2nd ed. New York: Oxford University Press, 1987.

Scheiber, Harry N. *American Law and the Constitutional Order: Historical Perspectives.* Cambridge, MA: Harvard University Press, 1978.

Wood, Gordon S. *The Creation of the American Republic, 1776–1787.* New York: W. W. Norton, 1972.

2

Creation of the Federal Republic

On June 12, 1776, five days after Richard Henry Lee had introduced the resolution of independence, the Second Continental Congress appointed a committee, chaired by John Dickinson of Pennsylvania, to draft a constitution for the new nation. One month later the committee submitted its draft of the Articles of Confederation. Immediately, opposition appeared because it made Congress stronger than the states. Due to the recent fight with Parliament over its authority to rule the colonies, most delegates feared a strong central government. Therefore they made major changes in the Dickinson draft and gave predominant power to the states, especially in Article II, which declared that "each state retains its sovereignty ... and every Power ... which is not ... delegated to the United States, in Congress assembled." Congress's authority was further circumscribed by its inability to levy taxes or regulate interstate commerce; these fiscal powers were given to the states. Without an executive branch to carry out its resolutions, the influence of the federal government on the people was severely restricted.

In fact, the delegates had thought little about federalism, the organization of a nation with both national and state governments, and none of them had considered dividing power between the two branches. Their main concern was the war, where each state was fighting to preserve its independence from England, though admittedly also "united" in a Continental Association to wage war, seek foreign support, and treat with the Indians in a unified way. They discussed and revised the Articles off and on for over a year and finally approved them on November 15, 1777.

The required unanimous consent for ratification by the states came slowly because many Americans still thought Congress's powers were too great. Only when postwar realities forced them to think nationally would they discard the lessons of their colonial past and invent new concepts to create a republican government, this time a federal republic. Another sticking point was control over western lands granted in the colonial charters of some states. In some cases these claims extended to the Mississippi River and beyond. The states of Maryland, Delaware, Pennsylvania, Rhode Island, and New Jersey, which lacked such grants, felt that such claims placed them in an unfair position, economically, in the new union. Maryland refused point blank to ratify unless Virginia surrendered its claims to land north of the Ohio River. In 1781, when Virginia acquiesced and gave these "Northwest Territories" to Congress, Maryland accepted the Articles, and they went into effect on March 1 of that year.

The fear of central power lingered, yet by the mid-1780s an increasing number of Americans were worried that Congress was too weak to govern, especially after an amendment sent to the states to give it more fiscal authority failed to achieve ratification. When Shays's Rebellion erupted in Massachusetts in the summer of 1786, it sparked the fear that the nation was drifting into anarchy—and Congress could do nothing to stop it.

Because of these developments, five states sent commissioners to a meeting in September at the temporary national capital at Annapolis, Maryland, to consider appropriate corrective remedies. They waited three weeks hoping that more states would send representatives, but when none showed up they sent a communiqué to Congress, then sitting in New York City. It stated that the difficulties with the Articles were so serious that a special convention should be called to meet in Philadelphia on the second Monday in May 1787 to investigate the situation and suggest a plan to correct the defects. Congress complied, and that spring fifty-five men from twelve states began to assemble in the state capitol of Pennsylvania, later known as Independence Hall.

Although no delegation had instructions from its state to write an entirely new frame of government, the general feeling among most delegates was that they were going to draft a new constitution, make it more like the state constitutions in structure, and give Congress more power to govern. As a first order of business they unanimously chose George Washington as presiding officer. Then, in part to avoid being recalled for violating their instructions merely to revise the Articles, they adopted a rule of secrecy. No official transcript of the debates would be taken, no publication of the proceedings would be allowed, and sentries were placed outside the building and at the door of the meeting room itself, which was moved to the second floor of the hall for greater security. They also decided that only seven states would be required for a quorum and that each state would have one vote.

Most delegates were property owners and men of substance. Many had been active in state governments after the war and had helped to write their state constitutions. Their occupational profile was diverse; although most were lawyers, there were merchants, planters, physicians, governors, and generals. Almost all were native born, and some were from families that had been in America for over a century. Half of them had attended college, and many had degrees. The delegations themselves varied in size, ranging from Virginia, with seven representatives, to New York, which had only three men, including the thirty-year-old Alexander Hamilton. The youngest delegate was twenty-six, and the oldest, Benjamin Franklin, was eighty-one. But the average age was forty-two, at that time just about the prime of life.

The debates lasted from May 25 until mid-September, with the average daily attendance numbering about thirty. The majority, later called Federalists and coming from the larger, more populous states and seacoast areas where commerce was important, wanted to strengthen the national government significantly. The minority, later known as Antifederalists, had little confidence in civic virtue, deeply distrusted central power, and were convinced that only the states could preserve liberty. They came from the small states and from areas on the frontier where farming, not commerce, was important; some were southern planters.

The Virginia Plan, largely the work of James Madison but introduced by Edmund Randolph on May 29, was a list of fifteen resolutions that would create a completely different, and much stronger, national government with separation of powers and checks and balances. Certain crucial powers, however, were beyond the control of Congress, such as state "police power" and regulating slavery. There would be a bicameral Congress, a president, and a federal judiciary. William Paterson of New Jersey introduced an alternative plan on June 13 that would merely have made modifications in the Articles. It proposed keeping a unicameral Congress, as before, and creating a plural executive and a supreme court, but no federal courts. It was defeated after only two days of discussion.

For the next six weeks most of the debates centered on the structure and powers of Congress, and debates over the plan were a prelude to the fight over federalism under the Constitution: What were the rights of the central government over and against the rights of the states? As James Madison summarized the issue on June 18, the central questions were what characteristics should be attached to the new federal plan and how it would operate on the people. Others, such as Alexander Hamilton, Rufus King, Luther Martin, and Oliver Ellsworth, presented their views on federal power. On September 12, George Mason suggested that a bill of rights be included, and Oliver Ellsworth formally moved for the adoption of such a bill. But the motion was defeated unanimously. Five days later the remaining thirty-nine delegates formally adopted the Constitution, signed it, and sent it out for ratification, with the proviso that it would go into effect when it was formally accepted by nine of the thirteen states.

Although ratification moved quickly, the process stalled in big states such as Virginia, New York, and Massachusetts, without whose support no successful new government might emerge. A host of factors, from competing concepts of republicanism to personal interest and political advantage, explained the delays, but the major stumbling block was the lack of a bill of rights in the new constitution. Why did the Federalists omit a bill of rights, which almost cost them a ratification victory? A combination of factors accounted for the mistake. First of all, they were tired and hot and the timing was bad. Some felt that the state constitutions had already done the job of protecting civil rights and that a federal bill of rights was unnecessary and redundant. Others thought that such a declaration was out of place because the Constitution was concerned only with the structure of government, not with enumerating the rights of the people. Alexander Hamilton worried that it would be impossible to enumerate all of those rights anyhow since the delegates were eager to adjourn and, consequently, some important rights might be omitted. Finally, it was argued that a bill of rights would be ineffective and would provide only a "paper barrier."

The ratification fight pitched the Federalists against the Antifederalists. The Federalist arguments are best seen in *The Federalist*, essays written by James Madison, Alexander Hamilton, and John Jay for the New York ratification contest. Their main purpose was to show how the Constitution contained important checks on Congress. They pointed out that legislation had to pass both houses to become law. They noted that the president could veto legislation. James Madison, in Federalist Number 10, argued that the energy of the American people over a vast area would check any abuse of congressional power by preventing standing majorities of any single interest from controlling the government. Alexander Hamilton, in Federalist Number 78, showed how the Supreme Court could check Congress by judicial review. He also showed how the federal judiciary would assure the fair and uniform application of the Constitution and federal laws. The Antifederalists, whose ideas are best expressed in Richard Henry Lee's "Federal Farmer" essays, dreaded the new power given to Congress and believed that the Constitution would lead the nation toward a consolidated, central despotism hostile to states' rights and liberty. In particular, Lee deplored the absence of a bill of rights and the undemocratic and inequitable structure of the Senate, where each state had two senators regardless of population.

The debates in the state ratification conventions were intense, and the outcomes were dangerously close. Massachusetts accepted the Constitution by a vote of 187 to 168. Virginia ratified by a vote of just 89 to 79. And New York, whose entrance in the union was crucial, approved the Constitution by a margin of only 30 to 27. Nevertheless, by July 1788, with the Federalists giving ironclad promises immediately to include a bill of rights as amendments, two-thirds of the states gave their consent and the first national elections were set for November. The nationalistic spirit that had prevailed during the ratification fight continued through the fall elections. Only a few Antifederalists ran for office, and so the first Congress was dominated by those who had wanted a stronger national government. The same spirit of consensus prevailed in the selection of the executive branch. When the Electoral College met in December it unanimously chose George Washington as president and gave John Adams thirty-four of its sixty-nine votes for the vice presidency, distributing the others among a variety of candidates.

By 1788, within a single generation, Americans had declared their political independence from England and then, in agreeing to the Constitution, threw off a number of sacred republican beliefs that had spawned that independence. They had begun, with the Articles, by severely limiting executive power; in the Constitution they created an independent executive. They had first made Congress subordinate to the states; now they agreed to a national government whose authority, based on the sovereignty of the people, was independent of the states. In 1776 they believed that liberty would survive only through civic virtue and that private interests would have to be conceded to public welfare; now they recognized that liberty would survive through a constant clash of the competition of diverse interest groups. But not all Americans had changed their minds. Many old revolutionaries still believed that only the states could preserve liberty, which to many if not most southerners also meant preserving the institution of slavery.

And so Americans turned to the task of launching what they called the "great experiment" with little precedent and no real experience with divided sovereignty, and with few assurances that government by the people would work. This portentous question was soon articulated by Thomas Jefferson when, in March 1801, in his First Inaugural Address, he said: "Sometimes it is said that man can not be trusted with the government of himself. Can he, then, be trusted with the government of others? Or have we found angels in the forms of kings to govern him? Let history answer this question." Over the next two centuries, it would.

DOCUMENTS

2.1.   The Virginia Plan

This plan was drafted by James Madison and introduced on the floor of the Constitutional Convention by Edmund Randolph, speaking for the Virginia delegation, on May 29, 1787. It became the basis for the ensuing debates over the new form of government during the following almost three months of deliberations.

1. Resolved that the Articles of Confederation ought to be so corrected and enlarged as to accomplish the objects proposed by their institution; namely "common defence, security of liberty and general welfare."

2. Resolved therefore that the rights of suffrage in the National Legislature ought to be proportioned to the Quotas of contribution, or to the number of free inhabitants, as the one or the other rule may seem best in different cases.

3. Resolved that the National Legislature ought to consist of two branches.

4. Resolved that the members of the first branch of the National Legislature ought to be elected by the people of the several States every   for the terms of   ; to be of the age of   years at least, to receive liberal stipends by which they may be compensated for the devotion of their time to public service, to be ineligible to any office established by a particular State, or under the authority of the United States, except those peculiarly belonging to the functions of the first branch, during the term of service, and for the space of   after its expiration; to be incapable of reelection for the space of   after the expiration of their term of service, and to be subject to recall.

5. Resolved that the members of the second branch of the National Legislature ought to be elected by those of the first, out of a proper number of persons nominated by the individual Legislatures, to be of the age of   years at least; to hold their offices for a term sufficient to ensure their independency; to receive liberal stipends, by which they may be compensated for the

devotion of their time to public service; and to be ineligible to any office established by a particular State, or under the authority of the United States, except those peculiarly belonging to the functions of the second branch, during the term of service, and for the space of   after the expiration thereof.

6. Resolved that each branch ought to possess the right of originating Acts; that the National Legislature ought to be impowered to enjoy the Legislature Rights vested in Congress by the Confederation and moreover to legislate in all cases to which the separate States are incompetent, or in which the harmony of the United States may be interrupted by the exercise of individual Legislation; to negative all laws passed by the several States, contravening in the opinion of the National Legislature the articles of Union; and to call forth the force of the Union against any member of the Union failing in its duty under the articles thereof.

7. Resolved that a National Executive be instituted; to be chosen by the National Legislature for the term of   years; to receive punctually, at stated times, a fixed compensation for the services rendered, in which no increase or diminution shall be made so as to affect the Magistracy, existing at the time of the increase or diminution, and to be ineligible a second time; and that besides a general authority to execute the National laws, it ought to enjoy the Executive rights vested in Congress by the Confederation.

8. Resolved that the Executive and a convenient number of the National Judiciary, ought to compose a Council or revision with authority to examine every act of the National Legislature before it shall operate, and every act of a particular Legislature before a Negative thereon shall be final; and that the dissent of the said Council shall amount to a rejection, unless the Act of the National Legislature be passed again, or that of a particular Legislature be again negatived by   of the members of each branch.

9. Resolved that a National Judiciary be established to consist of one or more supreme tribunals, and of inferior tribunals to be chosen by the National Legislature, to hold their offices during good behaviour; and to receive punctually at stated times fixed compensation for their services, in which no increase or diminution shall be made so as to affect the persons actually in office at the time of such increase or diminution. That the jurisdiction of the inferior tribunals shall be to hear and determine in the first instance, and of the supreme tribunal to hear and deter-

mine in the dernier resort, all piracies and felonies on the high seas, captures from an enemy; cases in which foreigners or citizens of other States applying to such jurisdictions may be interested, or which respect the collection of the National revenue; impeachments of any National officers, and questions which may involve the national peace and harmony.

10. Resolved that provision ought to be made for the admission of States lawfully arising within the limits of the United States, whether from a voluntary junction of Government and Territory or otherwise, with the consent of a number of voices in the National legislature less than the whole.

11. Resolved that a Republican Government and the territory of each State, except in the instance of a voluntary junction of Government and territory, ought to be guaranteed by the United States to each State.

12. Resolved that provision ought to be made for the continuance of Congress and their authorities and privileges, until a given day after the reform of the articles of Union shall be adopted, and for the completion of all their engagements.

13. Resolved that provision ought to be made for the amendment of the Articles of Union whensoever it shall seem necessary, and that the assent of the National Legislature ought not to be required thereto.

14. Resolved that the Legislative Executive and Judiciary powers within the several States ought to be bound by oath to support the articles of Union.

15. Resolved that the amendments which shall be offered to the Confederation, by the Convention ought at a proper time, or times, after the approbation of Congress to be submitted to an assembly or assemblies of Representatives, recommended by the several Legislatures to be expressly chosen by the people, to consider and decide thereon.

Source: James Madison, *Notes of Debates in the Federal Convention of 1787 Reported by James Madison* (New York: W. W. Norton, 1987), pp. 30–33. Reprint of *The Debates in the Federal Convention of 1787 Which Framed the Constitution of the United States*, edited by Gaillard Hunt and James Brown (New York: Oxford University Press, 1920).

2.2.   Debates in the Philadelphia Convention

The central focus of the discussions in the Philadelphia Convention, whether the delegates were discussing Congress, the executive branch, or the federal courts, was what powers would
be given to the new central government and what powers would
be retained by the states. The following excerpts from the debates include speeches on the floor by Alexander Hamilton and
Rufus King, both from New York, Luther Martin of Maryland,
and Oliver Ellsworth of Connecticut.

June 18, 1787

[Alexander Hamilton:] The great question is what provision shall we
make for the happiness of our Country? He would first make a comparative examination of the two plans—prove that there were essential
defects in both—and point out such changes as might render a *national
one*, efficacious.—The great & essential principles necessary for the support of Government. are 1. an active & constant interest in supporting
it. This principle does not exist in the States in favor of the federal Govt.
They have evidently in a high degree, the esprit de corps. They constantly pursue internal interests adverse to those of the whole. They have
their particular debts—their particular plans of finance &c. all these
when opposed to, invariably prevail over the requisitions & plans of
Congress. 2. the love of power, Men love power. The same remarks are
applicable to this principle. The States have constantly shewn a disposition rather to regain the powers delegated by them than to part with
more, or to give effect to what they had parted with. The ambition of
their demagogues is known to hate the controul of the Genl. Government. It may be remarked too that the Citizens have not that anxiety to
prevent a dissolution of the Genl. Govt as of the particular Govts. A
dissolution of the latter would be fatal: of the former would still leave
the purposes of Govt. attainable to a considerable degree. Consider what
such a State as Virga. will be in a few years, a few compared with the
life of nations. How strongly will it feel its importance & self-sufficiency?
3. an habitual attachment of the people. The whole force of this tie is on
the side of the State Govt. Its sovereignty is immediately before the eyes
of the people: its protection is immediately enjoyed by them. From its
hand distributive justice, and all those acts which familiarize & endear
Govt. to a people, are dispensed to them. 4. *Force* by which may be
understood a *coertion of laws or coertion of arms*. Congs. have not the former except in few cases. In particular States, this coercion is nearly suf-

ficient; tho' he held it in most cases, not entirely so. A certain portion of military force is absolutely necessary in large communities. Massts. is now feeling this necessity & making provision for it. But how can this force be exerted on the States collectively. It is impossible. It amounts to a war between the parties. Foreign powers also will not be idle spectators. They will interpose, the confusion will increase, and a dissolution of the Union ensue. 5. *influence.* he did not [mean] corruption, but a dispensation of those regular honors & emoluments, which produce an attachment to the Govt. almost all the weight of these is on the side of the States; and must continue so as long as the States continue to exist. All the passions then we see, of avarice, ambition, interest, which govern most individuals, and all public bodies, fall into the current of the States, and do not flow in the stream of the Genl. Govt. the former therefore will generally be an overmatch for the Genl. Govt. and render any confederacy, in its very nature precarious. Theory is in this case fully confirmed by experience. . . .

* * *

Mr. [Rufus] King, wished as everything depended on this proposition, that no objections might be improperly indulged agst. the phraseology of it. He conceived that the import of the terms "States" "Sovereignty" "*national*" "federal," had been often used & applied in the discussion inaccurately & delusively. The States were not "sovereigns" in the sense contended for by some. They did not possess the peculiar features of sovereignty. They could not make war, nor peace, nor alliances, nor treaties. Considering them as political Beings, they were dumb, for they could not speak to any forign Sovereign whatever. They were deaf, for they could not hear any propositions from such Sovereign. They had not even the organs or faculties of defence or offence, for they could not of themselves raise troops, or equip vessels, for war. On the other side, if the Union of the States comprises the idea of a confederation, it comprises that also of consolidation. A Union of the States is a union of the men composing them, from whence a *national* character results to the whole. Congs. can act alone without the States—they can act & their acts will be binding agst. the Instructions of the States. If they declare war, war is de jure declared, captures made in pursuance of it are lawful. No acts of the States can vary the situation, or prevent the judicial consequences. If the States therefore retained some portion of their sovereignty, they had certainly divested themselves of essential portions of it. If they formed a confederacy in some respects—they formed a Nation in others. The Convention could clearly deliberate on & propose any alterations that Congs. could have done under ye. federal articles. and could not Congs. propose by virtue of the last article, a change in any article whatever: And as well that relating to the equality of suffrage, as any other. He made these remarks to obviate some scruples which had been expressed. He doubted much the practicability of annihilating the States; but thought that much of their power ought to be taken from them.

* * *

June 28, 1787

Mr. L[uther] Martin resumed his discourse, contending that the Genl. Govt. ought to be formed for the States, not for individuals: that if the States were to have votes in proportion to their numbers of people, it would be the same thing whether their [representatives] were chosen by the Legislatures or the people; the smaller States would be equally en-slaved; that if the large States have the same interest with the smaller as was urged, there could be no danger in giving them an equal vote; they would not injure themselves, and they could not injure the large ones on that supposition without injuring themselves [and if the interests were not the same the inequality of suffrage wd—be dangerous to the smaller States.]: that it will be in vain to propose any plan offensive to the rulers of the States, whose influence over the people will certainly prevent their adopting it: that the large States were weak at present in proportion to their extent: & could only be made formidable to the small ones, by the weight of their votes; that in case a dissolution of the Union should take place, the small States would have nothing to fear from their power; that if in such a case the three great States should league themselves together, the other ten could do so too: & that he had rather see partial Confed-eracies take place, than the plan on the table. This was the substance of the residue of his discourse which was delivered with much diffuseness & considerable vehemence.

* * *

June 29, 1787

Mr. [Oliver] Elseworth moved that the rule of suffrage in the 2d. branch be the same with that established by the articles of confedera-tion". He was not sorry on the whole he said that the vote just passed, had determined against this rule in the first branch. He hoped it would become a ground of compromise with regard to the 2d. branch. We were partly national; partly federal. The proportional representation in the first branch was conformable to the national principle & would secure the large States agst. the small. An equality of voices was conformable to the federal principle and was necessary to secure the Small States agst. the large. He trusted that on this middle ground a compromise would take place. He did not see that it could on any other. And if no compro-mise should take place, our meeting would not only be in vain but worse than in vain. To the Eastward he was sure Massts. was the only State that would listen to a proposition for excluding the States as equal political Societies, from an equal voice in both branches. The others would risk every consequence rather than part with so dear a right. An attempt to deprive them of it, was at once cutting the body [of America] in two, and as he supposed would be the case, somewhere about this part of it. The large States he conceived would notwithstanding the equality of votes, have an influence that would maintain their superiority. . . . The existing confederation was founded on the equality of the States in the article of suffrage: was it meant to pay no regard to this antecedent plighted faith. Let a strong Executive, a Judiciary & Legislative power be created; but Let not too much be attempted; by which all may be lost. He was not in general a half-way man, yet he preferred doing half the good we could, rather than do nothing at all. The other half may be added, when the necessity shall be more fully experienced.

Source: Madison, *Debates*, pp. 129–32, 152–53, 203–204, 218.

2.3.   Letter from the Federal Farmer No. 1

> Richard Henry Lee, who had introduced the resolution moving for independence in the Second Continental Congress on June 7, 1776, became a leading opponent of the federal constitution. He published several essays, called "Letters," elaborating on his objections, the first of which appeared on October 8, 1787. In it, he warned against the dangers of a consolidated central government destroying the rights of the states.

October 8, 1787

The present moment discovers a new face in our affairs. Our object has been all along, to reform our federal system, and to strengthen our governments—to establish peace, order and justice in the community—but a new object now presents. The plan of government now proposed is evidently calculated totally to change, in time, our condition as a people. Instead of being thirteen republics, under a federal head, it is clearly designed to make us one consolidated government. Of this, I think, I shall fully convince you, in my following letters on this subject. This consolidation of the states has been the object of several men in this country for some time past. Whether such a change can ever be effected in any manner; whether it can be effected without convulsions and civil wars; whether such a change will not totally destroy the liberties of this country—time only can determine.

* * *

. . . September, 1786, a few men from the middle states met at Annapolis, and hastily proposed a convention to be held in May, 1787, for the purpose, generally, of amending the confederation—this was done before the delegates of Massachusetts, and of the other states arrived—still not a word was said about destroying the old constitution, and making a new one—The states still unsuspecting, and not aware that they were passing the Rubicon, appointed members to the new convention, for the sole and express purpose of revising and amending the confederation— and, probably, not one man in ten thousand in the United States, till within these ten or twelve days, had an idea that the old ship was to be destroyed, and he put to the alternative of embarking in the new ship presented, or of being left in danger of sinking—The States, I believe, universally supposed the convention would report alterations in the confederation, which would pass an examination in congress, and after being agreed to there, would be confirmed by all the legislatures, or be rejected. . . . Eleven states met in the convention, and after four months close attention presented the new constitution, to be adopted or rejected by the people. The uneasy and fickle part of the community may be prepared to receive any form of government; but, I presume, the enlightened and substantial part will give any constitution presented for their adoption, a candid and thorough examination; and silence those designing or empty men, who weakly and rashly attempt to precipitate the adoption of a system of so much importance. . . .

* * *

The plan proposed appears to be partly federal, but principally however, calculated ultimately to make the states one consolidated government.

The first interesting question, therefore suggested, is, how far the states can be consolidated into one entire government on free principles. In considering this question extensive objects are to be taken into view, and important changes in the forms of government to be carefully attended to in all their consequences. The happiness of the people at large must be the great object with every honest statesman, and he will direct every movement to this point. If we are so situated as a people, as not to be able to enjoy equal happiness and advantages under one government, the consolidation of the states cannot be admitted.

* * *

Independant of the opinions of many great authors, that a free elective government cannot be extended over large territories, a few reflections must evince, that one government and general legislation alone, never can extend equal benefits to all parts of the United States: Different laws, customs, and opinions exist in the different states, which by a uniform system of laws would be unreasonably invaded. The United States contain about a million of square miles, and in half a century will, probably, contain ten millions of people; and from the center to the extremes is about 800 miles.

Before we do away the state governments, or adopt measures that will tend to abolish them, and to consolidate the states into one entire government, several principles should be considered and facts ascertained:— These, and my examination into the essential parts of the proposed plan, I shall pursue in my next.

Yours's &c.
The Federal Farmer.

Source: Neil H. Cogan, *Contexts of the Constitution: A Documentary Collection on Principles of American Constitutional Law* (New York: Foundation Press, 1999), pp. 416–420.

2.4.   The Federalist, Numbers 10 and 78

To get the Constitution ratified by the New York Convention, 77 of a total of 105 essays were published in the New York newspapers under the pseudonym Publius. Fifty were written by Alexander Hamilton, fifty by James Madison, and five by John Jay. They argued that the system of checks and balances contained in the Constitution and the diversity of the American people would prevent the abuse of power by the central government.

Federalist Number 10

The two great points of difference between a Democracy and a Republic are, first, the delegation of the Government, in the latter, to a small number of citizens elected by the rest: secondly, the greater number of citizens, and greater sphere of country, over which the latter may be extended.

The effect of the first difference is, on the one hand to refine and enlarge the public views, by passing them through the medium of a chosen body of citizens, whose wisdom may best discern the true interest of their country, and whose patriotism and love of justice, will be least likely to sacrifice it to temporary or partial considerations. Under such a regulation, it may well happen that the public voice pronounced by the representatives of the people, will be more consonant to the public good, than if pronounced by the people themselves convened for the purpose. On the other hand, the effect may be inverted. Men of factious tempers, of local prejudices, or of sinister designs, may by intrigue, by corruption or by other means, first obtain the suffrages, and then betray the interests of the people. The question resulting is, whether small or extensive Republics are most favorable to the election of proper guardians of the public weal: and it is clearly decided in favor of the latter by two obvious considerations.

In the first place it is to be remarked that however small the Republic may be, the Representatives must be raised to a certain number, in order to guard against the cabals of a few; and that however large it may be, they must be limited to a certain number, in order to guard against the confusion of a multitude. Hence the number of Representatives in the two cases, not being in proportion to that of the Constituents, and being proportionally greatest in the small Republic, it follows, that if the proportion of fit characters, be not less, in the large than in the small Republic, the former will present a greater option, and consequently a greater possibility of a fit choice.

In the next place, as each Representative will be chosen by a greater number of citizens in the large than in the small Republic, it will be more difficult for unworthy candidates to practise with success the vicious arts, by which elections are too often carried; and the suffrages of the people being more free, will be more likely to centre on men who possess the most attractive merit, and the most diffusive and established characters.

* * *

The other point of difference is, the greater number of citizens and extent of territory which may be brought within the compass of Republican, than of Democratic Government; and it is this circumstance principally which renders factious combinations less to be dreaded in the former, than in the latter. The smaller the society, the fewer probably will be the distinct parties and interests composing it; the fewer the distinct parties and interests, the more frequently will a majority be found of the same party; and the smaller the number of individuals composing a majority, and the smaller the compass within which they are placed, the more easily will they concert and execute their plans of oppression. Extend the sphere, and you take in a greater variety of parties and interests; you make it less probable that a majority of the whole will have a common motive to invade the rights of other citizens; or if such a common motive exists, it will be more difficult for all who feel it to discover their own strength, and to act in unison with each other.

Federalist Number 78

Some perplexity respecting the right of the courts to pronounce legislative acts void, because contrary to the constitution, has arisen from an imagination that the doctrine would imply a superiority of the judiciary to the legislative power. It is urged that the authority which can declare the acts of another void, must necessarily be superior to the one whose acts may be declared void. As this doctrine is of great importance in all the American constitutions, a brief discussion of the grounds on which it rests cannot be unacceptable.

There is no position which depends on clearer principles, than that every act of a delegated authority, contrary to the tenor of the commission under which it is exercised, is void. No legislative act therefore contrary to the constitution can be valid. To deny this would be to affirm that the deputy is greater than his principal; that the servant is above his master; that the representatives of the people are superior to the people themselves; that men acting by virtue of powers may do not only what their powers do not authorise, but what they forbid.

If it be said that the legislative body are themselves the constitutional judges of their own powers, and that the construction they put upon them is conclusive upon the other departments, it may be answered, that this cannot be the natural presumption, where it is not to be collected from any particular provisions in the constitution. It is not otherwise to be supposed that the constitution could intend to enable the representatives of the people to substitute their will to that of their constituents. It is far more rational to suppose that the courts were designed to be an intermediate body between the people and the legislature, in order, among other things, to keep the latter within the limits assigned to their authority. The interpretation of the laws is the proper and peculiar province of the courts. A constitution is in fact, and must be, regarded by the judges as a fundamental law. It therefore belongs to them to ascertain its meaning as well as the meaning of any particular act proceeding from the legislative body. If there should happen to be an irreconcileable variance between the two, that which has the superior obligation and validity ought of course to be preferred; or in other words, the constitution ought to be preferred to the statute, the intention of the people to the intention of their agents.

Nor does this conclusion by any means suppose a superiority of the judicial to the legislative power. It only supposes that the power of the people is superior to both; and that where the will of the legislature declared in its statutes, stands in opposition to that of the people declared in the constitution, the judges ought to be governed by the latter, rather than the former. They ought to regulate their decisions by the fundamental laws, rather than by those which are not fundamental.

Source: Roy P. Fairfield, ed., *The Federalist Papers: A Collection of Essays Written in Support of the Constitution of the United States* (Garden City, NY: Doubleday, 1961), pp. 16–23, 226–233.

2.5.   Debates in the State Ratifying Conventions

> From November 1787 through July 1788, eleven states delib-
> erated the strengths and weaknesses of the new constitution,
> then voted to accept it. Federalists such as James Wilson of
> Pennsylvania argued in favor of the document and its system of
> checks and balances. The Antifederalists, such as Patrick Henry
> of Virginia, were deeply fearful of the great dangers of the fed-
> eral government. The vote was dangerously close in some states.
> The Federalists prevailed in Virginia by only ten votes and in
> New York by only three votes.

Pennsylvania, November 28, 1787

Mr. [James] Wilson. The secret is now disclosed, and it is discovered to be a dread that the boasted state sovereignties will, under this system, be disrobed of part of their power. Before I go into the examination of this point, let me ask one important question: Upon what principle is it contended that the sovereign power resides in the state governments? The honorable gentleman has said truly, that there can be no subordinate sovereignty. Now if there can not, my position is, that the sovereignty resides in the people. They have not parted with it; they have only dis-pensed such portions of power as were conceived necessary for the pub-lic welfare. This constitution stands upon this broad principle. I know very well, Sir, that the people have hitherto been shut out of the federal government, but it is not meant that they should any longer be dispos-sessed of their rights. In order to recognize this leading principle, the proposed system sets out with a declaration that its existence depends upon the supreme authority of the people alone. We have heard much about a consolidated government. I wish the honorable gentleman would condescend to give us a definition of what he meant by it. I think this the more necessary, because I apprehend that the term, in the numerous times it has been used, has not always been used in the same sense. It may be said, and I believe it has been said, that a consolidated govern-ment is such as will absorb and destroy the governments of the several States. If it is taken in this view, the plan before us is not a consolidated government, as I showed on a former day, and may, if necessary, show further on some future occasion. On the other hand, if it is meant that the general government will take from the state governments their power in some particulars, it is confessed and evident that this will be its operation and effect.

When the principle is once settled that the people are the source of authority, the consequence is that they may take from the subordinate governments powers with which they have hitherto trusted them, and place those powers in the general government, if it is thought that there they will be productive of more good. They can distribute one portion of power to the more contracted circle called State governments: they can also furnish another proportion to the government of the United States. Who will undertake to say as a state officer that the people may not give to the general government what powers and for what purposes they please? how comes it, Sir, that these State governments dictate to their superiors?—to the majesty of the people? When I say the majesty of the people, I mean the thing, and not a mere compliment to them. The honorable gentleman went a step further and said that the State governments were kept out of this government altogether. The truth is, and it is a leading principle in this system, that not the States only but the people also shall be here represented. And if this is a crime, I confess the general government is chargeable with it; but I have no idea that a safe system of power in the government, sufficient to manage the general interest of the United States, could be drawn from any other source or rested in any other authority than that of the people at large, and I consider this authority as the rock on which this structure will stand. If this principle is unfounded, the system must fall. If honorable gentlemen, before they undertake to oppose this principle, will show that the people have parted with their power to the State governments, then I confess I cannot support this constitution. It is asked, can there be two taxing powers? Will the people submit to two taxing powers? I think they will, when the taxes are required for the public welfare, by persons appointed immediately by their fellow citizens.

Virginia, June 14, 1788

Mr. [Patrick] HENRY entertained strong suspicions that great dangers must result from the [necessary and proper] clause under consideration . . . which gives them power to make all laws which shall be necessary to carry their laws into execution. By this they have a right to pass any law that may facilitate the execution of their acts. . . . If they think any law necessary for their personal safety, after perpetrating the most tyrannical and oppressive deeds, cannot they make it by this sweeping clause? If it be necessary to provide, not only for this, but for any department or officer of Congress, does not this clause enable them to make a law for the purpose? And will not these laws, made for those purposes, be paramount to the laws of the states? Will not this clause give them a right to keep a powerful army continually on foot, if they think it necessary to aid the execution of their laws? . . . However cautious you may be in the selection of your representatives, it will be dangerous to trust them with such unbounded powers. Shall we be told, when about to grant such illimitable authority, that it will never be exercised!

I conjure you once more to remember the admonition of that sage man who told you that, when you give power, you know not what you give. I know the absolute necessity of an energetic government. But is it consistent with any principle of prudence or good policy to grant unlimited, unbounded authority, which is so totally unnecessary that gentlemen say it will never be exercised? But gentlemen say that we must make experiments. A wonderful and unheard-of experiment it will be, to give unlimited power unnecessarily! I admit my inferiority in point of historical knowledge; but I believe no man can produce an instance of an unnecessary and unlimited power, given to a body independent of the legislature, within a particular district. Let any man in this Convention show me an instance of such separate and different powers of legislation in the same country—show me an instance where a part of the community was independent of the whole.

* * *

Mr. [James] MADISON. Mr. Chairman, I am astonished that the honorable member should launch out into such strong descriptions without any occasion. Was there ever a legislature in existence that held their sessions at a place where they had not jurisdiction? I do not mean such a legislature as they have in Holland; for it deserves not the name. Their powers are such as Congress have now, which we find not reducible to practice. If you be satisfied with the shadow and form, instead of the substance, you will render them dependent on the local authority. Suppose the legislature of this country should sit in Richmond, while the exclusive jurisdiction of the place was in some particular country; would this country think it safe that the general good should be subject to the paramount authority of a part of the community?

The honorable member asks, Why ask for this power, and if the subsequent clause be not fully competent for the same purpose. If so, what new terrors can arise from this particular clause? It is only a superfluity. If that latitude of construction which he contends for were to take place with respect to the sweeping clause, there would be room for those horrors. But it gives no supplementary power. It only enables them to execute the delegated powers. If the delegation of their powers be safe, no possible inconvenience can arise from this clause. It is at most but explanatory. For when any power is given, its delegation necessarily involves authority to make laws to execute it. Were it possible to delineate on paper all those particular cases and circumstances in which legislation by the general legislature would be necessary, and leave to the states all the other powers, I imagine no gentleman would object to it. But this is not within the limits of human capacity. The particular powers which are found necessary to be given are therefore delegated generally, and particular and minute specification is left to the legislature.

[Here Mr. Madison spoke of the distinction between regulation of police and legislation, but so low he could not be heard.]

When the honorable member objects to giving the general government jurisdiction over the place of their session, does he mean that it should be under the control of any particular state, that might, at a critical moment, seize it? I should have thought that this clause would have met with the most cordial approbation. As the consent of the state in which it may be must be obtained, and as it may stipulate the terms of the grant, should they violate the particular stipulations it would be an usurpation; so that, if the members of Congress were to be guided by the laws of their country, none of those dangers could arise.

[Mr. Madison made several other remarks, which could not be heard.]

Mr. HENRY replied that, if Congress were vested with supreme power of legislation, paramount to the constitution and laws of the states, the dangers he had described might happen; for that Congress would not be confined to the enumerated powers. This construction was warranted, in his opinion, by the addition of the word *department*, at the end of the clause, and that they could make any laws which they might think necessary to execute the powers of any department or officer of the government.

Source: Cogan, *Contexts of the Constitution*, pp. 493–494, 502–506.

ANNOTATED RESEARCH GUIDE

Books

Bailyn, Bernard. *Faces of Revolution: Personalities and Themes in the Struggle for American Independence*. New York: Alfred A. Knopf, 1990. Provides an excellent introduction for the beginning student of American independence of the major personalities (John Adams, Thomas Jefferson, Thomas Hutchinson, and Thomas Paine) and the lesser known figures (Andrew Eliot, Jonathan Mayhew, and Stephen Johnson). Bailyn also stresses the main historical themes of the Revolution first developed in his *Ideological Origins*.

————. *Ideological Origins of the American Revolution*. Cambridge, MA: Belknap Press of Harvard University Press, 1967. This major reinterpretation of the causes of the American Revolution and the framing of the Constitution maintains that, far from being "reluctant revolutionaries," as Clinton Rossiter had claimed, the founders framed the break from England and the Constitution itself on "abstract universals of natural rights."

Beard, Charles A. *An Economic Interpretation of the Constitution of the United States.* New York: Macmillan, 1914. This pioneering study of the Constitution spelled out what became known as the Beard thesis. It argues that the document was the reflection of the economic self-interests of the framers at the 1787 Philadelphia Convention. For a thoughtful revision of Beard's thesis, and a critical analysis of his methods and interpretations, see Lee Benson, *Turner and Beard: American Historical Writing Reconsidered* (New York: The Free Press, 1960).

Becker, Carl L. *The Declaration of Independence: A Study in the History of Political Ideas.* New York: Alfred A. Knopf, 1942. Provides a brilliant analysis of the political ideas that went into the Declaration as well as a thoughtful examination of the document's literary qualities.

Cornell, Saul. *The Other Founders: Anti-Federalism and the Dissenting Tradition in America, 1788–1828.* Chapel Hill: University of North Carolina Press, 1999. Explores the evolution of the tradition of dissenting public discourse about constitutionalism in the early Republic and emphasizes the persistence of certain fundamental themes in the Antifederalist texts.

Farrand, Max. *The Framing of the Constitution of the United States.* New Haven, CT: Yale University Press, 1913. The first full historical treatment of the debates and proceedings of the 1787 Philadelphia Constitutional Convention, from the calling of the convention in February 1787 to the completion of the final document in September.

Hoffman, Ronald, and Peter J. Albert, eds. *Launching the "Extended Republic": The Federalist Era.* Charlottesville: University Press of Virginia, 1996. Contains a valuable series of essays on the Federalist era by historians Gordon S. Wood, Bernard W. Sheehan, John L. Larson, and others.

Jensen, Merrill. *The New Nation: A History of the United States During the Confederation, 1781–1789.* Demonstrates that far from being a total failure, as had traditionally been thought, the nation achieved a number of significant accomplishments between the Treaty of Paris in 1783 and the ratification of the federal constitution in 1788.

Kenyon, Cecelia M., ed. *The Antifederalists.* Indianapolis: Bobbs-Merrill, 1966. Argues that the opponents of the Constitution were men "of little faith" who did not believe that a republican government could work over large geographic areas such as the United States.

Levy, Leonard W., ed. *Essays on the Making of the Constitution.* 2nd ed. New York: Oxford University Press, 1987. Points out that Madison's main concern to get a bill of rights added to the Constitution was political (to quiet the Antifederalists' criticisms) and not to protect civil liberties.

Madison, James. *Notes of Debates in the Federal Convention of 1787 Reported by James Madison.* New York: W. W. Norton, 1987. The only complete, firsthand account of the proceedings and debates of the convention by one of its own members.

Maier, Pauline. *American Scripture: Making the Declaration of Independence.* New York: Random House, 1998. A thoughtful revision of Becker's interpretation of the Declaration.

McDonald, Forrest. *Novus ordo seclorum: The Intellectual Origins of the Constitution.* Lawrence: University Press of Kansas, 1985. Stresses the power of ideas in the Constitutional Convention and portrays all of the delegates as being nationalists in that they were convinced that it was necessary to reorganize and strengthen the central government.

Peterson, Merrill D. *Jefferson and Madison and the Making of the Constitution.* Charlottesville: University Press of Virginia, 1987. Emphasizes an ongoing and intimate collaboration between Jefferson and Madison in applying the Constitution to the challenges of the new Republic.

Rakove, Jack N. *The Beginnings of National Politics.* New York: Alfred A. Knopf, 1979. Points out that the question of sovereignty, a dispute over the power of Congress, began almost immediately after declaring independence, and shows what the original American understanding of federalism was and how it was affected by events between 1774 and the Constitutional Convention of 1787.

Rossiter, Clinton L. *Seedtime of the Republic: The Origin of the American Tradition of Political Liberty.* New York: Harcourt, Brace, 1953. Argues that the patriots were "reluctant revolutionaries" who came to the decision for independence only after a desperate effort to find a place for the colonies within the British Empire.

Wood, Gordon S. *The Creation of the American Republic, 1776–1787.* New York: W. W. Norton, 1972. Pictures the founders as preeminently practical men, not naive utopians, who realistically approached their task with an unsentimental appreciation of human nature.

———. *The Radicalism of the American Revolution.* New York: Alfred A. Knopf, 1992. Demonstrates the radical nature of the decision taken in 1776 to create a new government that would rule a diverse and pluralistic society such as was found in America at the time. The Founding Fathers had to abandon Old World attachments and base a society on the ordinary desire of people to make money and pursue happiness—"new attachments befitting a republican people."

Nonprint Media

Web Sites

http://memory.loc.gov/ammem/bdsds/bdshome.html. A Library of Congress site from their Rare Book and Special Collections Division. The site is called "Documents from the Continental Congress and the Constitutional Convention 1774–1789." The Continental Congress Broadside Collection has 253 titles, and the Constitutional Convention Broadside Collection contains 274 documents.

http://webspaceinc.com/selectedquotes. "Selected Quotes from the Constitutional Convention." Has categorized and dated quotes from the convention.

http://1cwebz.loc.gov/const/ccongquery.html. Documents from the Continental Congress and the Constitutional Convention." The advantage of this site is that it allows a subject search.

www.louisville.edu/library/ . . . /goodsources/history/articles.html. Has the
   Articles of Confederation (Avalon Project) and Articles of Confederation
   (Teacher Link). Also has other related information about the Declaration
   of Independence and Confederation historical documents and history.
www.yale.edu/lawweb/Avalon/contcong/07–21–75.htm. Contains the Journals
   of the Continental Congress and Franklin's Articles of Confederation, July
   21, 1775.
ww.yale.edu/lawweb/Avalon/jeffauto.htm#artconfdebate. Contains Jefferson's
   account of his writing the Declaration and its acceptance in the Continental
   Congress. Also has his account of the initial debate on the Articles of
   Confederation when the Dickinson draft was presented to Congress on
   July 12, 1776.
ww.yale.edu/lawweb/Avalon/artconf.htm. "Articles of Confederation." Done
   under the Avalon Project at Yale Law School, it deals with the Annapolis
   Convention, Madison's notes of the debates, and the Federalist Papers.
www.memory.loc.gov/ammem/amlaw/lawhome.html. "A Century of Law-
   making for a New Nation: U.S. Congressional Documents and Debates
   1774–1873." Has law titles relating to the Continental Congress and the
   Constitutional Convention, Journals of the Continental Congress, Elliot's
   Debates, and Farrand's Record of the Constitutional Convention.

Videotape

Cooke, Alistair. *Inventing a Nation* [videorecording]. BBC-TV, and Time-Life
   Films. OCLC ID no. 09979696. A fifty-two minute analysis of the politics
   and government from 1783 to 1789 and of the Philadelphia Constitutional
   Convention.

3

The Sedition Act of 1798

In March 1789, as a first order of business, Congress set about adding a bill of rights to the Constitution and named James Madison chair of a House committee to draft the amendments. But surprisingly, from March until early June, Madison dragged his feet. He shared his concerns about proceeding with his assignment with Jefferson, who was still serving as the American minister to France. Madison worried that perhaps a bill of rights might imply federal powers not intended to be included in those enumerated to Congress in the Constitution. He suspected that in listing the civil rights some might be left out, and he was worried that once the amendment process got started the Antifederalists might use it to weaken the national government. But Madison realized that further delay was impossible when he found out that two states, Virginia and New York, had called for a second convention to write another constitution that would include a bill of rights.

On June 8, Madison gave one of his rare speeches on the floor of the House. He spoke on why there must be a federal bill of rights. Madison warned that all power can be abused, noting that Congress's power was especially dangerous because of the "necessary and proper" clause. True, he said, some states had bills of rights, but not all did, and some were "defective." To solve the problem of omitting important civil rights, he maintained that "covering amendments" could preserve these rights to the people and the states. He emphasized the political need to move quickly in order to reassure those who had objected to the omission of a bill of rights. By so adding them now, he said, these individuals would no longer have any "apprehensions" that the government intended "to deprive them of the liberty for which they valiantly fought and honorably bled." Many Americans fell into this category, and the federal government "ought not to disregard their inclination." Madison sifted through the many suggestions he received over the next two months, narrowing them down to eight amendments, which he submitted to the House, sitting as a Committee of the Whole, on July 21. Drawing heavily on the language of the Virginia Bill of Rights, he proposed to enlarge the Constitution by eight articles.

The House debated Madison's report, broadened protection against self-incrimination, added guarantees against unreasonable search and seizure, and inserted the words "or to the people" in what became the Tenth Amendment. On August 24, the House forwarded seventeen amendments to the Senate, which reduced the number to twelve in debates closed to the public. By September 25, both houses approved them and sent them to the president to be transmitted to the states. By December 1791, ten were ratified.

With the adoption of the Bill of Rights, Federalists were relieved that the potential dilution of federal power by the amendment process so hoped for by some Antifederalists had been circumvented and that the structure of the national government was unchanged. These ten amendments defined personal liberty in the United States. The First Amendment prohibited Congress from legislating any restriction to freedom of religion, speech, press, peaceable assembly, or petition. Other amendments stipulated procedural safeguards for those accused of a crime, such as the right to a jury trial and prohibition of illegal searches and seizures. Still others prohibited excessive bail and cruel and unusual punishment. The Ninth and Tenth Amendments were specifically designed to reserve to the people any unspecified rights and powers and to ameliorate fears that the new national government was given too much power over the states. The immediate impact of adding the Bill of Rights to the Constitution was salutary: the nation was physically completed by the admission of the two outstanding states, North Carolina (1789) and Rhode Island (1790). However, the adoption of the Bill of Rights, as events soon proved, did not guarantee that civil liberties would remain sacrosanct. This test came seven years later when Congress enacted a sedition act to curtail if not stamp out partisan opposition to the administration.

Such opposition first appeared during the early days of Washington's administration over economic policies advocated by Secretary of the Treasury Alexander Hamilton. Hamilton, to restructure the chaotic economy, proposed that Congress assume the responsibility of funding all public debt, both state and national, create a Bank of the United States to implement the funding and act as a fiscal agent for the federal government, and use congressional power to encourage manufacturing and commerce. But leaders of the opposition, Thomas Jefferson and James Madison, concluded that Hamilton's ideas dangerously expanded the potential use of federal power over the states, unjustly favored commercial interests and the wealthy, and jeopardized those of agriculture and the small, independent farmer. Moreover, they believed that their views represented the true spirit of the Revolution and that Hamilton and his supporters were bent on establishing a limited monarchy that would ultimately destroy the republic.

These opposing views of federal power came to a climax in Washington's cabinet in the spring of 1792, when the president had to decide whether or not to sign the bill creating the Bank of the United States into law. Hamilton argued that the bill should become law, while Jefferson, Washington's secretary of state, was against it. The president had both men put their positions in writing. Hamilton, asserting a "loose construction" of the Constitution, believed that the Bank was justified by the "implied powers" given Congress under the "necessary and proper" clause. Jefferson, believing in "strict construction," wrote that the Tenth Amendment reserved all powers not specifically given Congress "to the states, or to the people." Accordingly, if Congress wished to exercise a power not specifically entitled to it by the document, it must acquire that power through a constitutional amendment. Washington agreed with his secretary of the treasury and signed the bill.

In the 1796 presidential campaign, the strict constructionist opposition, calling themselves Republicans, openly challenged the administration and advanced Jefferson as their candidate. The administration, known as Federalists, preferred John Adams for the office. Unfortunately, in the late eighteenth century systematic political opposition was seen by many Americans as illegitimate in a republic, even a dangerous sign of corruption and subversion. Besides, factionalism had seriously hurt the Articles of Confederation and played a key role in their collapse. Understandably, then, the idea of an opposition party aroused deep concerns. Some felt that if it were allowed to grow unchecked it would weaken, if not destroy, the fabric of the fragile new Constitution. President Washington had endorsed this negative view of political opposition in his Farewell Address of September 17, 1796. In it, he pleaded for "unity of government" because it was "a main pillar in the edifice of . . . independence . . . of your prosperity, of that very Liberty, which you so highly prize." He warned solemnly of "the dangers of parties, in the state." They might be tolerated in monarchies, but in a republic they were to be "seen in . . . greatest rankness." Organized political opposition in "Governments purely elective . . . is a spirit not to be encouraged." It was a fire that, if not quenched by "a uniform vigilance," would burst "into a flame" and consume the nation.

Such concerns became acute among the Federalists when a crisis with France developed. In 1789 the French Revolution began to overthrow an oppressive monarchy and establish a republic. At first, most Americans supported the revolution, but by 1790 disquieting news arrived in the United States of radical violence breaking out in France, and when the king was executed in early 1793, the revolution was seen by some Americans as a perversion of republicanism. By that time, France, convinced that England was plotting with exiled French aristocrats to destroy the revolution, declared war on Britain. Despite the fact that the United States had a 1778 Treaty of Alliance with France, Washington issued a Proclamation of Neutrality that kept America out of the conflict.

But neither belligerent would accept this neutrality. Initially, England violated American neutral rights by impressing American seamen and curtailing American trade with the European continent. Washington avoided mounting public pressure for war by means of the Jay Treaty (1795). Although the treaty ignored the impressment issue, England gave the United States special trading privileges in the West Indies and promised to evacuate its troops still remaining in the Northwest Territory. Washington was disappointed that the treaty said nothing about America's neutral rights, but, fearing the mounting public pressure for reprisals against England, agreed to submit it to the Senate, where it passed by a bare two-thirds margin of 20 to 10. The House approved funding of the treaty by a straight party vote: Federalists in favor, Republicans against.

But no sooner had the neutrality question been settled with England than it surfaced with France. That country, outraged that the United States had not lived up to the 1778 Treaty of Alliance, attempted to cut off trade with England by confiscating American ships carrying English goods. By the spring of 1797 over 300 vessels had been detained. President Adams tried to imitate the diplomatic success Washington had achieved with the Jay Mission and sent three commissioners to Paris to reach a settlement. The negotiations collapsed when the French demanded a $250,000 bribe even before formal talks began. When Adams received the report of this insult in early March 1798, he recalled the commissioners and recommended that Congress prepare for war. It responded by passing appropriations to raise a standing army of 10,000 men, reactivate the Marine Corps, and begin construction of frigates.

In all these actions the Federalists voted to support the "quasi-war" with France and to use the incident of the bribe as an "insult" to the United States to stir anti-French feeling against the Republicans. The Republicans, on the other hand, voted against the war measures and expressed sympathy with the French position. In 1778, they said, the United States had signed the Treaty of Alliance and France had provided indispensable financial and military aid without which the Americans would not have won their independence. Now that France, a sister republic, was fighting for its life, the United States was obligated legally and morally to come to its aid.

Federalist newspapers soon began to accuse Republicans of being traitors "fit for stratagems and spoils." The Boston *Columbian Centennial* cried out that any American who "opposes the Administration is an Anarchist, a Jacobin, and a Traitor." It said that it was "patriotism to write in favor of our government—it is sedition to write against it." Congressional Federalists completely agreed and on July 17, 1798, passed a sedition law as a part of a package of four statutes known as the Alien and Sedition Acts. The targets of these laws were Republican editors, pamphleteers of French extraction, and foreign sympathizers with France, mainly Irish emigrants then living in the United States.

Although the Alien Acts were never enforced, the Sedition Act was, vigorously and against American citizens. Approved by a straight party vote in the House, 44 to 41, it provided heavy criminal penalties, a $2,000 fine, and up to two years in prison for anyone involved in "writing, printing, uttering or publishing any false, scandalous and malicious writing or writings against the government of the United States." It outlawed any conspiracy aimed at preventing the enforcement of federal laws and stipulated that the statute would remain in effect "until March 3, 1801, and no longer"—the last day that the Federalist administration would be in power.

The Federalists argued that such restrictions against free speech and press were "necessary and proper" because of the urgency of the situation. They said that the government had jurisdiction over the common law. They believed that the First Amendment did not restrict the federal government's right to pass a sedition act because it was not imposing prior restraint on either speech or the press. Besides, that amendment did not guarantee freedom from prosecution. Republicans argued that the Sedition Act was neither necessary nor proper. They noted that the Judiciary Act of 1789 stipulated that common law was not within the jurisdiction of the federal courts. Albert Gallatin of Pennsylvania expanded the scope of their argument. He insisted that criticism of public officials in the conduct of their jobs should not be punishable. Such criticism was not the same thing as attacking your neighbor's good name; that could be slander or libel. In a republic, Gallatin concluded, the government must allow the widest latitude of free speech and freedom of the press.

Over the following eighteen months, twenty-five men were arrested, all Republican politicians or editors. Fifteen were indicted and ten were convicted. Vice President Thomas Jefferson and James Madison left the capital, then temporarily located in Philadelphia, and returned to Virginia, where, secretly, they collaborated to try to stop what Jefferson called "the reign of witches." Since the Federalist judges enforcing the Sedition Act denied any of the accused the right to question its constitutionality, the two Virginians turned to the only agency of government left to defend the Bill of Rights, the state legislatures. They sent resolutions by courier to the Republican-controlled state legislatures in Richmond and Frankfort. Although there were slight differences between the resolutions (Madison wrote the Virginia document and Jefferson the Kentucky one), together they argued the same point. The Constitution was a compact among the states that gave specific and limited powers to the federal government. The Sedition Act had exceeded these limits and threatened liberty. Consequently, the states could interpose and prevent its enforcement. Accordingly, the resolutions declared the Sedition Act "unauthorative, void, and of no force" and requested other states to do the same thing.

But no other states endorsed the resolutions. One reason was that public fear of a threat of internal subversion had grown since the Whiskey Rebellion of 1794, during which western Pennsylvania farmers had violently resisted the enforcement of the federal Revenue Act of 1789. President Washington personally took command of 13,000 Pennsylvania militiamen to march against the 7,000 rebels organized near Pittsburgh. The successful suppression of the rebellion, without bloodshed, demonstrated to the public that challenges to federal power would be met vigorously. Moreover, some states said that the law was constitutional; others pointed out that the federal judiciary, not the states, had the power to decide constitutionality.

In the face of this rejection Jefferson drafted a second Kentucky Resolution, which was adopted on February 22, 1799. In it, he used more radical language in defiance of federal law, writing that "the several states who formed that instrument being sovereign and independent, have the unquestionable right to judge of the infraction; and that *a nullification of those sovereignties, of all unauthorized acts done under color of that instrument is the rightful remedy.*"

But by late February, just as Jefferson began to realize that his cause was becoming hopeless, he received astonishing news. Early in 1799 Adams announced another peace mission to France to end the war. Although the results of the mission would not be known for many months, news of the negotiations, and that France had expressed regret at the way the American commissioners had been treated in 1798, was enough to calm the war hysteria that had supported the Sedition Act. And when the French and Americans worked out an amicable settlement, the anti-French fever in the United States subsided.

This shift in public opinion encouraged Republicans to organize an open campaign against the Federalists in the upcoming national election. In marked contrast, the Federalists, by the summer of 1799, had become hopelessly divided between those who supported Adams's peace initiative and those, led by Hamilton, who were mortified by it. Even without (or because of) the quasi-war to cover their efforts to silence Republican newspapers and political opposition, the most ardent Federalists had pressed for more vigorous enforcement of the Sedition Act. Such desperation unmasked the Federalists' motives in the crisis and hurt them at the polls. In the final analysis, Adams's mission cost the Federalists the election in 1800, even though he was not hurt directly by the mission, since he ran ahead of other Federalists running for office. The Republicans, firmly united behind Jefferson and Aaron Burr, won the contest with 53 percent of the vote in the Electoral College and took control of both houses of Congress.

Still, Adams never regretted his decision and remained convinced the rest of his life that at the last minute he had saved the Bill of Rights. To one of the many critics who castigated the old man for having brought about the eventual destruction of his party (the Federalists never won another national election and by 1816 disappeared as a national party), he proclaimed, "I will defend my missions to France, as long as I have an eye to direct my hand." "I desire no other inscription over my gravestone," he wrote, "than 'Here lies John Adams, who took upon himself the responsibility of the peace with France in the year 1800.' " And this is his epitaph.

The subsequent history of eighteenth-century concepts of political sedition was short-lived. In 1812 the Supreme Court settled the constitutional question in *Hudson v. Goodwin* when Justice Joseph Story, writing the majority opinion, declared that Congress and the federal courts did not have common law jurisdiction in sedition; only the states had it. And in the open-ended political debates of the Age of Jackson, unrestrained political criticism was seen as an essential right of the people. What had been considered sedition in the 1790s became the accepted rhetoric and practice of Jacksonian democracy.

Nevertheless, the crisis of the Sedition Act and First Amendment rights caused many Americans, especially southern Republicans, to fear the potential abuse of federal power. And even though Jefferson's and Madison's resistance to what they condemned as an unconstitutional use of federal power in the Virginia and Kentucky Resolutions had failed to win any support, the doctrine of states' rights as a vehicle to stop the expansion and abuse of federal power had been planted—to be resurrected and reapplied by another generation in the Age of Jackson against Congress's alleged abuse of its fiscal authority.

DOCUMENTS

3.1.   Madison's Speech on the Bill of Rights, June 8, 1789

After some deliberation because of concerns that the Antifederalists might use the amendment process to weaken the federal government, James Madison delivered his first speech proposing a bill of rights on the floor of the House of Representatives on June 8, 1789. He was insistent that further delay be avoided at all costs because of rising public pressure for such amendments.

Mr. MADISON. This day Mr. Speaker, is the day assigned for taking into consideration the subject of amendments to the constitution. As I considered myself bound in honor and in duty to do what I have done on this subject, I shall proceed to bring the amendments before you as soon as possible, and advocate them until they shall be finally adopted or rejected by a constitutional majority of this house. With a view of drawing your attention to this important object, I shall move, that this house do now resolve itself into a committee of the whole, on the state of the union, by which an opportunity will be given, to bring forward some propositions which I have strong hopes, will meet the unanimous approbation of this house, after the fullest discussion and most serious regard. I therefore move you, that the house now go into a committee on this business. . . .

When I first hinted to the house my intention of calling their deliberations to this object, I mentioned the pressure of other important subjects, and submitted the propriety of postponing this till the more urgent business was dispatched; but finding that business not dispatched, when the order of the day for considering amendments arrived, I thought it a good reason for a farther delay, I moved the postponement accordingly. . . . But if we continue to postpone from time to time, and refuse to let the subject come into view, it may occasion suspicions, which, though not well founded, may tend to inflame or prejudice the public mind, against our decisions: they may think we are not sincere in our desire to incorporate such amendments in the constitution as will secure those rights, which they consider as not sufficiently guarded. . . .

. . . I will state my reasons why I think it proper to propose amendments; and state the amendments themselves, so far as I think they ought to be proposed. . . . It appears to me that this house is bound by every motive of prudence, not to let the first session pass over without proposing to the state legislatures some things to be incorporated into the constitution, as will render it as acceptable to the whole people of the United States, as it has been found acceptable to a majority of them. I wish, among other reasons why something should be done, that those who have been friendly to the adoption of this constitution, may have the opportunity of proving to those who were opposed to it, that they were as sincerely devoted to liberty and a republican government, as those who charged them with wishing the adoption of this constitution in order to lay the foundation of an aristocracy or despotism. It will be a desirable thing to extinguish from the bosom of every member of the community any apprehensions, that there are those among his countrymen who wish to deprive them of the liberty for which they valiantly fought and honorably bled. . . .

It cannot be a secret to the gentlemen in this house, that, notwithstanding the ratification of this system of government by eleven of the thirteen United States, in some cases unanimously, in others by large majorities; yet still there is a great number of our constituents who are dissatisfied with it; among whom are many respectable for their talents, their patriotism, and respectable for the jealousy they have for their liberty, which, though mistaken in its object, is laudable in its motive. There is a great body of the people falling under this description, who at present feel much inclined to join their support to the cause of federalism, if they were satisfied in this one point: We ought not to disregard their inclination, but, on principles of amity and moderation, conform to their wishes, and expressly declare the great rights of mankind secured under this constitution. . . .

But I will candidly acknowledge, that, over and above all these considerations, I do conceive that the constitution may be amended; that is to say, if all power is subject to abuse, that then it is possible the abuse of the powers of the general government may be guarded against in a more secure manner than is now done, while no one advantage, arising from the exercise of that power, shall be damaged or endangered by it. We have in this way something to gain, and, if we proceed with caution, nothing to lose; and in this case it is necessary to proceed with caution; for while we feel all these inducements to go into a revisal of the constitution, we must feel for the constitution itself, and make that revisal a moderate one. I should be unwilling to see a door opened for a reconsideration of the whole structure of the government, for a reconsideration of the principles and the substance of the powers given; because I doubt, if such a door was opened, if we should be very likely to stop at that point which would be safe to the government itself. . . .

There have been objections of various kinds made against the constitution: Some were levelled against its structure, because the president was without a council; because the senate, which is a legislative body, had judicial powers in trials on impeachments; and because the powers of that body were compounded in other respects, in a manner that did not correspond with a particular theory; because it grants more power than is supposed to be necessary for every good purpose; and controuls the ordinary powers of the state governments. I know some respectable characters who opposed this government on these grounds; but I believe that the great mass of the people who opposed it, disliked it because it did not contain effectual provision against encroachments on particular rights, and those safeguards which they have been long accustomed to have interposed between them and the magistrate who exercised the sovereign power: nor ought we to consider them safe, while a great number of our fellow citizens think these securities necessary.

Source: Neil H. Cogan, *Contexts of the Constitution: A Documentary Collection on Principles of American Constitutional Law* (New York: Foundation Press, 1999), pp. 803–806.

3.2.   Federalist Arguments for the Sedition Bill, July 1798

> Federalist representatives in the House, Samuel Otis of Massa-
> chusetts and Robert Harper of South Carolina, contended that
> the Sedition Act was justified by the necessary and proper clause
> of the Constitution, that the federal government had jurisdiction
> in common law cases of sedition, and that such an act was not
> a violation of the First Amendment.

Mr. Otis said . . . the present bill is perfectly harmless, and contains no provision which is not practised upon under the laws of the several States in which gentlemen had been educated, and from which they had drawn most of their ideas of jurisprudence, yet the gentleman continues to be dissatisfied with it.

The objections of the gentleman from Virginia, he believed, might be reduced to two inquiries. In the first place, had the Constitution given Congress cognizance over the offences described in this bill prior to the adoption of the amendments to the Constitution and, if Congress had that cognizance before that time have those amendments taken it away? With respect to the first question, it must be allowed that every inde-pendent Government has a right to preserve and defend itself against injuries and outrages which endanger its existence; for, unless it has this power, it is unworthy the name of a free Government, and must either fall or be subordinate to some other protection. Now some of the offences delineated in the bill are of this description. . . . From the nature of things, therefore, the National Government is invested with a power to protect itself against outrages of this kind, or it must be indebted to and dependent on an individual State for its protection, which is absurd. . . . The people of the individual States brought with them as a birthright into this country the common law of England, upon which all of them have founded their statute law. . . . When the people of the United States convened for the purpose of framing a federal compact, they were all habituated to this common law, to its usages, its maxims, and its definitions. . . . it will be natural to conclude that, in forming the Constitution, they kept in view the model of the common law, and that a safe recourse may be had to it in all cases that would otherwise be doubtful. Thus we shall find that one great end of this compact, as appears in the preamble, is the establishment of justice, and for this purpose a Judicial department is erected, whose powers are declared "to extend to all cases in law and equity, arising under the Constitution, the laws of the United States." &c. Justice, if the common law ideas of it are rejected, is susceptible of various constructions, but agreeably to the principles of that law, it affords redress for every injury, and provides a punishment for every crime that threatens to disturb the lawful operations of Government. . . . What other law can be contemplated but common law . . . ? It has been said by the gentleman that the Constitution has specified the only crimes that are cognizable under it; but other crimes had been made penal at an early period of the Government, by express statute, to which no exception had been taken. . . . Not because they are described in the Constitution, but because they are crimes against the United States—because laws against them are necessary to carry other laws into effect; because they tend to subvert the Constitution. . . .

. . . [T]his construction of the Constitution was abundantly supported by the act for establishing the Judicial Courts. That act, in describing certain powers of the District Court, contains this remarkable expression: "saving to suitors in all cases the right of a common law remedy, where the common law was competent to give it." . . .

It was, therefore, most evident to his mind, that the Constitution of the United States, prior to the amendments that have been added to it, secured to the National Government the cognizance of all the crimes enumerated in the bill, and it only remained to be considered whether those amendments divested it of this power. The amendment quoted by the gentleman from Virginia is in these words: "Congress shall make no law abridging the freedom of speech and of the press." . . . This freedom said Mr. O[tis], is nothing more than the liberty of writing, publishing, and speaking, one's thoughts, under the condition of being answerable to the injured party, whether it be the Government or an individual, for false, malicious, and seditious expressions, whether spoken or written;

and the liberty of the press is merely an exemption from all previous
restraints. . . .

* * *

[Mr. Harper said that] gentlemen who oppose the bill had said, that
hitherto the Government of the United States had existed and prospered
without a law of this kind, and then exultingly asked: "What change has
now taken place to render such a law necessary?" . . . The change, in his
opinion, consisted in this: that heretofore we had been at peace, and were
now on the point of being driven into a war with a nation which openly
boasts of its party among us, and its "diplomatic skill," as the most
effectual means of paralyzing our efforts, and bringing us to its own
terms. Of the operations of this skill among us, by means of corrupt
partisans and hired presses, he had no doubt; he was every day furnished with stronger reasons for believing in its existence, and saw
stronger indications of its systematic exertion. . . . He knew no reason
why we should not harbor traitors in our bosom as well as other nations;
and he did most firmly believe that France had a party in this country,
small, indeed, and sure to be disgraced and destroyed as soon as its
designs should become generally known, but, active, artful, and determined, and capable, if it could remain concealed, of effecting infinite
mischief. This party was the instrument of her "diplomatic skill." By this
party she hoped to stop "the wheels of our Government," enchain our
strength, enfeeble our efforts, and finally subdue us; and to repress the
enterprises of this party, he wished for a law against sedition and libels,
the two great instruments whereby France and her partisans had worked
for the destruction of other countries, and he had no doubt were now
working, he trusted unsuccessfully, for the destruction of this.

* * *

. . . The coat of mail which Congress was about to provide in this law,
might turn away the point of some dagger aimed at the heart of the
Government, and in that case it would, he said, be matter of rejoicing
that the bill had passed. . . .

It would be recollected, Mr. H[arper] said, that the gentleman from
Pennsylvania (Mr. Gallatin) had drawn an argument against this bill
from the manner in which juries are formed in Pennsylvania. In that
State juries are summoned by the sheriff; and, as the proceedings in the
Courts of the United States must conform to those of the State courts
respectively, the juries to try persons under this act, in Pennsylvania,
would be summoned by the marshal, who, holding his appointment at
the pleasure of the Executive, may select a jury pre-disposed to convict
the person accused. Such was the argument of the gentleman from Pennsylvania; but it should rather be an argument with that gentleman to use

his influence for obtaining a reform of this defect in the laws of his own State. Surely a defect in a State law, which it was in the power of that State to remove, could never be considered as a reason why the United States should not pass a law necessary for the safety, perhaps the existence, of the Government. This argument, moreover, would apply with as much force in one direction as in the other; for if, in the Federal courts, marshals appointed by the Executive should be inclined to pick juries against the accused, sheriffs, on the other hand, in the State courts, might be inclined to pick them in his favor. If, therefore, on the strength of this objection, the trial of libels and sedition should be left to the State courts, instead of being transferred, as the bill proposes, to the Courts of the United States, it would be running into Scylla, in our attempt to avoid Charybdis. There was, certainly, as much danger of partiality on one side as the other.

* * *

. . . They had contended that it was contrary to the third amendment to the Constitution, which provides "that Congress shall pass no law restraining the liberty of speech or the press." The gentleman from Pennsylvania had discovered that, independently of that amendment, Congress had no power to pass a law against sedition and libels none such being expressly given by the Constitution. But can there, said Mr. H[arper], be so great an absurdity, can such a political monster exist, as a Government which has no power to protect itself against sedition and libels? Has not the Constitution said that "Congress shall have power to make all laws which shall be necessary, or proper, for carrying into execution the foregoing powers, and all other powers vested by this Constitution in the Government of the United States, or in any department or officer thereof;" can the powers of a Government be carried into execution, if sedition for opposing its laws, and libels against its officers, itself, and its proceedings, are to pass unpunished? The idea, he said, appeared to him so monstrous and absurd, that he was astonished that any one should seriously advance it.

In the other objection, he admitted that there was more plausibility; the objection founded on that part of the Constitution which provides that "Congress shall pass no law to abridge the liberty of speech or of the press." He held this to be one of the most sacred parts of the Constitution, one by which he would stand the longest, and defend with the greatest zeal. But to what, he asked, did this clause amount? Did this liberty of the press include sedition and licentiousness? Did it authorize persons to throw, with impunity, the most violent abuse upon the President and both Houses of Congress? Was this what gentlemen meant by the liberty of the press? As well might it be said that the liberty of action implied the liberty of assault, trespass, or assassination. Every man possessed the liberty of action; but if he used this liberty to the detriment of others, by attacking their persons or destroying their property, he became liable to punishment for this licentious abuse of his liberty. The liberty of the press stood on precisely the same footing. Every man might publish what he pleased; but if he abused this liberty so as to publish slanders against his neighbor, or false, scandalous, and malicious libels against the magistrates, or the Government, he became liable to punishment. What did this law provide? That if "any person should publish any false, scandalous, and malicious libel against the President or Congress, or either House of Congress, with intent to stir up sedition, or to produce any other of the mischievous and wicked effects particularly described in the bill, he should, on conviction before a jury, be liable to fine and imprisonment. A jury is to try the offence, and they must determine, from the evidence and the circumstances of the case, first that the publication is *false*, secondly that it is *scandalous*, thirdly that it is *malicious*, and fourthly that it was made with the *intent* to do some one of the things particularly described in the bill. If in any one of these points the proof should fail, the man must be acquitted; and it is expressly provided that he may give the *truth* of the publication in evidence as a justification. Such is the substance of this law; and yet it is called a law abridging the liberty of the press! That is to say, that the liberty of the press implies the liberty of publishing, with impunity, false, scandalous, and malicious writings, with intent to stir up sedition, &c. As well might it be said that the liberty of *action* implies the liberty to rob and murder with impunity!

* * *

He had often heard in this place, and elsewhere, harangues on the liberty of the press as if it were to swallow up all other liberties; as if all law and reason, and every right, human and divine, was to fall prostrate before the liberty of the Press; whereas, the true meaning of it is no more than that a man shall be at liberty to print what he pleases, provided he does not offend against the laws, and not that no law shall be passed to regulate this liberty of the press. He admitted that a law which should say a man shall not slander his neighbor would be unnecessary; but it is perfectly within the Constitution to say, that a man shall not do this, or the other, which shall be injurious to the well being of society; in the same way that Congress had a right to make laws to restrain the personal liberty of man, when that liberty is abused by acts of violence on his neighbor.

He remembered a very respectable authority in this country (Dr. Franklin) had said, in an essay of his, called "the Court of the Press," that the liberty of the press could never be suffered to exist without the liberty of the cudgel; meaning no doubt to say, that as the use of the latter must be restrained, so must also the former, or else human life would be deplorable. Nor would the rational liberty of the press be restricted by a well defined law, provided persons have a fair trial by jury; but that liberty of the press which those who desire, who wish to overturn society, and trample upon everything not their own, ought not to be allowed, either in speaking or writing, in any country.

Mr. H[arper] knew the liberty of the press had been carried to a very considerable extent in this country. . . .

. . . It is time therefore, for the Government to take alarm; the long forbearance which it has shown ought to come to an end, since all its acts are represented in the vilest and foulest colors; and now they are sanctioned by the assertions of a person high in respectability, (he meant as to his situation in life,) and a law ought to pass to prevent such invitations as had been given to the people from producing their intended effects. It was for this reason that he wished a law to pass to punish treasonable and seditious writings.

. . . Because the seditious spirit which appeared in respectable quarters, was too long disregarded. If energetic laws had been passed in time, those deplorable effects would not have followed. He trusted they would not take place here. He hoped the most daring attempts to sow discontent among the people will now prove as ineffectual as they have heretofore done. He trusted the good sense and patriotism of the people would be their shield. He believed this, but he did not know it would be the case, and lest it should not, he wished a bill of this kind to pass.

Source: Annals of Congress, 5th Congress, 2nd Session, 1798, pp. 2145–2148, 2163–2168, 2101–2104.

3.3.   Republican Arguments Against the Sedition Bill, July 1798

Republican Albert Gallatin of Pennsylvania was one of the most eloquent opponents of the Sedition Act. He denied the constitutionality of the act and refuted the claim of federal jurisdiction. Most significantly, he stressed the dangers of Congress using the necessary and proper clause to justify legislation such as this act.

[Mr. Gallatin:] Was the bill, in its present shape, free from Constitutional objections? Supposing it to be Constitutional, was it expedient? or, to use the words of the Constitution, was it necessary and proper, at present, to pass this law? These were the two important questions which claimed the attention of the House.

The gentleman from Massachusetts (Mr. Otis) had attempted to prove the constitutionality of the bill by asserting, in the first place, that the power to punish libels was originally vested in Congress by the Constitution, and, in the next place, that the amendment to the Constitution, which declares that Congress shall not pass any law abridging the liberty of the press, had not deprived them of the power originally given. In order to establish his first position, the gentleman had thought it sufficient to insist that the jurisdiction of the Courts of the United States extended to the punishment of offences at common law. . . . That assertion was unfounded; for the judicial authority of those courts is, by the Constitution, declared to extend to cases of Admiralty, or affecting public Ministers; to suits between States, citizens of different States, or foreigners, and to cases arising under the Constitution, laws, and treaties, *made* under the authority of that Constitution; excluding, therefore, cases not arising under either—cases arising under the common law. . . . But, had that gentleman succeeded in proving the existence of the jurisdiction of the Federal Courts over offences at common law, and more particularly over libels, he would thereby have adduced the strongest argument against the passing of this bill; for, if the jurisdiction did exist, where was the necessity of now giving it? If the judicial authority of the Federal Courts, by the Constitution, extended to the punishment of libels, it was unnecessary to pass this law, which, modified as it is, was intended by its supporters for the sole purpose of enacting into a law of the United States the common law of libels. . . . The question was not whether the Courts of the United States had, without this law, the power to punish libels, but whether, supposing they had not the power, Congress had that of giving them this jurisdiction—whether Congress were vested by the Constitution with the authority of passing this bill?

. . . The people of the United States were not under the authority of a simple, or of one, but under two distinct Governments—that of the different States in which they respectively lived, and that of the Union. The Government of the Union was not a consolidated one, possessing general power; it was only a federal one, vested with specific powers, defined by the Constitution; and though it should seem that no one could, on reading that instrument, mistake its principle, yet, for greater security, it had been provided, by an amendment which now made a part of the Constitution, that the power not delegated to the United States, nor prohibited to the individual States, remained respectively with the States, or with the people. Hence it was that Congress had no undefined general legislative powers, but that it became necessary for them, whenever they passed a law, to show from what article of that charter under which they acted—from what specific power vested in them by the Constitution—

they derived the authority they claimed. In this instance, it must be shown that the Constitution has given them the power to pass a law for the punishment of libels. . . . But, so far from this being the case, it would be found that the Constitution had actually specified the cases in which Congress should have power either to define or to provide for the punishment of offences. . . .

It must be evident, from that enumeration, that the only clause of the Constitution which can give a color to the authority now claimed, is that already quoted, which gives Congress authority to make all laws which shall be necessary and proper for carrying into execution the power vested by the Constitution in the Government of the United States, or in any department or officer thereof.

But the language here used was strict and precise; it gave not a vague power, arbitrarily, to create offences against Government, or to take cognizance of cases which fall under the exclusive jurisdiction of the State courts. . . .

Mr. G[allatin] said that he had heretofore considered the Constitution as it originally stood, and that it must be evident that no law against libels could be passed by Congress, unless it was under color of carrying into effect some other distinct power vested in them. However improbable such an attempt might have appeared, the bill now under discussion justified the suspicions of those who, at the time of the adoption of the Constitution, had apprehended that the sense of that generally expressed clause might be distorted for that purpose. It was in order to remove these fears, that the amendment, which declares that Congress shall pass no law abridging the freedom of speech or the liberty of the press, was proposed and adopted—an amendment which was intended as an express exception to any supposed general power of *passing laws*, &c., vested in Congress by the other clause. The sense, in which he and his friends understood this amendment, was that Congress could not pass any law to punish any real or supposed abuse of the press. The construction given to it by the supporters of the bill was, that it did not prevent them to punish what they called the licentiousness of the press, but merely forbade their laying any previous restraints upon it. It appeared to him preposterous to say, that to punish a certain act was not an abridgement of the liberty of doing that act. It appeared to him that it was an insulting evasion of the Constitution for gentlemen to say, "We claim no power to abridge the liberty of the press; *that*, you shall enjoy unrestrained. You may write and publish what you please, but if you publish anything against us, we will punish you for it. . . .

. . . Finally, that construction was inconsistent with the amendment itself. That amendment provided against the passing of any law abridging either the liberty of the press or the freedom of speech; and a sound construction must be such as to be applicable to both. But that contended for, to wit, that the only prohibition was that of passing any law laying previous restraints upon either, was absurd, so far as it related to speech ...; no punishment should by law be inflicted upon it? But, admit the construction given to the amendment by the supporters of this bill, still must they recur to the original provisions of the Constitution—still is it incumbent on them to show that this bill is *necessary*, in order to carry into operation some of the powers of Government. . . . It is an obligation laid apon [sic] them by the Constitution itself, evidently, to prove that an alteration has taken place in the situation of this country, which impels us to pass this law. And yet they are silent. . . . Mr. G[allatin] would ask whether gentlemen did not believe themselves, that at no time had there been less to be apprehended from presses that circulated opinions in opposition to the measures of Government; that no reason could be adduced why this bill should pass, except that a party in the United States, feeling that they had more power, were not afraid of passing such a law, and would pass it, because they felt themselves so strong—so little in need of the assistance of that measure—that they expected to be supported by the people, even in that flagrant attack upon the Constitution?

* * *

[Mr. Gallatin:] Does the situation of the country, at this time, require that any law of this kind should pass? Do there exist such new and alarming symptoms of sedition, as render it necessary to adopt, in addition to the existing laws, any extraordinary measure for the purpose of suppressing unlawful combinations, and of restricting the freedom of speech and of the press? For such were the objects of the bill, whatever modifications it might hereafter receive.

The manner in which the principle of the bill had been supported, was perhaps more extraordinary still than the bill itself. The gentleman from Connecticut, (Mr. Allen,) in order to prove the existence of a combination against the Constitution and Government, had communicated to the House—what? a number of newspaper paragraphs. . . . His idea was to punish men for stating facts which he happened to disbelieve, or for enacting and avowing opinions, not criminal. . . .

* * *

Mr. G[allatin] acknowledged that some of the newspaper paragraphs quoted by Mr. Allen were of a very different nature from that letter. One of them, taken from the *Timepiece*, was extremely exceptionable; most of them contained sentiments different from his own, and expressed in a style he never would adopt. Yet in almost every one of them there was a mixture of truth and error; and what was the remedy proposed by the gentleman from Connecticut in order to rectify and correct error? Coercion: a law inflicting fine and imprisonment for the publication of erroneous opinions.

Was the gentleman afraid, or rather was Administration afraid, that in this instance error could not be successfully opposed by truth? The American Government had heretofore subsisted, it had acquired strength, it had grown on the affection of the people, it had been fully supported without the assistance of laws similar to the bill now on the table. It had been able to repel opposition by the single weapon of argument. And at present, when out of ten presses in the country nine were employed on the side of Administration, such is their want of confidence in the purity of their own views and motives, that they even fear the unequal contest, and require the help of force in order to suppress the limited circulation of the opinions of those who did not approve all their measures. . . .

. . . The only evidences brought by the supporters of this bill consist of writings expressing an opinion that certain measures of Government have been dictated by an unwise policy, or by improper motives, and that some of them were unconstitutional. This bill and its supporters suppose, in fact, that whoever dislikes the measures of Administration and of a temporary majority in Congress, and shall, either by speaking or writing, express his disapprobation and his want of confidence in the men now in power, is seditious, is an enemy, not of Administration, but of the Constitution, and is liable to punishment. That principle, Mr. G[allatin] said, was subversive of the principles of the Constitution itself. If you put the press under any restraint in respect to the measures of members of Government; if you thus deprive the people of the means of obtaining information of their conduct, you in fact render their right of electing nugatory; and this bill must be considered only as a weapon used by a party now in power, in order to perpetuate their authority and preserve their present places.

* * *

. . . In order to prove the necessity of the second section, which went to impose restraints on the liberty of speech and of the press, it was at least necessary to prove the existence of a seditious disposition amongst the people. The supporters of the bill had been unable to bring a single fact before this House, in support of that position. So long as they were compelled to resort only to newspaper paragraphs and speeches on this floor, in order to show the absolute necessity of passing sedition laws, he thought it useless to investigate more deeply the principles of this bill, and he trusted the weakness of their arguments would afford a sufficient proof to this House of the weakness of their cause, and was sufficient to insure a rejection of the bill.

* * *

Mr. Macon had no doubt on his mind that this bill was in direct opposition to the Constitution; and that if a law like this was passed, to
abridge the liberty of the press, Congress would have the same right to
pass a law making an establishment of religion, or to prohibit its free
exercise, as all are contained in the same clause of the Constitution; and,
if it be violated in one respect, it may as well be violated in others.
Several laws had been passed which he thought violated the spirit, but
none before this which directly violated the letter of the Constitution;
and, if this bill was passed, he should hardly think it worth while in
future to allege against any measure that it is in direct contradiction to
the Constitution.

Laws of restraint, like this, Mr. M[acon] said, always operate in a contrary direction from that which they were intended to take. The people
suspect something is not right, when free discussion is feared by Government. They know that truth is not afraid of investigation.

If, said Mr. M[acon], the people are so dissatisfied with Government
as some gentlemen would have it believed, but which he did not credit,
by passing a law like the present you will force them to combine together; they will establish corresponding societies throughout the Union,
and communications will be made in secret, instead of publicly, as had
been the case in other countries. He believed the people might be as
safely trusted with free discussion, as they whom they have chosen to
do their business.

* * *

The gentleman from Connecticut had read from a newspaper a paragraph which said, "that the Federalists are seeking to destroy the liberty
of the press;" but if this bill pass, he would venture to say, that where
that is heard once now, it will be heard a hundred times then. The idea
of abridging the liberty of the press would be so abhorrent to the feelings
of the people of this country, that he could not say what would be the
effect of it. This subject had been so well handled by our Envoys in their
reply to Mr. Talleyrand, that he wondered an attempt of this kind should
have been made. Nothing which he could say would be half so well said
as were their observations on this subject. They met with his entire approbation.

* * *

. . . The people of this country, almost to a man, understand the nature
both of the State and Federal Governments, which could not be said of
the great bulk of the people in Europe, who do not trouble themselves

about the concerns of Government. The people here will, therefore, much sooner discern and repel any encroachments upon their liberty, of which they, as freemen, ought to be extremely jealous.

Source: Annals of Congress, 1798, pp. 2107–2112, 2155–2162.

3.4.   Federalist Newspapers Attack the Republicans

> Astonishingly by today's standards, a large portion of the public in New England and the Middle Atlantic states enthusiastically supported the Sedition Act. Excerpts from several newspapers illustrate the tone and vehemence of their views of Republican opposition to the government.

Claypoole's American Daily Advertiser (Philadelphia) (April 16, 1798): "The Grand Inquest of the United States, for the district of Pennsylvania, to the President of the United States," dated April 13, 1798, a public address sent to Adams, denounced "characters in the United States who call themselves Americans, and who, with patriotism on their lips, and professions of regard for the Constitution of our Country, are endeavoring to poison the minds of the well-meaning citizens and to withdraw from the government the support of the people. . . . They are instruments of disorganization and sedition, many of whom are probably employed by that nation, whose rulers seek the destruction of America."

Porcupine's Gazette (Philadelphia) (June 22, 1798): "It is a fact not to be controverted at this day, that the French have done more toward the destruction of the government of Europe, by their political emissaries, preaching the vile doctrine of infidelity and atheism, and by their spies sent to create divisions among the people, and distinction between them and their government; they have done more by this means of intrigue, than by the combined strength of their armies or the bravery of their military force.—With this truth we cannot be too strongly impressed. Americans! Beware—at this moment beware of the diplomatic skill of the French republic."

Columbian Centinel (Boston) (July 11 and October 5, 1798): "Freedom of speech—let the revilers of our government have *rope* enough. For honest men of all parties the cord of friendship; for traitors and foreign spies the hangman's cord." "It is patriotism to write in favor of our government—it is sedition to write against it."

Connecticut Courant (Hartford) (August 13, 1798): "[When the Jacobins are quiet it is] ominous of evil. The murderer listens to see if all is quiet, then he begins. So it is with the J[a]cobins."

Gazette and General Advertiser (New York) (November 13, 1798): "[R]esistance and opposition to a really legitimate government is treason against the People, and deserves the severest punishment. [Republican newspapers] are the greatest curse to which free governments are liable. . . . Whoever does this is a foe—whoever countenances it is a traitor,— the PEOPLE should watch him with a jealous eye, and consider him ripe for '*treason stratagems and spoils*.' . . . They should be ferreted out of their lurking places, and condemned to the punishment merited by every patricide from the days of Adam to out [*sic*] own."

Albany Centinel (August 7, 1798): "The vile incendiary publications of foreign hirelings among us. . . . Such abominable miscreants deserve no place on the American soil. When the state is in danger and strong remedies are necessary . . . none but an ENEMY can resist their use. Such remedies have been provided by the late Session of Congress; and however long the partisans of France may declaim against them, every good citizen rejoices in the provision, and will aid in giving it efficacy."

Sources: Claypoole's American Daily Advertiser (Philadelphia), April 13 and 16, 1798; *Porcupine's Gazette* (Philadelphia), June 22, 1798; *Columbian Centinel* (Boston), July 11 and October 5, 1798; *Connecticut Courant* (Hartford), August 13, 1798; *Gazette and General Advertiser* (New York), November 13, 1798; *Albany Centinel*, August 7, 1798.

3.5.   Virginia and Kentucky Resolutions

Thomas Jefferson and James Madison collaborated in the writing of these documents, which they sent, unsigned, by courier to the legislatures of the two states. These states in turn formally passed the resolutions and sent them to the other states for endorsement, none of which supported the resolutions. They are the first public statements of the doctrines of states' rights and the use of these rights to block federal law. Madison wrote the Virginia Resolution and Jefferson the two Kentucky Resolutions, the second of which contained the explosive contention that states could nullify a federal law it considered unconstitutional.

KENTUCKY RESOLUTIONS
November 16, 1798

I. *Resolved*, that the several States composing the United States of America, are not united on the principle of unlimited submission to their general government; but that by compact under the style and title of a Constitution for the United States and of amendments thereto, they constituted a general government for special purposes, delegated to that government certain definite powers, reserving each State to itself, the residuary mass of right to their own self-government; and that whensoever the general government assumes undelegated powers, its acts are unauthoritative, void, and of no force. . . .

VIRGINIA RESOLUTIONS
December 24, 1798

Resolved, That the General Assembly of Virginia doth unequivocally express a firm resolution to maintain and defend the Constitution of the United States, and the Constitution of this state, against every aggression either foreign or domestic; and that they will support the Government of the United States in all measures warranted by the former.

That this Assembly most solemnly declares a warm attachment to the union of the states, to maintain which it pledges all its powers; and that, for this end, it is their duty to watch over and oppose every infraction of those principles which constitute the only basis of that Union, because a faithful observance of them can alone secure its existence and the public happiness.

That this Assembly doth explicitly and peremptorily declare that it views the powers of the Federal Government as resulting from the compact to which the states are parties, as limited by the plain sense and intention of the instrument constituting that compact; as no further valid than they are authorized by the grants enumerated in that compact; and that, in case of a deliberate, palpable, and dangerous exercise of other powers not granted by the said compact, the states, who are parties thereto, have the right and are in duty bound to interpose for arresting the progress of the evil, and for maintaining within their respective limits the authorities, rights, and liberties appertaining to them.

* * *

That the General Assembly doth particularly PROTEST against the palpable and alarming infractions of the Constitution in the two late cases of the "Alien and Sedition Acts," passed at the last session of Congress; the first of which exercises a power nowhere delegated to the Federal Government, and which, by uniting legislative and judicial powers to those of [the] *executive, subverts the general principles of free government, as well as the particular organization and positive provisions of the Federal Constitution: and the other of which acts exercises, in like manner, a power not delegated by the Constitution, but, on the contrary, expressly and positively forbidden by one of the amendments thereto,— a power which, more than any other, ought to produce universal alarm, because it is levelled against the right of freely examining public characters and measures, and of free communication among the people thereon, which has ever been justly deemed the only effectual guardian of every other right.*

* * *

... the General Assembly doth solemnly appeal to the like dispositions of the other states, in confidence that they will concur with this Commonwealth in declaring, as it does hereby declare, that the acts aforesaid are unconstitutional; and that the necessary and proper measures will be taken by each for co-operating with this state, in maintaining unimpaired the authorities, rights, and liberties reserved to the states respectively, or to the people. . . .

THE KENTUCKY RESOLUTIONS OF 1799
February 22, 1799

The representatives of the good people of this commonwealth, in General Assembly convened, having maturely considered the answers of sundry states in the Union, to their resolutions passed the last session, respecting certain unconstitutional laws of Congress, commonly called the Alien and Sedition Laws, would be faithless, indeed, to themselves and to those they represent, were they silently to acquiesce in the principles and doctrines attempted to be maintained in all those answers, that of Virginia only excepted. . . .

Resolved, That this commonwealth considers the federal Union, upon the terms and for the purposes specified in the late compact, conducive to the liberty and happiness of the several states: That it does now unequivocally declare its attachment to the Union, and to that compact, agreeably to its obvious and real intention, and will be among the last to seek its dissolution: That if those who administer the general government be permitted to transgress the limits fixed by that compact, by a total disregard to the special delegations of power therein contained, an annihilation of the state governments, and the creation upon their ruins of a general consolidated government, will be the inevitable consequence: That the principle and construction contended for by sundry of the state legislatures, that the general government is the exclusive judge of the extent of the powers delegated to it, stop not short of *despotism*— since the discretion of those who administer the government, and not the *Constitution*, would be the measure of their powers: That the several states who formed that instrument being sovereign and independent, have the unquestionable right to judge of the infraction; and, *That a nullification of those sovereignties, of all unauthorized acts done under color of that instrument is the rightful remedy*: That this commonwealth does, under the most deliberate reconsideration, declare, that the said Alien and Sedition Laws are, in their opinion, palpable violations of the said Constitution; and, however cheerfully it may be disposed to surrender its opinion to a majority of its sister states, in matters of ordinary or doubtful policy, yet, in momentous regulations like the present, which so vitally wound the best rights of the citizen, it would consider a silent acquiescence as highly criminal: That although this commonwealth, as a party to the federal compact, will bow to the laws of the Union, yet, it does, at the same time declare, that it will not now, or ever hereafter, cease to oppose in a constitutional manner, every attempt at what quarter soever offered, to violate that compact. And, finally, in order that no pretext or arguments may be drawn from a supposed acquiescence, on the part of this commonwealth in the constitutionality of those laws, and be thereby used as precedents for similar future violations of the federal compact— this commonwealth does now enter against them its solemn PROTEST.

Source: Henry Steale Commager, ed., *Documents of American History*, vol. 1, 8th ed. (New York: Appleton-Century-Crofts, 1968), pp. 178–184.

3.6. State Reaction to the Virginia and Kentucky Resolutions

To the consternation of Jefferson and Madison, awaiting the responses of the states at their homes in Virginia, not one supported the measures. Some simply declared that the Sedition Act was constitutional and must be obeyed. Others warned of the dangers inherent in a state deciding on the constitutional authority of a federal law; that decision should be made by the courts.

THE STATE OF RHODE ISLAND AND PROVIDENCE PLANTATIONS TO
VIRGINIA
February, 1799

Certain resolutions of the Legislature of Virginia, passed on the 21st of December last, being communicated to the Assembly,—

1. *Resolved*, That, in the opinion of this legislature, the second section of the third article of the Constitution of the United States, in these words, to wit,—"The judicial power shall extend to all cases arising under the laws of the United States,"—vests in the Federal Courts, exclu-

sively, and in the Supreme Court of the United States, ultimately, the authority of deciding on the constitutionality of any act or law of the Congress of the United States.

2. *Resolved*, That for any state legislature to assume that authority would be—

1st. Blending together legislative and judicial powers;

2d. Hazarding an interruption of the peace of the states by civil discord, in case of a diversity of opinions among the state legislatures; each state having, in that case, no resort, for vindicating its own opinions, but the strength of its own arm;

3d. Submitting most important questions of law to less competent tribunals; and,

4th. An infraction of the Constitution of the United States, expressed in plain terms.

3. *Resolved*, That, although, for the above reasons, this legislature, in their public capacity, do not feel themselves authorized to consider and decide on the constitutionality of the Sedition and Alien laws, (so called,) yet they are called upon, by the exigency of this occasion, to declare that, in their private opinions, these laws are within the powers delegated to Congress, and promotive of the welfare of the United States.

4. *Resolved*, That the governor communicate these resolutions to the supreme executive of the state of Virginia, and at the same time express to him that this legislature cannot contemplate, without extreme concern and regret, the many evil and fatal consequences which may flow from the very unwarrantable resolutions aforesaid, of the legislature of Virginia, passed on the twenty-first day of December last.

NEW HAMPSHIRE RESOLUTION ON THE VIRGINIA AND KENTUCKY
RESOLUTIONS
June 15, 1799

The legislature of New Hampshire, having taken into consideration certain resolutions of the General Assembly of Virginia, dated December 21, 1798; also certain resolutions of the legislature of Kentucky, of the 10th of November 1798:—

Resolved, That the legislature of New Hampshire unequivocally express a firm resolution to maintain and defend the Constitution of the United States, and the Constitution of this State, against every aggression, either foreign or domestic, and that they will support the government of the United States in all measures warranted by the former.

That the state legislatures are not the proper tribunals to determine the constitutionality of the laws of the general government; that the duty of such decision is properly and exclusively confided to the judicial department.

That, if the legislature of New Hampshire, for mere speculative purposes, were to express an opinion on the acts of the general government, commonly called "the Alien and Sedition Bills", that opinion would unreservedly be, that those acts are constitutional, and, in the present critical situation of our country, highly expedient.

That the constitutionality and expediency of the acts aforesaid have been very ably advocated and clearly demonstrated by many citizens of the United States, more especially by the minority of the General Assembly of Virginia. The legislature of New Hampshire, therefore, deem it unnecessary, by any train of arguments, to attempt further illustration of the propositions, the truth of which, it is confidently believed, at this day, is very generally seen and acknowledged.

Which report . . . was unanimously received and adopted, one hundred and thirty-seven members being present.

Source: Commager, *Documents of American History*, vol. 1, pp. 184–185.

ANNOTATED RESEARCH GUIDE

Books

Brant, Irving. *James Madison: The Virginia Revolutionary*. Indianapolis: Bobbs-Merrill, 1941. Focuses in part on Madison's crucial role as a leader of the Republican Party in the House of Representatives in framing the arguments against the passing of the Sedition Act of 1798.

Charles, Joseph. *The Origins of the American Party System*. Williamsburg, VA: Institute of Early American History and Culture, 1956. In this short (140-page) essay Charles convincingly shows that the formation of the two-party system in the 1790s was not a grassroots movement but started at the top of the government, in the cabinet and in Congress, where opposition emerged against the economic program of Alexander Hamilton and the Jay Treaty.

Dauer, Manning J. *The Adams Federalists*. Baltimore: Johns Hopkins University Press, 1968. Details how Adams, despite the open break with Hamilton and the High Federalists on the eve of the election of 1800, was able to hold on to the support of the majority of his own party and almost win reelection to the presidency.

Gilbert, Felix. *To the Farewell Address: Ideas of Early American Foreign Policy*. Princeton, NJ: Princeton University Press, 1961. Examines the political environment that led to Washington's Farewell Address as well as Alexander Hamilton's pivotal role in writing the text so as to use it to attack the legitimacy of party opposition to the Federalist administration.

Koch, Adrienne. *Jefferson and Madison: The Great Collaboration*. New York: Oxford University Press, 1964. Sees the political creed known as Jeffersonian as really a mixture of ideas, many of which were conceived by James Madison. Koch also wants her readers to appreciate that Madison's affirmation that that government is best which is least imperfect is not sufficiently understood by many American liberals.

Kurtz, Stephen G. *The Presidency of John Adams: The Collapse of Federalism, 1795–1800*. New York: A. S. Barnes, 1961. Attempts to rehabilitate the reputation of the Adams presidency, often considered a failure. Although admitting that Adams was not a heroic figure like Washington and that he lacked both Hamilton's driving ambition and Jefferson's confidence in the wisdom of the common man as the foundation of democratic government, Kurtz contends that his record was not as disastrous to the nation as is commonly believed.

Levy, Leonard W. *Constitutional Opinions: Aspects of the Bill of Rights*. New York: Oxford University Press, 1986. Considers the Sedition Act as causing a sudden change in thought on freedom of speech and the press. The Republicans, in opposing the act, suddenly advanced a radical new libertarian conception of First Amendment guarantees in stating that the widest toleration of these rights was essential in a government based on popular sovereignty.

Malone, Dumas. *Jefferson and the Ordeal of Liberty*. Boston: Little, Brown, 1962. In this volume, the third of his six-volume biography, this eminent historian tells the story of how Jefferson became the head of the Republican Party and how, as party leader, he championed individual freedom against the Sedition Act.

Miller, John C. *Crisis in Freedom: The Alien and Sedition Acts*. Boston: Little, Brown, 1951. A brief but readable introduction to the events that led to the passing and enforcing of the Sedition Act.

Smith, James Morton. *Freedom's Fetters: The Alien and Sedition Laws and American Civil Liberties*. Ithaca, NY: Cornell University Press, 1956. This definitive treatment of the Alien and Sedition Acts fully explores the crisis of 1798 but clearly is on the side of the Republicans and unsympathetic to the position of the Federalists.

Nonprint Media

Web Sites

www.optonline.com. Deals with the newspaper editors' and public speakers' strong criticism of President John Adams that led to the passing of the Sedition Act.

www.yale.edu. The Avalon Project at Yale Law School: The Virginia Resolution.

www.mayfieldpub.com. Newspaper Timeline. The Alien and Sedition Acts.

www.people.history.ohio-state.edu. Jefferson vs. Federalists; the Alien and Sedition Acts.

www2.gasou.edu/. The election of 1800.

4

Judicial Nationalism: The Marshall Court

Some historians call the election of 1800 a "revolution" because power changed hands peacefully and thereby assured constitutional government by the ballot rather than by an appeal to arms. Whether or not this transfer merits the designation revolutionary might be debated, but one fact remains uncontested: in the debate over federalism the parties switched sides. Now it was the Republicans, in office, who were anxious to expand the power of Congress and the Federalists who were the outspoken critics of such measures. Three events showed dramatically just how the political party positions had reversed themselves on the expansion of federal authority: the Louisiana Purchase, the Embargo Act, and the impeachment of Justice Samuel Chase. Equally significant, at the same time, the Supreme Court under the new Chief Justice, John Marshall, was giving the federal government broad constitutional authority to expand its power over the states.

In 1803 President Jefferson submitted the Livingston-Monroe Treaty, acquiring the Louisiana Territory from France, to the Senate for approval, despite the constitutional objections of the Federalists both in and out of Congress. Federalists opposed the treaty and pointed out that the Constitution contained no specific grant of authority to the president and Congress to make territorial acquisitions without approval of the states. The sheer size of the acquisition, they said, accentuated the constitutional question, and an amendment was required to clarify the issue. But quick ratification was necessary, Jefferson told his cabinet, lest Napoleon change his mind about the deal. Besides, Jefferson knew that the purchase was widely applauded by the public and that his fellow Republicans were hailing it as the greatest national event since the Declaration of Independence. The president pushed ahead.

Jefferson held all of the Republican senators in line and even pulled support from prominent Federalists such as Rufus King, Alexander Hamilton, and former President Adams's own son, John Quincy Adams. The Senate of eighteen Republicans and thirteen Federalists approved the treaty. The House, controlled by Republicans sixty-nine to thirty-six, passed an Enabling Act appropriating the necessary funds to reach the $15 million sale price. On October 21, 1803, President Jefferson signed the act and took possession of Louisiana. On December 20, formal transfer of the territory from France to the United States took place in the Cabildo in New Orleans. No other single event showed how fast the Republicans abandoned their states' rights and strict construction to a loose construction position and moved to a vigorous, pragmatic use of federal power.

Two years later, in order to preserve American neutrality during the Napoleonic Wars, the Republicans passed the Embargo Act. Clearing the Senate by a vote of 22 to 6 and the House by 82 to 44, it prohibited all American vessels from sailing to any foreign port and interdicted foreign vessels from taking on cargo in the United States. Federalist opposition erupted immediately. In New England, state legislatures discussed the calling of a convention for nullification of the act. The Connecticut legislature adopted a resolution reminiscent of the Virginia and Kentucky Resolutions that condemned the Republicans for "overleaping the prescribed bounds of their constitutional powers." It stated that it was "the duty of the state legislature to interpose their protecting shield between the right and liberty of the people, and the assumed power of the General Government." But Jefferson refused to consider repeal until just before he left office in March 1809. In fact, to the end of his life he continued to believe that if the embargo had been in place a little longer, American neutrality would have been respected and the War of 1812 with England avoided.

A third time where Jefferson and the Republicans extended congressional authority was in the so-called War on the Judiciary that resulted in impeachment proceedings against Justice Samuel Chase. Events leading to this episode began with Jefferson's inauguration as president. That day Adams, more petulant than usual, left the capital before dawn rather than attend the ceremony. But before he departed for Boston, he and the Federalists took political revenge and tried to ensure their place in the new order by increasing the power of the federal judiciary. Having lost both the presidency and Congress, in February they passed the Judiciary Act of 1801 and packed the judicial branch with loyal party members. The statute also reduced the Supreme Court from six justices to five, eliminated its duty to serve on the circuit courts, and increased the scope of federal judicial authority. Since the act did not become law until February 27, Adams spent his last hours in office hurriedly signing the "midnight appointments," the commissions for the new Federalist judges.

Jefferson considered the Judiciary Act an unconstitutional attempt to stack the cards against his administration by office-packing. He refused to deliver a batch of "midnight appointments" that still remained in the office of the secretary of state on inauguration day. Then the Republican-controlled Congress repealed the statute and replaced it with the Judiciary Act of 1802, which lowered the number of new judgeships to only five district court positions, restored circuit court responsibilities for the Supreme Court, and limited the time it could sit to hear cases. However, these measures did not satisfy the new president because he had disagreements not only with the existing personnel of the federal judiciary but also with its constitutional structure.

As far back as 1787, when Jefferson was still the American ambassador in Paris and had found out that Article III of the Constitution had established life tenure for federal judges, he was shocked. He felt that the practice was British and totally un-American, for it left the federal judiciary unaccountable to the people. He wrote to Madison that the Constitution must be amended to eliminate life tenure and allow Congress to remove judges by a majority vote instead of by impeachment. Later, the partisan conduct of the Federalist judges in enforcing the Sedition Act only confirmed in his mind the need for these changes.

Yet, as president, when he had the opportunity to ask Congress for the accountability amendment, he decided, in total contradiction to his pronouncements on strict construction and careful adherence to the Constitution, to bypass the amendment process and use impeachment to make the federal judiciary responsible to Congress. He and the Republicans ignored the narrow basis for impeachment, criminal conduct, and broadened it to include misconduct on the bench, and in the process opened the possibility of having judges removed by the political party in power. In short, the Jeffersonians were willing to threaten the independence of the judiciary to make it "accountable to the people."

To establish a precedent for such a radical measure, the Jeffersonians targeted John Pickering, a New Hampshire federal district judge who had earned the enmity of Republicans by berating them from the bench and abusing his judicial authority with partisan favors. Poor Pickering was a particularly vulnerable and pathetic victim. He was both deranged beyond recovery and an alcoholic, and even his family could not convince him to retire. In February 1803, House Republicans voted a bill of impeachment against Pickering and sent it to the Senate. The indictment contained no charge of criminal conduct, only evidence of an emotionally disturbed man. In March, the Senate, with eighteen Republicans for and thirteen Federalists against, secretly voted "guilty as charged," not, as the Constitution required, guilty of "high crimes and misdemeanors."

The same day that the Senate voted on Pickering the House began impeachment proceedings against Supreme Court Justice Samuel Chase for his vigorous prosecution of Republicans under the Sedition Act and specifically for his role in the trial of James Callender, a Virginia newspaper editor, for sedition. Chase, sitting as a trial judge in the Third Circuit Court, had refused to allow Callender's lawyers to prepare a defense, had repeatedly interfered to assist the prosecution, and had instructed the jury to bring in a guilty verdict, which it promptly did. If ever there was a prime example of judicial misconduct, the Jeffersonians thought, Chase was it. In January 1805, House Republicans voted to impeach and sent the charges to the Senate of twenty-five Republicans and only nine Federalists. Chase could easily have been convicted by the required two-thirds majority. But six northern Republicans deserted the president and voted not guilty, and Chase remained on the bench.

The Chase trial proved to be the high-water mark of Jefferson's constitutional radicalism. Not until the impeachment of President Andrew Johnson after the Civil War would the process again be used as a political weapon. Except for a confrontation with John Marshall in the treason trial of Aaron Burr, Jefferson left the judiciary alone. Nevertheless, the Supreme Court had come dangerously close to being politicized. As historian Samuel Eliot Morison observed, had "Chase been found guilty on the evidence presented, there is good reason to believe that the entire Supreme Court would have been purged."[1] As it turned out, the Court under Chief Justice John Marshall became the citadel of the Federalist view of federal power for the next three decades, long after the party itself had ceased to win elections and even after the Republicans achieved a majority on the bench in 1811.

John Adams appointed Marshall, a distant cousin of Jefferson, Chief Justice in January 1801 after Oliver Ellsworth resigned because of health reasons. Marshall embodied the Federalist view of the Constitution. He believed in loose construction, that Congress could pass laws that were necessary and proper. He saw the judiciary as an equal branch of the government and thought that the Supreme Court alone could interpret the Constitution as the "supreme law of the land." Just as important, he strengthened and unified the Court. The justices abandoned *seriatim* opinions where each justice wrote their separate opinions, and issued a single majority opinion so that the Court spoke with one voice. Marshall vastly increased its workload. Prior to 1801, the Court had decided only a handful of cases, notably *Chisholm v. Georgia* (1793) and *Ware v. Holden* (1796). Most federal suits were handled by the district and circuit courts without appeal. However, from 1801 to 1805 alone the Court's docket included twenty-six cases, all but two of them written by Marshall. And he established one of the most important of the Court's powers, judicial review. In his first important opinion, *Marbury v. Madison*, handed down in February 1803, the Court asserted the right to set aside a federal law. Between 1805 and 1832, in judicial review of state laws and court decisions, the Marshall Court established the principle of judicial nationalism, that the Supreme Court could vacate state laws and interpret the Constitution to assure that federal power and institutions were superior to the states.

The *Marbury* case grew out of the political turmoil of the midnight appointments and Jefferson's refusal to cede the undelivered commissions. William Marbury, one of the midnight appointees as justice of the peace of the District of Columbia, sued the secretary of state, James Madison, for his commission. He petitioned the Supreme Court to issue a writ of mandamus, a court order that had to be obeyed subject to punishment for contempt, requiring the president to release the commission. Marbury's request put Marshall in a difficult political position. If he issued the writ, Jefferson would probably ignore it and Marshall had no way to make him comply, short of issuing an arrest warrant. But if the Court denied the petition, it would appear that it was caving in to the Republicans and giving them an important victory.

He avoided the dilemma. He ruled that Marbury should have his appointment since it was his private property, a "vested right." However, Section 13 of the Judiciary Act of 1789, which gave the Court the power to issue that writ, went beyond the Constitution because no such prerogative was listed, or implied, by the document. Marshall wrote that it was "the essence of judicial duty" of the Court to follow the Constitution and concluded that Section 13 was "repugnant to the constitution" and void. In sum, he informed Marbury that while the Court believed he had a right to his commission, it did not have the authority to issue the requested writ.

The *Marbury* decision has stood as the classic example of the Court's power of "coordinate branch" judicial review, although it would not exercise it again until 1857 in the Dred Scott case. The more important form of judicial nationalism in regard to judicial review was the Marshall Court's vacating state laws and judicial opinions that conflicted with the Constitution. These rulings were handed down in six landmark cases where it ruled that state laws and court decisions were subordinate to the Constitution. The Court thereby fashioned what Edward S. Corwin called the "linchpin of the Constitution" that would hold the Union together. These decisions were *Fletcher v. Peck* (1810), *Dartmouth College v. Woodward* (1819), *McCulloch v. Maryland* (1819), *Cohens v. Virginia* (1821), *Gibbons v. Ogden* (1823), and *Worcester v. Georgia* (1832).

In *Fletcher v. Peck*, Marshall determined that the contract clause of the Constitution, Article I, Section 10, provided a shield of protection of property rights against state laws. In 1794 Georgia had issued land titles to a group of speculators called the Yazoo Land Company and authorized the sale of 35 million acres in present-day Alabama and Mississippi for 1.5 cents per acre. It was an immediate public scandal because most members of the legislature had been bribed to vote for the law, and the next legislature rescinded titles to the land. In the meantime, innocent buyers had purchased millions of acres from the Yazoo Company. One of them, Robert Fletcher, sued a seller, John Peck, for breach of warranty of title to challenge the 1796 rescission. The Court agreed and held that the original grant of land to the Yazoo Company was a contract within the meaning of the Constitution. Marshall determined that the second buyers had acquired titles in good faith and that the Rescinding Act of 1796 was an abridgment of the contract clause of the Constitution, and an impairment of the obligation of contract.

The Dartmouth College case, as it is often called, originated in 1816 when New Hampshire altered the charter of the college and made it into a state university. The trustees sued, and, on petition from the Federal District Court of New Hampshire, Daniel Webster argued their plea in *Dartmouth College v. Woodward*. He maintained that the college's charter was a contract within the meaning of the Constitution and that under the contract clause a change in the charter by the legislature impaired a contract originally made between the college and the royal governor of New Hampshire. The Court agreed by a vote of 5 to 1 that the contract clause prevented New Hampshire from impairing the obligations of the charter and that, as successor to the royal government, the state must comply with the Constitution. Marshall's ruling, in addition to establishing the supremacy of the Constitution over state law to protect private education from state interference, also construed the contract clause to limit state regulation of corporate charters and thereby imposed important limitations on state authority over the private economy.

McCulloch v. Maryland involved the question of whether Congress could legislate beyond the powers specifically enumerated in the Constitution. This issue was first raised in the debate over Hamilton's proposal to create the Bank of the United States in 1791 when he justified it as being "necessary and proper" for the economic recovery of the nation. Madison in Congress and Jefferson in the cabinet opposed it as unauthorized by the Constitution, arguing that if Congress wanted to create such a bank it needed an amendment to do so. In 1811, when the Bank's charter expired, the Jeffersonians allowed it to die. Five years later, under President Madison, they reversed themselves and chartered a Second Bank of the United States for twenty years. But many Republicans disagreed and continued to oppose the Second Bank on constitutional grounds as unjustified under the necessary and proper clause.

The issue came to a head in 1818 in Maryland. The president and cashier of the Baltimore branch of the Second Bank of the United States, James Buchanan and James McCulloch, engaged in blatantly fraudulent loan policies. The legislature in February tried to put it out of business by imposing a $15,000 annual licensing tax. McCulloch sued in the Maryland Court of Appeals on a writ of error, claiming that the legislature had erred in passing a tax against a federal institution. When that court upheld the law, McCulloch appealed to the Supreme Court. In his opinion Marshall dealt with two questions: Did Congress have constitutional power to establish a Bank of the United States? And could a state tax a federal institution? The lawyers for Maryland argued only the second question. They claimed that the Bank of the United States was not a federal institution because 60 percent of its stock was owned by private subscribers. In a unanimous decision the Court ruled for McCulloch. Marshall's opinion stated that the Bank was constitutional under the necessary and proper clause and that the Bank was a federal institution which a state could not tax because "the power to tax involves the power to destroy."

Cohens v. Virginia was a case where the Court reasserted a principle established in 1816 in *Martin v. Hunter's Lessee*—namely, that Section 25 of the Judiciary Act of 1789 was constitutional. But it went beyond *Martin* and ruled that the Eleventh Amendment allowed federal appellate courts to review cases from state courts. *Cohens* came about when a Virginia court challenged the ruling on federal power in *McCulloch v. Maryland* and tried to restrict the authority of federal courts. The Cohen brothers were convicted in a Virginia court for the crime of selling lottery tickets in the District of Columbia. Their lawyers argued that since they sold congressionally approved lottery tickets in the capital they were immune from the state's laws because of the supremacy clause. The Virginia courts ruled that the Eleventh Amendment did not permit the Supreme Court to take the case and that Section 25 of the Judiciary Act of 1789 did not give jurisdiction in this case. The courts further claimed that the Court could not review its criminal cases without the state's permission. Judge Spencer Roane of the Virginia Superior Court, in an essay signed "Algernon Sidney" and published in the *Richmond Enquirer* on May 29, 1821, argued that the Constitution operated on the people of Virginia only through its state laws. He also claimed that the Supreme Court could not overturn judgments of state courts. Marshall, in writing the unanimous opinion in *Cohens*, affirmed that Section 25 of the Judiciary Act of 1789 gave the federal courts appellate review over state courts. He wrote that the Court's power "as originally given, extends to all cases arising under the Constitution or a law of the United States, whoever may be the party." However, he ruled in support of Virginia's claim that the District Lottery Act did not exclude that state's law against lotteries. Most important, he affirmed that the Constitution operated directly on the people through the federal courts. He found that the Eleventh Amendment could not prevent appeals to the federal courts and thereby curtailed that amendment as a states' rights barrier to federal judicial authority.

Congressional control of interstate commerce was the issue in the "steamboat case," *Gibbons v. Ogden*, which resulted in the first loose construction interpretation of the Constitution by the Supreme Court. It involved a 1807 grant of a monopoly by New York to a steamboat company, owned by Robert Livingston and Robert Fulton and operated by Aaron Ogden, to have exclusive navigation on the Hudson River between New York City and New Jersey. When Thomas Gibbons began running competing boats between Manhattan and New Jersey, Ogden sued in the New York courts to stop the practice, and in 1811 the state courts upheld the monopoly. Gibbons then secured a federal license under the 1793 Coasting Act, and his lawyer, Daniel Webster, took his case to the Supreme Court on the grounds that the federal license took precedence over New York's monopoly statute. Webster argued that the power over interstate commerce was exclusively federal. L. Thomas Emmet, the lawyer for Ogden, insisted that states had legislated in the past on interstate matters and, therefore, had concurrent power with Congress over interstate commerce. By unanimous vote the Court held that Congress was ultimately supreme in all matters of interstate commerce and that commerce must be defined expansively as buying, selling, and transportation of goods. Marshall went on to define "to regulate" in the Constitution to mean congressional power to foster and protect interstate commerce.

Three years before Marshall retired, he handed down in *Worcester v. Georgia* his last opinion upholding federal power over the states. Georgia had arrested Samuel Worcester and Elizur Butler, Congregational missionaries to the Cherokee Nation, for failing to have a state license to live in Cherokee lands and for inciting them to resist Georgia's laws. The state court sentenced them to four years hard labor. Worcester, represented by William Wirt, sought an injunction in the federal district court to prevent the enforcement of state laws in the Indian nation and to contest the claim that Cherokees living on Georgia's land were subject to its laws. Wirt argued that Georgia had no jurisdiction over Cherokee lands within the state because they were protected by federal treaties. The Court ruled that Georgia's licensing laws were invalid because they not only violated the federal treaties but also contradicted the commerce clause of the Constitution. Marshall said that the Cherokee Nation were a distinct people with independent rights. Georgia simply ignored the Court. President Andrew Jackson refused to enforce the decision and went ahead with the removal of the Cherokees from Georgia to the Indian Territory in what is now Oklahoma, during which, on the "Trail of Tears," thousands perished.

By the end of the Jeffersonian era the pendulum of the federalism debate had swung well toward the expansion of national power. In the "era of good feelings," roughly coinciding with the presidency of James Monroe (1817–1825), the preeminent authority of national institutions and federal law seemed established over the states. Indeed, at the end of the era Henry Clay had cobbled together an even more vigorous program of federal power, the "American System." This term, coined by him in an 1824 speech on the floor of the House, called on Congress to pass a protective tariff to aid northern factories during the birth of the industrial revolution in the United States and to appropriate funds for a program of federal internal improvements (mainly turnpikes and canals) to develop new markets for American-made products in the West. By this time, too, the judicial nationalism of the Marshall Court had established the twin principles that federal institutions and federal law were superior over those of the states and that the expansive power given Congress in the necessary and proper clause was constitutional, principles that would endure to the Civil War and beyond despite attempts by Roger B. Taney, Marshall's successor as Chief Justice, to reverse them. But support for the vigorous federalism that emerged by the end of the era of good feelings met its most severe challenge almost immediately— in the states' rights reaction to the 1828 protective tariff and the nullification crisis of 1828–1833.

NOTE

1. Samuel Eliot Morison, Henry Steele Commager, and William Leuchtenburg, *The Growth of the American Republic*, vol. 1 (New York: Oxford University Press, 1969), p. 346.

DOCUMENTS

4.1.   *McCulloch v. Maryland,* 17 U.S. 316 (1819)

> In this milestone unanimous decision, with Chief Justice John
> Marshall writing the opinion, the Supreme Court upheld the
> constitutionality of the Second Bank of the United States and
> gave judicial sanction to the implied powers of Congress to en-
> act federal laws that were "necessary and proper." It also estab-
> lished the precedent that federal institutions were superior to the
> states and, therefore, that a Maryland tax placed upon a federal
> branch of the bank was unconstitutional because "the power to
> tax involves the power to destroy."

ERROR to the Court of Appeals of the State of Maryland.

This was in action of debt brought by the defendant in error, John
James, who sued as well for himself as for the State of Maryland, in
the County Court of Baltimore County, in the said State, against the
plaintiff in error, McCulloch, to recover certain penalties under the
act of the legislature of Maryland, hereafter mentioned. Judgment being
rendered against the plaintiff in error, upon the following statement
of facts, agreed and submitted to the Court by the parties, was affirmed
by the Court of Appeals of the State of Maryland, the highest Court of
law of said State, and the cause was brought, by writ of error, to this
Court.

* * *

OPINION: Mr. Chief Justice MARSHALL delivered the opinion of the
Court.

* * *

The first question made in the cause is, has Congress power to incorporate a bank?

It has been truly said, that this can scarcely be considered as an open
question, entirely unprejudiced by the former proceedings of the nation
respecting it. The principle now contested was introduced at a very early
period of our history, has been recognised by many successive legislatures, and has been acted upon by the judicial department, in cases of
peculiar delicacy, as a law of undoubted obligation.

* * *

The power now contested was exercised by the first Congress elected under the present constitution. The bill for incorporating the bank of the United States did not steal upon an unsuspecting legislature, and pass unobserved. Its principle was completely understood, and was opposed with equal zeal and ability. After being resisted, first in the fair and open field of debate, and afterwards in the executive cabinet, with as much persevering talent as any measure has ever experienced, and being supported by arguments which convinced minds as pure and as intelligent as this country can boast, it became a law. The original act was permitted to expire; but a short experience of the embarrassments to which the refusal to revive it exposed the government, convinced those who were most prejudiced against the measure of its necessity, and induced the passage of the present law. It would require no ordinary share of intrepidity to assert that a measure adopted under these circumstances was a bold and plain usurpation, to which the constitution gave no countenance.

* * *

In discussing this question, the counsel for the State of Maryland have deemed it of some importance, in the construction of the constitution, to consider that instrument not as emanating from the people, but as the act of sovereign and independent States. The powers of the general government, it has been said, are delegated by the States, who alone are truly sovereign; and must be exercised in subordination to the States, who alone possess supreme dominion.

It would be difficult to sustain this proposition. The Convention which framed the constitution was indeed elected by the State legislatures. But the instrument, when it came from their hands, was a mere proposal, without obligation, or pretensions to it. It was reported to the then existing Congress of the United States, with a request that it might "be submitted to a Convention of Delegates, chosen in each State by the people thereof, under the recommendation of its Legislature, for their assent and ratification." This mode of proceeding was adopted; and by the Convention, by Congress, and by the State Legislatures, the instrument was submitted to the people. They acted upon it in the only manner in which they can act safely, effectively, and wisely, on such a subject, by assembling in Convention. It is true, they assembled in their several States—and where else should they have assembled? No political dreamer was ever wild enough to think of breaking down the lines which separate the States, and of compounding the American people into one common mass. Of consequence, when they act, they act in their States. But the measures they adopt do not, on that account, cease to be the measures of the people themselves, or become the measures of the State governments.

From these Conventions the constitution derives its whole authority. The government proceeds directly from the people; is "ordained and established" in the name of the people; and is declared to be ordained, "in order to form a more perfect union, establish justice, ensure domestic tranquillity, and secure the blessings of liberty to themselves and to their posterity." The assent of the States, in their sovereign capacity, is implied in calling a Convention, and thus submitting that instrument to the people. But the people were at perfect liberty to accept or reject it; and their act was final. It required not the affirmance, and could not be negatived, by the State governments. The constitution, when thus adopted, was of complete obligation, and bound the State sovereignties.

* * *

The government of the Union, then, (whatever may be the influence of this fact on the case,) is, emphatically, and truly, a government of the people. In form and in substance it emanates from them. Its powers are granted by them, and are to be exercised directly on them, and for their benefit.

This government is acknowledged by all to be one of enumerated powers. The principle, that it can exercise only the powers granted to it, would seem too apparent to have required to be enforced by all those arguments which it[s] enlightened friends, while it was depending before the people, found it necessary to urge. That principle is now universally admitted. But the question respecting the extent of the powers actually granted, is perpetually arising, and will probably continue to arise, as long as our system shall exist.

In discussing these questions, the conflicting powers of the general and State governments must be brought into view, and the supremacy of their respective laws, when they are in opposition, must be settled.

If any one proposition could command the universal assent of mankind, we might expect it would be this—that the government of the Union, though limited in its powers, is supreme within its sphere of action. This would seem to result necessarily from its nature. It is the government of all; its powers are delegated by all; it represents all, and acts for all. Though any one State may be willing to control its operations, no State is willing to allow others to control them. The nation, on those subjects on which it can act, must necessarily bind its component parts. But this question is not left to mere reason: the people have, in express terms, decided it, by saying, "this constitution, and the laws of the United States, which shall be made in pursuance thereof," "shall be the supreme law of the land," and by requiring that the members of the

State legislatures, and the officers of the executive and judicial departments of the States, shall take the oath of fidelity to it.

The government of the United States, then, though limited in its powers, is supreme; and its laws, when made in pursuance of the constitution, form the supreme law of the land, "any thing in the constitution or
laws of any State to the contrary notwithstanding."

Among the enumerated powers, we do not find that of establishing a
bank or creating a corporation. But there is no phrase in the instrument
which, like the articles of confederation, excludes incidental or implied
powers; and which requires that every thing granted shall be expressly
and minutely described. Even the 10th amendment, which was framed
for the purpose of quieting the excessive jealousies which had been ex-
cited, omits the word "expressly," and declares only that the powers "not
delegated to the United States, nor prohibited to the States, are reserved
to the States or to the people;" thus leaving the question, whether the
particular power which may become the subject of contest has been delegated to the one government, or prohibited to the other, to depend on
a fair construction of the whole instrument. The men who drew and
adopted this amendment had experienced the embarrassments resulting
from the insertion of this word in the articles of confederation, and probably omitted it to avoid those embarrassments. A constitution, to contain
an accurate detail of all the subdivisions of which its great powers will
admit, and of all the means by which they may be carried into execution,
would partake of the prolixity of a legal code, and could scarcely be
embraced by the human mind. It would probably never be understood
by the public. Its nature, therefore, requires, that only its great outlines
should be marked, its important objects designated, and the minor in-
gredients which compose those objects be deduced from the nature of
the objects themselves. That this idea was entertained by the framers of
the American constitution, is not only to be inferred from the nature of
the instrument, but from the language. Why else were some of the limitations, found in the ninth section of the 1st article, introduced? It is
also, in some degree, warranted by their having omitted to use any restrictive term which might prevent its receiving a fair and just interpretation. In considering this question, then, we must never forget, that it
is a constitution we are expounding.

* * *

But the constitution of the United States has not left the right of Congress to employ the necessary means, for the execution of the powers
conferred on the government, to general reasoning. To its enumeration
of powers is added that of making "all laws which shall be necessary
and proper, for carrying into execution the foregoing powers, and all

other powers vested by this constitution, in the government of the United States, or in any department thereof."

* * *

But the argument on which most reliance is placed, is drawn from the peculiar language of this clause. Congress is not empowered by it to make all laws, which may have relation to the powers conferred on the government, but such only as may be "necessary and proper" for carrying them into execution. The word "necessary" is considered as controlling the whole sentence, and as limiting the right to pass laws for the execution of the granted powers, to such as are indispensable, and without which the power would be nugatory. That it excludes the choice of means, and leaves to Congress, in each case, that only which is most direct and simple.

Is it true, that this is the sense in which the word "necessary" is always used? Does it always import an absolute physical necessity, so strong, that one thing, to which another may be termed necessary, cannot exist without that other? We think it does not. If reference be had to its use, in the common affairs of the world, or in approved authors, we find that it frequently imports no more than that one thing is convenient, or useful, or essential to another. To employ the means necessary to an end, is generally understood as employing any means calculated to produce the end, and not as being confined to those single means, without which the end would be entirely unattainable. Such is the character of human language, that no word conveys to the mind, in all situations, one single definite idea; and nothing is more common than to use words in a figurative sense. Almost all compositions contain words, which, taken in their rigorous sense, would convey a meaning different from that which is obviously intended. It is essential to just construction, that many words which import something excessive, should be understood in a more mitigated sense—in that sense which common usage justifies. The word "necessary" is of this description. It has not a fixed character peculiar to itself. It admits of all degrees of comparison; and is often connected with other words, which increase or diminish the impression the mind receives of the urgency it imports. A thing may be necessary, very necessary, absolutely or indispensably necessary. To no mind would the same idea be conveyed, by these several phrases. This comment on the word is well illustrated, by the passage cited at the bar, from the 10th section of the 1st article of the constitution. It is, we think, impossible to compare the sentence which prohibits a State from laying "imposts, or duties on imports or exports, except what may be absolutely necessary for executing its inspection laws," with that which authorizes Congress "to make all laws which shall be necessary and proper for carrying into execution" the powers of the general government, without feeling a conviction that the convention understood itself to change materially the meaning of the word "necessary," by prefixing the word "absolutely." This word, then, like others, is used in various senses; and, in its construction, the subject, the context, the intention of the person using them, are all to be taken into view.

Let this be done in the case under consideration. The subject is the execution of those great powers on which the welfare of a nation essentially depends. It must have been the intention of those who gave these powers, to insure, as far as human prudence could insure, their beneficial execution. This could not be done by confiding the choice of means to such narrow limits as not to leave it in the power of Congress to adopt any which might be appropriate, and which were conducive to the end. This provision is made in a constitution intended to endure for ages to come, and, consequently, to be adapted to the various crises of human affairs. To have prescribed the means by which government should, in all future time, execute its powers, would have been to change, entirely, the character of the instrument. . . .

* * *

It being the opinion of the Court, that the act incorporating the bank is constitutional; and that the power of establishing a branch in the State of Maryland might be properly exercised by the bank itself, we proceed to inquire—

2. Whether the State of Maryland may, without violating the constitution, tax that branch?

That the power of taxation is one of vital importance; that it is retained by the States; that it is not abridged by the grant of a similar power to the government of the Union; that it is to be concurrently exercised by the two governments: are truths which have never been denied. But, such is the paramount character of the constitution, that its capacity to withdraw any subject from the action of even this power, is admitted. The States are expressly forbidden to lay any duties on imports or exports, except what may be absolutely necessary for executing their inspection laws. If the obligation of this prohibition must be conceded—if it may restrain a State from the exercise of its taxing power on imports and exports; the same paramount character would seem to restrain, as it certainly may restrain, a State from such other exercise of this power, as is in its nature incompatible with, and repugnant to, the constitutional laws of the Union. A law, absolutely repugnant to another, as entirely repeals that other as if express terms of repeal were used.

On this ground the counsel for the bank place its claim to be exempted from the power of a State to tax its operations. There is no express provision for the case, but the claim has been sustained on a principle which so entirely pervades the constitution, is so intermixed with the materials which compose it, so interwoven with its web, so blended with its texture, as to be incapable of being separated from it, without rending it into shreds.

This great principle is, that the constitution and the laws made in pursuance thereof are supreme; that they control the constitution and laws of the respective States, and cannot be controlled by them. From this, which may be almost termed an axiom, other propositions are deduced as corollaries, on the truth or error of which, and on their application to this case, the cause has been suppoed to depend. These are, 1st. That a power to create implies a power to preserve. 2nd. That a power to destroy, if wielded by a different hand, is hostile to, and incompatible with these powers to create and to preserve. 3d. That where this repugnancy exists, that authority which is supreme must control, not yield to that over which it is supreme.

* * *

The power of Congress to create, and of course to continue, the bank, was the subject of the preceding part of this opinion; and is no longer to be considered as questionable.

That the power of taxing it by the States may be exercised so as to destroy it, is too obvious to be denied. . . .

* * *

The sovereignty of a State extends to every thing which exists by its own authority, or is introduced by its permission; but does it extend to those means which are employed by Congress to carry into execution powers conferred on that body by the people of the United States? We think it demonstrable that it does not. Those powers are not given by the people of a single State. They are given by the people of the United States, to a government whose laws, made in pursuance of the constitution, are declared to be supreme. Consequently, the people of a single State cannot confer a sovereignty which will extend over them.

If we measure the power of taxation residing in a State, by the extent of sovereignty which the people of a single State possess, and can confer on its government, we have an intelligible standard, applicable to every case to which the power may be applied. We have a principle which leaves the power of taxing the people and property of a State unimpaired; which leaves to a State the command of all its resources, and which places beyond its reach, all those powers which are conferred by the people of the United States on the government of the Union, and all those means which are given for the purpose of carrying those powers into execution. We have a principle which is safe for the States, and safe for the Union. We are relieved, as we ought to be, from clashing sovereignty; from interfering powers; from a repugnancy between a right in one government to pull down what there is an acknowledged right in another to build up; from the incompatibility of a right in one government to destroy what there is a right in another to preserve. We are not driven to the perplexing inquiry, so unfit for the judicial department, what degree of taxation is the legitimate use, and what degree may amount to the abuse of the power. The attempt to use in one the means employed by the government of the Union, in pursuance of the constitution, is itself an abuse, because it is the usurpation of a power which the people of a single State cannot give.

* * *

If we apply the principle for which the State of Maryland contends, to the constitution generally, we shall find it capable of changing totally the character of that instrument. We shall find it capable of arresting all the measures of the government, and of prostrating it at the foot of the States. The American people have declared their constitution, and the laws made in pursuance thereof, to be supreme; but this principle would transfer the supremacy, in fact, to the States.

If the States may tax one instrument, employed by the government in the execution of its powers, they may tax any and every other instrument. They may tax the mail; they may tax the mint; they may tax patent rights; they may tax the papers of the custom-house; they may tax judicial process; they may tax all the means employed by the government, to an excess which would defeat all the ends of government. This was not intended by the American people. They did not design to make their government dependent on the States.

* * *

It has also been insisted, that, as the power of taxation in the general and State government is acknowledged to be concurrent, every argument which would sustain the right of the general government to tax banks chartered by the States, will equally sustain the right of the States to tax banks chartered by the general government.

But the two cases are not on the same reason. The people of all the States have created the general government, and have conferred upon it the general power of taxation. The people of all the States, and the States themselves, are represented in Congress, and, by their representatives, exercise this power. When they tax the chartered institutions of the States, they tax their constituents; and these taxes must be uniform. But, when a State taxes the operations of the government of the United States, it acts upon institutions created, not by their own constituents, but by people over whom they claim no control. It acts upon the measures of a government created by others as well as themselves, for the benefit of others in common with themselves. The difference is that which always exists, and always must exist, between the action of the whole on a part, and the action of a part on the whole—between the laws of a government declared to be supreme, and those of a government which, when in opposition to those laws, is not supreme.

* * *

The Court has bestowed on this subject its most deliberate consideration. The result is a conviction that the States have no power, by taxation or otherwise, to retard, impede, burden, or in any manner control, the operations of the constitutional laws enacted by Congress to carry into execution the powers vested in the general government. This is, we think, the unavoidable consequence of that supremacy which the constitution has declared.

We are unanimously of opinion, that the law passed by the legislature of Maryland, imposing a tax on the Bank of the United States, is unconstitutional and void.

Source: 4 Wheat. (17 U.S.) 316 (1819).

4.2.   States' Rights Asserted Against *McCulloch v. Maryland*

> John Taylor of Caroline County published *Construction Construed and Constitutions Vindicated* in 1820 to rebut the all-encompassing assertion of federal power over the states in the *McCulloch* ruling. Taylor's arguments represent an extreme, agrarian states' right doctrine. He warned that if Congress had the constitutional power to create a Bank of the United States it might claim the power to interfere in state institutions and free the slaves.

Previously to the union, the states were in the enjoyment of sovereignty or supremacy. Not having relinquished it by the union, in fact having then exercised it, there was no occasion, in declaring the supremacy of the constitution and laws made in pursuance thereof, to notice that portion of state supremacy, originally attached to, not severed from, and of course remaining with the powers not delegated to the federal government; whilst it was necessary to recognize that other portion of supremacy, attached to the special powers transferred from the states to the federal government. But, by recognizing the supremacy transferred, it was not intended to destroy the portion of supremacy not transferred. . . . The supremacy of the constitution is not confined to any particular department or functionary, but extends to our entire system of political

law. Under its protection, the federal senate has a right to defend itself
against the house of representatives; and the federal judicial power
against the federal legislative power; and if so, it seems impossible to
doubt, that the same sanction invests the state and federal judicial powers with a mutual right of self defence, against the aggressions of each
other.

I renounce the idea sometimes advanced, that the state governments
ever were or continue to be, sovereign or unlimited. If the people are
sovereign, their governments cannot also be sovereign. In the state
constitutions, some limitations are to be found; in the federal constitution, they are infinitely more abundant and explicit. Whatever arguments
can be urged against the sovereignty of state governments, stronger can
be urged against the sovereignty of the federal government. Both
governments are subjected to restrictions, and the power by which
both were constituted has entrusted neither with an exclusive power of
enforcing these restrictions upon the other, because it would have conceded its own supremacy by so doing, and parted with its inherent authority.

. . . If federal legislatures do not possess an absolute supremacy, federal judiciaries cannot possess it, since judgments cannot enforce that
which is not law. . . . And hence it results, that the right of construing
the constitution within their respective spheres, is mutual between the
state and general governments, because the latter have no supremacy
over the state powers retained, and the former no supremacy over the
federal powers delegated, except that which provides the stipulated
mode for amending the constitution.

* * *

Finally, it ought to be observed, that the constitution does not invest
the federal court with any jurisdiction, in cases of collision between either
the legislative or judicial powers of the state and federal governments;
and as such a jurisdiction would be infinitely more important than any
other with which it is endowed, the omission is not sufficiently accounted for by saying, either that the case was overlooked, as never
likely to happen, or, that though its occurrence was foreseen as extremely
probable, this important jurisdiction was bestowed by inference only,
whilst cases of jurisdiction comparatively insignificant were minutely expressed. But the omission is well accounted for, if we consider the constitution as having contemplated the state and federal governments as
its co-ordinate guardians, designed to check and balance each other;
since, having established that primary and important principle by the
division of powers between them, it would have been as obvious an
inconsistency to have bestowed a power on the federal courts to settle

collisions as to their mutual rights, as to have reserved the same supervising power to the state courts.

I hope the reader has perceived the propriety of my endeavours to ascertain the principles of our form of government, as preparatory to a consideration of the supremacy claimed for congress, supposed by the court to justify its decision; and as necessary to enable us to determine, whether the ground it has taken is real or imaginary.

Source: John Taylor, *Construction Construed and Constitutions Vindicated* (New York: Da Capo Press, 1970), pp. 142–145, 159. Facsimile of the University of North Carolina Library copy (Richmond, VA: Shepherd & Pollard, 1820).

4.3.   *Cohens v. Virginia* (1821)

This case was an attempt by southern states such as Virginia to challenge the assertion in *McCulloch v. Maryland* of the supremacy of federal law over the states. In this unanimous opinion written by the Chief Justice, Marshall stated that the Constitution made the Union supreme and that this document could only be interpreted by federal courts. The states were restricted to interpreting their own laws, and any federal issue arising in state action, according to the Judiciary Act of 1789, Section 25, must be decided in the federal courts.

OPINION: Mr. Chief Justice MARSHALL delivered the opinion of the Court.

This is a writ of error to a judgment rendered in the Court of Hustings for the borough of Norfolk, on an information for selling lottery tickets, contrary to an act of the Legislature of Virginia. In the State Court, the defendant claimed the protection of an act of Congress. A case was agreed between the parties, which states the act of Assembly on which the prosecution was founded, and the act of Congress on which the defendant relied, and concludes in these words: "If upon this case the Court shall be of opinion that the acts of Congress before mentioned were valid, and, on the true construction of those acts, the lottery tickets sold by the defendants as aforesaid, might lawfully be sold within the State of Virginia, notwithstanding the act or statute of the general assembly of Virginia prohibiting such sale, then judgment to be entered for the defendants: And if the Court should be of opinion that the statute or act of the General Assembly of the State of Virginia, prohibiting such sale, is valid, notwithstanding the said acts of Congress, then judgment to be entered that the defendants are guilty, and that the Commonwealth recover against them one hundred dollars and costs."

* * *

... The first question to be considered is, whether the jurisdiction of this Court is excluded by the character of the parties, one of them being a State, and the other a citizen of that State.

The second section of the third article of the constitution defines the extent of the judicial power of the United States. Jurisdiction is given to the Courts of the Union, in two classes of cases. In the first, their jurisdiction depends on the character of the cause, whoever may be the parties. This class comprehends "all cases in law and equity arising under this constitution, the laws of the United States, and treaties made, or which shall be made, under their authority." This clause extends the jurisdiction of the Court to all the cases described, without making in its terms any exception whatever, and without any regard to the condition of the party. If there be any exception, it is to be implied against the express words of the article.

In the second class, the jurisdiction depends entirely on the character of the parties. In this are comprehended "controversies between two or more States, between a State and citizens of another State," and "between a State and foreign States, citizens or subjects." If these be the parties, it is entirely unimportant what may be the subject of controversy. Be it what it may, these parties have a constitutional right to come into the courts of the Union. . . .

* * *

The American States, as well as the American people, have believed a close and firm union to be essential to their liberty and to their happiness. They have been taught by experience that this union cannot exist without a government for the whole; and they have been taught by the same experience that this government would be a mere shadow, that must disappoint all their hopes, unless invested with large portions of that sovereignty which belongs to independent States. Under the influence of this opinion, and thus instructed by experience, the American people, in the conventions of their respective States, adopted the present constitution.

If it could be doubted, whether, from its nature, it were not supreme in all cases where it is empowered to act, that doubt would be removed by the declaration, that "this constitution, and the laws of the United States which shall be made in pursuance thereof, and all treaties made, or which shall be made, under the authority of the United States, shall be the supreme law of the land; and the judges in every State shall be bound thereby, anything in the constitution or laws of any State to the contrary notwithstanding." This is the authoritative language of the American people; and, if gentlemen please, of the American States. It marks, with lines too strong to be mistaken, the characteristic distinction between the government of the Union, and those of the States. The general government, though limited as to its objects, is supreme with respect to those objects. This principle is a part of the constitution; and if there be any who deny its necessity, none can deny its authority.

* * *

One of the express objects, then, for which the judicial department was established, is the decision of controversies between States, and between a State and individuals. The mere circumstance, that a State is a party, gives jurisdiction to the Court. How, then, can it be contended, that the very same instrument, in the very same section, should be so construed, as that this same circumstance should withdraw a case from the jurisdiction of the court, where the constitution or laws of the United States are supposed to have been violated? . . . The mischievous consequences of the construction contended for on the part of Virginia, are also entitled to great consideration. It would prostrate, it has been said, the government and its laws at the feet of every State in the Union. And would not this be its effect? What power of the government could be executed by its own means, in any State disposed to resist its execution by a course of legislation? The laws must be executed by individuals acting within the several States. If these individuals may be exposed to penalties, and if the Courts of the Union cannot correct the judgments by which these penalties may be enforced, the course of the government may be, at any time, arrested by the will of one of its members. Each member will possess a *veto* on the will of the whole. . . .

* * *

That the United States form, for many and for most important purposes, a single nation, has not yet been denied. In war we are one people. In making peace we are one people. In all commercial regulations we are one and the same people. In many other respects the American people are one, and the government which is alone capable of controlling and managing their interests in all these respects, is the government of the Union. It is their government, and in that character they have no other. America has chosen to be, in many respects, and to many purposes, a nation; and for all these purposes her government is complete; to all these objects it is competent. The people have declared that in the exercise of all the powers given for these objects it is supreme. It can, then, in effecting these objects, legitimately control all individuals or governments within the American territory. The constitution and laws of a State, so far as they are repugnant to the constitution and laws of the United States, are absolutely void. These States are constituent parts of the United States. They are members of one great empire—for some purposes sovereign, for some purposes subordinate.

In a government so constituted is it unreasonable that the judicial power should be competent to give efficacy to the constitutional laws of the legislature? . . .

The propriety of intrusting the construction of the constitution, and laws made in pursuance thereof, to the judiciary of the Union, has not, we believe, as yet been drawn in question. It seems to be a corollary from this political axiom that the federal Courts should either possess exclusive jurisdiction in such cases, or a power to revise the judgment rendered in them by State tribunals. . . .

We are not restrained, then, by the political relations between the general and State governments from construing the words of the constitution defining the judicial power in their true sense. We are not bound to construe them more restrictively than they naturally import.

They give to the Supreme Court appellate jurisdiction in all cases arising under the constitution, laws, and treaties of the United States. The words are broad enough to comprehend all cases of this description, in whatever court they may be decided. . . .

After having bestowed upon this question the most deliberate consideration of which we are capable, the Court is unanimously of opinion that the objections to its jurisdiction are not sustained, and that the motion ought to be overruled.

Motion denied.

After the jurisdiction of the court was thus established the case was then heard and decided on its merits. The court held that the act of Congress authorizing the lottery was confined in its operation to the city of Washington and gave the defendants no right to sell lottery tickets in Virginia, and that the Norfolk court therefore had the right to convict the defendants for violating a law of Virginia, and its judgment was therefore affirmed.

Source: 6 Wheat. (19 U.S.) 264 (1821).

4.4.   Spencer Roane's "Sidney" Essays

Judge Spencer Roane of the Virginia Supreme Court wrote a series of letters to the editor of the *Richmond Enquirer* in 1821 challenging the *Cohens v. Virginia* ruling on federal judicial supremacy. Signed "Algernon Sidney," the May 29 essay argued that the Constitution operated on the people of Virginia through the state courts.

ON THE LOTTERY DECISION.
No. 2.

To the People of the United States:

The address of the supreme court is remarkable, fellow-citizens, in the very outset of their opinion. After stating that the controversy in question, arose under conflicting acts of the general and state governments, it adds, that, in the state court the plaintiff in error claimed the "protection" of the act of Congress. This word "protection", seems to import the entire innocence of that party. It also implies, that the act of the corporation of Washington, under which he acted, was entirely without blemish, and that the statute of Virginia, under which he was prosecuted was wholly indefensible. Nothing can be more remote from the truth than all of these positions: and all this is even admitted by the supreme court itself. But for the conflicting act of the city of Washington, dignified by the supreme court with the name of a statute of the United States, there is no pretense to say that the statute of Virginia was at all objectionable; and the court itself has admitted that the act of the city of Washington is incompetent to retard its execution. This last mentioned act is under the actual decision of the court a void authority when taken in relation to the territory of Virginia: it, therefore, affords no justification, nor can give any "protection" to the person who acts under it. . . .

The supreme court admits that the specification, in the second section of the third article of the constitution, does not extend to this case of a contest between a state and its own citizens; nor can an appellate jurisdiction be fairly inferred. If the jurisdiction, either original or appellate, had been intended to have been given in this delicate case, would it not have been provided for, and *that* in the first instance? The omission of this stronger or superior case shows that it was not intended to be given, under the undoubted rule of construction I have adverted to. If a cause of this kind is excluded from the original jurisdiction of the court, it can derive no aid from a matter which only arises in its progress, and on the merits. It is altogether casual and contingent, even upon the showing of the court itself, whether the cause will ever admit of an appeal or not.

This last idea is in entire unison with the famous provisions in the twenty-fifth section of the judicial act of the United States; and accordingly, that section has received the decided approbation of the court. That section exhibits the remarkable phenomenon, of the judgment of the supreme court of a state, being held to be final or not, according as it is rendered on one or the other side of a given question. It is founded upon a most unwarrantable jealousy of the state judiciaries, and finds nothing to warrant it in the constitution. This position has been justly exposed in all its various aspects, by the court of appeals of Virginia, in the case of *Hunter vs. Martin*. . . .

... The position here laid down by the court would lead to passive obedience and non-resistance by the states until their confederacy was completely overthrown and a consolidated government erected.

The court seems to consider that the constitution adopted by the "American people," expected that large portions of the sovereignty of the states would be given up. On this I have no other remark to make, than that as much of that sovereignty is given up, as has been given up, expressly, or by fair and necessary implication. All other powers are retained by the states and the people. As to the term "American people" used by the court, it seems to savor too much of consolidation. The constitution was adopted by them, not as *one* people, but by the several states, by the people thereof, respectively. In support of this idea I will refer to The Federalist, and to Madison's celebrated report, in almost every page. I will refer also to the Debates in the Convention of Virginia. The difference is not unimportant. In the last view, the idea of a confederation of the states is retained, and a check upon the proceedings of the other government is made more manifest. The expression now used seems to pave the way for the consolidation, which must flow from the principles now established.

... The supremacy yielded by the constitution, is to that constitution itself, and the laws duly made under it, but does not extend to unwarranted expositions thereof, by the courts of *one* of the contracting parties.

Source: William Edward, ed., *The John P. Branch Historical Papers of Randolph Macon College*, 5 vols. (Ashland, VA: Randolph-Macon College, 1905), vol. 2, pp. 78–113.

4.5. *Gibbons v. Ogden* (1824) and Federal Control of Interstate Commerce

In this unanimous decision the Supreme Court, thirty-five years after the ratification of the Constitution, in a clear statement of judicial nationalism, gave Congress predominant, but not exclusive, control over interstate commerce. The Court defined commerce as encompassing not merely the exchange of goods, but all matters of transportation, including steamboat traffic. This case was the first example of loose or broad construction of congressional power under the Constitution.

MARSHALL, C. J. The appellant contends that this decree is erroneous because the laws which purport to give the exclusive privilege it sustains are repugnant to the constitution and laws of the United States. They are said to be repugnant—1st. To that clause in the constitution which authorizes congress to regulate commerce. 2d. To that which authorizes congress to promote the progress of science and useful arts. . . .

As preliminary to the very able discussions of the constitution which we have heard from the bar, and as having some influence on its construction, reference has been made to the political situation of these states, anterior to its formation. It has been said that they were sovereign, were completely independent, and were connected with each other only by a league. This is true. But, when these allied sovereigns converted their league into a government, when they converted their congress of ambassadors, deputed to deliberate on their common concerns, and to recommend measures of general utility, into a legislature, empowered to enact laws on the most interesting subjects, the whole character in which the states appear underwent a change, the extent of which must be determined by a fair consideration of the instrument by which that change was effected.

This instrument contains an enumeration of powers expressly granted by the people to their government. It has been said that these powers ought to be construed strictly. But why ought they to be so construed? . . . What do gentlemen mean by a strict construction? If they contend only against that enlarged construction which would extend words beyond their natural and obvious import, we might question the application of the term, but should not controvert the principle. If they contend for that narrow construction which, in support of some theory not to be found in the constitution, would deny to the government those powers which the words of the grant, as usually understood, import, and which are consistent with the general views and objects of the instrument; for that narrow construction, which would cripple the government, and render it unequal to the objects for which it is declared to be instituted, and to which the powers given, as fairly understood, render it competent; then we cannot perceive the propriety of this strict construction, nor adopt it as the rule by which the constitution is to be expounded. As men whose intentions require no concealment, generally employ the words which most directly and aptly express the ideas they intend to convey, the enlightened patriots who framed our constitution, and the people who adopted it, must be understood to have employed words in their natural sense, and to have intended what they have said.

The words are: "congress shall have power to regulate commerce with foreign nations, and among the several States, and with the Indian tribes." The subject to be regulated is commerce; and our constitution being, as was aptly said at the bar, one of enumeration, and not of definition, to ascertain the extent of the power, it becomes necessary to settle the meaning of the word. The counsel for the appellee would limit it to traffic, to buying and selling, or the interchange of commodities, and do not admit that it comprehends navigation. This would restrict a general term, applicable to many objects, to one of its significations. Commerce, undoubtedly, is traffic, but it is something more,—it is intercourse. It describes the commercial intercourse between nations, and parts of nations, in all its branches, and is regulated by prescribing rules for carrying on that intercourse. . . .

If the opinion that "commerce," as the word is used in the constitution, comprehends navigation also, requires any additional confirmation, that additional confirmation is, we think, furnished by the words of the instrument itself. . . .

The word used in the constitution, then, comprehends, and has been always understood to comprehend, navigation within its meaning; and a power to regulate navigation is as expressly granted as if that term had been added to the word "commerce." . . .

* * *

We are now arrived at the inquiry, What is this power? It is the power to regulate; that is, to prescribe the rule by which commerce is to be governed. This power, like all others vested in congress, is complete in itself, may be exercised to its utmost extent, and acknowledges no limitations other than are prescribed in the constitution. These are expressed in plain terms, and do not affect the questions which arise in this case, or which have been discussed at the bar. If, as has always been understood, the sovereignty of congress, though limited to specified objects, is plenary as to those objects, the power over commerce with foreign nations, and among the several states, is vested in congress as absolutely as it would be in a single government, having in its constitution the same restrictions on the exercise of the power as are found in the constitution of the United States. . . . The power of congress, then, comprehends navigation within the limits of every state in the Union, so far as that navigation may be, in any manner, connected with "commerce with foreign nations, or among the several States, or with the Indian tribes." It may, of consequence, pass the jurisdiction line of New York, and act upon the very waters to which the prohibition now under consideration applies.

* * *

. . . [T]he court will enter upon the inquiry, whether the laws of New York, as expounded by the highest tribunal of that state, have, in their application to this case, come into collision with an act of congress, and deprived a citizen of a right to which that act entitles him. Should this collision exist, it will be immaterial whether those laws were passed in virtue of a concurrent power "to regulate commerce with foreign nations and among the several states," or in virtue of a power to regulate their domestic trade and police. In one case and the other the acts of New York must yield to the law of congress; and the decision sustaining the privilege they confer against a right given by a law of the Union, must be erroneous. . . . The nullity of any act inconsistent with the constitution is produced by the declaration that the constitution is supreme law. . . . In every such case the act of congress, or treaty, is supreme; and the law of the state, though enacted in the exercise of powers not controverted, must yield to it.

* * *

Powerful and ingenious minds, taking as postulates that the powers expressly granted to the government of the Union are to be contracted, by construction, into the narrowest possible compass, and that the original powers of the states are to be retained, if any possible construction will retain them, may, by a course of well-digested, but refined and metaphysical reasoning, founded on these premises, explain away the constitution of our country and leave it a magnificent structure indeed, to look at, but totally unfit for use. They may so entangle and perplex the understanding as to obscure principles which were before thought quite plain, and induce doubts where, if the mind were to pursue its own course none would be perceived. In such a case, it is peculiarly necessary to recur to safe and fundamental principles, to sustain those principles, and when sustained, to make them the tests of the arguments to be examined.

Decree of Court of New York reversed and annulled and bill of Aaron Ogden dismissed.

Source: 9 Wheat. (22 U.S.) 1 (1824).

4.6.   *Worcester v. Georgia* (1832)

The focus of the federal-state issue in this case was the right to protection against state law provided the Cherokee by federal treaties. The state of Georgia, in defiance of these treaties, had enacted laws that placed the Indians under state control. The Marshall Court, in this 1832 ruling and in a companion one of *Cherokee Nation v. Georgia* the previous year, found that the treaties made the Cherokees a "distinct community . . . in which the laws of Georgia can have no force." All matters dealing with this Indian nation and the United States fell under federal law.

March 1832

Mr. Chief Justice Marshall delivered the opinion of the Court.

This cause, in every point of view in which it can be placed, is of the deepest interest.

The defendant is a state, a member of the Union, which has exercised the powers of government over a people who deny its jurisdiction, and are under the protection of the United States.

The plaintiff is a citizen of the state of Vermont, condemned to hard labour for four years in the penitentiary of Georgia; under colour of an act which he alleges to be repugnant to the Constitution, laws, and treaties of the United States. . . .

The indictment charges the plaintiff in error, and others, being white persons, with the offence of "residing within the limits of the Cherokee nation without a license," and "without having taken the oath to support and defend the constitution and laws of the state of Georgia."

* * *

The indictment and plea in this case draw in question, we think, the validity of the treaties made by the United States with Cherokee Indians; if not so, their construction is certainly drawn in question; and the decision has been, if not against their validity, "against the right, privilege, or exemption, specially set up and claimed under them." They also draw into question the validity of a statute of the state of Georgia, "on the ground of its being repugnant to the Constitution, treaties, and laws of the United States, and the decision is in favour of its validity. . . ."

It has been said at the bar, that the acts of the legislature of Georgia seize on the whole Cherokee country, parcel it out among the neighbouring counties of the state, extend her code over the whole country, abolish its institutions and its laws, and annihilate its political existence.

* * *

The Cherokee nation, then, is a distinct community, occupying its own territory, with boundaries accurately described, in which the laws of Georgia can have no force, and which the citizens of Georgia have no right to enter, but with the assent of the Cherokees themselves, or in conformity with treaties, and with the acts of Congress. The whole intercourse between the United States and this nation, is, by our Constitution and laws, vested in the government of the United States.

The act of the state of Georgia, under which the plaintiff in error was prosecuted, is consequently void, and the judgment a nullity.

Source: 6 Peters (31 U.S.) 515 (1832).

4.7.   President Andrew Jackson's Seventh Annual Message to Congress, December 7, 1835

> Jackson refused to sustain Marshall's ruling in *Worcester v. Georgia* and, instead, adopted a policy of removing the Cherokees, as well as the Creeks, Choctaws, Chickasaws, and Seminoles, west of the Mississippi River. He had suggested such a plan in his 1830 message to Congress, but in 1835 he spelled it out in detail.

The plan of removing the aboriginal people who yet remain within the settled portions of the United States to the country west of the Mississippi River approaches its consummation. It was adopted on the most mature consideration of the condition of this race, and ought to be persisted in till the object is accomplished, and prosecuted with as much vigor as a just regard to their circumstances will permit, and as fast as their consent can be obtained. All preceding experiments for the improvement of the Indians have failed. It seems now to be an established fact that they can not live in contact with a civilized community and prosper. Ages of fruitless endeavors have at length brought us to a knowledge of this principle of intercommunication with them. The past we can not recall, but the future we can provide for. Independently of the treaty stipulations into which we have entered with the various tribes for the usufructuary rights they have ceded to us, no one can doubt the moral duty of the Government of the United States to protect and if possible to preserve and perpetuate the scattered remnants of this race which are left within our borders. In the discharge of this duty an extensive region in the West has been assigned for their permanent residence. It has been divided into districts and allotted among them. Many have already removed and others are preparing to go, and with the exception of two small bands living in Ohio and Indiana, not exceeding 1,500 persons, and of the Cherokees, all the tribes on the east side of the Mississippi, and extending from Lake Michigan to Florida, have entered into engagements which will lead to their transplantation.

The plan for their removal and reëstablishment is founded upon the knowledge we have gained of their character and habits, and has been dictated by a spirit of enlarged liberality. A territory exceeding in extent that relinquished has been granted to each tribe. Of its climate, fertility, and capacity to support an Indian population the representations are highly favorable. To these districts the Indians are removed at the expense of the United States, and with certain supplies of clothing, arms, ammunition, and other indispensable articles; they are also furnished gratuitously with provisions for the period of a year after their arrival at their new homes. In that time, from the nature of the country and of the products raised by them, they can subsist themselves by agricultural labor, if they choose to resort to that mode of life; if they do not they are upon the skirts of the great prairies, where countless herds of buffalo roam, and a short time suffices to adapt their own habits to the changes which a change of the animals destined for their food may require. Ample arrangements have also been made for the support of schools; in some instances council houses and churches are to be erected, dwellings constructed for the chiefs, and mills for common use. Funds have been set apart for the maintenance of the poor; the most necessary mechanical arts have been introduced, and blacksmiths, gunsmiths, wheelwrights, millwrights, etc., are supported among them. Steel and iron, and sometimes salt, are purchased for them, and plows and other farming utensils, domestic animals, looms, spinning wheels, cards, etc., are presented to them. And besides these beneficial arrangements, annuities are in all cases paid, amounting in some instances to more than $30 for each individual of the tribe, and in all cases sufficiently great, if justly divided and prudently expended, to enable them, in addition to their own exertions, to live comfortably. And as a stimulus for exertion, it is now provided by law that "in all cases of the appointment of interpreters or other persons employed for the benefit of the Indians a preference shall be given to persons of Indian descent, if such can be found who are properly qualified for the discharge of the duties."

Such are the arrangements for the physical comfort and for the moral improvement of the Indians. The necessary measures for their political advancement and for their separation from our citizens have not been neglected. The pledge of the United States has been given by Congress that the country destined for the residence of this people shall be forever "secured and guaranteed to them." A country west of Missouri and Arkansas has been assigned to them, into which the white settlements are not to be pushed. No political communities can be formed in that extensive region, except those which are established by the Indians themselves or by the United States for them and with their concurrence. A barrier has thus been raised for their protection against the encroachment of our citizens, and guarding the Indians as far as possible from those evils which have brought them to their present condition. Summary authority has been given by law to destroy all ardent spirits found in their country, without waiting the doubtful result and slow process of a legal seizure. I consider the absolute and unconditional interdiction of this article among these people as the first and great step in their melioration. Halfway measures will answer no purpose. These can not successfully contend against the cupidity of the seller and the overpowering appetite of the buyer. And the destructive effects of the traffic are marked in every page of the history of our Indian intercourse.

Source: Henry Steele Commager, ed., *Documents of American History*, vol. 1, 8th ed. (New York: Appleton-Century-Crofts, 1968), pp. 260–268.

ANNOTATED RESEARCH GUIDE

Books

Baker, Leonard. *John Marshall: A Life in Law*. New York: Macmillan, 1974. A reliable one-volume study of Marshall's public career with special emphasis on his years as Chief Justice.

Beveridge, Albert J. *The Life of John Marshall*. 4 vols. Boston: Houghton Mifflin, 1916–1919. Still stands as the main monument in the biographical literature on John Marshall.

Ellis, Richard E. *The Jeffersonian Crisis: Courts and Politics in the Young Republic*. New York: Oxford University Press, 1971. Deals with the conflict, both at the state and national level, within the Jeffersonian Republican Party between the radicals and the moderates over the relationship of an independent judiciary to the emerging American democracy in its earliest phase.

Horsnell, Margaret E. *Spencer Roane: Judicial Advocate of Jeffersonian Principles*. New York: Garland, 1986. Presents a reliable biography of this leading Virginia conservative and penetrating critic of Marshall's ruling in *McCulloch v. Maryland*.

Malone, Dumas. *Jefferson the President: First Term, 1801–1805*. Boston: Little, Brown, 1970; and *Jefferson the President: Second Term, 1805–1809*. Boston: Little, Brown, 1974. The two volumes stand as the most thorough scholarly treatment of Jefferson's stormy relationship with the federal judiciary in general and with Chief Justice John Marshall in particular.

Shalhope, Robert E. *John Taylor of Caroline: Pastoral Republican*. Columbia: University of South Carolina Press, 1980. Gives searching appraisal of this apostle of states' rights opposition to the threat of the "creeping consolidation" of the power of the national government.

Smith, Jean Edward. *John Marshall: Definer of a Nation*. New York: Henry Holt, 1996. In a lively biography, Smith draws a compelling portrait of this remarkable son of a Virginia yeoman who so profoundly shaped the Supreme Court during the first thirty-five years of the nineteenth century. Of compelling interest is his treatment of the deep personal animosities that flared up between President Jefferson and his distant cousin, the Chief Justice.

Stites, Francis N. *John Marshall: Defender of the Constitution*. New York: HarperCollins, 1981. Pictures Marshall as an adept political man who imposed his will on the nation by adapting the then ambiguous phrases of the Constitution to the issues brought before the Supreme Court to lay the foundations of "judicial nationalism."

White, G. Edward. *The Marshall Court and Cultural Change, 1815–1835*. New York:

Oxford University Press, 1991. This book, an abridged edition of White's monumental study of the Marshall Court published as two volumes (III and IV) in the *Oliver Wendell Holmes Devise History of the Supreme Court of the United States*, shows how the active reinterpretation of the Constitution by the Marshall Court was uniquely relevant to the rapidly changing American society of the Age of Jackson. White also stresses how, in handing down these landmark decisions, Marshall created the impression of a nonpartisan, objective Supreme Court.

Wolfe, Christopher. *The Rise of Modern Judicial Review: From Constitutional Interpretation to Judge-Made Law*. New York: Basic Books, 1986. Challenges the portrait of Marshall as committed to judicial activism and rather sees his contribution in reading the Constitution faithfully. It was later generations of Supreme Court justices who turned judicial review into a tool of activism far beyond the power that Marshall intended.

Nonprint Media

Web Sites

www.wwnorton.com/scww/sc-dec.html. Contains a collection of links to various resources offering Supreme Court decisions, such as "Selected Historic Decisions, Chief Justice John Marshall," which has biography and links to seminal Marshall cases included in this chapter.

www.encyclopedia.com/articles/0778.html. Has information on all the cases dealt with in this chapter.

http://stanley.feldbeerg.brandeis.edu/~pwol/14b99lec2.htm. Has Brandeis University lectures on the political climate of the *Marbury v. Madison* case.

http://history1700s.tqn.com/library/weekly/aa022898.htm. Examines the major opinions of the Marshall Court to show how they produced the nationalistic philosophy of John Marshall.

http://history.colstate.edu/Lupold/Miscell-GA/Theyaz~1.htm. "The Yazoo Scandal." Covers the events that led to *Fletcher v. Peck*.

Videotape

Equal Justice Under Law [videorecording]. Pittsburgh: WQED; Public Broadcasting Service, 1988.

5

The Nullification Crisis

By the 1820s the decisions of the Marshall Court, emphasizing as they did the constitutional supremacy of the federal government over the states, brought about a revival in the South of the states' rights arguments first put forth by Jefferson and Madison in the Virginia and Kentucky Resolutions, but this time they were used against Congress's fiscal power. The economic hard times brought on by the Panic of 1819 made many southerners see this power as hostile to slave-based, staple-crop agriculture. This rising phobia of federal authority reached a crisis in 1828 when Congress passed the "Tariff of Abominations."

The tariff actually was an accident, a freak of presidential politics. In the presidential campaign of 1828 the Jacksonian Democrats went along with a strategy devised by Martin Van Buren that would enable them to woo voters in the North (where the tariff was popular) and in the South (where it was adamantly opposed). As planned, that spring they introduced a high tariff bill in the House, where it passed with Democratic votes from the North and West. But they had placed such extraordinarily high duties on certain imports vital to New England textile factories that northern senators were expected to reject it, which, when combined with southern votes against the tariff, would ensure its defeat in the Senate. When that happened, Van Buren thought, Democrats could say in the North that their candidate, Andrew Jackson, was pro-tariff and claim in the South that he had wanted its defeat all along, hence was for free trade. Unexpectedly, Senator Daniel Webster found out what was going on, and he and other New England senators voted for the tariff. At the nadir of an economic depression, the Democrats had given the country a tariff wall of 41 percent, almost doubling taxes on the eve of the election! Quickly, Van Buren changed tactics. Democratic newspapers launched a vicious personal attack on President John Quincy Adams. In November Jackson polled 56 percent of the popular vote, and took the Electoral College by a vote of 178 to 83.

Many southerners hoped that the new president, himself a southern planter, would reduce the tariff. But John Calhoun, his vice president, wanted to make certain that everyone realized how strongly his section felt about the Tariff of Abominations. He retreated to his home in the South Carolina foothills, composed *The South Carolina Exposition and Protest*, and sent it to the legislature, which passed it in December. Citing Jefferson and Madison and using language of the Virginia and Kentucky Resolutions, Calhoun argued that the Union had been created by state governments; it was a compact where the powers of Congress were precisely limited. Consequently, a state could nullify any law that exceeded these enumerated powers. He targeted the Tariff of 1828 as "unconstitutional, unequal, and oppressive, and calculated to corrupt the public virtue and destroy the liberty of the country." It made southerners "the serfs of the system" and imposed a protective tax on southern planters exclusively for the benefit of northern factory owners. This was nothing more than the "despotism of the many" that made the rich richer and the poor poorer.

As vice president, Calhoun believed he had to keep his authorship of the *Exposition* anonymous and allowed others to argue his case. Early in 1830, as Calhoun solemnly presided over the Senate, a packed gallery listened to Senators Robert Y. Hayne of South Carolina and Daniel Webster of Massachusetts argue over Calhoun's ideas. He nodded in agreement as Hayne claimed that the North, in the "spirit of false philanthropy," wanted to destroy the South and dissolve the Union, just as it had tried to do in the Hartford Convention of 1814. He defended the right of the states to "interpose" their authority between the federal government and the people whenever Congress violated the Constitution.

Webster responded. Forget about the Hartford Convention, he said, that was history. In 1830 New England thought not in terms of states' rights but only about the welfare of the nation. Nullification was a false and dangerous doctrine that threatened national unity. The federal government, he intoned, was not a league of states but a manifestation of the will of the people, and the national interest transcended any sectional or state interest. He ended with a panegyric to the Union, one of the most quoted passages in the history of the Senate. He depicted in powerful language the outcome of nullification. It would leave "broken and dishonored fragments of a once glorious Union" with "States dissevered, discordant, belligerent; on a land rent with civil feuds, or drenched . . . in fraternal blood!" A rejection of nullification would see a rededication to a strong and perpetual Union "everywhere, spread all over in characters of living light, blazing on all its ample folds, as they float over the sea and over the land," flourishing under the sentiments "dear to every true American heart—Liberty *and* Union, now and forever, one and inseparable!"

Jackson, although in some instances an advocate of states' rights, condemned nullification outright. Within three months after the Webster-Hayne debate, the president discovered that Calhoun had written the *Exposition* and that Hayne had used it in the debate. Calhoun, caught between his loyalty to the Union as vice president and his instinctive devotion to states' rights doctrines as expressed in the document, resigned. He returned to South Carolina and was elected to the Senate. When Congress enacted a tariff in the fall of 1832 that reduced some protectionist duties but still kept high levels on textiles and iron, the South Carolina legislature called for the election of delegates to the Columbia Nullification Convention.

The convention, overwhelmingly dominated by the "nullifiers," used Calhoun's *Exposition* to justify its stand against federal power. Some historians contend that more than the tariff issue of federal power versus states' rights moved the South Carolina nullifiers to confront the president and Congress. Behind that issue lurked an intense fear of the possible use of federal power to destroy slavery. South Carolinians seemed especially sensitive to the security of their "peculiar institution" due to recent, alarming events involving slave unrest—the Denmark Vesey planned insurrection in Charleston in 1822, the publication in 1829 of David Walker's *Appeal to the Coloured Citizens of the World* with its call for a slave revolt, and the Nat Turner rebellion and massacre in Virginia in 1831. Moreover, the publication the same year as the Turner revolt of William Lloyd Garrison's radical abolitionist newspaper the *Liberator*, and increasing reports of slave violence and slave insurrections prevented in the nick of time, all combined to make the nullifiers' phobia of slave unrest and antislavery agitation acute. This was a mindset that overresponded to any external threat, such as the Tariff of 1828, that seemed to challenge states' rights, to them the only secure shield to preservation of slavery.

For a combination of reasons, therefore, on November 24, the nullifier-controlled South Carolina legislature passed the Ordinance of Nullification and declared the Tariff of 1828 null and void in South Carolina. State officers were forbidden to try to enforce the tarriff, and any appeal to the federal courts was prohibited. They also had to take an oath to support the ordinance or be removed from office. The ordinance warned that if the federal government used force to collect tariff duties, the citizens of South Carolina would automatically be relieved of all allegiance to the Union and the state would "proceed to organize a separate Government."

Jackson's response was swift and decisive. He threatened to hang Calhoun for treason and have the federal army enforce the law if nullifiers defied federal authority. On December 10 he issued a proclamation to the people of South Carolina that condemned nullification as destructive of the Union. He stated that the "Constitution of the United States . . . forms a *government*, not a league." The Union was perpetual, no state had the right to secede, and "disunion by armed force was treason." He dispatched General Winfield Scott to take command of federal troops in Charleston, sent a warship and seven revenue cutters to take up position in the harbor, and promised opponents of the nullifiers in South Carolina that the federal government would protect them should any civil strife break out. In January 1833, Congress passed the Force Bill, which allowed the president to use military force to override the Ordinance of Nullification.

But President Jackson, while taking these belligerent positions, urged Congress to reduce the tariff and, holding out the prospect of tariff reform through the government, isolated South Carolina from other southern states. Calhoun, realizing that he was getting no support in the South, reluctantly agreed to work in the Senate with Henry Clay to craft a compromise tariff. This bill, signed by Jackson on March 1, 1833, reduced import taxes to a 20 percent level over a ten-year period. South Carolina then repealed its Ordinance of Nullification, but not before, in a show of bravado, it nullified the Force Bill.

The nullification crisis was the first serious confrontation between a federal law and states' rights since the Sedition Act and the Virginia and Kentucky Resolutions. The nullifiers saw themselves as carrying on the same fight for liberty against oppression that Jefferson and Madison had championed in 1798 and the Patriots before them in 1776, but Calhoun's doctrine was too radical for most southerners to accept in 1832. However, the crisis showed that while there was no real support for nullification outside South Carolina, other southern states such as Georgia and Alabama supported the states' rights principles behind it. So, even though nullification was discredited, resistance to expanding federal power was not.

More ominous, the South never again dropped back into its old nationalistic way of thinking, and terms like states' rights, state sovereignty, and even secession increasingly became household words. Before the nullification showdown, the South had considered federal-state issues rationally, as seen in the Virginia and Kentucky Resolutions or in the writings of John Taylor of Caroline and Spencer Roane against the Marshall Court. Afterward, it became more and more emotional, increasingly fearful that it was becoming a helpless minority. Some, like nullifier William Harper, were convinced that the nation was "divided into slaveholding and non-slaveholding states," and that this was "the broad and marked distinction that must separate us at last." This feeling of isolation festered and grew during the decades after the nullification crisis. While nullification itself never revived, the threat of secession became a stronger and stronger refrain throughout the South as it came to see Congress as a threat to the future of its "peculiar institution."

DOCUMENTS

5.1.   *The South Carolina Exposition and Protest*, December 19, 1828

This anonymously published pamphlet was Vice President John
Calhoun's states' rights argument against Congress's power to
pass and enforce the Tariff of 1828. In it, he described an unavoidable economic conflict between the North and the South
because the North was industrial and the South was agricultural.
The South's condition after the Tariff of 1828 was intolerable.
The federal government might as well take one-third of its cotton
crop, and the region was helpless since it could not raise cotton
prices in a world market. The end result would be the creation
of a politically dominant industrial class that would pass federal
laws designed to ruin the agrarian South and destroy slavery to
benefit northern factories. South Carolina must use the power
given the states by the Constitution to nullify such an unconstitutional law. This power remained with the states, he reasoned,
simply because it had never been given to the federal government.

The Senate and House of Representatives of South Carolina, now met,
and sitting in General Assembly, through the Hon. William Smith and
the Hon. Robert Y. Hayne, their representatives in the Senate of the
United States, do, in the name and on behalf of the good people of the
said commonwealth, solemnly PROTEST against the system of protecting duties, lately adopted by the federal government, for the following
reasons:—

1st. *Because* the good people of this commonwealth believe that the
powers of Congress were delegated to it in trust for the accomplishment
of certain specified objects which limit and control them, and that every
exercise of them for any other purposes, is a violation of the Constitution
as unwarrantable as the undisguised assumption of substantive, independent powers not granted or expressly withheld.

2d. *Because* the power to lay duties on imports is, and in its very nature
can be, only a means of effecting objects specified by the Constitution;
since no free government, and least of all a government of enumerated
powers, can of right impose any tax, any more than a penalty, which is
not at once justified by public necessity, and clearly within the scope and

purview of the social compact; and since the right of confining appropriations of the public money to such legitimate and constitutional objects is as essential to the liberty of the people as their unquestionable privilege to be taxed only by their consent.

3d. *Because* they believe that the tariff law passed by Congress at its last session, and all other acts of which the principal object is the protection of manufactures, or any other branch of domestic industry; if they be considered as the exercise of a power in Congress to tax the people at its own good will and pleasure, and to apply the money raised to objects not specified in the Constitution, is a violation of these fundamental principles, a breach of a well-defined trust, and a perversion of the high powers vested in the federal government for federal purposes only.

4th. *Because* such acts, considered in the light of a regulation of commerce, are equally liable to objection; since, although the power to regulate commerce may, like all other powers, be exercised so as to protect domestic manufactures, yet it is clearly distinguishable from a power to do so *eo nomine*, both in the nature of the thing and in the common acception of the terms; and because the confounding of them would lead to the most extravagant results, since the encouragement of domestic industry implies an absolute control over all the interests, resources, and pursuits of a people, and is consistent with the idea of any other than a simple, consolidated government.

5th. *Because*, from the contemporaneous exposition of the Constitution in the numbers of the *Federalist*, (which is cited only because the Supreme Court has recognized its authority), it is clear that the power to regulate commerce was considered by the Convention as only incidentally connected with the encouragement of agriculture and manufactures; and because the power of laying imposts and duties on imports was not understood to justify in any case, a prohibition of foreign commodities, except as a means of extending commerce, by coercing foreign nations to a fair reciprocity in their intercourse with us, or for some *bona fide* commercial purpose.

6th. *Because*, whilst the power to protect manufacturers is nowhere expressly granted to Congress, nor can be considered as necessary and proper to carry into effect any specified power, it seems to be expressly reserved to the states, by the 10th section of the 1st article of the Constitution.

7th. *Because* even admitting Congress to have a constitutional right to protect manufactures by the imposition of duties, or by regulations of commerce, designed principally for that purpose, yet a tariff of which the operation is grossly unequal and oppressive, is such an abuse of power as is incompatible with the principles of a free government and the great ends of civil society, justice, and equality of rights and protection.

8th. *Finally*, because South Carolina, from her climate, situation, and peculiar institutions, is, and must ever continue to be, wholly dependent upon agriculture and commerce, not only for her prosperity, but for her very existence as a state; because the valuable products of her soil—the blessings by which Divine Providence seems to have designed to compensate for the great disadvantages under which she suffers in other respects—are among the very few that can be cultivated with any profit by slave labor; and if, by the loss of her foreign commerce, these products should be confined to an inadequate market, the fate of this fertile state would be poverty and utter desolation; her citizens, in despair, would emigrate to more fortunate regions, and the whole frame and constitution of her civil policy be impaired and deranged, if not dissolved entirely.

Deeply impressed with these considerations, the representatives of the good people of this commonwealth, anxiously desiring to live in peace with their fellow-citizens, and to do all that in them lies to preserve and perpetuate the union of the states, and liberties of which it is the surest pledge, but feeling it to be their bounden duty to expose and resist all encroachments upon the true spirit of the Constitution, lest an apparant acquiescence in the system of protecting duties should be drawn into precedent—do, in the name of the commonwealth of South Carolina, claim to enter upon the Journal of the Senate their *protest* against it as unconstitutional, oppressive, and unjust.

Source: Henry Steele Commager, ed., *Documents of American History*, vol. 1, 8th ed. (New York: Appleton-Century-Crofts, 1968), pp. 249–251.

5.2.   Webster's Second Reply, January 26, 1830

> Webster replied to Senator Robert Y. Hayne of South Carolina and the states' rights argument that southern states could "interpose" to prevent the enforcement of an unconstitutional law. It was one of his most eloquent speeches on the floor of the Senate and a powerful oration in defense of federal power and the preservation of the Union.

There yet remains to be performed, Mr. President, by far the most grave and important duty, which I feel to be devolved on me by this occasion. It is to state, and to defend, what I conceive to be the true principles of the Constitution under which we are here assembled. . . .

I understand the honorable gentleman from South Carolina to maintain, that it is a right of the State legislatures to interfere, whenever, in their judgment, this government transcends its constitutional limits, and to arrest the operation of its laws.

I understand him to maintain this right, as a right existing *under* the Constitution, not as a right to overthrow it on the ground of extreme necessity, such as would justify violent revolution.

I understand him to maintain an authority, on the part of the States, thus to interfere, for the purpose of correcting the exercise of power by the general government, of checking it, and of compelling it to conform to their opinion of the extent of its powers.

I understand him to maintain, that the ultimate power of judging of the constitutional extent of its own authority is not lodged exclusively in the general government, or any branch of it; but that, on the contrary, the States may lawfully decide for themselves, and each State for itself, whether, in a given case, the act of the general government transcends its power.

I understand him to insist, that, if the exigency of the case, in the opinion of any State government, require it, such State government may, by its own sovereign authority, annul an act of the general government which it deems plainly and palpably unconstitutional.

This is the sum of what I understand from him to be the South Carolina doctrine, and the doctrine which he maintains. I propose to consider it, and compare it with the Constitution. . . .

* * *

. . . I say, the right of a State to annul a law of Congress cannot be maintained. . . . I do not admit, that, under the Constitution and in conformity with it, there is any mode in which a State government, as a member of the Union, can interfere and stop the progress of the general government, by force of her own laws, under any circumstances whatever.

* * *

There are other proceedings of public bodies which have already been alluded to, and to which I refer again, for the purpose of ascertaining more fully what is the length and breadth of that doctrine, denominated the Carolina doctrine, which the honorable member has now stood up on this floor to maintain. In one of them I find it resolved, that "the tariff of 1828, and every other tariff designed to promote one branch of industry at the expense of others, is contrary to the meaning and intention of the federal compact; and such a dangerous, palpable, and deliberate usurpation of power, by a determined majority, wielding the general government beyond the limits of its delegated powers, as calls upon the

States which compose the suffering minority, in their sovereign capacity, to exercise the powers which, as sovereigns, necessarily devolve upon them, when their compact is violated."

Observe, Sir, that this resolution holds the tariff of 1828, and every other tariff designed to promote one branch of industry at the expense of another, to be such a dangerous, palpable, and deliberate usurpation of power, as calls upon the States, in their sovereign capacity, to interfere by their own authority. . . .

* * *

I wish now, Sir, to make a remark upon the Virginia resolutions of 1798. I cannot undertake to say how these resolutions were understood by those who passed them. Their language is not a little indefinite. In the case of the exercise by Congress of a dangerous power not granted to them, the resolutions assert the right, on the part of the State, to interfere and arrest the progress of the evil. This is susceptible of more than one interpretation. It may mean no more than that the States may interfere by complaint and remonstrance, or by proposing to the people an alteration of the Federal Constitution. This would all be quite unobjectionable. Or it may be that no more is meant than to assert the general right of revolution, as against all governments, in cases of intolerable oppression. This no one doubts, and this, in my opinion, is all that he who framed the resolutions could have meant by it; for I shall not readily believe that he was ever of opinion that a State, under the Constitution and in conformity with it, could, upon the ground of her own opinion of its unconstitutionality, however clear and palpable she might think the case, annul a law of Congress, so far as it should operate on herself, by her own legislative power.

I must now beg to ask, Sir, Whence is this supposed right of the States derived? Where do they find the power to interfere with the laws of the Union? Sir, the opinion which the honorable gentleman maintains is a notion founded in a total misapprehension, in my judgment, of the origin of this government, and of the foundation on which it stands. I hold it to be a popular government, erected by the people; those who administer it, responsible to the people; and itself capable of being amended and modified, just as the people may choose it should be. It is as popular, just as truly emanating from the people, as the State governments. It is created for one purpose; the State governments for another. It has its own powers; they have theirs. There is no more authority with them to arrest the operation of a law of Congress, than with Congress to arrest the operation of their laws. We are here to administer a Constitution emanating immediately from the people, and trusted by them to our administration. . . . Sir, the very chief end, the main design, for which the whole Constitution was framed and adopted, was to establish a government that should not be obliged to act through State agency, or depend on State opinion and State discretion. The people had had quite enough of that kind of government under the Confederation. Under that system, the legal action, the application of law to individuals, belonged exclusively to the States. Congress could only recommend; their acts were not of binding force, till the States had adopted and sanctioned them. Are we in that condition still? Are we yet at the mercy of State discretion and State construction? Sir, if we are, then vain will be our attempt to maintain the Constitution under which we sit.

* * *

I have not allowed myself, Sir, to look beyond the Union, to see what might lie hidden in the dark recess behind. I have not coolly weighed the chances of preserving liberty when the bonds that unite us together shall be broken asunder. I have not accustomed myself to hang over the precipice of disunion, to see whether, with my short sight, I can fathom the depth of the abyss below; nor could I regard him as a safe counsellor in the affairs of this government, whose thoughts should be mainly bent on considering, not how the Union may be best preserved, but how tolerable might be the condition of the people when it should be broken up and destroyed. While the Union lasts, we have high, exciting, gratifying prospects spread out before us, for us and our children. Beyond that I seek not to penetrate the veil. God grant that in my day, at least, that curtain may not rise! God grant that on my vision never may be opened what lies behind! When my eyes shall be turned to behold for the last time the sun in heaven, may I not see him shining on the broken and dishonored fragments of a once glorious Union; on States dissevered, discordant, belligerent; on a land rent with civil feuds, or drenched, it may be, in fraternal blood! Let their last feeble and lingering glance rather behold the gorgeous ensign of the republic, now known and honored throughout the earth, still full high advanced, its arms and trophies streaming in their original lustre, not a stripe erased or polluted, nor a single star obscured, bearing for its motto, no such miserable interrogatory as "What is all this worth?" nor those other words of delusion and folly, "Liberty first and Union afterwards"; but everywhere, spread all over in characters of living light, blazing on all its ample folds, as they float over the sea and over the land, and in every wind under the whole heavens, that other sentiment, dear to every true American heart,—Liberty *and* Union, now and for ever, one and inseparable!

Source: Daniel Webster, *The Writings and Speeches of Daniel Webster* (Boston: Little, Brown, 1903), vol. 6, pp. 50–51, 60, 71–75.

5.3.   Andrew Jackson to Robert Y. Hayne, February 8, 1831

President Jackson rebutted the states' right assertion of nullification. The president believed that the people, by their franchise, would bring about the repeal of any unconstitutional law.

For the rights of the states, no one has a higher regard and respect than myself; none would go farther to maintain them: It is only by maintaining them faithfully that the Union can be preserved.

But how I ask, is this to be effected? Certainly not by conceding to one state authority to declare an act of Congress void, and meet all the consequences and hazard that such a course would produce, far from it; there is a better remedy, one which has heretofore proved successful in the worst of times, and all must admit its power. If Congress, and the Executive, feeling power, and forgetting right, shall overleap the powers the Constitution bestows, and extend their sanction to laws which the power granted to them does not permit, the remedy is with the people— not by avowed opposition—not thro open and direct resistance, but thro the more peaceful and reasonable course of submitting the whole matter to them at their elections, and they by their free suffrage at the polls, will always in the end, bring about the repeal of any obnoxious laws which violate the Constitution. Such abuses as these cannot be of long duration in our enlightened country where the people rule. Let all contested matters be brought to that tribunal, and it will decree correctly.

This is, in general political questions, the only course that should be pursued, and which the Constitution contemplates. That a state has the power to nullify the Legislative enactments of the General Government I never did believe, nor have I ever understood Mr. Jefferson to hold such an opinion. That ours is a Government of laws, and depends on a will of the majority, is the true reading of the Constitution; the time I hope is far distant when the abuse of power on the part of Congress will be so great as to justify a state to stand forth in open violation and resistance to its measures; In all Republics the voice of a Majority must prevail, consent to this, and act upon it, and harmony will prevail; oppose it, and disagreement, difference and danger will certainly follow. Assert that a state may declare acts passed by Congress inoperative and void, and revolution with all of its attendant evils in the end must be looked for and expected—compromise, mutual concessions, and friendly forbearance between different interests, and sections of our happy Country must be regarded and nourished by all who desire to perpetuate the blessings we enjoy.

Source: John Spencer Basset and J. Franklin Jameson, eds., *The Correspondence of Andrew Jackson*, 7 vols. (Carnegie Institution of Washington, 1926–1935; reprint, New York: Kraus Reprint, 1969), vol. 4, pp. 241–242.

5.4.   South Carolina's Ordinance of Nullification, 1832

A special nullification convention called by the governor met at Columbia and on November 24 passed the following ordinance nullifying the Tariffs of 1828 and 1832. It threatened armed resistance and secession if the federal government tried to collect the duties.

An Ordinance to Nullify certain acts of the Congress of the United States, purporting to be laws laying duties and imposts on the importation of foreign commodities.

Whereas the Congress of the United States, by various acts, purporting to be acts laying duties and imposts on foreign imports, but in reality intended for the protection of domestic manufactures, and the giving of bounties to classes and individuals engaged in particular employments, at the expense and to the injury and oppression of other classes and individuals, and by wholly exempting from taxation certain foreign commodities, such as are not produced or manufactured in the United States, to afford a pretext for imposing higher and excessive duties on articles similar to those intended to be protected, hath exceeded its just powers under the Constitution, which confers on it no authority to afford such protection, and hath violated the true meaning and intent of the Constitution, which provides for equality in imposing the burthens of taxation upon the several States and portions of the Confederacy: *And whereas* the said Congress, exceeding its just power to impose taxes and collect revenue for the purpose of effecting and accomplishing the specific objects and purposes which the Constitution of the United States authorizes it to effect and accomplish, hath raised and collected unnecessary revenue for objects unauthorized by the Constitution:—

We, therefore, the people of the State of South Carolina in Convention assembled, do declare and ordain . . . That the several acts and parts of acts of the Congress of the United States, purporting to be laws for the imposing of duties and imposts on the importation of foreign commodities . . . and, more especially . . . [the tariff acts of 1828 and 1832] . . . are unauthorized by the Constitution of the United States, and violate the true meaning and intent thereof, and are null, void, and no law, nor binding upon this State, its officers or citizens; and all promises, contracts, and obligations, made or entered into, or to be made or entered into, with purpose to secure the duties imposed by the said acts, and all judicial proceedings which shall be hereafter had in affirmance thereof, are and shall be held utterly null and void.

And it is further Ordained, That it shall not be lawful for any of the constituted authorities, whether of this State or of the United States, to enforce the payment of duties imposed by the said acts within the limits of this State; but it shall be the duty of the Legislature to adopt such measures and pass such acts as may be necessary to give full effect to this Ordinance, and to prevent the enforcement and arrest the operation of the said acts and parts of acts of the Congress of the United States within the limits of this State, from and after the 1st day of February next. . . .

And it is further Ordained, That in no case of law or equity, decided in the courts of this State, wherein shall be drawn in question the authority of this ordinance, or the validity of such act or acts of the Legislature as may be passed for the purpose of giving effect thereto, or the validity of the aforesaid acts of Congress, imposing duties, shall any appeal be taken or allowed to the Supreme Court of the United States, nor shall any copy of the record be printed or allowed for that purpose; and if any such appeal shall be attempted to be taken, the courts of this State shall proceed to execute and enforce their judgments, according to the laws and usages of the State, without reference to such attempted appeal, and the person or persons attempting to take such appeal may be dealt with as for a contempt of the court.

And it is further Ordained, That all persons now holding any office of honor, profit, or trust, civil or military, under this State, (members of the Legislature excepted), shall, within such time, and in such manner as the Legislature shall prescribe, take an oath well and truly to obey, execute, and enforce, this Ordinance, and such act or acts of the Legislature as may be passed in pursuance thereof, according to the true intent and meaning of the same; and on the neglect or omission of any such person or persons so to do, his or their office or offices shall be forthwith vacated . . . and no person hereafter elected to any office of honor, profit, or trust, civil or military, (members of the Legislature excepted), shall, until the Legislature shall otherwise provide and direct, enter on the execution of his office . . . until he shall, in like manner, have taken a similar oath; and no juror shall be empannelled in any of the courts of this State, in any cause in which shall be in question this Ordinance, or any act of the Legislature passed in pursuance thereof, unless he shall first, in addition to the usual oath, have taken an oath that he will well and truly obey, execute, and enforce this Ordinance, and such act or acts of the Legislature as may be passed to carry the same into operation. . . .

And we, the People of South Carolina, to the end that it may be fully understood by the Government of the United States, and the people of the co-States, that we are determined to maintain this, our Ordinance and Declaration, at every hazard, *Do further Declare* that we will not submit to the application of force, on the part of the Federal Government, to reduce this State to obedience; but that we will consider the passage, by Congress, of any act . . . to coerce the State, shut up her ports, destroy or harass her commerce, or to enforce the acts hereby declared to be null and void, otherwise than through the civil tribunals of the country, as inconsistent with the longer continuance of South Carolina in the Union: and that the people of this State will thenceforth hold themselves absolved from all further obligation to maintain or preserve their political connexion with the people of the other States, and will forthwith proceed to organize a separate Government, and do all other acts and things which sovereign and independent States may of right to do.

Source: *Statutes at Large of South Carolina* (Columbia, SC: A. S. Johston, 1836), vol. 1, pp. 329–330.

5.5.   President Jackson's "December Proclamation"

> This proclamation of December 10, 1832, was preceded by a more moderate attack on nullification in Jackson's December 4 Annual Message to Congress. In this second statement he blasted the doctrine of nullification and the threats of the nullifiers at Columbia. He said that the government of the United States was a government of the people, not merely a league of states. He proclaimed that no state had the right to secede and that disunion by armed force was treason. He backed up this proclamation with a threat of force.

To preserve this bond of our political existence from destruction, to maintain inviolate this state of national honor and prosperity, and to justify the confidence my fellow-citizens have reposed in me, I, Andrew Jackson, President of the United States, have thought proper to issue this my proclamation, stating my views of the Constitution and laws applicable to the measures adopted by the convention of South Carolina and to the reasons they have put forth to sustain them, declaring the course which duty will require me to pursue, and, appealing to the understanding and patriotism of the people, warn them of the consequences that must inevitably result from an observance of the dictates of the convention. . . .

The ordinance is founded, not on the indefeasible right of resisting acts which are plainly unconstitutional and too oppressive to be endured, but on the strange position that any one State may not only declare an act of Congress void, but prohibit its execution; that they may do this consistently with the Constitution; that the true construction of that instrument permits a State to retain its place in the Union and yet be bound by no other of its laws than those it may choose to consider as constitutional. . . . But reasoning on this subject is superfluous when our social compact, in express terms, declares that the laws of the United States, its Constitution, and treaties made under it are the supreme law of the land, and, for greater caution, adds "that the judges in every State shall be bound thereby, anything in the constitution or laws of any State to the contrary notwithstanding." And it may be asserted without fear of refutation that no federative government could exist without a similar provision. . . .

If this doctrine had been established at an earlier day, the Union would have been dissolved in its infancy. . . .

* * *

I consider, then, the power to annul a law of the United States, assumed by one State, *incompatible with the existence of the Union, contradicted expressly by the letter of the Constitution, unauthorized by its spirit, inconsistent with every principle on which it was founded, and destructive of the great object for which it was formed.*

* * *

This right to secede is deduced from the nature of the Constitution, which, they say, is a compact between sovereign States who have preserved their whole sovereignty and therefore are subject to no superior; that because they made the compact they can break it when in their opinion it has been departed from by the other States. Fallacious as this course of reasoning is, it enlists State pride and finds advocates in the honest prejudices of those who have not studied the nature of our Government sufficiently to see the radical error on which it rests. . . .

The Constitution of the United States, then, forms a *government*, not a league; and whether it be formed by compact between the States or in any other manner, its character is the same. It is a Government in which all the people are represented, which operates directly on the people individually, not upon the States; they retained all the power they did not grant. But each State, having expressly parted with so many powers as to constitute, jointly with the other States, a single nation, can not, from that period, possess any right to secede, because such secession does not break a league, but destroys the unity of a nation; and any injury to that unity is not only a breach which would result from the contravention of a compact, but it is an offense against the whole Union.

To say that any State may at pleasure secede from the Union is to say that the United States are not a nation, because it would be a solecism to contend that any part of a nation might dissolve its connection with the other parts, to their injury or ruin, without committing any offense. Secession, like any other revolutionary act, may be morally justified by the extremity of oppression; but to call it a constitutional right is confounding the meaning of terms, and can only be done through gross error or to deceive those who are willing to assert a right, but would pause before they made a revolution or incur the penalties consequent on a failure.

. . . Disunion by armed force is *treason*. Are you really ready to incur its guilt? If you are, on the heads of the instigators of the act be the dreadful consequences; on their heads be the dishonor, but on yours may fall the punishment. On your unhappy State will inevitably fall all the evils of the conflict you force upon the Government of your country. It can not accede to the mad project of disunion, of which you would be the first victims. . . .

Fellow-citizens of the United States, the threat of unhallowed disunion, the names of those once respected by whom it is uttered, the array of military force to support it, denote the approach of a crisis in our affairs on which the continuance of our unexampled prosperity, our political existence, and perhaps that of all free governments may depend. The conjuncture demanded a free, a full, and explicit enunciation, not only of my intentions, but of my principles, of action; and as the claim was asserted of a right by a State to annul the laws of the Union, and even to secede from it at pleasure, a frank exposition of my opinions in relation to the origin and form of our Government and the construction I give to the instrument by which it was created seemed to be proper. Having the fullest confidence in the justness of the legal and constitutional opinion of my duties which has been expressed, I rely with equal confidence on your undivided support in my determination to execute the laws, to preserve the Union by all constitutional means, to arrest, if possible, by moderate and firm measures the necessity of a recourse to force; and if it be the will of Heaven that the recurrence of its primeval curse on man for the shedding of a brother's blood should fall upon our land, that it be not called down by any offensive act on the part of the United States.

Fellow-citizens, the momentous case is before you. On your undivided support of your Government depends the decision of the great question it involves—whether your sacred Union will be preserved and the blessing it secures to us as one people shall be perpetuated. No one can doubt that the unanimity with which that decision will be expressed will be such as to inspire new confidence in republican institutions, and that the prudence, the wisdom, and the courage which it will bring to their defense will transmit them unimpaired and invigorated to our children.

May the Great Ruler of Nations grant that the signal blessings with which He has favored ours may not, by the madness of party or personal ambition, be disregarded and lost; and may His wise providence bring those who have produced this crisis to see the folly before they feel the misery of civil strife, and inspire a returning veneration for that Union which, if we may dare to penetrate His designs, He has chosen as the only means of attaining the high destinies to which we may reasonably aspire.

ANDREW JACKSON.

Source: Commager, *Documents*, vol. 1, pp. 263–268.

5.6.   South Carolina's Reply to the "December Proclamation"

On December 20, 1832, the Nullification Convention's Committee on Federal Relations recommended the following response to Jackson's bold assertion of federal constitutional and military power. It denounced his arguments and actions as "erroneous and dangerous" federalism that would mean the creation of a "consolidated government in the stead of our free confederacy." It denounced the president's statements on the Union as "subversive of the rights of the states and liberties of the people." A final confrontation between South Carolina and the federal government was avoided with the passage of the Compromise Tariff signed into law by Jackson on March 1, 1833.

The Committee on federal relations, to which was referred the proclamation of the President of the United States, has had it under consideration, and recommends the adoption of the following resolutions:

Resolved, That the power vested by the Constitution and laws in the President of the United States, to issue his proclamation, does not authorize him in that mode, to interfere whenever he may think fit, in the affairs of the respective states, or that he should use it as a means of promulgating executive expositions of the Constitution, with the sanction of force thus superseding the action of other departments of the general government.

Resolved, That it is not competent to the President of the United States, to order by proclamation the constituted authorities of a state to repeal their legislation, and that the late attempt of the President to do so is unconstitutional, and manifests a disposition to arrogate and exercise a power utterly destructive of liberty.

Resolved, That the opinions of the President, in regard to the rights of the States, are erroneous and dangerous, leading not only to the establishment of a consolidated government in the stead of our free confederacy, but to the concentration of all powers in the chief executive.

Resolved, That the proclamation of the President is the more extraordinary, that he had silently, and as it is supposed, with entire approbation, witnessed our sister state of Georgia avow, act upon, and carry into effect, even to the taking of life, principles identical with those now denounced by him in South Carolina.

Resolved, That each state of the Union has the right, whenever it may deem such a course necessary for the preservation of its liberties or vital interests, to secede peaceably from the Union, and that there is no constitutional power in the general government, much less in the executive department, of that government, to retain by force such state in the Union.

Resolved, That the primary and paramount allegiance of the citizens of this state, native or adopted, is of right due to this state.

Resolved, That the declaration of the President of the United States in his said proclamation, of his personal feelings and relations towards the State of South Carolina, is rather an appeal to the loyalty of subjects, than to the patriotism of citizens, and is a blending of official and individual character, heretofore unknown in our state papers, and revolting to our conception of political propriety.

Resolved, That the undisguised indulgence of personal hostility in the said proclamation would be unworthy of the animadversion of this legislature, but for the seldom and official form of the instrument which is made its vehicle.

Resolved, That the principles, doctrines and purposes, contained in the said proclamation are inconsistent with any just idea of a limited government, and subversive of the rights of the states and liberties of the people, and if submitted to in silence would lay a broad foundation for the establishment of monarchy.

Resolved, That while this legislature has witnessed with sorrow such a relaxation of the spirit of our institutions, that a President of the United States dare venture upon this high handed measure, it regards with indignation the menaces which are directed against it, and the concentration of a standing army on our borders—that the state will repel force by force, and relying upon the blessings of God, will maintain its liberty at all hazards.

Resolved, That copies of these resolutions be sent to our members in Congress, to be laid before that body.

Source: Commager, *Documents*, vol. 1, pp. 268–269.

ANNOTATED RESEARCH GUIDE

Books

Coit, Margaret L. *John C. Calhoun, American Portrait*. Cambridge, MA: The Riverside Press, 1950. This Pulitzer Prize–winning biographer believes that Calhoun in the nullification crisis was motivated by a deep desire to preserve the Union, not by a radical urge to dissolve it. She has high praise for his courageous return to Washington, D.C., in January 1833 after being elected to the Senate to help work out a settlement of the crisis in the Compromise Tariff of 1833.

Dangerfield, George. *The Era of Good Feelings*. New York: Harcourt, Brace and World, 1952. This Pulitzer Prize–winning monograph is a distinguished account of the transition from Jeffersonian republicanism to Jacksonian democracy and has a fine chapter on the immediate cause of the nullification crisis titled "Abominations."

Ellis, Richard E. *The Union at Risk: Jacksonian Democracy, States' Rights, and the Nullification Crisis*. New York: Oxford University Press, 1987. Stresses the point that President Jackson's attitude toward Calhoun's version of nullification and states' rights is essential to a full understanding of the crisis. Put simply by Jackson himself, he declared the doctrine of nullification to be "incompatible with the existence of the Union." Ellis agrees and thinks that Calhoun was really advocating the doctrine of secession, an idea more radical than the legal concept that a state could refuse to obey a federal law.

Freehling, William W. *Prelude to Civil War: The Nullification Movement in South Carolina, 1816–1832*. New York: Harper and Row, 1966. Another outstanding monograph on the nullification issue and how it developed in the unique political climate of South Carolina, with a recognition that the slavery issue influenced the South Carolinians' thinking on nullification.

Latner, Richard B. *The Presidency of Andrew Jackson: White House Politics, 1829–1837*. Athens: University of Georgia Press, 1979. Provides a solid administrative history of Old Hickory's battles with the emerging Whig opposition, his confrontation with Calhoun, and the war on the Second Bank of the United States.

Peterson, Merrill D. *Olive Branch and the Sword: The Compromise of 1833*. Baton Rouge: Louisiana State University Press, 1982. A first-rate discussion of the various forces that converged in Washington after Jackson's reelection in 1832 to bring about the settlement of the nullification crisis in the passing of the Compromise Tariff of 1833.

Remini, Robert V. *Andrew Jackson and the Course of American Democracy, 1833–1845*. New York: Harper and Row, 1977. The leading biographer of Andrew Jackson praises the man for maintaining the Union and strengthening the federal government in the nullification crisis. He also praises Jackson for successfully setting forth the principle that the Union was perpetual and indivisible. Remini's *Henry Clay: Statesman for the Union* (New York: W. W. Norton, 1991) is the most recent scholarly biography of the "Great Pacificator."

Van Deusen, Glyndon G. *The Jacksonian Era, 1828–1848*. New York: Harper and
    Row, 1959. This survey of events of the period was originally published
    as part of the New American Nation series and still serves as the standard
    introduction to the Age of Jackson.

Nonprint Media

Web Sites

www.sciway.net/hist/documents.htm. Lists twelve historical documents related
    to South Carolina, including the Ordinance of Nullification.
http://216.202.17.223/hwdebate.htm. "The Webster-Hayne Debate." Transcribes
    in full the debates of January 1830 and includes an outline of the debates
    and a point-by-point paraphrase of each speech.
www.yale.edu/lawweb/Avalon/states/sc/ordnull.htm. "South Carolina Ordi-
    nance of Nullification, November 24, 1832." Fully transcribes the original
    document.
www.nv.cc.va.us/home/nvsageh/Hist121/Part3/JacksonProSC.htm. "Andrew
    Jackson on Nullification." Transcribes in full President Jackson's "Procla-
    mation to the People of South Carolina."
http://sailor.qutenberg.org/etext96/jccrs10.txt and http://jollyroger.nbci.com/
    library/JohnC.CalhounsRemarkstotheSenateebook.html. Both transcribe
    in full John C. Calhoun, "On Nullification and the Force Bill," U.S. Senate,
    February 15, 1833.
www.jmu.edu/madison/nullification/jacksonletter.htm. "A Letter from Andrew
    Jackson." Letter of January 13, 1833, from Andrew Jackson to Martin Van
    Buren discussing the nullification crisis. Shows the original letter, scanned
    from the Martin Van Buren Papers, not a transcription.
http://press-pubs.uchicago.edu/founders/documents/v1ch3s14.html.   Letter
    from James Madison to Daniel Webster, March 15, 1833, regarding Web-
    ster's speech on nullification. From *The Writings of James Madison*, ed. Gail-
    lard Hunt.

Videotape

Remini, Robert V. *Andrew Jackson* [videorecording]. West Lafayette, IN: C-SPAN
    Archives, 1999.

6

The Compromise of 1850

During the thirty years following the ratification of the Constitution, Congress largely avoided the issue of slavery, except for passing the federal Fugitive Slave Act in 1793 and a statute in 1807 that outlawed the international slave trade, effective January 1, 1808. But in 1819, when the territory of Missouri requested admission as a slave state, the future of the "peculiar institution" furtively entered national politics. Beginning in 1792 with Kentucky, eight new states had been added to the Union, and in 1819 it stood in equilibrium, eleven free and eleven slave. Missouri's petition raised a fundamental sectional problem for many northerners. If slavery were extended there, it might eventually spread throughout the rest of the Louisiana Territory, the area acquired as the Louisiana Purchase from France in 1803.

In its most deceptive form, therefore, the "Missouri question" involved future control of the entire Mississippi Valley, and beyond. Consequently, the question of the power of the federal government over slavery, once raised, never disappeared. An almost unbroken sequence of increasingly emotional events ensued involving slavery, federal power, and states' rights—the rise of abolitionism and the attempt to thwart the 1793 Fugitive Slave Act, the fight over the annexation of Texas, and reactions to the Wilmot Proviso—that led to one of the most dramatic events ever seen in the Senate over federalism, a forensic display that resulted in the Compromise of 1850 and the preservation of the Union, for a while.

All this began almost casually in February 13, 1819, when, during the debate over the Missouri Enabling Act, Congressman James Tallmadge of New York proposed an amendment that prohibited "the further introduction of slavery" into Missouri and freed all slaves born there at the age of twenty-five. The Tallmadge Amendment passed the House but was defeated in the Senate, and Congress was deadlocked. Southerners opposed the Tallmadge Amendment for a variety of reasons. First, most of Missouri's population, estimated at 60,000, were southerners, many of whom owned slaves, and it seemed undemocratic not to let them decide the question. Others charged that the North would destroy the Union if it tried to use federal power to prevent the natural expansion of slavery. As Thomas Cobb of Georgia put it, only "seas of blood" could extinguish the conflagration that was starting. Still others argued that slavery was property, protected by the Constitution, and masters had a vested right to take their property into the territories.

Northerners, both old-line Federalists and Jeffersonian Republicans, cried out that the South was infringing on the political sphere of the North. Missouri, as a slave state, would stick up like a sore thumb into the "free" area of the nation established by the Northwest Ordinance of 1787 and marked by the tumbling boundary of the Ohio River. They argued important constitutional issues. The federal government had the power to exclude slavery from a territory because of the precedent of the 1787 Northwest Ordinance. And Congress had the right to impose conditions on the admission of new states.

Under pressure from the Speaker of the House, Henry Clay, Congress worked out a compromise that maintained the equilibrium in the Senate between slave and free states. Senator Jesse Thomas of Illinois proposed that Missouri be admitted with slavery but that it be "forever prohibited" north of the latitude of 36°30' westward to the Red River border with Mexico. In the meantime, Maine had come in as a free state, thereby making the Senate twelve to eleven in favor of the free states. So admitting Missouri as a slave state would restore the balance in the Senate, twelve to twelve. Northerners accepted the plan because it gave them the rest of the Louisiana Territory, by then called the Missouri Territory. Southerners went along because the Missouri Compromise line allowed them access to present-day Arkansas and Oklahoma as well as the possibility of land in the Mexican province of Texas, into which southern planters were already immigrating across the Sabine River.

Despite the quick resolution of the Missouri question, the federal issue raised by it, Congress's authority over slavery, lingered. Southerners began to fear for the security of slavery, and northerners were apprehensive about its unrestricted spread. Some Americans were deeply pessimistic about the future of the Union. Thomas Jefferson wrote that this "momentous question, like a firebell in the night, awakened and filled me with terror." Secretary of State John Quincy Adams confided in his diary, "I take it for granted that the present question is a mere preamble—a title page to a great and tragic volume."

For almost a decade after the Missouri Compromise antislavery opinion in the North remained compartmentalized. Although northerners would not tolerate slavery spreading beyond where it was in 1820, they felt no compelling need to attack it where it existed under state laws. Individuals who advocated abolition of slavery were rare and were seen as radical extremists. In the 1830s, however, the abolitionist movement began to take shape. William Lloyd Garrison began publication of his uncompromising newspaper *The Liberator* in 1831 that demanded an immediate end to slavery. In 1833 he and others founded the New England Anti-Slavery Society. Funded by two wealthy Manhattan businessmen, Arthur and Lewis Tappan, they launched a moral crusade against the institution. Revivalists such as Theodore Dwight Weld sent out "holy bands" of abolitionists to preach for "immediate" emancipation "gradually achieved." They demanded that Congress stop the interstate slave trade, refuse to admit any more slave states, and abolish slavery in the nation's capital. The Anti-Slavery Society, using new high-speed printing presses, inundated the country with 1.1 million pieces of propaganda. Former slave Frederick Douglass joined the society and became one of its most eloquent spokesmen for the use of any means, including the underground railroad, to liberate those in bondage. Free-born black David Walker published his provocative pamphlet *Appeal to the Coloured Citizens of the World* (1829), which denounced white Americans, North and South, as racists and prophesied a final day of reckoning when God would bring them justice and these "tyrants" would "wish they were never born!"

Random opposition to the abolitionists appeared in the North when hostile crowds disrupted their meetings. In 1837 Elijah P. Lovejoy was murdered in Alton, Illinois, for publishing antislavery arguments in his newspaper. In Boston, Harrison Gray Otis denounced the abolitionists as subversive and the Anti-Slavery Society as "revolutionary." He predicted they would infect the political parties and precipitate a disaster. "What will become of the Union?" he asked.

In the South crowds stopped the distribution of antislavery literature, sometimes intercepting and destroying the mailings. In 1835 the South Carolina legislature passed a law that prohibited the circulation of abolitionist propaganda and imposed severe penalties for printing or speaking anything that would incite a slave insurrection. Several southern states requested that the federal government stop the delivery through the mail of any abolitionist literature. Postmaster General Amos Kendall, though, wrote to the postmaster of South Carolina that he had "no legal authority to exclude newspapers from the mail, nor prohibit their carriage or delivery on account of their character or tendency, real or supposed." But President Jackson, in his 1835 Annual Message to Congress, asked for a law to stop the circulation through the mail of "incendiary publications." And John Calhoun introduced such a measure into the Senate, where the "Mail Bill" was defeated. Even so, pro-southern administrators afterwards gave southern postmasters the right to interdict abolitionist tracts from the mails.

Some northern states, such as Pennsylvania, passed personal liberty laws to prevent the return of runaway slaves under the 1793 Fugitive Slave Act, by refusing to allow state officials to participate in the capture and return to slavery of alleged fugitives. In 1842 the Supreme Court, in *Prigg v. Pennsylvania*, declared the 1793 law constitutional and vacated the Pennsylvania statute. The Court ruled that power over fugitive slaves belonged exclusively to Congress and was "uncontrolled and uncontrollable by State sovereignty or State legislation." The effect of the ruling was to prevent states from obstructing the recovery of slave "property" but also to remove from states the responsibility to do so. The implication of the ruling, realized in 1850, was that the federal government would have to assume primary responsibility for recovering slaves who had escaped across state lines.

During the 1830s, as the abolitionists assaulted slavery where it existed, the issue of its spread westward once again appeared, this time in the matter of Texas. In the Transcendental Treaty of 1819 with Spain the international boundary of the United States and Mexico had been drawn at the Sabine River. Yet only months after the treaty was ratified thousands of Americans, led by Stephen F. Austin and other "empressarios" or recruiters, moved across the river into the Texas plains to grow cotton in their fertile soil. The Mexican government, as an enticement, offered free land and local self-government to the Americans. By 1830, there were 20,000 white Americans and 2,000 slaves living there. The sheer number of immigrants caused the authorities in Mexico City to reconsider the original agreement, revoke local self-government, and bring the Americans into compliance with Mexican laws that prohibited slavery and required everyone to pay taxes for the support of the Catholic Church.

When the Mexican government outlawed slavery in Texas, it set in motion a series of events that finally led Americans to declare their independence in March 1836. The next month a Texas army led by Sam Houston defeated troops under General Antonio Lopez de Santa Anna at San Jacinto. In October, the Texans elected Houston president and approved a plebiscite favoring annexation by the United States. But neither President Jackson nor his successor, Martin Van Buren, would touch the request because they knew it would stir up the controversy over slavery, already inflamed by the abolitionists. The problem was that annexing Texas as a territory would open the possibility of creating from it perhaps five or more slave states, since it was about the same size as the Northwest Territory from which had been carved Ohio, Indiana, Illinois, and the Michigan Territory.

Abolitionists cried out that the annexation would encourage southerners to extend slavery to the Far West, directly violating the understanding of the Missouri Compromise, which limited its expansion to the Red River. They said that the South would never accept geographic containment of slavery and would inveterately conspire to extend it in order to have enough power in Congress to protect the peculiar institution from federal attack. Some northern politicians pointed out that annexation of Texas would mean war with Mexico, and no American blood should be shed to spread slavery. Southerners replied that such charges were nonsense, and to prove their point a southern president, John Tyler, drew up an annexation treaty that limited the expansion of the "slave power" in the Senate to just two senators. Texas would come in as a state, skipping the territorial stage, and thereby eliminate the possibility of creating any more slave states.

The annexation issue festered until the presidential election of 1844. That year the Democrats nominated James K. Polk on a campaign promise of "Manifest Destiny." The Democratic platform contained curious but politically effective language. It demanded "reannexation" of Texas (implying it had been a part of the Louisiana Purchase) and "reoccupation" of Oregon (an end to the joint occupation of the area provided for in the Convention of 1818 agreement). The Whig candidate, Henry Clay, refused to take a position on the Texas question, and his waffling cost him the election. The first antislavery political party, the Liberty Party, nominated abolitionist journalist James G. Birney, who drew enough votes away from Clay in New York to swing its thirty-six electoral votes to Polk and elect him president. Polk's victory was taken by President Tyler as a mandate for Texas annexation. He had Congress annex it by a joint resolution, instead of by a two-thirds vote in the Senate, just before he left office in March 1845. As opponents of annexation had predicted, Mexico immediately broke off diplomatic relations with the United States, and within three months the two countries were at war.

During the first summer of the war, Pennsylvania congressman David Wilmot added a proviso to a military appropriations bill. It stated that neither slavery nor involuntary servitude could exist in any territories acquired in the conflict, and thereby injected the explosive issue of the future of slavery into the mainstream of national politics. Debate on the Wilmot Proviso continued for four years. It passed the House twice but failed twice in the Senate. In the meantime, General Zachary Taylor, "Old Rough and Ready" and a hero of the war with Mexico, had been elected president, the second Whig candidate chosen for that office. In his inaugural address he stated his position on the Mexican cession. As a slaveowner and a states' rights southerner, he sympathized with that section's position that only states, not Congress or a territorial government, could decide to ban slavery. His formula was both simple and, to the South, even southern Whigs, totally and shockingly unacceptable. He asked Congress to admit California as a state immediately, skipping the territorial stage, and to do the same thing for New Mexico, the other half of the Mexican cession, in the near future. He reasoned that if the South insisted on allowing only states the power to deal with slavery, he would give them the state governments to decide the question.

Southerners reacted immediately, furious because slavery had been illegal in Mexico since 1821, when that country was formed out of the Spanish Empire, and because, with virtually no slaveowners living there it was obvious that slavery would be excluded in California. So the president unwittingly was giving the opponents of slavery expansion all the benefits of the Wilmot Proviso without ever passing it! Mississippi voters were so outraged that they called for a convention of southern states to meet in Nashville to deal with the crisis, and southern extremists throughout the region talked about secession.

These tumultuous events culminated in the great debate over slavery and federalism in the Senate during the winter of 1850. There, the "Great Triumvirate"—Henry Clay, John Calhoun, and Daniel Webster—argued the pros and cons of federal power over the peculiar institution. On the floor of the Senate in January, Clay, the seventy-three-year-old architect of the Missouri Compromise and defuser of the nullification crisis with the Tariff of 1833, put forth his plan. Congress should admit California as a free state. It had already drafted a constitution that outlawed slavery, and that position clearly represented the wishes of most Californians. The other half of the Mexican cession would be divided into two territories, New Mexico and Utah, without the Wilmot Proviso, under the doctrine of popular sovereignty. He argued that slavery did not exist there now and was excluded "by nature," meaning geography, from being extended there in the future. When the voters of these territories exercised their popular sovereignty and ruled on slavery, the courts should decide if they had the power to act on it. As a gesture to the North, Clay proposed that Congress abolish the slave trade, but not slavery itself, in the District of Columbia. As a gesture to the South, he asked Congress to enact a stronger fugitive slave law to guarantee southerners unobstructed reclaiming of runaway slaves. He also denied Congress's power to interfere with the interstate slave trade. On January 29, he put all these ideas, plus provisions that adjusted the eastern boundaries of New Mexico and Utah, into an omnibus bill.

John C. Calhoun responded to Clay's plan on March 4, his last presentation to the Senate before his death on March 31. Too ill to deliver the speech, he sat silent and wrapped in a black cloak while a colleague,

Senator James M. Mason of Virginia, read the testament. It began by expressing Calhoun's profound fear of disunion over the present agitation of the slavery question. Many southerners, he stated, felt that they could no longer stay in the Union as things were. Why? Because the balance between the free and slave states no longer existed and the South had become a self-conscious, helpless minority. There were three ways by which it was being deprived of its strength and security. One was exclusion of slavery from the "public domain" in the Missouri Compromise line. The second was the unfair way in which the federal government had interfered in the section's economy with protective tariffs and internal improvements that had made the North more attractive and prosperous. And third, there had been an alteration in the theory of government whereby a group of sovereign states was being changed into a centralized federal government ruled by a simple majority. How could the Union be saved? He had no compromise to offer, only a list of demands on Congress that would help restore to the South its original rights: cease the antislavery crusade by outlawing abolitionist literature in the mails; give the South an equal share of the public domain; pass a stringent fugitive slave law; and agree to a constitutional amendment giving the South the power to protect itself as it was able to do in 1787, that is, a nullification amendment. He closed by threatening that if California came in as a free state, the South would take this as a sign that the North, and Congress, would not meet these demands.

Webster spoke next, on March 7. In one of the most effective speeches of his career, he opened with a plea for compromise to preserve the Union. Although he did condemn slavery as a "moral wrong," he felt that the extremist opinions of the abolitionists were harmful. But he also condemned the self-righteousness of extremists in the South. He went on to argue, agreeing with Clay, that California and New Mexico were predestined by climate to be free states and that a prohibition against slavery in the territories was unnecessary; indeed, the Wilmot Proviso needlessly aggravated the South. He defended a more stringent fugitive slave law because return of slave property was a constitutional duty. Webster concluded by warning that secession was synonymous with war.

Extremists in Congress from both the North and the South combined to reject the Omnibus Bill. Clay, exhausted, allowed Democrat Stephen A. Douglas of Illinois to take over the laborious task of rallying the forces for compromise. Fortunately, events favored compromise. Calhoun's death left the delegates at the convention in Nashville without a dynamic leader. Webster's March 7 oration had considerable impact on moderates and brought many to support compromise, although abolitionists had branded him a traitor. Then there was the solid economic prosperity of the times. A majority of Americans did not want to upset it by what they saw as an academic dispute over slavery. Northern manufacturers wanted to keep both southern cotton and southern markets, and southern planters did not want to disrupt the Atlantic trade routes. Lastly, on July 4, 1850, sixty-five-year-old "Rough and Ready" was subjected to two hours of patriotic oratory under a broiling sun. He then tried to cool off by gulping enormous numbers of chilled cherries washed down by iced milk. He quickly developed acute indigestion that Washington physicians diagnosed as "cholera morbus," deadly cholera. If he had been left alone the president probably would have recovered. But the physicians subjected him to a regimen that killed him. They drugged him with opium, calomel, and quinine. They bled and blistered him. In desperation, when his condition worsened, they gave him the "Indian remedy," a concoction of crude petroleum and snakeweed. Taylor died on July 9.

After an appropriate period of mourning for the president, Douglas began the yeoman's task of submitting the portions of Clay's compromise one by one for a successful vote. The provisions on admission of California and abolishing the slave trade in the capital passed with the least trouble, with northern support. Southerners rallied to the organization of Utah and New Mexico territories without the Wilmot Proviso and to the commitment to a new fugitive slave law. By September 17, Douglas had successfully passed all of the parts of the Compromise of 1850, and the new president, Millard Fillmore, signed the bill.

Historians agree that the Compromise of 1850 really settled nothing, that extremists in neither the North nor the South conceded anything. It only bought more time for the nation. More significantly, perhaps, there were two fatal flaws in the settlement that during the 1850s exacerbated sectional hostilities. The idea of having New Mexico and Utah settle the slavery question through popular sovereignty was vague: could slavery extend itself to these territories in the interim, before the territorial legislatures acted? And the Fugitive Slave Act of 1850, intended as a gesture of compromise toward the South, actually aroused more anti-southern feeling in the North in the way it was enforced because it was perceived as sending free northern blacks into slavery and forced otherwise uncommitted northerners to "dirty their hands" in the slave-catching business or suffer arrest and fines for obstructing the capture of alleged fugitives. To many northern minds, the new Fugitive Slave Act was part of a vast "slave power conspiracy" that jeopardized northerners' civil liberties and threatened to carry slavery everywhere in the Union. To southerners, the refusal of the North to honor the Compromise by supporting the Fugitive Slave Act and suppressing antislavery activism "proved" that northerners could not be trusted. The Compromise, therefore, fostered suspicion rather than settling the slavery question. Thus began the decade of the irreconcilable conflict and steady, though not inevitable, drift to secession and civil war.

Consequently, federalism issues persisted during the 1850s. Abolitionist newspapers assaulted the Fugitive Slave Act as violating basic constitutional rights such as trial by jury and the opportunity to present evidence and cross-examine witnesses. They denounced the act because it gave a financial incentive to capture runaways and return them to bondage. Abolitionists organized public protest meetings in at least five states, and a Boston mob rescued a fugitive slave from a federal marshal. In 1854, in the celebrated Burns case, emotions were further exacerbated. Anthony Burns, a Virginia slave, had escaped to Boston as a stowaway on a ship. Believing he was safe, he wrote to a relative back in Virginia, also a slave. The letter was intercepted, Burns was discovered and arrested as a fugitive, and federal marshals detained him in the city's federal courthouse. Abolitionists gathered at the building demanding his freedom. President Franklin Pierce telegraphed state officials to demand the Fugitive Slave Law be fully executed, and dispatched military units to Boston which escorted Burns from the courthouse to the harbor and back to slavery. The cost of Burns's return to bondage was a phenomenal $100,000.

In January 1854, Congress passed Stephen Douglas's Kansas-Nebraska Bill, opening the entire Kansas and Nebraska territories to slavery even though that area was above the Missouri Compromise line. Abolitionists charged that southerners were engaging in a slave power conspiracy to spread the institution all the way to Canada. Reacting to this sinister prospect, northern states between 1855 and 1859 passed personal liberty laws that would prevent the enforcement of the Fugitive Slave Act by giving legal counsel to runaway slaves and requiring a jury trial before deportation to the South. The outcome was an ironic reversal of the two sections on the issue of federal power: the South now applauded the federal authority to return fugitive slaves without obstruction, while the North enacted states' rights laws that would prevent the return of slaves.

In March 1857, the Supreme Court further angered northerners in its decision in *Dred Scott v. Sandford*, which gave the "slave power" a major victory. Chief Justice Roger B. Taney's opinion, among other things, declared that the Constitution did not give Congress the authority to exclude slavery from a territory. In 1859 the Supreme Court, in *Ableman v. Booth*, again sided with the southern view of federalism. Here the Wisconsin Supreme Court released Sherman M. Booth, an abolitionist editor of a Milwaukee newspaper, who had been arrested for violating the Fugitive Slave Act by aiding and abetting the escape of a fugitive slave. But Booth was then tried in a federal court and sentenced to a fine and imprisonment. Then the Wisconsin Supreme Court once more released him on the ruling that the Fugitive Slave Act was unconstitutional. The Supreme Court heard the case on a writ of error, and Chief Justice Taney's unanimous opinion condemned the ruling of the state supreme court as subverting the foundations of the government, a sweeping assertion of federal power over states' rights. Now no state had judicial authority to remove a person from federal custody. Many northerners saw *Ableman v. Booth* as marking the end of any constitutional way to stop the slave power.

DOCUMENTS

6.1.   John Calhoun's Senate Speech, March 4, 1850

> On March 4, a terminally ill Calhoun (he was to die on March
> 31) sat ghostlike in the Senate while a fellow senator read his
> warning on the impending disunion of the country. After item-
> izing the ways that the North had forced the South to become
> a helpless minority, he laid down three ultimata that must be
> complied with by the North in order to save the Union. He
> threatened that if California became a free state, then disunion,
> although by "the work of time," was inevitable.

I have, Senators, believed from the first that the agitation of the subject
of slavery would, if not prevented by some timely and effective measure,
end in disunion. Entertaining this opinion, I have, on all proper occasions, endeavored to call the attention of both the two great parties which
divide the country to adopt some measure to prevent so great a disaster,
but without success. The agitation has been permitted to proceed, with
almost no attempt to resist it, until it has reached a point when it can
no longer be disguised or denied that the Union is in danger. You have
thus had forced upon you the greatest and the gravest question that can
ever come under your consideration—How can the Union be preserved?
    . . . Now I ask, Senators, what is there to prevent its further progress,
until it fulfils the ultimate end proposed, unless some decisive measure
should be adopted to prevent it? Has any one of the causes, which has
added to its increase from its original small and contemptible beginning
until it has attained its present magnitude, diminished in force? Is the
original cause of the movement—that slavery is a sin, and ought to be
suppressed—weaker now than at the commencement? Or is the abolition
party less numerous or influential, or have they less influence with, or
control over the two great parties of the North in elections? Or has the
South greater means of influencing or controlling the movements of this
Government now, than it had when the agitation commenced? To all
these questions but one answer can be given: No—no—no. The very
reverse is true. Instead of being weaker, all the elements in favor of
agitation are stronger now than they were in 1835, when it first commenced, while all the elements of influence on the part of the South are
weaker. Unless something decisive is done, I again ask, what is to stop

this agitation, before the great and final object at which it aims—the abolition of slavery in the States—is consummated? Is it, then, not certain, that if something is not done to arrest it, the South will be forced to choose between abolition and secession? Indeed, as events are now moving, it will not require the South to secede, in order to dissolve the Union. Agitation will of itself effect it, of which its past history furnishes abundant proof—as I shall next proceed to show.

It is a great mistake to suppose that disunion can be effected by a single blow. The cords which bound these States together in one common Union, are far too numerous and powerful for that. Disunion must be the work of time. It is only through a long process, and successively, that the cords can be snapped, until the whole fabric falls asunder. Already the agitation of the slavery question has snapped some of the most important, and has greatly weakened all the others, as I shall proceed to show.

The cords that bind the States together are not only many, but various in character. Some are spiritual or ecclesiastical; some political; others social. Some appertain to the benefit conferred by the Union, and others to the feeling of duty and obligation.

* * *

The strongest cord, of a political character, consists of the many and powerful ties that have held together the two great parties which have, with some modifications, existed from the beginning of the Government. They both extended to every portion of the Union, and strongly contributed to hold all its parts together. But this powerful cord has fared no better than the spiritual. It resisted, for a long time, the explosive tendency of the agitation, but has finally snapped under its force—if not entirely, in a great measure. Nor is there one of the remaining cords which has not been greatly weakened. To this extent the Union has already been destroyed by agitation, in the only way it can be, by sundering and weakening the cords which bind it together.

If the agitation goes on, the same force, acting with increased intensity, as has been shown, will finally snap every cord, when nothing will be left to hold the States together except force. But, surely, that can, with no propriety of language, be called a Union, when the only means by which the weaker is held connected with the stronger portion is *force*. It may, indeed, keep them connected; but the connection will partake much more of the character of subjugation, on the part of the weaker to the stronger, than the union of free, independent, and sovereign States, in one confederation, as they stood in the early stages of the Government, and which only is worthy of the sacred name of Union. . . .

Source: Richard C. Crallé, ed., *The Works of John C. Calhoun*, 6 vols. (New York: D. Appleton, 1854–1857), vol. 4, pp. 542–559.

6.2.   Daniel Webster's March 7 Oration

Webster's oration to the Senate against extremists in both the South and North, and his plea for moderation to save the Union, did much to move public opinion toward a compromise over the question of the future of slavery in the Mexican cession. He spoke not as a "Northern man" but as an American "for the preservation of the Union." "Hear me for my cause," he pleaded. Webster's speech alone was not enough, however, and seven months of exhaustive efforts by Henry Clay and Stephen Douglas, combined with the deaths of Calhoun and President Zachary Taylor, enabled an omnibus compromise package to be brought before Congress.

Mr. President,—I wish to speak to-day, not as a Massachusetts man, nor as a Northern man, but as an American, and a member of the Senate of the United States. . . .

* * *

But we must view things as they are. Slavery does exist in the United States. It did exist in the States before the adoption of this Constitution, and at that time. Let us, therefore, consider for a moment what was the state of sentiment, North and South, in regard to slavery, at the time this Constitution was adopted. A remarkable change has taken place since; but what did the wise and great men of all parts of the country think of slavery then? In what estimation did they hold it at the time when this Constitution was adopted? It will be found, Sir, if we will carry ourselves by historical research back to that day, and ascertain men's opinions by authentic records still existing among us, that there was then no diversity of opinion between the North and the South upon the subject of slavery. It will be found that both parts of the country held it equally an evil,—a moral and political evil. . . . The great ground of objection to it was political; that it weakened the social fabric; that, taking the place of free labor, society became less strong and labor less productive; and therefore we find from all the eminent men of the time the clearest expression of their opinion that slavery is an evil. They ascribed its existence here, not without truth, and not without some acerbity of temper and force of language, to the injurious policy of the mother country, who, to favor the navigator, had entailed these evils upon the Colonies. I need hardly refer, Sir, particularly to the publications of the day. They are matters of history on the record. The eminent men, the most eminent men, and

nearly all the conspicuous politicians of the South, held the same sentiments,—that slavery was an evil, a blight, a scourge, and a curse. . . .

* * *

Now, as to California and New Mexico, I hold slavery to be excluded
from those territories by a law even superior to that which admits and
sanctions it in Texas. I mean the law of nature, of physical geography,
the law of the formation of the earth. That law settles for ever, with a
strength beyond all terms of human enactment, that slavery cannot exist
in California or New Mexico. Understand me, Sir; I mean slavery as we
regard it; the slavery of the colored race as it exists in the Southern States.
I shall not discuss the point, but leave it to the learned gentlemen who
have undertaken to discuss it; but I suppose there is no slavery of that
description in California now. I understand that *peonism*, a sort of penal
servitude, exists there, or rather a sort of voluntary sale of a man and
his offspring for debt, an arrangement of a peculiar nature known to the
law of Mexico. But what I mean to say is, that it is as impossible that
African slavery, as we see it among us, should find its way, or be introduced, into California and New Mexico, as any other natural impossibility. California and New Mexico are Asiatic in their formation and
scenery. They are composed of vast ridges of mountains, of great height,
with broken ridges and deep valleys. The sides of these mountains are
entirely barren; their tops capped by perennial snow. There may be in
California, now made free by its constitution, and no doubt there are,
some tracts of valuable land. But it is not so in New Mexico. Pray, what
is the evidence which every gentleman must have obtained on this subject, from information sought by himself or communicated by others? I
have inquired and read all I could find, in order to acquire information
on this important subject. What is there in New Mexico that could, by
any possibility, induce anybody to go there with slaves? There are some
narrow strips of tillable land on the borders of the rivers; but the rivers
themselves dry up before midsummer is gone. All that the people can
do in that region is to raise some little articles, some little wheat for their
tortillas, and that by irrigation. And who expects to see a hundred black
men cultivating tobacco, corn, cotton, rice, or any thing else, on lands in
New Mexico, made fertile only by irrigation?

I look upon it, therefore, as a fixed fact, to use the current expression
of the day, that both California and New Mexico are destined to be free,
so far as they are settled at all, which I believe, in regard to New Mexico,
will be but partially for a great length of time; free by the arrangement
of things ordained by the Power above us. . . . I would not take pains
uselessly to reaffirm an ordinance of nature, nor to re-enact the will of
God. I would put in no Wilmot Proviso for the mere purpose of a taunt
or a reproach. I would put into it no evidence of the votes of superior
power, exercised for no purpose but to wound the pride, whether a just

and a rational pride, or an irrational pride of the citizens of the Southern States. . . .

* * *

Now, Mr. President, I have established, so far as I proposed to do so, the proposition with which I set out, and upon which I intend to stand or fall; and that is, that the whole territory within the former United States, or in the newly acquired Mexican provinces, has a fixed and settled character, now fixed and settled by law which cannot be repealed,— in the case of Texas without a violation of public faith, and by no human power in regard to California or New Mexico; that, therefore, under one or other of these laws, every foot of land in the States or in the Territories has already received a fixed and decided character.

. . . I will allude to other complaints of the South, and especially to one which has in my opinion just foundation; and that is, that there has been found at the North, among individuals and among legislators, a disinclination to perform fully their constitutional duties in regard to the return of persons bound to service who have escaped into the free States. In that respect, the South, in my judgment, is right, and the North is wrong. Every member of every Northern legislature is bound by oath, like every other officer in the country, to support the Constitution of the United States; and the article of the Constitution which says to these States that they shall deliver up fugitives from service is as binding in honor and conscience as any other article. No man fulfils his duty in any legislature who sets himself to find excuses, evasions, escapes from this constitutional obligation. . . .

* * *

Then, Sir, there are the Abolition societies, of which I am unwilling to speak, but in regard to which I have very clear notions and opinions. I do not think then useful. I think their operations for the last twenty years have produced nothing good or valuable. . . . I do not mean to impute gross motives even to the leaders of these societies; but I am not blind to the consequences of their proceedings. I cannot but see what mischiefs their interference with the South has produced. . . .

* * *

There are also complaints of the North against the South. I need not go over them particularly . . . They complain, therefore, that, instead of slavery being regarded as an evil, as it was then, an evil which all hoped would be extinguished gradually, it is now regarded by the South as an institution to be cherished, and preserved, and extended; an institution which the South has already extended to the utmost of her power by the acquisition of new territory.

. . . Why, who are the laboring people of the North? They are the whole North. They are the people who till their own farms with their own hands; freeholders, educated men, independent men. . . . And what can these people think when so respectable and worthy a gentleman as the member from Louisiana undertakes to prove that the absolute ig- norance and the abject slavery of the South are more in conformity with the high purposes and destiny of immortal, rational human beings, than the educated, the independent free labor of the North?

* * *

Mr. President, I should much prefer to have heard from every member on this floor declarations of opinion that this Union could never be dis- solved, than the declaration of opinion by anybody, that, in any case under the pressure of any circumstances, such a dissolution was possible. I hear with distress and anguish the word "secession," especially when it falls from the lips of those who are patriotic, and known to the country, and known all over the world, for their political services. Secession! Peaceable secession! Sir, your eyes and mine are never destined to see that miracle. The dismemberment of this vast country without convul- sion! The breaking up of the fountains of the great deep without ruffling the surface! Who is so foolish, I beg everybody's pardon, as to expect to see any such thing? Sir, he who sees these States, now revolving in har- mony around a common centre, and expects to see them quit their places and fly off without convulsion, may look the next hour to see the heav- enly bodies rush from their spheres, and jostle against each other in the realms of space, without causing the wreck of the universe. There can be no such thing as a peaceable secession. Peaceable secession is an utter impossibility. Is the great Constitution under which we live, covering this whole country,—is it to be thawed and melted away by secession, as the snows on the mountain melt under the influence of a vernal sun, disappear almost unobserved, and run off? No, Sir! No, Sir! I will not state what might produce the disruption of the Union; but, Sir, I see as plainly as I see the sun in heaven what that disruption itself must pro- duce; I see that it must produce war, and such a war as I will not de- scribe, *in its twofold character.*

* * *

And now, Mr. President, instead of speaking of the possibility or util- ity of secession, instead of dwelling in those caverns of darkness, instead of groping with those ideas so full of all that is horrid and horrible, let us come out into the light of day; let us enjoy the fresh air of Liberty and Union; let us cherish those hopes which belong to us; let us devote ourselves to those great objects that are fit for our consideration and our action; let us raise our conceptions to the magnitude and the importance of the duties that devolve upon us; let our comprehension be as broad as the country for which we act, our aspirations as high as its certain destiny; let us not be pygmies in a case that calls for men. Never did there devolve on any generation of men higher trusts than now devolve upon us, for the preservation of this Constitution and the harmony and peace of all who are destined to live under it. Let us make our generation one of the strongest and brightest links in that golden chain which is destined, I fondly believe, to grapple the people of all the States to this Constitution for ages to come. We have a great, popular, constitutional government, guarded by law and by judicature, and defended by the affections of the whole people. No monarchical throne presses these States together, no iron chain of military power encircles them; they live and stand under a government popular in its form, representative in its character, founded upon principles of equality, and so constructed, we hope, as to last for ever. In all its history it has been beneficent; it has trodden down no man's liberty; it has crushed no State. Its daily respiration is liberty and patriotism; its yet youthful veins are full of enterprise, courage, and honorable love of glory and renown. Large before, the country has now, by recent events, become vastly larger. This republic now extends, with a vast breadth, across the whole continent. The two great seas of the world wash the one and the other shore. We realize, on a mighty scale, the beautiful description of the ornamental border of the buckler of Achilles:—

"Now, the broad shield complete, the artist crowned
With his last hand, and poured the ocean round;
In living silver seemed the waves to roll,
And beat the bucker's verge, and bound the whole."

Source: Edward Everett, ed., *The Speeches and Orations of Daniel Webster* (Boston, 1902), pp. 604–605, 615–624.

6.3.   The Compromise of 1850

The eight resolutions introduced by Henry Clay on January 29, 1850, were the basis of the final compromise worked out by September. Other provisions were added to the final settlement, such as the Texas and New Mexico boundary settlement, the Utah Act, the Fugitive Slave Act of September 18, 1850, and the abolition of the slave trade in the nation's capital. These are presented in the documents below.

1. CLAY'S RESOLUTIONS
January 29, 1850
(*U.S. Senate Journal*, 31st Congress, 1st Session, p. 118 ff.)

It being desirable, for the peace, concord, and harmony of the Union of these States, to settle and adjust amicably all existing questions of controversy between them arising out of the institution of slavery upon a fair, equitable and just basis: therefore,

1. *Resolved*, That California, with suitable boundaries, ought, upon her application to be admitted as one of the States of this Union, without the imposition by Congress of any restriction in respect to the exclusion or introduction of slavery within those boundaries.

2. *Resolved*, That as slavery does not exist by law, and is not likely to be introduced into any of the territory acquired by the United States from the republic of Mexico, it is inexpedient for Congress to provide by law either for its introduction into, or exclusion from, any part of the said territory; and that appropriate territorial governments ought to be established by Congress in all of the said territory, not assigned as the boundaries of the proposed State of California, without the adoption of any restriction or condition on the subject of slavery.

* * *

5. *Resolved*, That it is inexpedient to abolish slavery in the District of Columbia whilst that institution continues to exist in the State of Maryland, without the consent of that State, without the consent of the people of the District, and without just compensation to the owners of slaves within the District.

6. *But, resolved*, That it is expedient to prohibit, within the District, the slave trade in slaves brought into it from States or places beyond the limits of the District, either to be sold therein as merchandise, or to be transported to other markets without the District of Columbia.

7. *Resolved*, That more effectual provision ought to be made by law, according to the requirement of the constitution, for the restitution and delivery of persons bound to service or labor in any State, who may escape into any other State or Territory in the Union. And,

8. *Resolved*, That Congress has no power to promote or obstruct the trade in slaves between the slaveholding States; but that the admission or exclusion of slaves brought from one into another of them, depends exclusively upon their own particular laws.

2. THE TEXAS AND NEW MEXICO ACT
September 9, 1850
(*U.S. Statutes at Large*, Vol. IX, p. 446 ff.)

An Act proposing to the State of Texas the Establishment of her Northern and Western Boundaries, the Relinquishment by the said State of all Territory claimed by her exterior to said Boundaries, and of all her claims upon the United States, and to establish a territorial Government for New Mexico.

Be it enacted, That the following propositions shall be, and the same hereby are, offered to the State of Texas, which, when agreed to by the said State, and in an act passed by the general assembly, shall be binding and obligatory, upon the United States, and upon the said State of Texas: *Provided*, The said agreement by the said general assembly shall be given on or before the first day of December, eighteen hundred and fifty....

* * *

SEC. 2. And that all that portion of the Territory of the United States bounded as follows [boundaries] ... is hereby erected into a temporary government, by the name of the Territory of New Mexico: *Provided*, That nothing in this act contained shall be construed to inhibit the government of the United States from dividing said Territory into two or more Territories, in such manner and at such times as Congress shall deem convenient and proper, or from attaching any portion thereof to any other Territory or State: *And provided, further*, That, when admitted as a State, the said Territory, or any portion of the same, shall be received into the Union, with or without slavery, as their constitution may prescribe at the time of their admission.

3. THE UTAH ACT
September 9, 1850
(*U.S. Statutes at Large*, Vol. IX, p. 453 ff.)

An Act to establish a Territorial Government for Utah
Be it enacted, That all that part of the territory of the United States included within the following limits, to wit: bounded on the west by the State of California, on the north by the Territory of Oregon, and on the east by the summit of the Rocky Mountains, and on the south by the thirty-seventh parallel of north latitude, be, and the same is hereby, created into a temporary government, by the name of the Territory of Utah; and, when admitted as a State, the said Territory, or any portion of the same, shall be received into the Union, with or without slavery, as their constitution may prescribe at the time of their admission: *Provided*, That nothing in this act contained shall be construed to inhibit the government of the United States from dividing said Territory into two or more Territories, in such manner and at such times as Congress shall deem convenient and proper, or from attaching any portion of said Territory to any other State or Territory of the United States....

4. FUGITIVE SLAVE ACT
September 18, 1850
(*U.S. Statutes at Large*, Vol. IX, p. 462 ff.)

An Act to amend, and supplementary to, the Act entitled "An Act respecting Fugitives from Justice, and Persons escaping from the Service of their Masters," approved—[February 12, 1793].
... SEC. 5. That it shall be the duty of all marshals and deputy marshals to obey and execute all warrants and precepts issued under the

provisions of this act, when to them directed; and should any marshal or deputy marshal refuse to receive such warrant, or other process, when tendered, or to use all proper means diligently to execute the same, he shall, on conviction thereof, be fined in the sum of one thousand dollars, to the use of such claimant . . . and after arrest of such fugitive, by such marshal or his deputy, or whilst at any time in his custody under the provisions of this act, should such fugitive escape, whether with or without the assent of such marshal or his deputy, such marshal shall be liable, on his official bond, to be prosecuted for the benefit of such claimant, for the full value of the service or labor of said fugitive in the State, Territory, or District whence he escaped: and the better to enable the said commissioners, when thus appointed, to execute their duties faithfully and efficiently, in conformity with the requirements of the Constitution of the United States and of this act, they are hereby authorized and empowered, within their counties respectively, to appoint . . . any one or more suitable persons, from time to time, to execute all such warrants and other process as may be issued by them in the lawful performance of their respective duties; with authority to such commissioners, or the persons to be appointed by them, to execute process as aforesaid, to summon and call to their aid the bystanders, or *posse comitatus* of the proper country, when necessary to ensure a faithful observance of the clause of the Constitution referred to, in conformity with the provisions of this act; and all good citizens are hereby commanded to aid and assist in the prompt and efficient execution of this law, whenever their services may be required, as aforesaid, for that purpose; and said warrants shall run, and be executed by said officers, any where in the State within which they are issued.

SEC. 6. That when a person held to service or labor in any State or Territory of the United States, has heretofore or shall hereafter escape into another State or Territory of the United States, the person or persons to whom such service or labor may be due . . . may pursue and reclaim such fugitive person, either by procuring a warrant from some one of the courts, judges, or commissioners aforesaid, of the proper circuit, district, or country, for the apprehension of such fugitive from service or labor, or by seizing and arresting such fugitive, where the same can be done without process, and by taking, or causing such person to be taken, forthwith before such court, judge, or commissioner, whose duty it shall be to hear and determine the case of such claimant in a summary manner; and upon satisfactory proof being made, by deposition or affidavit, in writing, to be taken and certified by such court, judge, or commissioner, or by other satisfactory testimony, duly taken and certified by some court . . . and with proof, also by affidavit, of the identity of the person whose service or labor is claimed to be due as aforesaid, that the person so arrested does in fact owe service or labor to the person or persons claiming him or her, in the State or Territory from which such fugitive may have escaped as aforesaid, and that said person escaped, to make out and deliver to such claimant, his or her agent or attorney, a certificate setting forth the substantial facts as to the service or labor due from such fugitive to the claimant, and of his or her escape from the State or Territory in which he or she was arrested, with authority to such claimant . . . to use such reasonable force and restraint as may be necessary, under the circumstances of the case, to take and remove such fugitive person back to the State or Territory whence he or she may have escaped as aforesaid. In no trial or hearing under this act shall the testimony of such alleged fugitive be admitted in evidence; and the certificates in this and the first [fourth] section mentioned, shall be conclusive of the right of the person or persons in whose favor granted, to remove such fugitive to the State or Territory from which he escaped, and shall prevent all molestation of such person or persons by any process issued by any court, judge, magistrate, or other person whomsoever.

SEC. 7. That any persons who shall knowingly and willingly obstruct, hinder, or prevent such claimant, his agent or attorney, or any person or persons lawfully assisting him, her, or them, from arresting such a fugitive from service or labor, either with or without process as aforesaid, or shall rescue, or attempt to rescue, such fugitive from service or labor, from the custody of such claimant . . . or other person or persons lawfully assisting as aforesaid, when so arrested . . . or shall aid, abet, or assist such person so owing service or labor as aforesaid, directly or indirectly, to escape from such claimant . . . or shall harbor or conceal such fugitive, so as to prevent the discovery and arrest of such person, after notice or knowledge of the fact that such person was a fugitive from service or labor . . . shall, for either of said offences, be subject to a fine not exceeding one thousand dollars, and imprisonment not exceeding six months . . . ; and shall moreover forfeit and pay, by way of civil damages to the party injured by such illegal conduct, the sum of one thousand dollars, for each fugitive so lost as aforesaid. . . .

SEC. 9. That, upon affidavit made by the claimant of such fugitive . . . that he has reason to apprehend that such fugitive will be rescued by force from his or their possession before he can be taken beyond the limits of the State in which the arrest is made, it shall be the duty of the officer making the arrest to retain such fugitive in his custody, and to remove him to the State whence he fled, and there to deliver him to said claimant, his agent, or attorney. And to this end, the officer aforesaid is hereby authorized and required to employ so many persons as he may deem necessary to overcome such force, and to retain them in his service so long as circumstances may require. . . .

SEC. 10. That when any person held to service or labor in any State or

Territory, or in the District of Columbia, shall escape therefrom, the party to whom such service or labor shall be due ... may apply to any court of record therein ... and make satisfactory proof to such court ... of the escape aforesaid, and that the person escaping owed service or labor to such party. Whereupon the court shall cause a record to be made of the matters so proved, and also a general description of the person so escaping, with such convenient certainty as may be; and a transcript of such record ... being produced in any other State, Territory, or district in which the person so escaping may be found ... shall be held and taken to be full and conclusive evidence of the fact of escape, and that the service or labor of the person escaping is due to the party in such record mentioned. And upon the production by the said party of other and further evidence if necessary, either oral or by affidavit, in addition to what is contained in the said record of the identity of the person escaping, he or she shall be delivered up to the claimant. And the said court, commissioner, judge, or other person authorized by this act to grant certificates to claimants of fugitives, shall, upon the production of the record and other evidences aforesaid, grant to such claimant a certificate of his right to take any such person identified and proved to be owing service or labor as aforesaid, which certificate shall authorize such claimant to seize or arrest and transport such person to the State or Territory from which he escaped. ...

5. ACT ABOLISHING THE SLAVE TRADE IN THE DISTRICT OF COLUMBIA
September 20, 1850
(*U.S. Statutes at Large*, Vol. IX, p. 467 ff.)

An Act to suppress the Slave Trade in the District of Columbia.

Be it enacted ... That from and after January 1, 1851, it shall not be lawful to bring into the District of Columbia any slave whatever, for the purpose of being sold, or for the purpose of being placed in depot, to be subsequently transferred to any other State or place to be sold as merchandize. And if any slave shall be brought into the said District by its owner, or by the authority or consent of its owner, contrary to the provisions of this act, such slave shall thereupon become liberated and free.

SEC. 2. That it shall and may be lawful for each of the corporations of the cities of Washington and Georgetown, from time to time, and as often as may be necessary, to abate, break up, and abolish any depot or place of confinement of slaves brought into the said District as merchandize, contrary to the provisions of this act, by such appropriate means as may appear to either of the said corporations expedient and proper. And the same power is hereby vested in the Levy Court of Washington county, if any attempt shall be made, within its jurisdictional limits, to establish a depot or place of confinement for slaves brought into the said District as merchandize for sale contrary to this act.

Source: Henry Steele Commager, ed., *Documents of American History*, vol. 1, 8th ed. (New York: Appleton-Century-Crofts, 1968), pp. 319–323.

6.4.   The Georgia Platform, 1850

At a convention at Milledgeville, Georgia, Unionists in the state met to evaluate the Compromise of 1850 and adopted this platform. It reiterated the argument that henceforth the states' rights principles of the "original Compact" must be respected, that the Compromise would be accepted as the final settlement of the slavery question in the territories, and that the North must fully comply with the enforcement of the new Fugitive Slave Act. The Unionist position showed that, even among "friends" of the Union in the South, loyalty to the Union was conditional.

To the end that the position of this State may be clearly apprehended by her Confederates of the South and of the North, and that she may be blameless of all future consequences—

Be it resolved by the people of Georgia in Convention assembled, First. That we hold the American Union secondary in importance only to the rights and principles it was designed to perpetuate. That past associations, present fruition, and future prospects, will bind us to it so long as it continues to be the safe-guard of those rights and principles.

Second. That if the thirteen original Parties to the Compact, bordering the Atlantic in a narrow belt, while their separate interests were in embryo, their peculiar tendencies scarcely developed, their revolutionary trials and triumphs still green in memory, found Union impossible without compromise, the thirty-one of this day may well yield somewhat in the conflict of opinion and policy, to preserve that Union which has extended the sway of Republican Government over a vast wilderness to another ocean, and proportionately advanced their civilization and national greatness.

Third. That in this spirit the State of Georgia has maturely considered the action of Congress, embracing a series of measures for the admission of California into the Union, the organization of Territorial Governments for Utah and New Mexico, the establishment of a boundary between the latter and the State of Texas, the suppression of the slave-trade in the District of Columbia, and the extradition of fugitive slaves, and (connected with them) the rejection of propositions to exclude slavery from the Mexican Territories, and to abolish it in the District of Columbia; and, whilst she does not wholly approve, will abide by it as a permanent adjustment of this sectional controversy.

Fourth. That the State of Georgia, in the judgment of this Convention, will and ought to resist, even (as a last resort) to a disruption of every tie which binds her to the Union, any future Act of Congress abolishing Slavery in the District of Columbia, without the consent and petition of the slave-holders thereof, or any Act abolishing Slavery in places within the slave-holding States, purchased by the United States for the erection of forts, magazines, arsenals, dockyards, navy-yards, and other like purposes; or in any Act suppressing the slave-trade between slave-holding States; or in any refusal to admit as a State any Territory applying because of the existence of Slavery therein; or in any Act prohibiting the introduction of slaves into the Territories of Utah and New Mexico; or in any Act repealing or materially modifying the laws now in force for the recovery of fugitive slaves.

Fifth. That it is the deliberate opinion of this Convention, that upon the faithful execution of the Fugitive Slave Bill by the proper authorities, depends the preservation of our much loved Union.

Source: Commager, *Documents*, vol. 1, pp. 323–324.

ANNOTATED RESEARCH GUIDE

Books

Donald, David H. *Liberty and Union: The Crisis of Popular Government, 1830–1890.* Boston: Little, Brown, 1978. Argues that compromise and pragmatic solutions to sectional crises failed to avert war, a lesson that led to pragmatic politics by the end of the century.

Fehrenbacher, Don E. *Sectional Crisis and Southern Constitutionalism.* Baton Rouge: Louisiana State University Press, 1995. Covers the Missouri Compromise, the Wilmot Proviso, and the constitutional history of southern states to show how the federal government became involved in slavery.

Filler, Louis. *The Crusade Against Slavery: Friends, Foes, and Reforms, 1820–1860.* New York: Harper and Row, 1960. Still stands as a solid introduction to the history of abolitionism.

Freehling, William. *The Road to Disunion: Secessionists at Bay, 1776–1854.* New York: Oxford University Press, 1990. A general narrative history of the deep divisions in the South over secession.

Greenberg, Kenneth S. *Masters and Statesmen: The Political Culture of American Slavery.* Baltimore: Johns Hopkins University Press, 1985. Examines the ways southerners responded to northern assertions of power.

Hamilton, Holman. *Prologue to Conflict: The Crisis and Compromise of 1850.* Lexington: University Press of Kentucky, 1964. The fullest treatment of events leading up to, and the story of the passing of, the Compromise.

Johannsen, Robert W. *Stephen A. Douglas*. Urbana: University of Illinois Press, 1997. The definitive biography of the leader of the Democratic Party, who became the preeminent spokesman for popular sovereignty during the decade preceding secession.

Nye, Russel. *Fettered Freedom: Civil Liberties and the Slave Controversy, 1830–1860*. East Lansing: Michigan State University Press, 1964. Shows how the "slave power conspiracy" developed and how it and the South's determination to preserve the peculiar institution unchanged became a threat to republican government.

Pease, Jane H. *The Fugitive Slave Law and Anthony Burns: A Problem in Law Enforcement*. Philadelphia: Lippincott, 1975. Describes the arrest of Burns in Boston, his attempted rescue by an angry mob, and his march back to slavery in Virginia, an episode that led to the passing of Massachusetts's Personal Liberty Law in 1855.

Potter, David M. *The Impending Crisis, 1848–1861*. New York: Harper and Row, 1976. The classic account of the political and constitutional issues of the period.

Quarles, Benjamin. *Black Abolitionists*. New York: Oxford University Press, 1969. The only scholarly history of this influential section of the abolitionist movement, some of whose leaders advocated violence as a means of eliminating slavery in the South. It significantly advances the historical understanding of Frederick Douglass.

Shryock, Richard H. *Georgia and the Union in 1850*. Durham, NC: Duke University Press, 1926. Covers the reaction to the Compromise of 1850 in Georgia, focusing on the role of pro-Union Georgians in the writing of the "Georgia Platform."

Stewart, James B. *Holy Warriors: The Abolitionists and American Slavery*. Rev. ed. New York: Hill and Wang, 1996. An important survey of the abolitionist movement and the men and women who led it.

Nonprint Media

Web Sites

www.americanpresident.org/KoTrain/Courses/JP/JP   DomesticAffairs.htm. Companion Web site to the American President Series. This biographical section on James K. Polk outlines the issues surrounding the Wilmot Proviso.

http://lcweb.loc.gov/exhibits/treasures/trm043.html. The Library of Congress provides a look at the originals of John C. Calhoun's speech against the Compromise of 1850 and Daniel Webster's speech in favor of it.

http://www.pbs.org/wgbh/aia/part4/4p2951.html. PBS online presents information about the Compromise of 1850, including the Fugitive Slave Law. Offers a detailed explanation of the issues involved in the Compromise.

http://www.spartacus.schoolnet.co.uk/USASfugitive.htm. This educational re-

source offers a profile of the legislation passed in 1850 and provides reactions written by former slaves.

Videotapes

The American President, Episode 10: The Balance of Power [videorecording]. PBS.
Contains information about James K. Polk's presidency and the Wilmot
Proviso. Companion Web site: see above.

Africans in America, Part Four: Judgment Day [videorecording]. PBS. Describes the
abolitionists' crusade and southern reaction to the attack on slavery.
Covers the Compromise of 1850 and the Fugitive Slave Law. Companion
Web site: http://www.pbs.org/africansinamerica

Cooke, Alistair. *A Firebell in the Night* [videorecording]. BBC-TV and Time-Life
Films. Fifty-two minutes of coverage of slavery and the South, plantation
life, the "King Cotton" economy, the factory system in the North, expansion of slavery, the Missouri Compromise, the Mexican War, and the Compromise of 1850.

7

Plessy v. Ferguson: From Emancipation to Segregation

During the Civil War the power of the federal government over the states expanded in a significant number of areas. In 1862 Congress passed the Morrill Land Grant Act, which granted each state 30,000 acres of federal land for each of its congressional districts to finance education in agriculture, engineering, and military sciences. Eventually, the act helped to establish sixty-nine new colleges and universities. At the start of the war Lincoln, who believed that the emergency justified unprecedented use of executive power, authorized appropriations for a major shipbuilding program without consulting Congress. The National Banking Acts of 1863, 1864, and 1865 marked an extraordinary increase in federal fiscal authority. Now, for the first time, the country had a uniform currency in the form of national banknotes. They superseded the more than 7,000 kinds of notes issued by state banks, on which Congress, in 1865, imposed a prohibitive tax, forcing most of them to join the national banking system. In 1861 Lincoln suspended the writ of habeas corpus between the capital and Philadelphia to ensure Maryland's loyalty to the Union. Then he suspended it in other critical areas, mainly along the border states. By war's end over 13,000 citizens had been arrested and held without trial. Although state courts continued to function regularly, military courts sometimes put civilians on trial without juries.

But none of these new assertions of federal power in areas in the hands of the states before the war was as sweeping as the emancipation of the slaves. On September 22, 1862, following the Union victory at the Battle of Antietam, President Abraham Lincoln published the Emancipation

Proclamation, which declared that after January 1, 1863, all slaves in regions still in rebellion against the United States would be free. He did so under his war power authority as commander-in-chief, using military necessity as the constitutional cover for an extraordinary assertion of federal power in an area once the almost exclusive province of states. The Proclamation did not apply to areas of the South already under the control of the Union Army or to the loyal border states, and no slave was freed by it. Still, everyone understood at the time that the Emancipation Proclamation fundamentally altered the character and purpose of the war. Union victory now meant the end of slavery, "a new birth of freedom" for a new nation.

Making emancipation a war aim raised a number of legal questions. How could a wartime measure continue after the conflict was over? What would be the citizenship status of the freed slaves? What would be their civil rights? These questions prompted Lincoln in June 1864 to have the Republican Party put in its platform the passing of a constitutional amendment abolishing slavery. The Republican delegates quickly adopted such a plank, and in Congress the following year they passed the Thirteenth Amendment and sent it to the states for ratification. The language of the amendment ended slavery forever. But more than ending slavery, Section 2, the enabling clause, gave the federal government sweeping authority to enforce the amendment in any state unwilling to comply. This provision, and similar sections in the two other "freedom amendments," the Fourteenth and Fifteenth, provided the legal foundation for Congress in the postwar years to use federal law to guarantee the freed slaves their civil rights.

The immediate impact of the ratification of the Thirteenth Amendment on December 6, 1865, was the passing of legislation to make certain it was obeyed. Such federal laws were necessary after the war, the Radicals argued, because it was apparent that southern states were quickly putting in place race laws, or "black codes," specifically designed to circumvent the amendment. These codes allowed blacks to own property and sue and be sued in court but imposed high penalties for vagrancy and prohibited them from voting, from working in many nonagricultural jobs, and from bearing arms. In response, Congress created the Freedmen's Bureau, a federal agency, independent of state control, to deal with the economic and social problems facing the 4 million freed slaves and to prepare them for citizenship. During its existence it established over 100 hospitals, distributed 20 million packets of food rations, and operated 4,000 schools for 600,000 black children. In 1866 Congress also passed the first Civil Rights Act to give the Thirteenth Amendment specific definition. It declared blacks full citizens and guaranteed them the right to make contracts, testify in court, and hold property.

But by the time the Civil Rights Act was enacted, Congress was on a collision course with the president over the question of how to bring the South back into the Union. Lincoln, claiming constitutional authority as commander-in-chief, on December 8, 1863, had issued a wartime proclamation that became known as his Ten Percent Plan of Reconstruction. He told the Confederate states that if they stopped fighting they could come back into the Union by taking a simple loyalty oath and by accepting the abolition of slavery. Then, when a number of citizens in the state equal to 10 percent of the number of adult males who had voted in the 1860 election had taken the oath, new state governments could be organized, so long as they recognized emancipation. Only high Confederate officials would be disfranchised. The following year the Radicals in Congress, who had taken a firm position against the Ten Percent Plan as too lenient toward the South, offered their own, much harsher, Wade-Davis bill. It required 50 percent of the adult males to take an "ironclad" oath and disfranchised anyone who had fought against the Union. The president pocket-vetoed the measure. By the time of Lincoln's assassination he and the Congress had reached a standoff, though Lincoln's thinking on Reconstruction was not fixed.

Andrew Johnson, the new president in April 1865, only exacerbated the differences between presidential and congressional Reconstruction. In his Amnesty Proclamation of May 29, 1865, he excluded the wealthy planter class from power as well as high-ranking Confederate officers and politicians. All other adult white males just had to swear a loyalty oath to receive an amnesty. He appointed provisional governors in each state to convene constitutional conventions to write documents that would both denounce secession and eliminate slavery. When that was completed the states could hold congressional elections and be restored to the Union. Southern states proceeded with the president's plan but restored Confederate leaders to high office, with Georgians even electing the former vice president of the Confederacy, Alexander Stephens, to the Senate. In December 1865, Johnson, who embraced white supremacy, accepted the results and said that Reconstruction was now complete.

Republicans countered. They acted partly out of a personal dislike for the man, whose language was intemperate and whose dealings with congressmen were at best inept. Another reason was that by 1866 all southern states, in addition to returning high Confederate officials to power, had in place stringent black codes that restored the freedman to a condition of virtual bondage. On April 9, 1866, Congress repassed the Civil Rights Act over a presidential veto by a two-thirds majority. It was the first time that Congress overrode a veto of a major piece of legislation. Shortly afterwards, it overrode Johnson's veto of the Freedmen's Bureau bill. After these victories Congress, not the president, largely controlled Reconstruction planning, though the president still played a vital role by refusing to enforce congressional Reconstruction policy and by removing military and civil officers sympathetic to Republican Reconstruction. Accordingly, to assure blacks their civil rights under the Constitution, and to try to remove several issues from political jockeying thereafter, the Republicans passed the Fourteenth Amendment.

It became the cornerstone of their Reconstruction plan. Of its four far-reaching provisions, the first was the most important, given the subsequent history of the amendment. It conferred citizenship on the former slaves and prohibited states from infringing on their "privileges and immunities" as citizens. It prohibited states from depriving a citizen his or her life, liberty, or property "without due process of law" and guaranteed "equal protection of the laws." The second section took aim at the black codes' denial of the franchise. It penalized any state that abridged a citizen's right to vote by reducing its representation in the House of Representatives proportionately. The third section forbade any official who had joined the Confederacy to hold state or federal office. The fourth repudiated the Confederate debt. Section 5 reiterated the power of the federal government to enforce the amendment in the same language as the Thirteenth Amendment's enabling clause. And Congress made acceptance of the amendment a precondition for a "seceded" state's readmission to the Union.

Johnson went on a speaking tour to block ratification in a "swing around the circle" that began in the East and went through the Midwest. But he received little response and returned discredited for badgering hecklers and accusing Republican leaders of treason, even more so when every southern state except Tennessee refused to ratify the amendment. Moreover, the very Radicals that Johnson had denounced in his tour received resounding victories in the 1866 elections. And, with huge Republican majorities in both houses, they turned their full attention on the South.

Determined to assert full federal control over the former Confederate states, on March 2, 1867, Congress passed the First Reconstruction Act. This law virtually destroyed southern state governments and divided the Confederacy (except for Tennessee, because it had accepted the Fourteenth Amendment) into five military districts under the command of a major general. These officers had sweeping authority to guarantee the civil rights of "all persons," to suppress insurrection, and to oversee the administration of military justice. The act disfranchised all classes of southerners identified in the Fourteenth Amendment. It stated that the freedmen could vote for, and serve in, state constitutional conventions. If the constitution was approved by Congress and if the state then accepted the Fourteenth Amendment, martial law would end and the state would be admitted to the Union. Johnson vetoed the law, and Congress easily overrode it.

Then Johnson counterattacked. He limited the power of the military commanders in the five districts and removed other officers who were enforcing the Reconstruction Act. The Radicals, to prevent Johnson from sabotaging their program, restricted presidential authority. Congress passed a law removing his traditional prerogative to summon Congress into session. It limited his control over the military by requiring him to issue all military orders with the approval of Ulysses S. Grant, the General of the Army. In the Tenure of Office Act, they forbade the president to remove any cabinet member without the approval of the Senate. Using Johnson's alleged violation of this act when he unilaterally removed Secretary of War Edwin Stanton, the House of Representatives passed a bill of impeachment against the president. But on May 16, 1868, the Senate fell one vote short of the necessary two-thirds majority to convict him of "high crimes and misdemeanors."

The Republican-controlled Congress was determined to stamp out all southern resistance to federal authority and at the same time avoid the possibility of Democratic "unreconstructed" southern states being readmitted to Congress. It passed the Second Reconstruction Act on March 23, 1867, and the Third Reconstruction Act on July 19. These acts authorized the army to register black voters and to supervise state elections.

Southern defiance increased. Because the acts stipulated that the new state constitutions had to be approved by a majority vote, whites refused to vote and prevented ratification. Congress then changed the procedure in the Fourth Reconstruction Act of March 11, 1868, and had the constitutions ratified just by "a majority of those voting."

In 1869, to guarantee success in imposing its will on the South, Congress passed the Fifteenth Amendment and presented it to the states for ratification. It prohibited states from denying the right to vote "on account of race, color, or previous condition of servitude." Most southern states, under federal pressure, swiftly accepted the amendment, and it was ratified on February 3, 1870. It became law on paper only, because southern whites subverted it with violence and intimidation of black voters and Republicans. Later, conservative whites would effectively disfranchise blacks by imposing literacy tests, poll taxes, and residency and registration requirements that discriminated against blacks in practice.

Nevertheless, between 1868 and 1872, the South lived under "Black Republican" Reconstruction. Former slaves voted, always for Republicans, held office, and enjoyed the protection of the Fourteenth and Fifteenth Amendments. Numerous blacks held minor offices and served in state legislatures. Eighteen were elected to Congress. Black politicians were aided by southern white "scalawags" who cooperated with the Republicans and by "carpetbaggers," northern idealists, some of whom were black, who came to the South to help the freedmen and build a "new South" on a northern model.

Under these circumstances, and dominated by the Republican Party, southern states wrote new constitutions that adopted a number of democratic reforms, such as the removal of property qualifications for voting and for officeholding. Republican-controlled legislatures appropriated funds for public schools and hospitals for the mentally ill, the blind, and the deaf. They built orphanages. They broadened women's property rights and made divorce more accessible for them. They increased taxes to provide money to rebuild railroad networks and restored levees along the rivers. Republican governments also promoted industry with subsidies, expanded banking, and encouraged a pro-business climate with regulation. Manufacturing increased. But Radical Reconstruction could not last, because for Republican governments to stay in power they had to have the support of a large percentage of the white voters. And this proved impossible.

Federal Reconstruction was undermined and then thwarted in three ways: by systematic violence by southern whites, by emerging states' rights conservativism among Republicans in Congress, and by Supreme Court rulings that undermined federal authority. Violence and terror were practiced by paramilitary organizations such as the Ku Klux Klan, which was founded in Tennessee in 1865, assassinated Republican leaders, broke up Republican Party meetings, and frightened blacks into abstaining from voting. Congress in 1870 and 1871 passed two Enforcement Acts and an anti-Klan law in a vain effort to curb these violent campaigns. But federal officials in the South used these statutes only selectively, mainly in Mississippi and the Carolinas; in other parts of the South they were ignored, and violence continued unabated. Even when arrests were made southern juries refused to convict in two-thirds of the cases brought to trial. So, even when the Klan disbanded in 1873, the violence kept up with new organizations such as the Red Shirts and rifle clubs.

At the same time that southerners were "redeeming" their state governments from Republican control, in Congress a number of influential but conservative Republicans challenged the legitimacy of Reconstruction by attacking the idea that the Thirteenth, Fourteenth, and Fifteenth Amendments had made the federal government the protector of the civil rights of the freed slave. For example, Senator Lyman Trumbull of Illinois considered the anti-Klan laws an infringement on the constitutional rights of the states to be the guardians of individual rights under their "police power." Trumbull and others feared a dangerous precedent had been established where, under such increasing congressional authority over individual rights, there would be such a centralization and consolidation of federal power as to eliminate eventually the need for any state governments whatsoever.

The Supreme Court, in a series of decisions that ultimately led to its sanctioning of racial segregation in the 1896 decision *Plessy v. Ferguson*, steadily undermined the use of the Fourteenth Amendment and congressional laws to guarantee black civil rights. The narrowing of the interpretation of the amendment began in 1873 with the *Slaughterhouse Cases*. In 1869 the Republican-controlled legislature in Louisiana had passed a law that conferred a monopoly of all slaughtering in New Orleans on the Crescent City Live-Stock Landing & Slaughterhouse Company. It required all butchers to rent space from the Crescent City company, claiming that this would provide improved health conditions in the industry. The Republicans argued that the law was a legitimate regulation under the "police powers" given the states. The butchers, most of whom were Democrats, contended that the monopoly violated the Fourteenth Amendment, which had been ratified in 1868.

They sued in the state courts and then in the Louisiana Supreme Court, arguing that the Fourteenth Amendment prohibited states from passing "any law which shall abridge the privileges or immunities of citizens of the United States," which to them meant their unrestricted right to do business. They maintained that under the due process clause of the amendment only the courts could do this. They argued that the monopoly law had also transgressed its inherent powers of legislation and violated the state constitution and, moreover, had created a monopoly for the sole purpose of private profit, not for the good of the community. Lawyers for the Republican legislature argued that the Fourteenth Amendment only applied to the freed blacks and that the legislature had authority to create a monopoly under the "police power" of the Constitution. The state supreme court found in favor of the monopoly. The butchers appealed to the United States Supreme Court.

Its 5 to 4 decision, handed down on April 14, 1873, and written by Justice Samuel Miller, held that the Louisiana law was constitutional because "the purpose of the Fourteenth Amendment was to guarantee freedom of the former negro slaves, not to transfer control over the entire domain of civil rights from the states to the Federal government." Miller pointed out that there were two types of citizenship, national and state. National citizenship meant only the right to travel from state to state. State citizenship dealt with civil rights—the right to vote, to use public accommodations, to work, and housing. Miller wrote that the police power clause gave the states full authority over industries inside the state. Therefore, the Court ruled that the Fourteenth Amendment did not apply in this case. Congress reacted to the decision by enacting a second Civil Rights Act in February 1875. This law made blacks "equal before the law" and gave them the right to serve on juries. It also mandated desegregation of all public facilities.

The following year the Court further limited the Fourteenth Amendment's ability to protect the civil rights of the freedmen in *United States v. Cruikshank*. This case involved the "Colfax Massacre" in Louisiana, where an armed white militia had attacked and killed over 100 black men during a gubernatorial election. Three militiamen were indicted and found guilty for violating the 1870 Force Act. They appealed to the Supreme Court. As in the *Slaughterhouse* ruling, the Court found that there were distinctions between the rights of federal citizens and state citizens. Chief Justice Morrison R. Waite wrote the unanimous opinion, which held that the Fourteenth Amendment limited *state* action against civil rights but not actions by *individuals* against each other. He also concluded that there was no evidence that the white defendants' actions were motivated by race.

The day after the *Cruikshank* opinion was handed down, in *United States v. Reese*, the Court, in an 8 to 1 majority decision, ruled that states had the power to deny suffrage on account of race because, Waite wrote, it was "within the power of a State to exclude citizens of the United States from voting on account of race as it was on account of property or education." He stated that the "Fifteenth Amendment does not confer the right of suffrage upon any one, it only prevents the states . . . from giving preference . . . to one citizen . . . over another on account of race, color, or previous condition of servitude." Finally, Waite declared that the 1870 Force Act did not come under the "appropriate legislation" of the freedom amendments and, consequently, was "unauthorized" by the Constitution. The Court had to intervene when Congress "steps outside of its constitutional limitations, and attempts that which is beyond its reach" and encroaches "upon the reserved power of the States and the people."

In October 1883, the Court denied the legitimacy of the Civil Rights Act of 1875 in the *Civil Rights Cases*. Justice Joseph Bradley wrote: "Until some State law has been passed, or some State action through its officers or agents has been taken, adverse to the rights of citizens sought to be protected by the Fourteenth Amendment, no legislation of the United States under said amendment, nor any proceeding under such legislation can be called into activity; for the prohibitions of the amendment are against State laws and acts done under State authority." Justice John Marshall Harlan stated in his lone dissent that in the majority ruling "the substance and spirit of the recent amendments of the Constitution have been sacrificed by a subtle and ingenious verbal criticism." In essence, the decision in the *Civil Rights Cases* withdrew the federal government from the enforcement of the freedom amendments, and it would not return to that area until the mid-twentieth century.

In 1896 the Court gave blanket constitutional approval for state racial segregation laws in *Plessy v. Ferguson*. In New Orleans a group of blacks and Creoles organized into a citizens' committee to test the constitutionality of a 1890 Louisiana statute, the Separate Car Act. On June 7, 1892, Homer Plessy, a shoemaker who was one-eighth black, purchased a first-class ticket on the East Louisiana Railway from New Orleans to Covington, entered the train, and took a seat in a coach reserved for white passengers. The conductor ordered him to move to the black car or be ejected and arrested. Plessy refused. The police forcibly took him to the New Orleans parish jail, where he was charged with violating the Separate Car Act. Plessy had been put on the train by the citizens' committee, and its lawyer, Albion Tourgée, put up $500 in bail money for Plessy, who was then arraigned before the criminal district court for the parish of New Orleans, presided over by Judge John Howard Ferguson.

Plessy's new lawyer, James Walker, argued that the state law was null and void because it conflicted with the U.S. Constitution. He said that neither the state nor any railroad company had the right to deny Plessy his "liberty" on the basis of race. He claimed that Plessy was a citizen and that the Fourteenth Amendment forbade "abridgment of privileges or immunities of any citizen of the United States." Judge Ferguson rejected the plea and ruled that Louisiana had a legal right to regulate railroad companies that operated only within the state. He went on to write that Plessy was not deprived of his liberty but "simply deprived of the liberty of doing as he pleased, and of violating a penal statute with impunity."

The case went to the Supreme Court, where Albion Tourgée again represented Plessy. Tourgée reiterated the earlier arguments against the constitutionality of the Separate Car Act. By a 7 to 1 majority, with one abstention, the Court ruled against Plessy. Justice Henry Billings Brown wrote the opinion, in which he rejected the assumption that "social prejudices may be overcome by legislation," and claimed that "equal rights cannot be secured to the negro except by an enforced commingling of the two races." "Legislation is powerless to eradicate racial instincts or to abolish distinctions based upon physical differences," he went on, "and the attempt to do so can only result in accentuating the differences of the present situation." He stated that transportation was like education, and thereby expanded the application of the Court's decision. He concluded that if "the civil and political rights of both races be equal, one cannot be inferior to the other civilly or politically." He further wrote, "If one race be inferior to the other socially, the Constitution of the United States cannot put them upon the same plane." Justice Harlan's ringing dissent rejected the "separate but equal" doctrine. He wrote that "in view of the Constitution, in the eye of the law, there is in this country no superior, dominant, ruling class of citizens. . . . There is no caste here. . . . Our Constitution is color-blind, and neither knows nor tolerates classes among citizens." "In respect of civil rights," Marshall asserted, "all citizens are equal before the law." But back in New Orleans, on January 11, 1897, Plessy paid a $25 fine to Judge Ferguson's district court clerk.

Without either congressional or judicial support, southern whites solidified the system of racial segregation that they had begun with the black codes after the Civil War. During the twenty years following *Plessy*, Jim Crow laws proliferated throughout the region and created two separate societies, one white, the other black. These laws prohibited racial mixing in public transportation facilities. They segregated hotels, theaters, and parks. State laws and local ordinances separated the races at drinking fountains and toilets. Blacks were confined to separate parts of hospitals and cemeteries. Neighborhoods were legally designated as "colored" or "white." Some cities had curfews that had blacks off the streets by ten o'clock at night. Different Bibles were used in courtrooms to swear in black and white witnesses. There were separate schools.

By 1896, then, the attempt by Republican politicians in Congress to use the federal power to guarantee the civil rights of the former slaves had failed. The Fourteenth and Fifteenth Amendments, combined with federal statutes designed to weaken, if not eliminate, the authority of the southern states over blacks, had marked a new and dramatic use of federal power to prevent unrepentant Confederates, almost all of them Democrats, from taking over their state governments and denying basic freedoms to their former slaves. For a few years this imposed federalism on the South worked, but even then there was unmistakable, persistent white resistance.

The waning of the reforming impulse in the Republican Party and the rise of states' rights conservatives in its ranks, the new materialism of the Gilded Age, which cynically subordinated the plight of the freedmen to the advancement of business prosperity, the lack of experience and training among black leaders and voters in the South—all melded to bring about a full retreat of Reconstruction federalism. The retreat was encouraged by a deep-seated racism, not only in the South but also in the North, that made most northern whites cynically disinterested in black rights. Then, too, new ideas about Social Darwinism and "survival of the fittest," and new fears about "dark-skinned" immigrants crowding into America made many native-born northern whites sympathetic to southern whites' arguments that social harmony depended on white dominance. In any case, Social Darwinism held that federal laws did not have the power to undo social habits and remake racial attitudes, and northern interest in the "Negro problem" was exhausted by the mid-1870s.

Historically, then, the descent of the freedmen between 1866 and 1896 from emancipated "citizens" whose civil rights were fully backed by the authority of the federal government to a state-mandated and enforced racial segregation and second-class citizenship exposed to harassment and violence seemed almost inevitable. By 1896 the nation was ready to lapse into what historian C. Vann Woodward called the "capitulation to racism." But something had been done during Reconstruction to strengthen the power of the federal government, if not for its own day, then certainly for future generations of Americans. During Reconstruction, the fundamental language of civil rights—"the privileges or immunities of citizens of the United States," "due process of law," and "equal protection of the law"—had been added to the Constitution. This language would be indispensable when American reformers would once again resurrect the Republican idea of equality.

DOCUMENTS

7.1.   Howell Cobb: An Unreconstructed Southerner

> Cobb was a major general in the Confederate army. Before the
> war, he was an influential Georgia attorney as well as a Dem-
> ocratic member of, and Speaker of, the U.S. House of Repre-
> sentatives, a governor of Georgia, and secretary of the treasury
> under President James Buchanan. He was typical of most former
> Confederates in that he deeply resented the stationing of federal
> troops in the South as a means for federal reconstruction of that
> section's political and social life.

We of the ill-fated South realize only the mournful present whose lesson
teaches us to prepare for a still gloomier future.... The people of the
south, conquered, ruined, impoverished, and oppressed, bear up with
patient fortitude under the heavy weight of their burdens. Disarmed and
reduced to poverty, they are powerless to protect themselves against
wrong and injustice; and can only await with broken spirits that destiny
which the future has in store for them. At the bidding of their more
powerful conquerors they laid down their arms, abandoned a hopeless
struggle, and returned to their quiet homes under the plighted faith of
a soldier's honor that they should be protected so long as they observed
the obligations imposed upon them of peaceful law-abiding citizens.

* * *

Since the close of the war they have taken our property of various
kinds, sometimes by seizure, and sometimes by purchase,—and when
we have asked for remuneration have been informed that the claims of
rebels are never recognized by the Government. To this decision necessity compels us to submit; but our conquerors express surprise that we
do not see in such ruling the evidence of their kindness and forgiving
spirit.

They have imposed upon us in our hour of distress and ruin a heavy
and burdensome tax, peculiar and limited to our impoverished section.
Against such legislation we have ventured to utter an earnest appeal,
which to many of their leading spirits indicates a spirit of insubordina-
tion which calls for additional burdens. They have deprived us of the
protection afforded by our state constitutions and laws, and put life,

liberty and property at the disposal of absolute military power. Against this violation of plighted faith and constitutional right we have earnestly and solemnly protested, and our protests have been denounced as insolent;—and our restlessness under the wrong and oppression which have followed these acts has been construed into a rebellious spirit, demanding further and more stringent restrictions of civil and constitutional rights. They have arrested the wheels of State government, paralyzed the arm of industry, engendered a spirit of bitter antagonism on the part of our negro population towards the white people with whom it is the interest of both races they should maintain kind and friendly relations, and are now struggling by all the means in their power both legal and illegal, constitutional and unconstitutional, to make our former slaves *our masters*, bringing these Southern states under the power of *negro supremacy*.

* * *

With an Executive who manifests a resolute purpose to defend with all his power the constitution of his country from further aggression, and a Judiciary whose unspotted record has never yet been tarnished with a base subserviency to the unholy demands of passion and hatred, let us indulge the hope that the hour of the country's redemption is at hand, and that even in the wronged and ruined South there is a fair prospect for better days and happier hours when our people can unite again in celebrating the national festivals as in the olden time.

Source: Howell Cobb to J. D. Hoover, January 4, 1868, in *The Correspondence of Robert Toombs, Alexander H. Stephens, and Howell Cobb*, ed. Ulrich B. Philips (Washington, DC: American Historical Association, 1913), pp. 690–694.

7.2. Congressional House and Senate Debates on the Fourteenth Amendment, 1866

Excerpts from the House and Senate debates cover important questions and considerations regarding federalism and civil rights. One was whether or not the federal Bill of Rights applied to the states. Another was whether the word "persons" in the amendment applied not only to blacks but to women as well. And a third was what limits should be put on federal power to enforce civil rights guarantees. The drafting and ratification of the amendment did not end the debates as to the full extent and meaning of federal power and civil rights, which remain unsettled even to this day.

February 27, 1866

Mr. [Robert] Hale [New York]. What is the effect of the amendment which the committee on reconstruction propose for the sanction of this House and the States of the Union? I submit that it is in effect a provision under which all State legislation, in its codes of civil and criminal jurisprudence and procedure, affecting the individual citizen, may be overridden, may be repealed or abolished, and the law of Congress established instead. I maintain that in this respect it is an utter departure from every principle ever dreamed of by the men who framed our Constitution.

Mr. [Thaddeus] Stevens [Pennsylvania]. Does the gentleman mean to say that, under this provision, Congress could interfere in any case where the legislation of a State was equal, impartial to all? Or is it not simply to provide that, where any State makes a distinction in the same law between different classes of individuals, Congress shall have power to correct such discrimination and inequality? Does this proposition mean anything more than that?

Mr. Hale. I will answer the gentleman. In my judgment it does go much further than the remarks of the gentleman would imply: but even if it goes no further than that—and I will discuss this point more fully before I conclude—it is still open to the same objection, that it proposes an entire departure from the theory of the Federal Government in meddling with these matters of State jurisdiction at all.

Now, I say to the gentleman from Pennsylvania [Mr. Stevens] that reading the language in its grammatical and legal construction it is a grant of the fullest and most ample power to Congress to make all laws "necessary and proper to secure to all persons in the several States protection in the rights of life, liberty, and property," with the simple proviso that such protection shall be equal. It is not a mere provision that when the States undertake to give protection which is unequal Congress may equalize it: it is a grant of power in general terms—a grant of the right to legislate for the protection of life, liberty and property, simply qualified with the condition that it shall be equal legislation. That is my construction of the proposition as it stands here. It may differ from that of other gentlemen.

Mr. [Charles] Eldridge [Wisconsin]. Mr. Speaker, let me go a little further here. If it be true that the construction of this amendment, which I understand to be claimed by the gentleman from Ohio, [Mr. Bingham] who introduced it, and which I infer from his question is claimed by the gentleman from Pennsylvania. [Mr. Stevens:] if it be true that that is the true construction of this article, is it not even then introducing a power never before intended to be conferred upon Congress. For we all know it is true that probably every State in this Union fails to give equal protection to all persons within its borders in the rights of life, liberty, and property. It may be a fault in the States that they do not do it. A reformation may be desirable, but by the doctrines of the school of politics in which I have been brought up, and which I have been taught to regard was the best school of political rights and duties in this Union, reforms of this character should come from the States, and not be forced upon them by the centralized power of the Federal Government.

* * *

May 8, 1866

Mr. Stevens. Let us now refer to the provisions of the proposed amendment.

The first section prohibits the States from abridging the privileges and immunities of citizens of the United States, or unlawfully depriving them of life, liberty, or property, or of denying to any person within their jurisdiction the "equal" protection of the laws.

I can hardly believe that any person can be found who will not admit that every one of these provisions is just. They are all asserted, in some form or other, in our DECLARATION or organic law. But the Constitution limits only the action of Congress, and is not a limitation on the States. This amendment supplies that defect, and allows Congress to correct the unjust legislation of the States, so far that the law which operates upon one man shall operate *equally* upon all. Whatever law punishes a white man for a crime shall punish the black man precisely in the same way and to the same degree. Whatever law protects the white man shall afford "equal" protection to the black man. Whatever means of redress is afforded to one shall be afforded to all. Whatever law allows the white man to testify in court shall allow the man of color to do the same. These are great advantages over their present codes. Now different degrees of punishment are inflicted, not on account of the magnitude of the crime, but according to the color of the skin. Now color disqualifies a man from testifying in courts, or being tried in the same way as white men. I need not enumerate these partial and oppressive laws. Unless the Constitution should restrain them those States will all, I fear, keep up this discrimination, and crush to death the hated freedmen. Some answer, "Your civil rights bill secures the same things." That is partly true, but a law is repealable by a majority. And I need hardly say that the first time that the South with their copperhead allies obtain the command of Congress it will be repealed. The veto of the President and their votes on the bill are conclusive evidence of that.

May 23, 1866

Mr. [Jacob] Howard [Michigan]. The first clause of this section relates to the privileges and immunities of citizens of the United States as such, and as distinguished from all other persons not citizens of the United States.

It would be a curious question to solve what are the privileges and immunities of citizens of each of the States in the several States. I do not propose to go at any length into that question at this time. It would be a somewhat barren discussion. But it is certain the clause was inserted in the Constitution for some good purpose. It has in view some results beneficial to the citizens of the several States, or it would not be found there; yet I am not aware that the Supreme Court have ever undertaken to define either the nature or extent of the privileges and immunities thus guaranteed. Indeed, if my recollection serves me, that court, on a certain occasion not many years since, when this question seemed to present itself to them, very modestly declined to go into a definition of them, leaving questions arising under the clause to be discussed and adjudicated when they should happen practically to arise. . . .

Such is the character of the privileges and immunities spoken of in the second section of the fourth article of the Constitution. To these privileges and immunities, whatever they may be—for they are not and cannot be fully defined in their entire extent and precise nature—to these should be added the personal rights guaranteed and secured by the first eight amendments of the Constitution; such as the freedom of speech and of the press; the right of the people peaceably to assemble and petition the Government for a redress of grievances, a right appertaining to each and all the people; the right to keep and to bear arms; the right to be exempted from the quartering of soldiers in a house without the consent of the owner; the right to be exempt from unreasonable searches and seizures, and from any search or seizure except by virtue of a warrant issued upon a formal oath or affidavit: the right of an accused person to be informed of the nature of the accusation against him, and his right to be tried by an impartial jury of the vicinage; and also the right to be secure against excessive bail and against cruel and unusual punishments.

Now, sir, here is a mass of privileges, immunities, and rights, some of them secured by the second section of the fourth article of the Constitution, which I have recited, some by the first eight amendments of the Constitution; and it is a fact well worthy of attention that the course of decision of our courts and the present settled doctrine is, that all these immunities, privileges, rights, thus guaranteed by the Constitution or recognized by it, are secured to the citizen solely as a citizen of the United States and as a party in their courts. They do not operate in the slightest degree as a restraint or prohibition upon State legislation. States are not affected by them, and it has been repeatedly held that the restriction contained in the Constitution against the taking of private property for public use without just compensation is not a restriction upon State legislation, but applies only to the legislation of Congress.

Now, sir, there is no power given in the Constitution to enforce and to carry out any of these guarantees. They are not powers granted by the Constitution to Congress, and of course do not come within the sweeping clause of the Constitution authorizing Congress to pass all laws necessary and proper for carrying out the foregoing or granted powers, but they stand simply as a bill of rights in the Constitution, without power on the part of Congress to give them full effect; while at the same time the States are not restrained from violating the principles embraced in them except by their own local constitutions, which may be altered from year to year. The great object of the first section of this amendment is, therefore, to restrain the power of the States and compel them at all times to respect these great fundamental guarantees.

Source: Kermit L. Hall, *Major Problems in American Constitutional History*. Volume 1: *The Colonial Era Through Reconstruction* (Lexington, MA: D. C. Heath, 1992), pp. 535–544.

7.3.   Principles of the Ku Klux Klan (1868)

The Ku Klux Klan was the most important, and the largest, paramilitary secret society that organized to oppose Reconstruction through terrorism and violence. It was first organized in Pulaski, Tennessee, in 1865 and rapidly spread throughout the former Confederacy after Republican Reconstruction went into effect in 1868. The Klan directed its intimidation and violence against Republicans and blacks to undo Republican governments and force blacks back into a subordinate role in society. Although the Klan was broken up by the federal Force Act of 1870, it achieved its principal purpose of disrupting Republican governments and driving Republican voters from the polls. The Klan and other such paramilitary organizations bequeathed a legacy of violence to southern politics that lasted more than a generation.

Creed

We, the Order of the ***, reverentially acknowledge the majesty and supremacy of the Divine Being, and recognize the goodness and providence of the same. And we recognize our relation to the United States Government, the supremacy of the Constitution, the Constitutional Laws thereof, and the Union of States thereunder.

Character and Objects of the Order

This is an institution of Chivalry, Humanity, Mercy, and Patriotism; embodying in its genius and its principles all that is chivalric in conduct, noble in sentiment, generous in manhood, and patriotic in purpose; its peculiar objects being

First: To protect the weak, the innocent, and the defenseless, from the indignities, wrongs, and outrages of the lawless, the violent, and the brutal; to relieve the injured and oppressed; to succor the suffering and unfortunate, and especially the widows and orphans of Confederate soldiers.

Second: To protect and defend the Constitution of the United States, and all laws passed in conformity thereto, and to protect the States and the people thereof from all invasion from any source whatever.

Third: To aid and assist in the execution of all constitutional laws, and to protect the people from unlawful seizure, and from trial except by their peers in conformity to the laws of the land.

Titles

Sec. 1. The officers of this Order shall consist of a Grand Wizard of the Empire, and his ten Genii; a Grand Dragon of the Realm, and his eight Hydras; a Grand Titan of the Dominion, and his six Furies; a Grand Giant of the Province, and his four Goblins; a Grand Cyclops of the Den, and his two Night Hawks; a Grand Magi, a Grand Monk, a Grand Scribe, a Grand Exchequer, a Grand Turk, and a Grand Sentinel.

Sec. 2. The body politic of this Order shall be known and designated as "Ghouls."

* * *

Interrogations to be asked

1st. Have you ever been rejected, upon application for membership in the ***, or have you ever been expelled from the same?

2d. Are you now, or have you ever been, a member of the Radical Republican party, or either of the organizations known as the "Loyal League" and the "Grand Army of the Republic?"

3d. Are you opposed to the principles and policy of the Radical party, and to the Loyal League, and the Grand Army of the Republic, so far as you are informed of the character and purposes of those organizations?

4th. Did you belong to the Federal army during the late war, and fight against the South during the existence of the same?

5th. Are you opposed to negro equality, both social and political?

6th. Are you in favor of a white man's government in this country?

7th. Are you in favor of Constitutional liberty, and a Government of equitable laws instead of a Government of violence and oppression?

8th. Are you in favor of maintaining the Constitutional rights of the South?

9th. Are you in favor of the re-enfranchisement and emancipation of the white men of the South, and the restitution of the Southern people to all their rights, alike proprietary, civil, and political?

10th. Do you believe in the inalienable right of self-preservation of the people against the exercise of arbitrary and unlicensed power?

Source: J. C. Lester and K. L. Wilson, *The Klu Klux Klan: Its Origin, Growth and Disbandment*, ed. W. L. Fleming (New York: Neale, 1905), p. 154.

7.4. The Republicans Lose Mississippi (1875)

> H. R. Revels, former U.S. senator from Mississippi, describes the conditions that led to the Democratic "Redeemers" regaining control of their state governments from the Republicans, conditions that were mirrored in most of the other southern states by the mid-1870s.

Since reconstruction, the masses of my people have been . . . enslaved in mind by unprincipled adventurers, who, caring nothing for country, were willing to stoop to anything, no matter how infamous, to secure power to themselves and perpetuate it. My people are naturally republicans and always will be, but as they grow older in freedom so do they in wisdom. A great portion of them have learned that they were being used as mere tools, and, as in the late election, not being able to correct the existing evil among themselves, they determined, by casting their ballots against these unprincipled adventurers, to overthrow them; and now that they have succeeded in defeating these unprincipled adventurers, they are organizing for a republican victory in 1876; that we will

be successful there cannot be a doubt. There are many good white republicans in the State who will unite with us, and who have aided us
in establishing ourselves as a people. In almost every instance these men
who have aided us have been cried down by the so-called republican
officials in power in the State. My people have been told by these schem-
ers when men were placed upon the ticket who were notoriously corrupt
and dishonest, that they must vote for them; that the salvation of the
party depended upon it; that the man who scratched a ticket was not a
republican. This is only one of the many means these unprincipled demagogues have devised to perpetuate the intellectual bondage of my people. To defeat this policy at the late election men irrespective of race,
color, or party affiliation united and voted together against men known
to be incompetent and dishonest. I cannot recognize, nor do the masses
of my people who read recognize, the majority of the officials who have
been in power for the past two years as republicans. We do not believe
that republicanism means corruption, theft, and embezzlement. These
three offenses have been prevalent among a great portion of our office-
holders; to them must be attributed the defeat of the republican party in
the State if defeat there was; but I, with all the lights before me, look
upon it as an uprising of the people, the whole people to crush out
corrupt rings and men from power. Mississippi is to-day as much republican as it ever was, and in November, 1876, we will roll up a rousing
majority for the republican candidate for President. . . .

The great masses of the white people have abandoned their hostility
to the General Government and republican principles, and to-day accept
as a fact that all men are born free and equal, and I believe are ready to
guarantee to my people every right and privilege guaranteed to an
American citizen. The bitterness and hate created by the late civil strife
has, in my opinion, been obliterated in this State, except, perhaps, in
some localities, and would have long since been entirely obliterated were
it not for some unprincipled men who would keep alive the bitterness
of the past and inculcate a hatred between the races, in order that they
may aggrandize themselves by office and its emoluments to control my
people, the effect of which is to degrade them. As an evidence that party-
lines in this State have been obliterated, men were supported without
regard to their party affiliations, their birth, or their color by those who
heretofore have acted with the democratic party, by this course giving
an evidence of their sincerity that they have abandoned the political issues of the past, and were only desirous of inaugurating an honest State
government and restoring a mutual confidence between the races. . . .
Had our State administration adhered to republican principles and stood
by the platform upon which it was elected, the State to-day would have
been on the highway of prosperity. Peace would have prevailed within
her borders, and the republican party would have embraced within its

folds thousands of the best and purest citizens of which Mississippi can boast, and the election just passed would have been a republican victory of not less than eighty to a hundred thousand majority; but the dishonest course which has been pursued has forced into silence and retirement nearly all of the leading republicans who organized and have heretofore led the party to victory. A few who have been bold enough to stand by republican principles and condemn dishonesty, corruption and incompetency, have been supported and elected by overwhelming majorities. If the State administration had adhered to republican principles, advanced patriotic measures, appointed only honest and competent men to office, and sought to restore confidence between the races, blood-shed would have been unknown, peace would have prevailed, Federal interference been unthought of; harmony, friendship, and mutual confidence would have taken the place of the bayonet.

In conclusion, let me say to you, and through you, to the great republican party of the North, that I deemed it my duty, in behalf of my people, that I present these facts in order that they and the white people (their former owners) should not suffer the misrepresentations which certain demagogues seemed desirous of encouraging.

Source: Walter L. Fleming, *Documentary History of Reconstruction, Political, Military, Social, Religious, Educational & Industrial, 1865 to the Present Time* (Cleveland: A. H. Clark Co., 1906–1907), pp. 402–404.

7.5. Jim Crow Cars

> This excerpt from a U.S. Senate "Report on Labor and Capital" (1883) portrays the rise of racial discrimination in Alabama and the South in transportation facilities, particularly in railroad passenger cars. This situation was the target of the court action by the new Orleans citizens' committee on the Louisiana Separate Car Law that led to *Plessy v. Ferguson*.

There has been a universal discrimination here in Alabama, and, indeed, all over the South, in the treatment of the colored people as to cars they are permitted to ride in. The white people have always labored under the impression that whenever a colored man attempted to go into a ladies' car, he did it simply because it was a car for white people. Now if the white people looked at it as we look at it, taking a common-sense view of it, they would see that that idea is erroneous and false. We go into those cars simply because there are better acommodations there, and because we secure better protection in the ladies' car, for the general sentiment of the white men certainly protects their ladies. But in the cars allotted to the colored people a white man comes in and smokes cigars, and chews tobacco, and curses and swears, and all that kind of thing, and the conductors on the various roads don't exercise their powers for the protection of the colored passengers. We made these complaints to the railroad commission, and the president of the commission told us that it was a matter within their jurisdiction, and that they would take cognizance of it, and would see that those complaints were looked into, and those evils remedied. We asked simply for equal accommodation and protection with the white people in riding on the railroads, and the 22d day of this month was set for a final hearing, and the superintendent of railroads was summoned to be there at the final hearing of the matter, and we have the assurance of the gentlemen of the commission that the subject will be acted upon promptly, and that the vexed question—for this is one of the most vexed questions that we have to deal with in the South—will be settled. We expect, therefore, that so far as Alabama is concerned, the people of both races will have equal accommodation. Our people do not care whether they are put in the front of the train or in the middle or at the tail end, so long as they have proper accommodation and proper protection.

Source: Fleming, *Documentary History of Reconstruction*, pp. 446–447. From *Senate "Report on Labor and Capital,"* vol. 4 (1883), p. 382.

7.6.   *Plessy v. Ferguson* (1896)

> The majority opinion of this 7 to 1 decision (with Justice David Brewer abstaining), written by Justice Henry Billings Brown, contained the language that would dominate federal-state relations over black civil rights until the 1954 Supreme Court desegregation case of *Brown v. Board of Education.* Plessy unequivocally removed the federal government from interfering in segregated facilities in the South so long as these facilities were "separate but equal."

OPINION: MR. JUSTICE BROWN, after stating the case, delivered the opinion of the court.

This case turns upon the constitutionality of an act of the General Assembly of the State of Louisiana, passed in 1890, providing for separate railway carriages for the white and colored races. Acts 1890, No. 111, p. 152.

* * *

The constitutionality of this act is attacked upon the ground that it conflicts both with the Thirteenth Amendment of the Constitution, abolishing slavery, and the Fourteenth Amendment, which prohibits certain restrictive legislation on the part of the States.

* * *

... By the Fourteenth Amendment, all persons born or naturalized in the United States, and subject to the jurisdiction thereof, are made citizens of the United States and of the State wherein they reside; and the States are forbidden from making or enforcing any law which shall abridge the privileges or immunities of citizens of the United States, or shall deprive any person of life, liberty or property without due process of law, or deny to any person within their jurisdiction the equal protection of the laws.

The proper construction of this amendment was first called to the attention of this court in the Slaughter-house cases ... which involved, however, not a question of race, but one of exclusive privileges. The case did not call for any expression of opinion as to the exact rights it was intended to secure to the colored race, but it was said generally that its main purpose was to establish the citizenship of the negro; to give definitions of citizenship of the United States and of the States, and to protect from the hostile legislation of the States the privileges and immunities of citizens of the United States, as distinguished from those of citizens of the States.

The object of the amendment was undoubtedly to enforce the absolute equality of the two races before the law, but in the nature of things it could not have been intended to abolish distinctions based upon color, or to enforce social, as distinguished from political equality, or a commingling of the two races upon terms unsatisfactory to either. Laws permitting, and even requiring, their separation in places where they are liable to be brought into contact do not necessarily imply the inferiority of either race to the other, and have been generally, if not universally, recognized as within the competency of the state legislatures in the exercise of their police power. The most common instance of this is connected with the establishment of separate schools for white and colored children, which has been held to be a valid exercise of the legislative power even by courts of States where the political rights of the colored race have been longest and most earnestly enforced.

* * *

... [W]here a statute of Louisiana required those engaged in the transportation of passengers among the States to give to all persons travelling within that State, upon vessels employed in that business, equal rights and privileges in all parts of the vessel, without distinction on account of race or color, and subjected to an action for damages the owner of such a vessel, who excluded colored passengers on account of their color from the cabin set aside by him for the use of whites, it was held to be so far as it applied to interstate commerce, unconstitutional and void. The court in this case, however, expressly disclaimed that it had anything whatever to do with the statute as a regulation of internal commerce, or affecting anything else than commerce among the States.

* * *

While we think the enforced separation of the races, as applied to the internal commerce of the State neither abridges the privileges or immunities of the colored man, deprives him of his property without due process of law, nor denies him the equal protection of the laws, within the meaning of the Fourteenth Amendment. . . .

* * *

We consider the underlying fallacy of the plaintiff's argument to consist in the assumption that the enforced separation of the two races stamps the colored race with a badge of inferiority. If this be so, it is not by reason of anything found in the act, but solely because the colored race chooses to put that construction upon it. The argument necessarily assumes that if, as has been more than once the case, and is not unlikely to be so again, the colored race should become the dominant power in the state legislature, and should enact a law in precisely similar terms, it would thereby relegate the white race to an inferior position. We imagine that the white race, at least, would not acquiesce in this assumption. The argument also assumes that social prejudices may be overcome by legislation, and that equal rights cannot be secured to the negro except by an enforced commingling of the two races. We cannot accept this proposition. If the two races are to meet upon terms of social equality, it must be the result of natural affinities, a mutual appreciation of each other's merits and a voluntary consent of individuals. As was said by the Court of Appeals of New York in People v. Gallagher, 93 N.Y. 438, 448, "this end can neither be accomplished nor promoted by laws which conflict with the general sentiment of the community upon whom they are designed to operate. When the government, therefore, has secured to each of its citizens equal rights before the law and equal opportunities for improvement and progress, it has accomplished the end for which it was organized and performed all of the functions respecting social advantages with which it is endowed." Legislation is powerless to eradicate racial instincts or to abolish distinctions based upon physical differences, and the attempt to do so can only result in accentuating the difficulties of the present situation. If the civil and political rights of both races be equal one cannot be inferior to the other civilly or politically. If one race be inferior to the other socially, the Constitution of the United States cannot put them upon the same plane.

Source: 163 U.S. 537 (1896).

7.7.   Harlan's Dissent

> Justice John Marshall Harlan's lone dissent in *Plessy* was a "voice in the wilderness" when he condemned the pernicious effects that the majority opinion would have on race relations in the United States. He eloquently proclaimed that even though the white race was "dominant," the "Constitution is color-blind, and neither knows nor tolerates classes among citizens."

It is one thing for railroad carriers to furnish, or to be required by law to furnish, equal accommodations for all whom they are under a legal duty to carry. It is quite another thing for government to forbid citizens of the white and black races from travelling in the same public conveyance, and to punish officers of railroad companies for permitting persons of the two races to occupy the same passenger coach. It a State can prescribe, as a rule of civil conduct, that whites and blacks shall not travel as passengers in the same railroad coach, why may it not so regulate the use of the streets of its cities and towns as to compel white citizens to keep on one side of a street and black citizens to keep on the other? Why may it not, upon like grounds, punish whites and blacks who ride together in street cars or in open vehicles on a public road or street? Why may it not require sheriffs to assign whites to one side of a court-room and blacks to the other? And why may it not also prohibit the commingling of the two races in the galleries of legislative halls or in public assemblages convened for the considerations of the political questions of the day? Further, if this statute of Louisiana is consistent with the personal liberty of citizens, why may not the State require the separation in railroad coaches of native and naturalized citizens of the United States, or of Protestants and Roman Catholics?

* * *

The white race deems itself to be the dominant race in this country. And so it is, in prestige, in achievements, in education, in wealth and in power. So, I doubt not, it will continue to be for all time, if it remains true to its great heritage and holds fast to the principles of constitutional liberty. But in view of the Constitution, in the eye of the law, there is in this country no superior, dominant, ruling class of citizens. There is no caste here. Our Constitution is color-blind, and neither knows nor tolerates classes among citizens. In respect of civil rights, all citizens are equal before the law. The humblest is the peer of the most powerful. The law regards man as man, and takes no account of his surroundings or of his color when his civil rights as guaranteed by the supreme law of the land are involved. It is, therefore, to be regretted that this high tribunal, the final expositor of the fundamental law of the land, has reached the conclusion that it is competent for a State to regulate the enjoyment by citizens of their civil rights solely upon the basis of race.

Source: 163 U.S. 537 (1896).

ANNOTATED RESEARCH GUIDE

Books

Belz, Herman Julius. *A New Birth of Freedom: The Republican Party and Freedmen's Rights, 1861–1866.* Westport, CT: Greenwood Press, 1976. Traces the patterns of race relations and civil rights in the first year of Reconstruction, focusing on the Freedmen's Bureau Act of 1865, civil rights, and the Thirteenth Amendment.

Brock, William R. *An American Crisis: Congress and Reconstruction, 1865–1867.* New York: Harper and Row, 1966. Advances the proposition that Radical Republicans such as Thaddeus Stevens and Charles Sumner held racial ideology that was in conflict with the thinking of a majority of Americans. These men thought that the freed black must be treated equally by the law.

Cox, LaWanda, and John H. Cox. *Politics, Principle, and Prejudice, 1865–1866: Dilemma of Reconstruction America.* New York: Macmillan, 1963. Argues that most Republicans supported the Reconstruction principle of giving the freed slaves equal legal rights. The authors are also highly critical of the blatant racism of President Andrew Johnson and his supporters.

Current, Richard N. *Those Terrible Carpetbaggers.* New York: Oxford University Press, 1988. Examines the altruistic and sincere motives of those northerners who came into the South to rebuild and diversify its economy.

Fireside, Harvey. *Plessy v. Ferguson: Separate but Equal?* Springfield, NJ: Enslow Publishers, 1997. Analyzes in detail the trial, litigation, and the segregation laws in Louisiana that were involved in the Supreme Court case that challenged a state's right to require separate but equal facilities for the two races in railroad accommodations.

Foner, Eric. *Reconstruction: America's Unfinished Revolution, 1863–1877.* New York: Harper and Row, 1988. Part of the New American Nation series, this is the best starting point for a full narrative of the status of southern blacks from the coming of emancipation through the Redeemers' victory at the end of Reconstruction in 1877.

Hyman, Harold M. *A More Perfect Union: The Impact of the Civil War and Reconstruction on the Constitution.* New York: Alfred A. Knopf, 1973. The second half of this book treats the constitutional issues involved in Reconstruction. Includes an excellent bibliographical essay.

Lafgren, Charles A. *The Plessy Case: A Legal-Historical Interpretation*. New York: Oxford University Press, 1987. The definitive study of the law and interests behind the case.

McFeely, William S. *Grant: A Biography*. New York: W. W. Norton, 1982. McFeely admits that the Republicans built an impressive constitutional machine to protect the rights of black citizenry and applauds Grant's crucial role in winning passage of the Ku Klux Klan Act of 1871. But he concedes that Grant was unable to make the laws effective and was reluctant to use the federal army to enforce them.

McKitrick, Eric L. *Andrew Johnson and Reconstruction*. Chicago: University of Chicago Press, 1963. Sees President Johnson's assertive use of executive power as the key force in beginning Reconstruction. McKitrick maintains that when he acted he did so in full knowledge of all the choices before him.

McPherson, James M. *The Struggle for Equality: Abolitionists and the Negro in the Civil War and Reconstruction*. Princeton, NJ: Princeton University Press, 1964. Argues that the failure of Radical Republicans and former abolitionists to give blacks in the South free land left them open to economic exploitation and accounts for the failure of Reconstruction.

Simpson, Brooks D. *The Reconstruction Presidents*. Lawrence: University Press of Kansas, 1998. Presents lucid coverage of Presidents Lincoln, Johnson, and Grant and is a fine introduction to the federal issues involved in presidential Reconstruction.

Stampp, Kenneth M. *The Era of Reconstruction, 1865–1877*. New York: Alfred A. Knopf, 1965. Argues that Radical Reconstruction must be related to national events and that the carpetbaggers were not all either ignorant or corrupt nor were the scalawags all scamps, degraded poor whites, and cynical opportunists.

Williamson, Joel. *After Slavery: The Negro in South Carolina During Reconstruction, 1861–1877*. Chapel Hill: University of North Carolina Press, 1965. Examines how and why segregation was adopted in South Carolina as a vehicle to replace slavery to enforce racial separation upon the freed blacks.

Woodward, C. Vann. *The Strange Career of Jim Crow*. New York: Oxford University Press, 1966. Offers a classic view of how state-mandated segregation entered southern society at a date later than Reconstruction, between 1877 and the early 1900s.

Nonprint Media

Web Sites

http://www.civilwarhome.com/lincolnandproclamation.htm. Explains what the Emancipation Proclamation did and did not do.

http://www.infoplease.com/ce6/history/A0841309.html. Covers Lincoln's and Johnson's reconstruction plans, early congressional legislation, the Reconstruction Acts, Radical Republican governments in the South, and Reconstruction's end.

http://www.stanford.edu/~paherman/reconstruction.htm. Sections include: debates over Reconstruction, presidential Reconstruction, congressional Reconstruction; Republican state governments, opposition to Reconstruction, and the end of Reconstruction.

Videotape

Benedict, Michael. *Andrew Johnson* [videorecording]. West Lafayette, IN: CSPAN Archives, 1999.

8

New Deal Federalism

The New Deal was President Franklin Delano Roosevelt's response to the Great Depression, the longest and most severe economic decline in United States history, which left millions of Americans out of work, with no hope of finding a job, and with their confidence in American free enterprise and democracy shaken. The president, inaugurated on March 4, 1933, believed that only the federal government, in cooperation with the states, had the ability to cope with the emergency. Although without any clear-cut plan of action, he set about to use federal power through congressional legislation and executive agencies to do whatever worked to save the nation. Historians can see, despite its pragmatic, almost helter-skelter nature, especially during the "First 100 Days" of his administration, that Roosevelt ended up creating the New Deal, a three-point attack on the Depression: economic recovery stimulated by new federal laws, federal relief for those in need, and federal reforms that would prevent future depressions. He achieved success in the last two, but not the first—only the economic stimulation resulting from America's entry into World War II would restore full employment and bring about economic expansion.

The impact of the Depression was staggering. After the stock market crashed in October 1929, factories slashed production when new orders stopped coming in and inventories piled up. As Americans rushed to withdraw their savings to meet expenses, banks folded. In the remaining three months of 1929, 659 closed; 1,350 more shut down in 1930, followed by 2,293 in 1931 and 1,453 in 1932. Unemployment skyrocketed to staggering figures. By the spring of 1930, 120,000 of the 280,000 textile workers in New England had no jobs. From 12 to 15 million workers out of a work force of 48,830,000 were permanently laid off. In some cities the figure was disastrous. In Cleveland, 50 percent of the work force was let go, in Akron the figure was 60 percent, and in Toledo it was 80 percent. Fear of the breadline drifted up into the middle class as universities graduated thousands of teachers, engineers, architects, and lawyers who had no prospect of finding employment.

President Herbert Hoover, who had won easily against the Democratic candidate Al Smith in the 1928 election, initially sounded encouraging, in large part because Secretary of the Treasury Andrew Mellon advised him to simply allow "the slump to liquidate itself." Hoover predicted that the crisis was only temporary, and stated that the economy was fundamentally sound. Prosperity would return, he said, as soon as there was a "restoration of confidence." Hoover, although a Progressive who had confidence in a federal-state partnership, shied away from expanding it to have the federal government aid individuals hit by the Depression. Instead, he asked businessmen to maintain employment, keep wages steady, and have their people work harder. He had the Federal Reserve Board lower interest rates for loans. Even as the Depression deepened, he refused to help the unemployed directly.

Hoover's program for recovery was a mixture of federal, state, and private measures. In 1930 he created the President's Organization on Unemployment Relief (POUR) to raise money from private contributions to help those out of work. He urged Congress to cut taxes in order to increase consumer purchasing power. He called for federal appropriations for established public works projects, such as the Hoover and Grand Coulee Dams. He approved the Agricultural Marketing Act of 1929, which was supposed to help farmers, whose income collapsed from $25.5 billion in 1920 to $5.5 billion, through its Federal Farm Board. It was supposed to support crop prices by purchasing surplus products to keep them off the market, but it was inadequately funded. In 1932, in a bold action to assist banks, Hoover had Congress create the Reconstruction Finance Corporation (RFC) with a $2 billion budget to make loans to banks and their corporate debtors. That same year the Glass-Steagall Banking Act put $2 billion of new money in circulation. To protect American markets from foreign competition, Hoover signed the Hawley-Smoot Tariff, which raised import taxes 30 percent. But the tariff caused European nations to retaliate with their own tariffs on American products, and that dried up what was left of the market for the nation's export goods. Above all, Hoover continued to condemn direct federal unemployment relief. He called it a "dole" that would unbalance the federal budget, invite reckless spending on useless projects, and destroy the moral character of the recipients by creating a permanent class of public wards. The most he was willing to do in terms of a federal relief program was to sign the Emergency Relief and Construction Act (ERCA). This law permitted the RFC to authorize up to $1.5 billion for "reproductive" projects that would pay for themselves. The ERCA appropriated another $300 million to go to states to augment their relief programs, but this amounted to only about 3 cents a day for the average recipient.

By the fall of 1932 events had shown Hoover's assumptions about the severity of the crisis to be wrong. Private charity and state and local governments were all but broke. Many families had nothing coming in, no savings left, and no hope for a job in the future. By then, a quarter of the nation was in a position where the only sure thing they could count on was hunger. In the cities, men and women lined up on the sidewalks to receive food from soup kitchens. Some families, utterly destitute, dug for food in city dumps. In Appalachia they ate weeds and roots. In empty lots on the edges of the larger cities they built crude shelters out of packing crates and metal and called them Hoovervilles. In July, the president ordered the army to assist the police in evacuating the 2,000 participants in the Bonus Army protest who had encamped on the Mall in Washington, D.C.

In this blighted environment the Democratic Party nominated Governor Franklin Delano Roosevelt of New York as its presidential candidate. Although he had no real plan as an alternative to what Hoover had done, he boldly scolded Hoover's response to the rising unemployment and insisted that the federal government must actively experiment with new ways to bring about relief. He promised "bold and persistent experimentation to give a new deal to the forgotten man." He formed a "Brain Trust" of university professors and lawyers to come up with innovative federal plans to fight the "economics of scarcity." Hoover only reiterated his earlier efforts to cope with the Depression and restated his faith in "rugged individualism" and the "American System." On election day FDR won all but six states, with 57 percent of the popular vote and 89 percent of the Electoral College. Both the House and the Senate went Democratic.

In his inaugural address Roosevelt demanded federal action, immediately, to deal with "nameless, unreasoning, unjustified terror which paralyzes needed efforts to convert retreat into advance." He addressed the emergency of "a host of unemployed citizens [who] face the grim problem of existence, and an equally great number [who] toil with little return." He promised the strongest type of executive leadership and urged complete cooperation from Congress. However, he threatened that if Congress did not respond he would ask for "the one remaining instrument to meet the crisis—broad executive power to wage a war against the emergency as great as the power that would be given me if we were in fact invaded by a foreign foe." But Congress did respond.

After the inauguration Roosevelt summoned Congress into emergency session, imposed a four-day "holiday" closing all banks, and turned his full attention to the ways in which federal law could bring about economic recovery. Historians have called this vast legislative output between 1933 and 1934 the First New Deal. Of the fifteen important federal statutes enacted during the first hundred days of the Roosevelt administration, two laws, the Agriculture Adjustment Act (AAA) and the National Industrial Recovery Act (NIRA), became the cornerstones of federal help for farmers and factory workers.

In the AAA, Congress, for the first time, established the principle of "parity" for farmers who voluntarily enrolled in the program and cut back production. Essentially, parity meant having the federal government make up the difference between the market value of farm produce and the actual income that farmers needed to make a profit.

The NIRA did for workers what the AAA did for farmers—it provided a guaranteed minimum wage. The law created the Public Works Administration (PWA) and the National Recovery Administration (NRA). The PWA was intended to use federal funds to stimulate consumer purchasing power and provide jobs in a $3.3 billion public works program. But its director, Harold Ickes, did not use the funds fast enough to stimulate the stricken economy. The NRA and its director, Hugh Johnson, wanted to end cutthroat competition by requiring businesses to comply with "codes of fair practices" drafted by individuals representing the federal government, business, labor unions, and consumers. These codes fixed prices, limited production, and listed rules of fair competition. Section 7(a) of the NIRA guaranteed unions the right to organize and to collective bargaining. The NRA, like the PWA, failed to achieve its goals. First, the program was voluntary, and some businesses refused to comply. Some who did developed codes that just benefitted business. There were not enough NRA inspectors to supervise the program. For example, they could not enforce the codes requiring collective bargaining, and even the support of labor unions for NRA waned.

Two other bold programs of the New Deal marked a dramatic extension of federal power into the lives of American citizens never before touched by the federal government. One was the Tennessee Valley Authority (TVA). Begun in 1933, it was a federal authority that built and ran a series of dams along the Tennessee River from Paducah, Kentucky, to Knoxville, Tennessee, to Muscle Shoals, Alabama, that created electric power facilities for factories, businesses, and homes, and controlled floods. The TVA was a colossal expansion of federal power over the states, specifically Virginia, North Carolina, Georgia, Alabama, Kentucky, and Tennessee, and federal representatives controlled the production and pricing of electric power.

The second program, the Social Security Act of August 1935, gave federal help to people who could not help themselves, such as the elderly, the handicapped, dependent children, and the unemployed. It was a cooperative federal-state program. Old age insurance was in part funded by a payroll tax on employers and workers that would provide a pension to individual participants in the program, run by the states, over the age of sixty-five. Employers were taxed to supplement federal appropriations for a state-administered unemployment insurance program. But Roosevelt knew he had to hold on to the support of southern Democrats, and the Social Security Act ignored farm workers and domestic servants, many of whom were southern blacks. This exclusion pointed out Roosevelt's reluctance in all of the New Deal measures to challenge southerners who dominated, indeed often controlled, important congressional committees, and his willingness to mollify these conservative Democrats from the states' rights South by conceding significant local authority in the administration of New Deal programs.

Despite its limitations, the Social Security Act was a historic development in the history of federalism. It was the first contract between the federal government and the people in which the government took on the responsibility of preserving individual social rights, a commitment heretofore seen only in pensions given to veterans and their families. Such programs had been limited and temporary; Social Security was comprehensive and permanent. It was the foundation legislation of the welfare state.

Less dramatic parts of the New Deal included the Civilian Conservation Corps (CCC), Federal Housing Administration (FHA), and the Home Owners' Loan Corporation (HOLC). The CCC employed over 2 million men aged eighteen to twenty-five in federal conservation projects. The FHA and HOLC put the federal government into the area of financing home construction and mortgages for the first time. The New Deal strengthened public confidence in the stock exchanges through the Federal Securities Act (1933), which mandated full disclosure of new stock issues, and the Securities Exchange Act (1934), which created the Securities and Exchange Commission to place trading practices under federal regulation. It extended federal supervision to banks in the Banking Act (1933), which established the Federal Deposit Insurance Corporation (FDIC) to insure bank deposits. In labor law, in the summer of 1935 Congress passed the National Labor Relations (Wagner) Act, which used federal authority to guarantee workers the right to unionize and to collective bargaining and created a five-member National Labor Relations Board to administer the law to prevent unfair labor practices and assure fair union elections.

Critics on the right and left, in and out of Congress, were furious at the New Deal. They condemned the AAA for making farmers plow under 10.4 million acres of cotton and annually destroy 6 million hogs at a time when many Americans were poorly fed and some on the edge of starvation. They argued that the NRA codes subverted individual initiative and self-reliance. They charged that the NRA prices were inflated and favored large companies over small factories. Demagogues such as Dr. Francis E. Townsend, Senator Huey Long, and Father Charles Coughlin attacked the New Deal from the left and right, and condemned Roosevelt for not using federal power vigorously enough. Townsend called for a $200 monthly federal pension for any retired person over the age of sixty, paid in scrip, with the requirement that it be spent within thirty days. Long's "Share Our Wealth" scheme would have had the federal government attach all incomes over $1 million by taxation and confiscate all inheritances over $5 million. Then it could give every family a $5,000 homestead allowance and an annual stipend of $2,000. In his weekly radio addresses Father Coughlin, a Canadian-born Roman Catholic priest, moved from support of the New Deal to vehement opposition. By 1934 the "Radio Priest" was calling the NRA "abortive" and the AAA a "Pagan Deal." Roosevelt, he claimed, was surrounded by "Drain Trust sycophants." He demanded the creation of a National Union for Social Justice to replace capitalism with socialism.

From other quarters criticism mounted. The sheer size of the TVA was an alarming example of the federal expansion and spending gone wild. The Social Security Act was targeted because the tax that funded it was regressive, since the more workers earned, the smaller the share of their wages that went to the fund. Besides, it was deflationary to tax money from people who would not be repaid for years. It was discriminatory because it excluded domestic servants, workers in restaurants and hospitals, farm workers, most women, and almost all blacks.

The whole conflict between New Deal federalism and conservative states' rights objections to it reached a crisis point in the Supreme Court. In May 1935, in *Schechter Poultry Corp. v. United States*, the Court declared the NIRA unconstitutional on the grounds that "Congress cannot delegate legislative power to the President to exercise an unfettered discretion" in matters of trade and commerce. It stated that the law invaded states' rights. Chief Justice Charles Evans Hughes, writing the unanimous opinion, declared that commerce was separate from manufacturing and that Congress, although it could regulate interstate commerce, could not regulate production; only the states could do that. In July, Congress replaced the NIRA with the National Labor Relations Act, commonly known as the Wagner Act, which set up a board with the power to investigate union complaints of "unfair labor practices," issue cease-and-desist orders, and arbitrate labor disputes. Roosevelt waited to see what the Court would do to his New Deal. In January 1936, in *United States v. Butler*, by a vote of 6 to 3, it vacated the AAA. Justice Owen Roberts, writing for the majority, stated that the act amounted to federal statutory regulation and control of agricultural production that invaded the reserved powers of the states. He further decided that the AAA was an unconstitutional tax on one part of the community, consumers, for the benefit of another, farmers. Finally, Roberts declared that the "general welfare" and "necessary and proper" clauses did not allow Congress to do everything it wanted to do.

After the *Butler* decision Roosevelt feared that the Court would likely cancel the Social Security Act. Consequently, following his landslide reelection in 1936, in which he took every state except Maine and Vermont, he tried to change the Court's conservative balance. In his Judiciary Reorganization Bill of February 1937, he asked Congress for an addition of "younger blood" on the Court by allowing him to appoint one new justice, up to a maxim of six, for every justice who had passed the age of seventy and failed to retire. Since there were six members then on the Court over that age, four of them solid core conservatives, he was asking Congress to cooperate in creating a Supreme Court favorable to the New Deal.

In Congress, both liberal Republicans and conservative Democrats opposed the scheme as a dangerous attack on the independence of the judiciary. During the winter and spring of 1937, while debate continued in Congress and in the press, public opinion steadily mounted against the idea. In the end Roosevelt suffered the most damaging political defeat in his presidency when the Senate Judiciary Committee's report rejected the plan in language so strong that "it will never again be presented to the free representatives of the free people of America."

Meanwhile, the Court handed down a surprising decision that made Roosevelt's packing plan seem moot. In March, in *West Coast Hotel Co. v. Parrish*, by a 5 to 4 decision, it sustained a Washington State minimum wage law. Roosevelt dubbed it "the switch in time that saved nine." In April, again by a 5 to 4 vote, in *NLRB v. Jones & Laughlin Steel Corp.*, the Court held that Congress's authority to regulate interstate commerce included the power to regulate manufacturing of goods involved in interstate commerce. Chief Justice Hughes's majority opinion also found that labor conditions at a plant that produced nationally distributed goods had a direct impact on interstate commerce. In the "Social Security Cases" that same spring, the Court upheld the Social Security Act as constitutional. In May, in *Stewart Machine Co. v. Davis*, by another vote of 5 to 4, it reasoned that federal unemployment compensation was a valid exercise of congressional authority under the Constitution to "tax and spend" the people's money for the general welfare. For the same reason it upheld federal old-age benefits provisions of the Social Security Act in *Helvering v. Davis*. Other key provisions of the New Deal eventually won Court approval. In 1941 it sustained the constitutionality of the National Fair Labor Standards Act in *United States v. Darby*. The following year the second AAA (1938) received constitutional approval in *Wickard v. Filburn* when newly appointed justice Robert Jackson, in writing the unanimous opinion, set aside the distinction between production and commerce and ruled that the federal government could regulate almost any type of commercial activity under the interstate commerce clause.

The New Deal, and the Supreme Court opinions that upheld it, established an unprecedented expansion of the constitutional power of the federal government. It could now permanently regulate the nation's economy. Congress could legislate as a social engineer under the fiscal power given it by the Constitution, and take responsibility for curing social as well as economic ills, a sharp and pivotal break from traditional laissez-faire assumptions that had dominated federalism in peacetime since the end of the Civil War. Even so, the states were important partners in the administration of almost all New Deal programs. Historian James T. Patterson and others identified a number of important, specific changes in state politics brought about by the New Deal. It stimulated governors to sponsor merit systems and promote civil service in dispensing federal jobs to the desperate jobless. It demonstrated that the federal government's programs could produce positive results and "forced politicians to recognize that states' rights without state activism must perish."[1] It stimulated an increase in voting among groups such as unskilled workers and immigrants who before had largely stayed out of politics. The New Deal caused states to expect extensive federal dollars to underwrite their expensive programs in highway construction, education, and public health. At the same time, the New Deal forced states to adopt a progressive attitude on taxation, welfare responsibilities, and labor law. However, one of the most striking features of New Deal federalism was the constraints imposed on it by the persistence of the ideas of states' rights and strict constructionism. Consequently, in the final analysis, instead of the New Deal becoming a force for radical change, it was better at preserving diversity and developing coordinated federal-state cooperation in achieving its main, if also sometimes contradictory, goals of relief, recovery, and reform.

Despite its undisputed importance in the long run in expanding the use of federal power beyond the Progressives' idea of regulating the national economy, the New Deal's most significant immediate impact was profound. By the time the United States unexpectedly entered World War II in December 1941, it had provided the federal government with constitutional authority to regulate industry without having to rely on emergency war powers to justify regulation of the country's industrial war programs. Another legacy of the New Deal was in what it ignored and left exclusively to the states—race relations. President Roosevelt, as seen in the Social Security Act, for the pragmatic political need to keep conservative southern Democrats in line, refused to use the federal government to move against Jim Crow laws in the South. That exercise of federal power awaited a much different America after World War II, and a much different Democratic resident.

NOTE

1. James T. Patterson, *The New Deal and the States: Federalism in Transition* (Princeton, NJ: Princeton University Press, 1969), p. 197.

DOCUMENTS

8.1.   President Herbert Hoover's Press Statement on Federal Relief, February 1931

President Hoover distributed this written statement to the press on February 3, 1931, to clarify his views against using federal funds for "charitable purposes." He vehemently opposed using federal monies because it would "break down [the] sense of responsibility of individual generosity." Such measures, he claimed, would strike at "the roots of self-government" and throw the nation into the "abyss" of dependency upon the federal government for charity "in some form or other."

Certain senators have issued a public statement to the effect that unless the President and the House of Representatives agree to appropriations from the Federal Treasury for charitable purposes they will force an extra session of Congress.

I do not wish to add acrimony to a discussion, but would rather state this case as I see its fundamentals.

This is not an issue as to whether people shall go hungry or cold in the United States. It is solely a question of the best method by which hunger and cold shall be prevented. It is a question as to whether the American people on one hand will maintain the spirit of charity and mutual self help through voluntary giving and the responsibility of local government as distinguished on the other hand from appropriations out of the Federal Treasury for such purposes. My own conviction is strongly that if we break down this sense of responsibility of individual generosity to individual and mutual self help in the country in times of national difficulty and if we start appropriations of this character we have not only impaired something infinitely valuable in the life of the American people but have struck at the roots of self-government. Once this has happened it is not the cost of a few score millions but we are faced with the abyss of reliance in future upon Government charity in some form or other. The money involved is indeed the least of the costs to American ideals and American institutions.

* * *

Unemployment Relief

In the matter of unemployment outside of the drought areas important economic measures of mutual self help have been developed such as those to maintain wages, to distribute employment equitably, to increase construction work by industry, to increase Federal construction work from a rate of about $275,000,000 a year prior to the depression to a rate now of over $750,000,000 a year; to expand state and municipal construction—all upon a scale never before provided or even attempted in any depression. But beyond this to assure that there shall be no suffering, in every town and county voluntary agencies in relief of distress have been strengthened and created and generous funds have been placed at their disposal. They are carrying on their work efficiently and sympathetically.

But after and coincidentally with voluntary relief, our American system requires that municipal, county and state governments shall use their own resources and credit before seeking such assistance from the Federal Treasury.

I have indeed spent much of my life in fighting hardship and starvation both abroad and in the southern states. I do not feel that I should be charged with lack of human sympathy for those who suffer but I recall that in all the organizations with which I have been connected over these many years, the foundation has been to summon the maximum of self help. I am proud to have sought the help of Congress in the past for nations who were so disorganized by war and anarchy that self help was impossible. But even these appropriations were but a tithe of that which was coincidentally mobilized from the public charity of the United States and foreign countries. There is no such paralysis in the United States and I am confident that our people have the resources, the initiative, the courage, the stamina and kindliness of spirit to meet this situation in the way they have met their problems over generations.

I will accredit to those who advocate Federal charity a natural anxiety for the people of their states. I am willing to pledge myself that if the time should ever come that the voluntary agencies of the country together with the local and state governments are unable to find resources with which to prevent hunger and suffering in my country, I will ask the aid of every resource of the Federal Government because I would no more see starvation amongst our countrymen than would any senator or congressman. I have the faith in the American people that such a day will not come.

The American people are doing their job today. They should be given a chance to show whether they wish to preserve the principles of individual and local responsibility and mutual self help before they embark on what I believe is a disastrous system. I feel sure they will succeed if given the opportunity.

Source: William Dudley, *The Great Depression: Opposing Viewpoints* (San Diego, CA: Greenhaven Press, 1994), pp. 26–30.

8.2.   Roosevelt's First Inaugural Address, March 4, 1933

> In this ringing assertion of his commitment to use the full power of the federal government to meet the crisis of the Great Depression, Roosevelt leveled with the American people. He told them that in a "national emergency" as grave as if the United States had been invaded by a foreign enemy, he would demand that Congress, in a special session, take immediate action. If it did not, he warned, "I shall ask the Congress for the one remaining instrument to meet the crisis—broad executive power to wage a war against the emergency."

President Hoover, Mr. Chief Justice, my friends:

This is a day of national consecration, and I am certain that my fellow-Americans expect that on my induction into the Presidency I will address them with a candor and a decision which the present situation of our nation impels.

This is pre-eminently the time to speak the truth, the whole truth, frankly and boldly. Nor need we shrink from honestly facing conditions in our country today. This great nation will endure as it has endured, will revive and will prosper.

So first of all let me assert my firm belief that the only thing we have to fear is fear itself—nameless, unreasoning, unjustified terror which paralyzes needed efforts to convert retreat into advance.

In every dark hour of our national life a leadership of frankness and vigor has met with that understanding and support of the people themselves which is essential to victory. I am convinced that you will again give that support to leadership in these critical days.

In such a spirit on my part and on yours we face our common difficulties. They concern, thank God, only material things. Values have shrunken to fantastic levels; taxes have risen; our ability to pay has fallen, government of all kinds is faced by serious curtailment of income; the means of exchange are frozen in the currents of trade; the withered leaves of industrial enterprise lie on every side; farmers find no markets for their produce; the savings of many years in thousands of families are gone.

More important, a host of unemployed citizens face the grim problem of existence, and an equally great number toil with little return. Only a foolish optimist can deny the dark realities of the moment.

* * *

. . . This nation asks for action, and action now.

Our greatest primary task is to put people to work. This is no unsolvable problem if we face it wisely and courageously.

It can be accomplished in part by direct recruiting by the government itself, treating the task as we would treat the emergency of a war, but at the same time, through this employment, accomplishing greatly needed projects to stimulate and reorganize the use of our natural resources.

* * *

. . . We must act, and act quickly.

Finally, in our progress toward a resumption of work we require two safeguards against a return of the evils of the old order; there must be a strict supervision of all banking and credits and investments; there must be an end to speculation with other people's money, and there must be provision for an adequate but sound currency.

These are the lines of attack. I shall presently urge upon a new Congress in special session detailed measures for their fulfillment, and I shall seek the immediate assistance of the several States.

Through this program of action we address ourselves to putting our own national house in order and making income balance outgo.

* * *

This I propose to offer, pledging that the larger purposes will bind upon us all as a sacred obligation with a unity of duty hitherto evoked only in time of armed strife.

With this pledge taken, I assume unhesitatingly the leadership of this great army of our people, dedicated to a disciplined attack upon our common problems.

Action in this image and to this end is feasible under the form of government which we have inherited from our ancestors.

Our Constitution is so simple and practical that it is possible always to meet extraordinary needs by changes in emphasis and arrangement without loss of essential form.

That is why our constitutional system has proved itself the most superbly enduring political mechanism the modern world has produced. It has met every stress of vast expansion of territory, of foreign wars, of bitter internal strife, of world relations.

It is to be hoped that the normal balance of executive and legislative authority may be wholly adequate to meet the unprecedented task before us. But it may be that an unprecedented demand and need for undelayed action may call for temporary departure from that normal balance of public procedure.

I am prepared under my constitutional duty to recommend the measures that a stricken nation in the midst of a stricken world may require.

These measures, or such other measures as the Congress may build out of its experience and wisdom, I shall seek, within my constitutional authority, to bring to speedy adoption.

But in the event that the Congress shall fail to take one of these two courses, and in the event that the national emergency is still critical, I shall not evade the clear course of duty that will then confront me.

I shall ask the Congress for the one remaining instrument to meet the crisis—broad executive power to wage a war against the emergency as great as the power that would be given me if we were in fact invaded by a foreign foe.

For the trust reposed in me I will return the courage and the devotion that befit the time. I can do no less.

We face the arduous days that lie before us in the warm courage of national unity; with the clear consciousness of seeking old and precious moral values; with the clean satisfaction that comes from the stern performance of duty by old and young alike.

We aim at the assurance of a rounded and permanent national life.

We do not distrust the future of essential democracy. The people of the United States have not failed. In their need they have registered a mandate that they want direct, vigorous action.

They have asked for discipline and direction under leadership. They have made me the present instrument of their wishes. In the spirit of the gift I take it.

In this dedication of a nation we humbly ask the blessing of God. May He protect each and every one of us! May He guide me in the days to come!

Source: F. D. Roosevelt's First Inaugural Address, March 4, 1933, Pamphlet (Washington, DC: Government Printing Office, 1933).

8.3.   Senator Huey P. Long's "Share Our Wealth" Plan, 1935

Senator Long of Louisiana in May 1935 wrote a letter that was published in the *Congressional Record* detailing his radical plan to have the federal government redistribute tax funds to help Americans out of the Depression. He wanted the federal government to "shoulder the obligation which it owes to every child born on earth—that is, a fair chance to life, liberty, and happiness."

For 20 years I have been in the battle to provide that, so long as America has, or can produce, an abundance of the things which make life comfortable and happy, that none should own so much of the things which he does not need and cannot use as to deprive the balance of the people of a reasonable proportion of the necessities and conveniences of life. The whole line of my political thought has always been that America must face the time when the whole country would shoulder the obligation which it owes to every child born on earth—that is, a fair chance to life, liberty, and happiness.

* * *

It was after my disappointment over the Roosevelt policy, after he became President, that I saw the light. I soon began to understand that, regardless of what we had been promised, our only chance of securing the fulfillment of such pledges was to organize the men and the women of the United States so that they were a force capable of action, and capable of requiring such a policy from the lawmakers and from the President after they took office. That was the beginning of the Share Our Wealth Society movement. . . .

The Problem

It is impossible for the United States to preserve itself as a republic or as a democracy when 600 families own more of this Nation's wealth—in fact, twice as much—as all the balance of the people put together. Ninety-six per cent of our people live below the poverty line, while 4 per cent own 87 per cent of the wealth. American can have enough for all to live in comfort and still permit millionaires to own more than they can ever spend and to have more than they can ever use; but America cannot allow the multimillionaires and the billionaires, a mere handful of them, to own everything unless we are willing to inflict starvation upon 125,000,000 people.

* * *

The Share Our Wealth Program

Here is the whole sum and substance of the Share Our Wealth movement:

1. Every family to be furnished by the Government a homestead allowance, free of debt, of not less than one-third the average family wealth of the country, which means, at the lowest, that every family shall have the reasonable comforts of life up to a value of from $5,000 to

$6,000. No person to have a fortune of more than 100 to 300 times the average family fortune, which means that the limit to fortunes is between $1,500,000 and $5,000,000, with annual capital levy taxes imposed on all above $1,000,000.

2. The yearly income of every family shall not be less than one-third of the average family income, which means that, according to the estimates of the statisticians of the United States Government and Wall Street, no family's annual income would be less than from $2,000 to $2,500. No yearly income shall be allowed to any person larger than from 100 to 300 times the size of the average family income, which means that no person would be allowed to earn in any year more than from $600,000 to $1,800,000, all to be subject to present income-tax laws.

3. To limit or regulate the hours of work to such an extent as to prevent overproduction; the most modern and efficient machinery would be encouraged, so that as much would be produced as possible so as to satisfy all demands of the people, but to also allow the maximum time to the workers for recreation, convenience, education, and luxuries of life.

4. An old age pension to the persons over 60.

5. To balance agricultural production with what can be consumed according to the laws of God, which includes the preserving and storage of surplus commodities to be paid for and held by the Government for the emergencies when such are needed. Please bear in mind, however, that when the people of America have had money to buy things they needed, we have never had a surplus of any commodity. This plan of God does not call for destroying any of the things raised to eat or wear, nor does it countenance wholesale destruction of hogs, cattle, or milk.

6. To pay the veterans of our wars what we owe them and to care for their disabled.

7. Education and training for all children to be equal in opportunity in all schools, colleges, universities, and other institutions for training in the professions and vocations of life; to be regulated on the capacity of children to learn, and not upon the ability of parents to pay the costs. Training for life's work to be as much universal and thorough for all walks in life as has been the training in the arts of killing.

8. The raising of revenue and taxes for the support of this program to come from the reduction of swollen fortunes from the top, as well as for the support of public works to give employment whenever there may be any slackening necessary in private enterprise.

The Call for Support

I now ask those who read this circular to help us at once in this work of giving life and happiness to our people—not a starvation dole upon which someone may live in misery from week to week. Before this miserable system of wreckage has destroyed the life germ of respect and culture in our American people let us save what was here, merely by having none too poor and none too rich. The theory of the Share Our Wealth Society is to have enough for all, but not to have one with so much that less than enough remains for the balance of the people.

Source: Congressional Record, 74th Congress, 2nd Session, vol. 79, no. 107 (May 23, 1935): 8333–8336.

8.4.   The Republican Party Platform, 1936

In 1936 the Republican Party charged that the Democrats' New Deal program threatened to unbalance government. The Republican platform asserted a conservative, states' rights opposition to the New Deal legislation and predicted the demise of free government if the program was not stopped. Insomuch as the election of 1936 was a referendum on the New Deal, Roosevelt's landslide victory over the Republicans proclaimed an important shift in public thinking about the role of the federal government in the economy and the responsibility of government to ensure a "just" society.

America is in peril. The welfare of American men and women and the future of our youth are at stake. We dedicate ourselves to the preservation of their political liberty, their individual opportunity and their character as free citizens, which today for the first time are threatened by Government itself.

For three long years the New Deal Administration has dishonored American traditions and flagrantly betrayed the pledges upon which the Democratic Party sought and received public support.

The powers of Congress have been usurped by the President.

The integrity and authority of the Supreme Court have been flouted.

The rights and liberties of American citizens have been violated.

Regulated monopoly has displaced free enterprise.

The New Deal Administration constantly seeks to usurp the rights reserved to the States and to the people.

It has insisted on the passage of laws contrary to the Constitution.

It has intimidated witnesses and interfered with the right of petition.

It has dishonored our country by repudiating its most sacred obligations.

It has been guilty of frightful waste and extravagance, using public funds for partisan political purposes.

It has promoted investigations to harass and intimidate American citizens, at the same time denying investigations into its own improper expenditures.

It has created a vast multitude of new offices, filled them with its favorites, set up a centralized bureaucracy, and sent out swarms of inspectors to harass our people.

It has bred fear and hesitation in commerce and industry, thus discouraging new enterprises, preventing employment and prolonging the depression.

It secretly has made tariff agreements with our foreign competitors, flooding our markets with foreign commodities.

It has coerced and intimidated voters by withholding relief from those opposing its tyrannical policies.

It has destroyed the morale of many of our people and made them dependent upon Government.

Appeals to passion and class prejudice have replaced reason and tolerance.

To a free people these actions are insufferable. This campaign cannot be waged on the traditional differences between the Republican and Democratic parties. The responsibility of this election transcends all previous political divisions. We invite all Americans, irrespective of party, to join us in defense of American institutions.

Constitutional Government and Free Enterprise

We Pledge Ourselves:

1. To maintain the American system of constitutional and local self government, and to resist all attempts to impair the authority of the Supreme Court of the United States, the final protector of the rights of our citizens against the arbitrary encroachments of the legislative and executive branches of Government. There can be no individual liberty without an independent judiciary.

2. To preserve the American system of free enterprise, private competition, and equality of opportunity, and to seek its constant betterment in the interests of all.

Reemployment

The only permanent solution of the unemployment problem is the absorption of the unemployed by industry and agriculture. To that end, we advocate:

Removal of restrictions on production.

Abandonment of all New Deal policies that raise production costs, increase the cost of living, and thereby restrict buying, reduce volume and prevent reemployment.

Encouragement instead of hindrance to legitimate business.

Withdrawal of Government from competition with private payrolls.

Elimination of unnecessary and hampering regulations.

Adoption of such policies as will furnish a chance for individual enterprise, industrial expansion, and the restoration of jobs.

Relief

The necessities of life must be provided for the needy, and hope must be restored pending recovery. The administration of relief is a major failure of the New Deal. It has been faithless to those who most deserve our sympathy. To end confusion, partisanship, waste and incompetence.
We Pledge:

1. The return of responsibility for relief administration to nonpolitical local agencies familiar with community problems.
2. Federal grants-in-aid to the States and Territories while the need exists, upon compliance with these conditions: (a) a fair proportion of the total relief burden to be provided from the revenues of States and local governments; (b) all engaged in relief administration to be selected on the basis of merit and fitness; (c) adequate provision to be made for the encouragement of those persons who are trying to become self-supporting.
3. Undertaking of Federal public works only on their merits and separate from the administration of relief.
4. A prompt determination of the facts concerning relief and unemployment.

Security

Real security will be possible only when our productive capacity is sufficient to furnish a decent standard of living for all American families and to provide a surplus for future needs and contingencies. For the attainment of that ultimate objective, we look to the energy, self-reliance and character of our people, and to our system of free enterprise.

Society has an obligation to promote the security of the people, by affording some measure of protection against involuntary unemployment and dependency in old age. The New Deal policies, while purporting to provide social security, have, in fact, endangered it.

We propose a system of old age security. . . .

We propose to encourage adoption by the States and Territories of honest and practical measures for meeting the problems of unemployment insurance.

The unemployment insurance and old age annuity sections of the present Social Security Act are unworkable and deny benefits to about two-thirds of our adult population, including professional men and women and all those engaged in agriculture and domestic service, and the self employed, while imposing heavy tax burdens upon all. The so-called reserve fund estimated at forty-seven billion dollars for old age insurance is no reserve at all, because the fund will contain nothing but the Government's promise to pay, while the taxes collected in the guise of premiums will be wasted by the Government in reckless and extravagant political schemes.

Labor

The welfare of labor rests upon increased production and the prevention of exploitation. We pledge ourselves to:

Protect the right of labor to organize and to bargain collectively through representatives of its own choosing without interference from any source.

Prevent governmental job holders from exercising autocratic powers over labor.

Support the adoption of State laws and interstate compacts to abolish sweatshops and child labor, and to protect women and children with respect to maximum hours, minimum wages and working conditions. We believe that this can be done within the Constitution as it now stands.

Agriculture

The farm problem is an economic and social, not a partisan problem, and we propose to treat it accordingly.... Our paramount object is to protect and foster the family type of farm, traditional in American life, and to promote policies which will bring about an adjustment of agriculture to meet the needs of domestic and foreign markets. As an emergency measure, during the agricultural depression, Federal benefit payments or grants-in-aid when administered within the means of the Federal Government are consistent with a balanced budget.

We Propose:

1. To facilitate economical production and increased consumption on a basis of abundance instead of scarcity.

2. A national land-use program, including the acquisition of abandoned and non-productive farm lands by voluntary sale or lease, subject to approval of the legislative and executive branches of the States concerned, and the devotion of such land to appropriate public use, such as watershed protection and flood prevention, reforestation, recreation, and conservation of wild life.

3. That an agricultural policy be pursued for the protection and restoration of the land resources, designed to bring about such a balance between soil-building and soil-depleting crops as will permanently insure productivity, with reasonable benefits to co-operating farmers on family-type farms, but so regulated as to eliminate the New Deal's destructive policy towards the dairy and live-stock industries.

4. To extend experimental aid to farmers developing new crops suited to our soil and climate. . . .

Regulation of Business

We recognize the existence of a field within which governmental regulation is desirable and salutary. The authority to regulate should be vested in an independent tribunal acting under clear and specific laws establishing definite standards. Their determinations on law and facts should be subject to review by the Courts. We favor Federal regulation, within the Constitution, of the marketing of securities to protect investors. We favor also Federal regulation of the interstate activities of public utilities. . . .

Government Finance

The New Deal Administration has been characterized by shameful waste and general financial irresponsibility. It has piled deficit upon deficit. It threatens national bankruptcy and the destruction through inflation of insurance policies and savings bank deposits.

We Pledge Ourselves To:

Stop the folly of uncontrolled spending.

Balance the budget—not by increasing taxes but by cutting expenditures, drastically and immediately.

Revise the Federal tax system and coordinate it with State and local tax systems.

Use the taxing power for raising revenue and not for punitive or political purposes.

Money and Banking

We advocate a sound currency to be preserved at all hazards.

The first requisite to a sound and stable currency is a balanced budget.

We oppose further devaluation of the dollar.

We will restore to the Congress the authority lodged with it by the Constitution to coin money and regulate the value thereof by repealing all the laws delegating this authority to the Executive.

We will cooperate with other countries toward stabilization of currencies as soon as we can do so with due regard for our national interests and as soon as other nations have sufficient stability to justify such action.

Conclusion

We assume the obligations and duties imposed upon Government by modern conditions. We affirm our unalterable conviction that, in the future as in the past, the fate of the nation will depend, not so much on the wisdom and power of Government, as on the character and virtue, self-reliance, industry and thrift of the people and on their willingness to meet the responsibilities essential to the preservation of a free society.

Finally, as our party affirmed in its first Platform in 1856: "Believing that the spirit of our institutions as well as the Constitution of our country guarantees liberty of conscience and equality of rights among our citizens, we oppose all legislation tending to impair them," and "we invite the affiliation and cooperation of the men of all parties, however differing from us in other respects, in support of the principles herein declared."

The acceptance of the nomination tendered by this Convention carries with it, as a matter of private honor and public faith, an undertaking by each candidate to be true to the principles and program herein set forth.

Source: David E. Shi and Holly A. Mayer, *For the Record: A Documentary History of America* (New York: W. W. Norton, 1999), vol. 2, pp. 228–231.

8.5.   President Roosevelt's Plan to Change the Supreme Court

---

The Supreme Court's decisions in *Schechter* and other cases, striking down the basic legislation of the New Deal, caused Roosevelt to come up with a plan to "pack" the Court with enough new liberal justices to permit Congress to protect New Deal policies with new legislation. Roosevelt outlined his plan in a message to Congress on February 5, 1937. Mathematically, the scheme was simple. Congress should permit him to add six new justices, all of whom would, presumably, be supportive of the New Deal, thus changing the existing six to three majority in favor of conservative justices to nine to six in favor of the liberals. The Court-packing scheme represented not only Roosevelt's effort to secure the New Deal but also a view on the new powers an activist federal government should have.

At the present time the Supreme Court is laboring under a heavy burden. Its difficulties in this respect were superficially lightened some years ago by authorizing the court, in its discretion, to refuse to hear appeals in many classes of cases. This discretion was so freely exercised that in the last fiscal year, although 867 petitions for review were presented to the Supreme Court, it declined to hear 717 cases. If petitions in behalf of the Government are excluded, it appears that the court permitted private litigants to prosecute appeals in only 108 cases out of 803 applications. Many of the refusals were doubtless warranted. But can it be said that full justice is achieved when a court is forced by the sheer necessity of keeping up with its business to decline, without even an explanation, to hear 87 percent of the cases presented to it by private litigants?

It seems clear, therefore, that the necessity of relieving present congestion extends to the enlargement of the capacity of all the federal courts.

* * *

. . . The modern tasks of judges call for the use of full energies.

Modern complexities call also for a constant infusion of new blood in the courts, just as it is needed in executive functions of the Government and in private business. A lowered mental or physical vigor leads men to avoid an examination of complicated and changed conditions. Little by little, new facts become blurred through old glasses fitted, as it were, for the needs of another generation; older men, assuming that the scene is the same as it was in the past, cease to explore or inquire into the present or the future. . . .

Life tenure of judges, assured by the Constitution, was designed to place the courts beyond temptations or influences which might impair their judgments: it was not intended to create a static judiciary. A constant and systematic addition of younger blood will vitalize the courts and better equip them to recognize and apply the essential concepts of justice in the light of the needs and the facts of an ever-changing world. . . .

* * *

In the uncertain state of the law, it is not difficult for the ingenious to devise novel reasons for attacking the validity of new legislation or its application. While these questions are laboriously brought to issue and debated through a series of courts, the Government must stand aside. It matters not that the Congress has enacted the law, that the Executive has signed it and that the administrative machinery is waiting to function. Government by injunction lays a heavy hand upon normal processes; and no important statute can take effect—against any individual or organization with the means to employ lawyers and engage in wide-flung litigation—until it has passed through the whole hierarchy of the courts. Thus the judiciary, by postponing the effective date of Acts of the

Congress, is assuming an additional function and is coming more and more to constitute a scattered, loosely organized and slowly operating third house of the National Legislature. . . .

* * *

Draft of Proposed Bill

SEC. 1. (a) When any judge of a court of the United States, appointed to hold his office during good behavior, has heretofore or hereafter attained the age of seventy years and has held a commission or commissions as judge of any such court or courts at least ten years, continuously or otherwise, and within six months thereafter has neither resigned nor retired, the President, for each such judge who has not so resigned or retired, shall nominate, and by and with the advice and consent of the Senate, shall appoint one additional judge to the court to which the former is commissioned. Provided, That no additional judge shall be appointed hereunder if the judge who is of retirement age dies, resigns or retires prior to the nomination of such additional judge.

(b) The number of judges of any court shall be permanently increased by the number appointed thereto under the provisions of subsection (a) of this section. No more than fifty judges shall be appointed thereunder, nor shall any judge be so appointed if such appointment would result in (1) more than fifteen members of the Supreme Court of the United States, (2) more than two additional members so appointed to a circuit court of appeals, the Court of Claims, the United States Court of Customs and Patent Appeals, or the Customs Court, or (3) more than twice the number of judges now authorized to be appointed for any district or, in the case of judges appointed for more than one district, for any such group of districts.

(c) That number of judges which is at least two-thirds of the number of which the Supreme Court of the United States consists, or three-fifths of the number of which the United States Court of Appeals for the District of Columbia, the Court of Claims or the United States Court of Customs and Patent Appeals consists, shall constitute a quorum of such court. . . .

SEC. 5 (a) The term "judge of retirement age" means a judge of a court of the United States, appointed to hold his office during good behavior, who has attained the age of seventy years and has held a commission or commissions as judge of any such court or courts at least ten years, continuously or otherwise, and within six months thereafter, whether or not he is eligible for retirement, has neither resigned nor retired. . . .

(d) The term "judge" includes justice.

Source: 1937 Public Papers and Addresses of Franklin Roosevelt 51 (Washington, DC: Government Printing Office, 1941).

8.6.   Senate Response to Roosevelt's Court-Packing Plan, 1937

The 1937 Report of the Senate Judiciary Committee summarized the reasons behind the Senate's opposition to Roosevelt's formula to change the Supreme Court and its potential to politicize this judicial body and destroy the separation of powers. Roosevelt's plan found few takers outside ardent New Deal supporters. Opponents of the plan, and the New Deal, used the Court-packing crisis to charge New Dealers with overstepping the bounds of federal authority and undermining the constitutional balance of power.

The Committee on the Judiciary, to whom was referred the bill to reorganize the judicial branch of the Government, after full consideration, having unanimously amended the measure, hereby report the bill adversely with the recommendation that it do not pass. . . .

The Argument

The committee recommends that the measure be rejected for the following primary reasons:

I. The bill does not accomplish any one of the objectives for which it was originally offered.

II. It applies force to the judiciary and in its initial and ultimate effect would undermine the independence of the courts.

III. It violates all precedents in the history of our Government and would in itself be a dangerous precedent for the future.

IV. The theory of the bill is in direct violation of the spirit of the American Constitution and its employment would permit alteration of the Constitution without the people's consent or approval; it undermines the protection our constitutional system gives to minorities and is subversive of the rights of individuals.

* * *

Object of Plan Acknowledged

No amount of sophistry can cover up this fact. The effect of this bill is not to provide for an increase in the number of Justices composing the Supreme Court. The effect is to provide a forced retirement or, failing in this, to take from the Justices affected a free exercise of their independent judgment. . . .

Let us, for the purpose of the argument, grant that the Court has been wrong, wrong not only in that it has rendered mistaken opinions but wrong in the far more serious sense that it has substituted its will for the congressional will in the matter of legislation. May we nevertheless safely punish the Court?

Today it may be the Court which is charged with forgetting its constitutional duties. Tomorrow it may be the Congress. The next day it may be the Executive. If we yield to temptation now to lay the lash upon the Court, we are only teaching others how to apply it to ourselves and to the people when the occasion seems to warrant. Manifestly, if we may force the hand of the Court to secure our interpretation of the Constitution, then some succeeding Congress may repeat the process to secure another and a different interpretation and one which may not sound so pleasant in our ears as that for which we now contend.

* * *

But, if the fault of the judges is not so grievous as to warrant impeachment, if their offense is merely that they have grown old, and we feel, therefore, that there should be a "constant infusion of new blood," then obviously the way to achieve that result is by constitutional amendment fixing definite terms for the members of the judiciary or making mandatory their retirement at a given age. Such a provision would indeed provide for the constant infusion of new blood, not only now but at all times in the future. The plan before us is but a temporary expedient which operates once and then never again, leaving the Court as permanently expanded to become once more a court of old men, gradually year by year falling behind the times. . . .

A Measure Without Precedent

This bill is an invasion of judicial power such as has never before been attempted in this country. . . .

. . . And never in the history of the country has there been such an act. The present bill comes to us, therefore, wholly without precedent.

It is true that the size of the Supreme Court has been changed from time to time, but in every instance after the Adams administration, save one, the changes were made for purely administrative purposes in aid of the Court, not to control it. . . .

A Precedent of Loyalty to the Constitution

Shall we now, after 150 years of loyalty to the constitutional ideal of an untrammeled judiciary, duty bound to protect the constitutional rights of the humblest citizen even against the Government itself, create the vicious precedent which must necessarily undermine our system? The only argument for the increase which survives analysis is that Congress should enlarge the Court so as to make the policies of this administration effective.

* * *

Even if the case were far worse than it is alleged to be, it would still be no argument in favor of this bill to say that the courts and some judges have abused their power. The courts are not perfect, nor are the judges. The Congress is not perfect, nor are Senators and Representatives. The Executive is not perfect. These branches of government and the office[s] under them are filled by human beings who for the most part strive to live up to the dignity and idealism of a system that was designed to achieve the greatest possible measure of justice and freedom for all the people. We shall destroy the system when we reduce it to the imperfect standards of the men who operate it. We shall strengthen it and ourselves, we shall make justice and liberty for all men more certain when, by patience and self-restraint, we maintain it on the high plane on which it was conceived.

Inconvenience and even delay in the enactment of legislation is not a heavy price to pay for our system. Constitutional democracy moves forward with certainty rather than with speed. The safety and the permanence of the progressive march of our civilization are far more important to us and to those who are to come after us than the enactment now of any particular law. The Constitution of the United States provides ample opportunity for the expression of popular will to bring about such reforms and changes as the people may deem essential to their present and future welfare. It is the people's charter of the powers granted those who govern them. . . .

Summary

We recommend the rejection of this bill as a needless, futile, and utterly dangerous abandonment of constitutional principle.

* * *

It would subjugate the courts to the will of Congress and the President and thereby destroy the independence of the judiciary, the only certain shield of individual rights.

* * *

Its ultimate operation would be to make this Government one of men rather than one of law, and its practical operation would be to make the Constitution what the executive or legislative branches of the Government choose to say it is—an interpretation to be changed with each change of administration.

It is a measure which should be so emphatically rejected that its parallel will never again be presented to the free representatives of the free people of America.

Source: Kermit L. Hall, ed., *Major Problems in American Constitutional History*, Volume 11: *From 1870 to the Present* (Lexington, MA: D. C. Heath, 1992), pp. 206–213.

ANNOTATED RESEARCH GUIDE

Books

Badger, Anthony J. *The New Deal: The Depression Years, 1933–1940*. New York: Farrar, Straus and Giroux, 1989. Provides a recent and reliable overview of the New Deal that emphasizes the limited aspects of Roosevelt's liberal reforms.

Barber, William J. *Designs Within Disorder: Franklin D. Roosevelt, the Economists, and the Shaping of American Economic Policy, 1933–1945*. New York: Cambridge University Press, 1996. Stresses the liberal ideology of the emerging welfare state that can be seen in the seemingly helter-skelter legislation of the first and second New Deals.

Braeman, John, et al., eds. *The New Deal: The State and Local Levels*. Columbus: Ohio State University Press, 1975. A fine collection of essays that examine the New Deal in local communities.

Brinkley, Alan. *Voices of Protest: Huey Long, Father Coughlin, and the Great Depression*. New York: Alfred A. Knopf, 1982. The best treatment of the critics of the New Deal from the political left.

Burns, James MacGregor. *Roosevelt: The Lion and the Fox*. New York: Harcourt, Brace, 1956. Emphasizes Roosevelt's inability to create substantial political and social reforms.

Hacker, Louis M. *American Problems of Today*. New York: F. S. Crofts and Co., 1938. A contemporary historian's view of the New Deal that labeled it "a political program in behalf of agricultural landlords and big commercial farmers, organized trade unionists, and overseas investors and imperialist promoters."

Hofstadter, Richard. *The Age of Reform: From Bryan to F.D.R.* New York: Alfred A. Knopf, 1955. An analysis of the New Deal as a significant break with previous reform traditions in America.

Leuchtenburg, William E. *Franklin D. Roosevelt and the New Deal*. New York: Harper and Row, 1963. A full narrative of the New Deal from 1932 to 1940 that shows how much the personality of Roosevelt dominated his administration and points out that it is the conservative character of the New Deal and FDR that is most significant.

McElvaine, Robert S. *The Great Depression: America, 1929–1941*. New York: Random House, 1984. The best single-volume treatment of the Great Depression, particularly in its analysis of the origins and first years of the most serious economic crisis in American history.

Patterson, James T. *The New Deal and the States: Federalism in Transition*. Princeton, NJ: Princeton University Press, 1969. A thoughtful appraisal of the new federalism between 1929 and 1940 with an emphasis on the persistence of the doctrines of states' rights and strict construction as a restraint on the New Deal.

Perkins, Dexter. *The Age of Franklin Roosevelt, 1932–1945*. Chicago: University of Chicago Press, 1957. Views the New Deal as an effective and successful experiment in democratic federalism.

Schlesinger, Arthur M., Jr. *The Age of Roosevelt*. 3 vols. Boston: Houghton Mifflin, 1957–1960. The most comprehensive and sympathetic interpretation of the New Deal. Portrays it as an attempt to preserve democracy from the threat of powerful business interests at home and totalitarianism abroad.

Sitkoff, Harvard. *A New Deal for Blacks*. New York: Oxford University Press, 1981. Examines the meager accomplishments made by black Americans during the New Deal because of the racism that characterized most of its programs.

Terkel, Studs. *Hard Times: An Oral History of the Great Depression*. New York: Pantheon Books, 1970. The most revealing oral history of the Depression. Presents a wide range of experiences during the crisis.

Nonprint Media

Web Sites

http://www.nscds.pvt.k12.il.us/nscds/us/apushist/roosevelt/newdeal.html. Summarizes the agencies of the New Deal.

http://newdeal.feri.org/index.htm. Offers a list of homepages and sites about Roosevelt and the New Deal.

http://www.socialstudieshelp.com/CourtCases.htm. "Historic Supreme Court Cases" includes a summary of *Schechter* and *Jones & Laughlin*.

Videotapes

The American Experience: The Democrats. PBS Video Series, 750 minutes on four discs. 4PK (DVD Video). Code: V4617.

The American Experience: The Presidents. PBS Video Series, 1,350 minutes on eight discs. 8PK (DVD Video). Code: PRM0001.

The American Experience: The Presidents Collection. Deals with TR and FDR. PBS Video Series, 510 minutes on four tapes. Code: A2767.

The Great Depression Set. Shows the impact of the Depression. A&E/History Channel series, 200 minutes, set of four videos.

9

Brown v. Board of Education: Federalism and Civil Rights

The New Deal was mainly for white Americans. The vast majority of blacks did not benefit directly from its programs, though they did not escape the administration of New Deal policies that altered farming and industrial work. In fact, during the Great Depression most blacks saw their condition worsen, and in the South, where about 75 percent of blacks lived, they were more than ever disfranchised, economically exploited, and segregated. There, they could not vote, could not serve on juries, and were excluded from most universities, hospitals, swimming pools, and public parks. They attended woefully underfunded separate public schools. In the cities and towns they worked in the most menial jobs, and in the rural areas they often were propertyless sharecroppers and tenants, caught in a cycle of poverty and disease. Lynching continued unabated. In 1929 seven black men were hanged by mobs, and in 1933 the figure escalated to twenty-four. In the North blacks were discriminated against in all jobs, and black unemployment during the Depression reached almost 50 percent. The Republican Party was lily-white. And President Franklin D. Roosevelt, determined to keep the loyalty of southern Democrats behind his New Deal legislation, refused to make a commitment to laws against lynching and the abolition of the poll tax.

Many New Deal programs hurt blacks rather than helped them. For example, the Agricultural Adjustment Act (AAA) forced many black tenant farmers off the land. The Civilian Conservation Corps (CCC) initially excluded blacks. The loan programs of the Federal Housing Administration (FHA) promoted racial and social segregation by denying mortgages for blacks in white neighborhoods, and vice versa. All skilled jobs in the Tennessee Valley Authority (TVA) went to whites. And the Fair Labor Standards Act did not cover the unskilled jobs held mostly by blacks, such as waiters, cooks, janitors, and farm hands.

But the experience of fighting the racism of Nazism in World War II and the mounting Cold War pressures on the United States after the war changed the views of many white Americans on racial segregation. The problem was obvious. How could the United States stand as the leader of the free world against the tyranny of communism if it practiced racism at home? Furthermore, how could Americans show the emerging nations of Africa and Asia that the United States was the world's leader in protecting human rights if white Americans subjected black Americans to racial separation and denied them basic civil rights? Moreover, during the war 1.5 million blacks left the South to work in war industries in the North and West, thereby nationalizing what had until then been a regional issue, namely, racial segregation.

President Harry S. Truman saw these compelling international and national pressures to end racism. But more than that, he personally believed that every American should enjoy full rights of citizenship, regardless of color. In December 1946, he signed Executive Order 9808, establishing the President's Committee on Civil Rights. He proclaimed that the preservation of civil rights was guaranteed by the Constitution and was "essential to domestic tranquility, national security, the general welfare, and the continued existence of our free institutions." The order directed the committee to investigate the status of civil rights and submit a report on its recommendations for ways the federal government could guarantee "more adequate and effective means and procedures" to protect "the civil rights of the people of the United States."

The following year the committee's report, *To Secure These Rights*, was published. It set the goals of the civil rights movement for the next twenty years. It demanded strengthening the Civil Rights Section of the Justice Department. It called for federal laws against lynching. It recommended federal laws to eliminate the poll tax and to protect the right to vote against racial discrimination by states. It wanted Congress to enact a federal Fair Employment Practices Act prohibiting discrimination in hiring. It wanted an end to educational discrimination in public schools. In a sweeping conclusion, it demanded the "elimination of segregation, based on race, color, creed, or national origin, from American life."

On February 2, 1948, President Truman took the committee's findings to Congress in his Civil Rights Message. Standing before a joint session, he asserted his belief that all men were created equal and that they had the right to equal justice under law. He talked about the "flagrant examples" of discrimination that existed in America and stated that the

"Federal Government has a clear duty to see that constitutional guaranties of individual liberties and of equal protection under the laws are not denied or abridged anywhere in our Union." He ended with a clear reference to the relationship of segregation and America's role in the Cold War. "If we wish to inspire the peoples of the world whose freedom is in jeopardy," he said, "if we wish to restore hope to those who have already lost their civil liberties, if we wish to fulfill the promise that is ours, we must correct the remaining imperfections in our practice of democracy."

When Congress, controlled by an alliance of conservative southern Democrats and Republicans, refused to act on Truman's message, he moved on his own. He issued Executive Order 9981, establishing equal opportunity in the armed forces "without regard to race, color, religion or national origins." He created the President's Committee on Equality of Treatment and Opportunity in the Armed Services to examine and then eliminate segregation. He ordered racial discrimination ended in all federal civil service jobs. He instructed the Justice Department to act on behalf of blacks to end segregation. It immediately filed suits in federal district courts to eliminate racial segregation in colleges and universities, housing, restaurants, and hotels in Washington, D.C., and in public education.

Meanwhile, the struggle for equal opportunity and equal protection of the laws for blacks received the backing of the Supreme Court. In 1944, in *Smith v. Allwright*, it struck down the all-white primary election laws. In 1948, in a unanimous decision in *Shelley v. Kraemer*, the Court ruled against restrictive covenants in the sale of real estate. Such covenants, Chief Justice Frederick Vinson stated, excluded blacks and Jews from purchasing property and denied to the excluded groups the equal protection of the laws required by the Fourteenth Amendment. Afterward, restrictive covenants could not be used to keep neighborhoods segregated. In 1950, in *Sweatt v. Painter*, the Court again unanimously ruled that the separate but equal standard was not attainable in state universities and implied that the doctrine was also unattainable in other public areas. In the same session the Court, in *McLaurin v. Oklahoma State Regents*, unanimously concluded that separate but equal in graduate education was unattainable.

In the late 1930s the Legal Defense Fund of the National Association for the Advancement of Colored People (NAACP) challenged the separate but equal doctrine of *Plessy v. Ferguson* that legalized racial segregation in public schools in the South. Led by Charles Houston until 1950, and then by Thurgood Marshall (who would become the first black justice of the Court in 1967), it argued that the literal interpretation of the doctrine was unconstitutional because it violated the equal protection clause of the Fourteenth Amendment. In 1951 a three-judge district court, in *Briggs v. Elliott*, ruled against separate black schools in South Carolina because they were inherently unequal and inferior. By 1952 Marshall had won similar cases in Kansas, Virginia, Delaware, and the District of Columbia.

At that point Marshall consolidated all of them into an appellants' brief to the Supreme Court. His arguments contained the essential points that he soon would present in original oral arguments in *Brown v. Board of Education* (Brown I). Put simply, Jim Crow schools violated a student's right to equality before the law. The Fourteenth Amendment, Marshall said, "precludes a state from imposing distinctions or classifications based upon race and color alone." Segregated public schools must be eliminated and integrated schools opened in their place. All of these points were buttressed with social and scientific evidence. Just before the Supreme Court heard Marshall's arguments, Chief Justice Vinson died from a heart attack, and President Dwight D. Eisenhower appointed Earl Warren in his place. Warren, attorney general of California from 1939 to 1942 and governor of the state since then, was known as a "law and order" conservative who had pushed for relocation of Japanese Americans during World War II. But as Chief Justice, he became a champion of black civil rights.

Brown I was argued on December 9, 1952, reargued on December 8, 1953, and decided on May 17, 1954, by a unanimous vote. As in the appellants' brief, Marshall used both law and social science. He maintained that the original intent of the Fourteenth Amendment's equal protection clause was to prevent segregation. He presented sociological, historical, and statistical facts to prove the unequal effects of segregated school systems and their detrimental impact on black children. Warren wrote the opinion. In an unusually short but brisk statement, only ten pages in length, he launched a legal and social revolution in race relations in the United States and marked a new and unexpectedly liberal way in which the Court would interpret the Constitution to expand the power of the federal government over state laws. He said that although the cases came to the Court from four different states and were premised on different facts and conditions, "a common legal question justifies their consideration together in this consolidated opinion." The common question was the contention by the NAACP that "segregated public schools are not 'equal' and cannot be made 'equal,' and that hence [the plaintiffs] are deprived of the equal protection of the law." He went on to write that the Court "must consider public education in the light of its full development and its present place in American life throughout the nation," because education "is perhaps the most important function of state and local governments." He asked, "Does segregation of children in public schools solely on the basis of race . . . deprive the children of the minority group of equal educational opportunities?" His answer: "We believe that it does." The Chief Justice contended that "in the field of public education the doctrine of 'separate but equal' has no place." "Separate educational facilities," he wrote, "are inherently unequal." "Such segregation is a denial of the equal protection of the laws."

Even so, the ruling provided no Court direction as to how to change the segregated public schools. It only asked Marshall to submit such a solution in the next session of the Court. The following year, in *Brown v. Board of Education of Topeka* (Brown II), it ordered that desegregation proceed with "all deliberate speed." It gave school authorities the "primary responsibility for elucidating, assessing, and solving these problems" and told the federal courts to oversee the fastest way to achieve desegregation in their own jurisdictions.

Unfortunately, Brown II was an ambiguous ruling, encouraged delay, and reflected the justices' fear that any immediate implementation of a desegregation plan would invite southern hostility and even violence. They were right. Southern legislatures openly refused to integrate their schools. And ninety-six congressmen signed a "declaration on Integration" that advocated resistance to desegregation. Published in the *New York Times*, it condemned "the decision of the Supreme Court in the school cases as clear abuse of judicial power," characterizing it as part of "a trend in the Federal judiciary undertaking to legislate, in derogation of the authority of Congress, and to encroach upon the reserved rights of the states and the people." They pledged "to use all lawful means to bring about a reversal of this decision which is contrary to the Constitution and to prevent the use of force in its implementation."

Over the next two years southern resistance, called "massive resistance," to the Supreme Court's order to integrate intensified. Georgia made it a felony to spend tax money for desegregated schools. Mississippi forbade any organization to file a desegregation action in the courts. North Carolina withheld funds from desegregated schools. Prince Edward County, Virginia, closed its schools and enrolled white children in segregated private schools. In September 1957, at Little Rock, Arkansas, Governor Orval Faubus, the day before integration was to begin, called out the National Guard to prevent black students from entering the city's high school. When a federal district judge ordered the troops to withdraw, an angry crowd gathered at the school. President Eisenhower went on television and called the city leaders "demagogic extremists" who were encouraging "disorderly mobs" for the sole purpose of "preventing the carrying out of the Court's order relating to the admission of Negro children to that school." He then announced that he was federalizing the Arkansas National Guard and would deploy U.S. Army paratroopers to keep the peace and protect the black children. City officials reacted by closing all schools to prevent integration, and a federal district court ordered a delay of integration for two-and-a-half years.

The NAACP appealed the district court's decision to the Supreme Court, which in September 1958 handed down a unanimous decision in *Cooper v. Aaron*. It denounced the governor and legislature of Arkansas for failure to obey federal court orders "resting on this Court's considered interpretation of the United States Constitution." It pointed out that no "state legislator or executive or judicial officer can war against the Constitution without violating his undertaking to support it." The civil rights of black students "are not to be sacrificed or yielded to the violence and disorder which have followed upon the actions of the Governor and Legislature" of Arkansas. The "Brown case can neither be nullified openly and directly by state legislators or state executive or judicial officers, nor nullified indirectly by them through evasive schemes for segregation." Finally, it declared that the "right of a student not to be segregated on racial grounds in schools so maintained is indeed so fundamental and pervasive that it is embraced in the concept of due process of law." But educational segregation remained largely unchanged.

In the face of the white backlash against *Brown*, and the inability of the federal courts to end segregation, blacks developed their own nonjudicial assault on segregation, first with the economic pressure of a boycott. In December 1955, in Montgomery, Alabama, Rosa Parks, a department store clerk and black activist, refused to surrender her seat to a white man on a bus, as required by an Alabama Jim Crow law, and was arrested. A number of local black women, friends of hers, organized a boycott by blacks of the city's bus system. This same group chose Martin Luther King, Jr., the minister at the Dexter Street Baptist Church, to lead the boycott. The white community retaliated. They refused to insure automobiles that transported blacks to work in carpools. Someone exploded a bomb in the front yard of King's home. Ninety blacks were arrested for organizing what city officials claimed was an illegal conspiracy. The standoff lasted a year, nearly crippled the bus company, and forced many city businesses into bankruptcy. Throughout the contest, King urged perseverance and nonviolence. In November 1956, the Supreme Court declared the Montgomery bus law illegal, the boycott ended, and the buses were integrated.

With the Montgomery boycott the contest between the federal government and southern states over integration moved beyond education and court decisions to become a national crusade to end Jim Crow in the South and to establish equality for blacks in all aspects of public life. Under King, who founded the Southern Christian Leadership Conference (SCLC), new offensives were developed against racism that moved the fight beyond the South, although the main focus of the struggle still remained in that region. But blacks frustrated with racism did not need King to guide them, and they embarked on "direct action" efforts to bring down Jim Crow and gain basic civil rights. "Sit-ins" began at

Greensboro, North Carolina, in February 1960 when black college students refused to leave a "whites only" lunch counter. Within days, some 300 students joined them. The strategy quickly spread to sit-ins at Durham, Winston-Salem, Charlotte, and High Point, then to Portsmouth, Virginia, and across the South.

Uplifted by the public attention that the sit-ins received throughout out the nation, black college and high school students in the spring founded the Student Non-violent Coordinating Committee (SNCC) and marched to demonstrate against segregation singing their anthem, "We Shall Overcome." Blacks started another key organization against racism in 1960, the Congress of Racial Equality (CORE), with James Farmer as its director. It put together in the spring of 1961 a "freedom ride" made up of blacks and whites to travel on a bus from Washington, D.C., to New Orleans to focus national attention on racism in the South and to test the efficacy of federal law prohibiting discrimination in interstate travel. They met a violent reception, and some were beaten by mobs. The violence forced a reluctant Kennedy administration, which did not want to get entangled in civil rights cases in the South, to broker a deal to protect the riders. The fight continued over civil rights during the 1960s, sometimes degenerating into violent episodes reminiscent of Klan terrorist activities during Reconstruction. Some southern governors such as George C. Wallace of Alabama and Ross Barnett of Mississippi grandstanded against the federal government by personally defying federal court orders to end segregation at their state universities. At the University of Mississippi, mob violence became so severe in 1962 that President John F. Kennedy had to send in the army to restore order and force compliance to federal law, at the cost of two dead and 375 wounded.

The rational, judicial challenge to segregation in public education by the NAACP culminating in the Supreme Court's *Brown* decision was a pivotal event in the history of racism in the United States. It forced the nation to come to grips with an issue that had been too often ignored since its founding: to realize that the morality, not to say the future of our society, demanded an end to racial inequality. In so doing, *Brown* unequivocally put the authority of federal law against state segregated facilities. Southern state legislatures and southern whites in general stood behind states' rights to oppose intrusion into these areas never before touched by the federal government, not even during the New Deal. Whatever might be said about the failure of the *Brown* decision to achieve integration, the course of race relations in the South, and eventually in the nation, was forever changed. One all-important fact remained after *Brown*. The doctrine of separate but equal, handed down in the 1896 *Plessy v. Ferguson* decision that provided the legal basis for Jim Crow laws in southern states for sixty years, was vacated. The Constitution, as interpreted by the Court, would now be used by the federal government to end segregation, not to condone it.

The fight over civil rights had resulted in a significant expansion of federal authority over the states, and in court-ordered busing it opened all areas of public accommodations to federal sanctions against segregation. No better example of this unprecedented extension of federal power into the daily lives of American citizens can be found than the Civil Rights Act of 1964. President Kennedy, a few months before his assassination, realized that if ever racial discrimination were to be overcome, the federal government needed greater authority to combat it. He asked Congress to enact a law guaranteeing "the kind of equality of treatment which we would want ourselves." But southerners in Congress blocked the bill, and it was not passed until the new president, Lyndon Baines Johnson, using deep public sympathy for the fallen president, combined with his own brilliant legislative skills, moved the bill through Congress and signed it into law on July 2, 1964.

The Civil Rights Act of 1964, along with the Voting Rights Act of 1965, significantly expanded federal authority in ensuring civil rights, including the right to vote. The Civil Rights Act established a federal standard and empowered the government, through the courts and other agencies, to enforce the principle of equality before the law in employment, access to public services, public accommodations, and education. The law ended state-mandated and -maintained Jim Crow. It also ushered in the new age of federal responsibility for ensuring citizens' rights in an increasing range of activities. The law was the foundation of the "rights revolution" that marked the last decades of the twentieth century.

DOCUMENTS

9.1.   President Truman's Civil Rights Message to Congress, February 2, 1949

Using the Report of the Committee on Civil Rights as the basis for his address, President Harry S. Truman asked Congress to pass the measures it recommended. His address to a Congress dominated by conservative Republicans and southern Democrats produced no new legislation, but it dramatized to the American public the existing, but ignored, inequities in race relations in the United States.

To the Congress of the United States:

In the state of the Union message on January 7, 1948, I spoke of five great goals toward which we should give strive in our constant effort to strengthen our democracy and improve the welfare of our people. The first of these is to secure fully our essential human rights. I am now presenting to the Congress my recommendations for legislation to carry us forward toward that goal.

This Nation was founded by men and women who sought these shores that they might enjoy greater freedom and greater opportunity than they had known before. The founders of the United States proclaimed to the world the American belief that all men are created equal, and that governments are instituted to secure the inalienable rights with which all men are endowed. In the Declaration of Independence and the Constitution of the United States they eloquently expressed the aspirations of all mankind for equality and freedom.

These ideals inspired the peoples of other lands, and their practical fulfillment made the United States the hope of the oppressed everywhere. Throughout our history men and women of all colors and creeds, of all races and religions, have come to this country to escape tyranny and discrimination. Millions strong, they have helped build this democratic Nation and have constantly reinforced our devotion to the great ideals of liberty and equality. With those who preceded them they have helped to fashion and strengthen our American faith—a faith that can be simply stated:

We believe that all men are created equal and that they have the right to equal justice under law.

We believe that all men have the right to freedom of thought and of expression and the right to worship as they please.

We believe that all men are entitled to equal opportunities for jobs, for homes, for good health, and for education.

We believe that all men should have a voice in their government, and that government should protect, not usurp, the rights of the people.

These are the basic civil rights which are the source and the support of our democracy.

Today the American people enjoy more freedom and opportunity than ever before. Never in our history has there been better reason to hope for the complete realization of the ideals of liberty and equality.

We shall not, however, finally achieve the ideals for which this Nation was founded so long as any American suffers discrimination as a result of his race, or religion, or color, or the land of origin of his forefathers.

Unfortunately there still are examples—flagrant examples—of discrimination which are utterly contrary to our ideals. Not all groups of our population are free from the fear of violence. Not all groups are free to live and work where they please or to improve their conditions of life by their own efforts. Not all groups enjoy the full privileges of citizenship and participation in the Government under which they live.

We cannot be satisfied until all our people have equal opportunities for jobs, for homes, for education, for health, and for political expression, and until all our people have equal protection under the law. . . .

The protection of civil rights is the duty of every government which derives its powers from the consent of the people. This is equally true of local, State, and National Governments. There is much that the States can and should do at this time to extend their protection of civil rights. Wherever the law-enforcement measures of State and local governments are inadequate to discharge this primary function of government, these measures should be strengthened and improved.

The Federal Government has a clear duty to see that constitutional guaranties of individual liberties and of equal protection under the laws are not denied or abridged anywhere in our Union. That duty is shared by all three branches of the Government, but it can be fulfilled only if the Congress enacts modern, comprehensive civil-rights laws, adequate to the needs of the day, and demonstrating our continuing faith in the free way of life.

I recommend, therefore, that the Congress enact legislation at this session directed toward the following specific objectives:

(1) Establishing a permanent Commission on Civil Rights, a Joint Congressional Committee on Civil Rights, and a Civil Rights Division in the Department of Justice.

(2) Strengthening existing civil-rights statutes.

(3) Providing Federal protection against lynching.

(4) Protecting more adequately the right to vote.

(5) Establishing a Fair Employment Practice Commission to prevent unfair discrimination in employment.

(6) Prohibiting discrimination in interstate transportation facilities.

* * *

The legislation I have recommended for enactment by the Congress at the present session is a minimum program if the Federal Government is to fulfill its obligation of insuring the Constitutional guaranties of individual liberties and of equal protection under the law.

* * *

It is the settled policy of the United States Government that there shall be no discrimination in Federal employment or in providing Federal services and facilities. Steady progress has been made toward this objective in recent years. I shall shortly issue an Executive order containing a comprehensive restatement of the Federal nondiscrimination policy, together with appropriate measures to ensure compliance.

During the recent war and in the years since its close we have made such progress toward equality of opportunity in our armed services without regard to race, color, religion, or national origin. I have instructed the Secretary of Defense to take steps to have the remaining instances of discrimination in the armed services eliminated as rapidly as possible. The personnel policies and practices of all the services in this regard will be made consistent.

* * *

The position of the United States in the world today makes it especially urgent that we adopt these measures to secure for all our people their essential rights.

The peoples of the world are faced with the choice of freedom or enslavement, a choice between a form of government which harnesses the state in the service of the individual and a form of government which chains the individual to the needs of the state.

We in the United States are working in company with other nations who share our desire for enduring world peace and who believe with us that, above all else, men must be free. We are striving to build a world family of nations—a world where men may live under governments of their own choosing and under laws of their own making.

As part of that endeavor, the Commission of Human Rights of the United Nations is now engaged in preparing an international bill of human rights by which the nations of the world may bind themselves by

international covenant to give effect to basic human rights and fundamental freedoms. We have played a leading role in this undertaking
designed to create a world order of law and justice fully protective of
the rights and the dignity of the individual.

To be effective in these efforts, we must protect our civil rights so that
by providing all our people with the maximum enjoyment of personal
freedom and personal opportunity we shall be a stronger nation—
stronger in our leadership, stronger in our moral position, stronger in
the deeper satisfactions of a united citizenry.

We know that our democracy is not perfect. But we do know that it
offers a fuller, freer, happier life to our people than any totalitarian nation has ever offered.

If we wish to inspire the peoples of the world whose freedom is in
jeopardy, if we wish to restore hope to those who have already lost their
civil liberties, if we wish to fulfill the promise that is ours, we must
correct the remaining imperfections in our practice of democracy.

We know the way. We need only the will.

HARRY S TRUMAN.

Source: 80th Congress, 2nd Session, House Doc. No. 516 (1948).

9.2.   *Brown v. Board of Education* (1954)

The Court unanimously reversed *Plessy v. Ferguson*'s separate
but equal doctrine and held that racially segregated public
schools violated the Fourteenth Amendment's equal protection
clause. Chief Justice Earl Warren's opinion was clear, nontech-
nical, and short—only ten pages. The decision, as Warren anticipated, ignited a legal and social revolution in the history of
black-white relations in the United States. It also marked the
beginning of the Warren Court's "judicial activism," that is, using the Court's interpretation of the Constitution to bring about
important changes in American society.

Mr. Chief Justice Warren delivered the opinion of the Court.

These cases come to us from the States of Kansas, South Carolina,
Virginia, and Delaware. They are premised on different facts and different local conditions, but a common legal question justifies their consideration together in this consolidated opinion.

In each of the cases, minors of the Negro race, through their legal
representatives, seek the aid of the courts in obtaining admission to the
public schools of their community on a nonsegregated basis. In each

instance, they had been denied admission to schools attended by white children under laws requiring or permitting segregation according to race. This segregation was alleged to deprive the plaintiffs of the equal protection of the laws under the Fourteenth Amendment. In each of the cases other than the Delaware case, a three-judge federal district court denied relief to the plaintiffs on the so-called "separate but equal" doctrine announced by this Court in *Plessy* v. *Ferguson*, 163 U.S. 537. Under that doctrine, equality of treatment is accorded when the races are provided substantially equal facilities, even though these facilities be separate. In the Delaware case, the Supreme Court of Delaware adhered to that doctrine, but ordered that the plaintiffs be admitted to the white schools because of their superiority to the Negro schools.

The plaintiffs contend that segregated public schools are not "equal" and cannot be made "equal," and that hence they are deprived of the equal protection of the laws. . . .

* * *

In the first cases in this Court construing the Fourteenth Amendment, decided shortly after its adoption, the Court interpreted it as proscribing all state-imposed discriminations against the Negro race. The doctrine of "separate but equal" did not make its appearance in this Court until 1896 in the case of *Plessy* v. *Ferguson, supra,* involving not education but transportation. American courts have since labored with the doctrine for over half a century. In this Court, there have been six cases involving the "separate but equal" doctrine in the field of public education. In *Cumming* v. *County Board of Education,* 175 U.S. 528, and *Gong Lum* v. *Rice,* 275 U.S. 78, the validity of the doctrine itself was not challenged. In more recent cases, all on the graduate school level, inequality was found in that specific benefits enjoyed by white students were denied to Negro students of the same educational qualifications. *Missouri ex rel. Gaines* v. *Canada,* 305 U.S. 337; *Sipuel* v. *Oklahoma,* 332 U.S. 631; *Sweatt* v. *Painter,* 339 U.S. 629; *McLaurin* v. *Oklahoma State Regents,* 339 U.S. 637. In none of these cases was it necessary to re-examine the doctrine to grant relief to the Negro plaintiff. And in *Sweatt* v. *Painter, supra,* the Court expressly reserved decision on the question whether *Plessy* v. *Ferguson* should be held inapplicable to public education.

In the instant cases, that question is directly presented. Here, unlike *Sweatt* v. *Painter,* there are findings below that the Negro and white schools involved have been equalized, or are being equalized, with respect to buildings, curricula, qualifications and salaries of teachers, and other "tangible" factors. Our decision, therefore, cannot turn on merely a comparison of these tangible factors in the Negro and white schools involved in each of the cases. We must look instead to the effect of segregation itself on public education.

In approaching this problem, we cannot turn the clock back to 1868, when the Amendment was adopted, or even to 1896 when *Plessy* v. *Ferguson* was written. We must consider public education in the light of its full development and its present place in American life throughout the nation. Only in this way can it be determined if segregation in public schools deprives these plaintiffs of the equal protection of the laws.

Today, education is perhaps the most important function of state and local governments. Compulsory school attendance laws and the great expenditures for education both demonstrate our recognition of the importance of education to our democratic society. It is required in the performance of our most basic public responsibilities, even service in the armed forces. It is the very foundation of good citizenship. Today it is a principal instrument in awakening the child to cultural values, in preparing him for later professional training, and in helping him to adjust normally to his environment. In these days, it is doubtful that any child may reasonably be expected to succeed in life if he is denied the opportunity of an education. Such an opportunity, where the state has undertaken to provide it, is a right which must be made available to all on equal terms.

We come then to the question presented: Does segregation of children in public schools solely on the basis of race, even though the physical facilities and other "tangible" factors may be equal, deprive the children of the minority group of equal educational opportunities? We believe that it does.

In *Sweatt* v. *Painter, supra*, in finding that a segregated law school for Negroes could not provide them equal educational opportunities, this Court relied in large part on "those qualities which are incapable of objective measurement but which make for greatness in a law school." In *McLaurin* v. *Oklahoma State Regents, supra*, the Court, in requiring that a Negro admitted to a white graduate school be treated like all other students, again resorted to intangible considerations: ". . . his ability to study, to engage in discussions and exchange views with other students, and, in general, to learn his profession." Such considerations apply with added force to children in grade and high schools. To separate them from others of similar age and qualifications solely because of their race generates a feeling of inferiority as to their status in the community that may affect their hearts and minds in a way unlikely ever to be undone. . . . Whatever may have been the extent of psychological knowledge at the time of *Plessy* v. *Ferguson*, this finding is amply supported by modern authority. Any language in *Plessy* v. *Ferguson* contrary to this finding is rejected.

We conclude that in the field of public education the doctrine of "separate but equal" has no place. Separate educational facilities are inherently unequal. Therefore, we hold that the plaintiffs and others similarly situated for whom the actions have been brought are, by reason of the segregation complained of, deprived of the equal protection of the laws guaranteed by the Fourteenth Amendment. This disposition makes unnecessary any discussion whether such segregation also violates the Due Process Clause of the Fourteenth Amendment.

Because these are class actions, because of the wide applicability of this decision, and because of the great variety of local conditions, the formulation of decrees in these cases presents problems of considerable complexity. On reargument, the consideration of appropriate relief was necessarily subordinated to the primary question—the constitutionality of segregation in public education. We have now announced that such segregation is a denial of the equal protection of the laws. In order that we may have the full assistance of the parties in formulating decrees, the cases will be restored to the docket, and the parties are requested to present further argument on Questions 4 and 5 previously propounded by the Court for the reargument this Term. The Attorney General of the United States is again invited to participate. The Attorneys General of the states requiring or permitting segregation in public education will also be permitted to appear as *amici curiae* upon request to do so by September 15, 1954, and submission of briefs by October 1, 1954.

It is so ordered.

May 17, 1954

Source: 347 U.S. 483 (1954).

9.3. Southern Congressmen's Declaration on Integration, March 12, 1956

> Reacting to the *Brown* II decision in 1955 ordering integration be accomplished "with all deliberate speed," ninety-six southern congressmen put out this declaration. It was published in the *New York Times* on March 12, 1956. They condemned the Court for violating the Constitution and the rights of the states, and urged their states to defy it "by all lawful means."

We regard the decision of the Supreme Court in the school cases as clear abuse of judicial power. It climaxes a trend in the Federal judiciary undertaking to legislate, in derogation of the authority of Congress, and to encroach upon the reserved rights of the states and the people.

The original Constitution does not mention education. Neither does the Fourteenth Amendment nor any other amendment. The debates preceding the submission of the Fourteenth Amendment clearly show that there was no intent that it should affect the systems of education maintained by the states.

The very Congress which proposed the amendment subsequently provided for segregated schools in the District of Columbia.

When the amendment was adopted in 1868, there were thirty-seven states of the Union. Every one of the twenty-six states that had any substantial racial differences among its people either approved the operation of segregated schools already in existence or subsequently established such schools by action of the same law-making body which considered the Fourteenth Amendment.

As admitted by the Supreme Court in the public school case (*Brown v. Board of Education*), the doctrine of separate but equal schools "apparently originated in Roberts v. City of Boston (1849), upholding school segregation against attack as being violative of a state constitutional guarantee of equality." This constitutional doctrine began in the North—not in the South—and it was followed not only in Massachusetts but in Connecticut, New York, Illinois, Indiana, Michigan, Minnesota, New Jersey, Ohio, Pennsylvania and other northern states until they, exercising their rights as states through the constitutional processes of local self-government, changed their school systems.

In the case of Plessy v. Ferguson in 1896 the Supreme Court expressly declared that under the Fourteenth Amendment no person was denied any of his rights if the states provided separate but equal public facilities. This decision has been followed in many other cases. It is notable that the Supreme Court, speaking through Chief Justice Taft, a former President of the United States, unanimously declared in 1927 in Lum v. Rice that the "separate but equal" principle is ". . . within the discretion of the state in regulating its public schools and does not conflict with the Fourteenth Amendment."

This interpretation, restated time and again, became a part of the life of the people of many of the states and confirmed their habits, customs, traditions and way of life. It is founded on elemental humanity and common sense, for parents should not be deprived by Government of the right to direct the lives and education of their own children.

Though there has been no constitutional amendment or act of Congress changing this established legal principle almost a century old, the Supreme Court of the United States, with no legal basis for such action, undertook to exercise their naked judicial power and substituted their personal political and social ideas for the established law of the land.

This unwarranted exercise of power by the court, contrary to the Constitution, is creating chaos and confusion in the states principally affected. It is destroying the amicable relations between the white and

Negro races that have been created through ninety years of patient effort by the good people of both races. It has planted hatred and suspicion where there has been heretofore friendship and understanding.

Without regard to the consent of the governed, outside agitators are threatening immediate and revolutionary changes in our public school systems. If done, this is certain to destroy the system of public education in some of the states.

With the gravest concern for the explosive and dangerous condition created by this decision and inflamed by outside meddlers:

We reaffirm our reliance on the Constitution as the fundamental law of the land.

We decry the Supreme Court's encroachments on rights reserved to the states and to the people, contrary to established law and to the Constitution.

We commend the motives of those states which have declared the intention to resist forced integration by any lawful means.

We appeal to the states and people who are not directly affected by these decisions to consider the constitutional principles involved against the time when they too, on issues vital to them, may be the victims of judicial encroachment.

Even though we constitute a minority in the present Congress, we have full faith that a majority of the American people believe in the dual system of government which has enabled us to achieve our greatness and will in time demand that the reserved rights of the states and of the people be made secure against judicial usurpation.

We pledge ourselves to use all lawful means to bring about a reversal of this decision which is contrary to the Constitution and to prevent the use of force in its implementation.

In this trying period, as we all seek to right this wrong, we appeal to our people not to be provoked by the agitators and troublemakers invading our states and to scrupulously refrain from disorder and lawless acts.

Source: "Southern Congressmen's Declaration of Integration," *New York Times*, March 12, 1956.

9.4.   President Eisenhower's Address on the Little Rock Crisis

On September 24, 1957, President Dwight D. Eisenhower appeared on television to condemn the violence in Little Rock over integration. It was the first time that the president had spoken out on civil rights and southern resistance to integration.

My Fellow Citizens. . . . I must speak to you about the serious situation that has arisen in Little Rock. . . . In that city, under the leadership of demagogic extremists, disorderly mobs have deliberately prevented the carrying out of proper orders from a federal court. Local authorities have not eliminated that violent opposition and, under the law, I yesterday issued a proclamation calling upon the mob to disperse.

This morning the mob again gathered in front of the Central High School of Little Rock, obviously for the purpose of again preventing the carrying out of the court's order relating to the admission of Negro children to that school.

Whenever normal agencies prove inadequate to the task and it becomes necessary for the executive branch of the federal government to use its powers and authority to uphold federal courts, the President's responsibility is inescapable.

In accordance with that responsibility, I have today issued an Executive Order directing the use of troops under federal authority to aid in the execution of federal law at Little Rock, Arkansas. This became necessary when my Proclamation of yesterday was not observed, and the obstruction of justice still continues.

It is important that the reasons for my action be understood by all our citizens.

As you know, the Supreme Court of the United States has decided that separate public educational facilities for the races are inherently unequal and therefore compulsory school segregation laws are unconstitutional. . . .

During the past several years, many communities in our southern states have instituted public school plans for gradual progress in the enrollment and attendance of school children of all races in order to bring themselves into compliance with the law of the land.

They thus demonstrated to the world that we are a nation in which laws, not men, are supreme.

I regret to say that this truth—the cornerstone of our liberties—was not observed in this instance. . . .

Here is the sequence of events in the development of the Little Rock school case.

In May of 1955, the Little Rock School Board approved a moderate plan for the gradual desegregation of the public schools in that city. It provided that a start toward integration would be made at the present term in the high school, and that the plan would be in full operation by 1963. . . . Now this Little Rock plan was challenged in the courts by some who believed that the period of time as proposed in the plan was too long.

The United States Court at Little Rock, which has supervisory responsibility under the law for the plan of desegregation in the public schools, dismissed the challenge, thus approving a gradual rather than an abrupt change from the existing system. The court found that the school board had acted in good faith in planning for a public school system free from racial discrimination.

Since that time, the court has on three separate occasions issued orders directing that the plan be carried out. All persons were instructed to refrain from interfering with the efforts of the school board to comply with the law.

Proper and sensible observance of the law then demanded the respectful obedience which the nation has a right to expect from all its people. This, unfortunately, has not been the case at Little Rock. Certain misguided persons, many of them imported into Little Rock by agitators, have insisted upon defying the law and have sought to bring it into disrepute. The orders of the court have thus been frustrated.

The very basis of our individual rights and freedoms rests upon the certainly that the President and the Executive Branch of Government will support and insure the carrying out of the decisions of the federal courts, even, when necessary with all the means at the President's command. . . .

Mob rule cannot be allowed to override the decisions of our courts.

Now, let me make it very clear that federal troops are not being used to relieve local and state authorities of their primary duty to preserve the peace and order of the community. . . .

The proper use of the powers of the Executive Branch to enforce the orders of a federal court is limited to extraordinary and compelling circumstances. Manifestly, such an extreme situation has been created in Little Rock. This challenge must be met and with such measures as will preserve to the people as a whole their lawfully protected rights in a climate permitting their free and fair exercise.

The overwhelming majority of our people in every section of the country are united in their respect for observance of the law—even in those cases where they may disagree with that law. . . .

A foundation of our American way of life is our national respect for law.

In the South, as elsewhere, citizens are keenly aware of the tremendous disservice that has been done to the people of Arkansas in the eyes of the nation, and that has been done to the nation in the eyes of the world.

At a time when we face grave situations abroad because of the hatred that communism bears toward a system of government based on human rights, it would be difficult to exaggerate the harm that is being done to the prestige and influence, and indeed to the safety, of our nation and the world.

Our enemies are gloating over this incident and using it everywhere to misrepresent our whole nation. We are portrayed as a violator of those standards of conduct which the peoples of the world united to proclaim in the Charter of the United Nations. There they affirmed "faith in fundamental human rights" and "in the dignity and worth of the human person" and they did so "without distinction as to race, sex, language or religion."

And so, with deep confidence, I call upon the citizens of the State of Arkansas to assist in bringing to an immediate end all interference with the law and its processes. If resistance to the federal court orders ceases at once, the further presence of federal troops will be unnecessary and the City of Little Rock will return to its normal habits of peace and order and a blot upon the fair name and high honor of our nation in the world will be removed.

Thus will be restored the image of America and of all its parts as one nation, indivisible, with liberty and justice for all.

Source: Public Papers of the Presidents: Dwight D. Eisenhower, no. 198 (1957).

9.5.   *Cooper v. Aaron* (1958)

> This unanimous decision was the Supreme Court's response to the situation in Little Rock in particular, and to southern defiance of the *Brown* rulings in general. It flatly denied the states the right to interpret the Constitution and refuse compliance with decisions of the Court.

Opinion of the Court by the Chief Justice, Mr. Justice Black, Mr. Justice Frankfurter, Mr. Justice Douglas, Mr. Justice Burton, Mr. Justice Clark, Mr. Justice Harlan, Mr. Justice Brennan, and Mr. Justice Whittaker:

As this case reaches us it raises questions of the highest importance to the maintenance of our federal system of government. It necessarily involves a claim by the governor and legislature of a state that there is no duty on state officials to obey federal court orders resting on this Court's considered interpretation of the United States Constitution. Specifically it involves actions by the governor and legislature of Arkansas upon the premise that they are not bound by our holding in Brown v. Board of Education, 347 U.S. 483. . . .

On May 17, 1954, this Court decided that enforced racial segregation in the public schools of a state is a denial of the equal protection of the laws enjoined by the Fourteenth Amendment. Brown v. Board of Education.

The Court postponed, pending further argument, formulations of a decree to effectuate this decision. That decree was rendered May 31, 1955. Brown v. Board of Education, 349 U.S. 294. In the formulation of that decree the Court recognized that good faith compliance with the principles declared in Brown might in some situations "call for elimination of a variety of obstacles in making the transition to school systems operated in accordance with the constitutional principles set forth in our May 17, 1954, decision." . . .

Under such circumstances, the district courts were directed to require "a prompt and reasonable start toward full compliance," and to take such action as was necessary to bring about the end of racial segregation in the schools "with all deliberate speed." . . .

* * *

One may well sympathize with the position of the Board in the face of the frustrating conditions which have confronted it, but, regardless of the Board's good faith, the actions of the other state agencies responsible for those conditions compel us to reject the Board's legal position. . . .

The constitutional rights of respondents are not to be sacrificed or yielded to the violence and disorder which have followed upon the actions of the Governor and Legislature. . . .

. . . the constitutional rights of children not to be discriminated against in school admission on grounds of race or color declared by this Court in the Brown case can neither be nullified openly and directly by state legislators or state executive or judicial officers, nor nullified indirectly by them through evasive schemes for segregation whether attempted "ingeniously or ingenuously." Smith v. Texas, 311 U.S. 128.

* * *

Article VI of the Constitution makes the Constitution the "supreme Law of the Land." In 1803, Chief Justice Marshall, speaking for a unanimous Court, referring to the Constitution as "the fundamental and paramount law of the nation," declared in the notable case of Marbury v. Madison that "It is emphatically the province and duty of the judicial department to say what the law is." This decision declared the basic principle that the federal judiciary is supreme in the exposition of the law of the Constitution, and that principle has ever since been respected by this Court and the country as a permanent and indispensable feature of our constitutional system. It follows that the interpretation of the Fourteenth Amendment enunciated by this Court in the Brown case is the supreme law of the land. . . .

No state legislator or executive or judicial officer can war against the Constitution without violating his undertaking to support it. . . .

It is, of course, quite true that the responsibility for public education is primarily the concern of the states, but it is equally true that such responsibilities, like all other state activity, must be exercised consistently with federal constitutional requirements as they apply to state action.

The Constitution created a government dedicated to equal justice under law. The Fourteenth Amendment embodied and emphasized that ideal. State support of segregated schools through any arrangement, management, funds, or property cannot be squared with the Amendment's command that no state shall deny to any person within its jurisdiction the equal protection of the laws. The right of a student not to be segregated on racial grounds in schools so maintained is indeed so fundamental and pervasive that it is embraced in the concept of due process of law. Bolling v. Sharpe, 347 U.S. 497. The basic decision in Brown was unanimously reached by this Court only after the case had been briefed and twice argued and the issue had been given the most serious consideration. Since the first Brown opinion three new Justices have come to the Court. They are at one with the Justices still on the Court who participated in that basic decision as to its correctness, and that decision is now unanimously reaffirmed. The principles announced in that decision and the obedience of the states to them, according to the command of the Constitution, are indispensable for the protection of the freedoms guaranteed by our fundamental charter for all of us. Our constitutional ideal of equal justice under law is thus made a living truth.

Source: 358 U.S. 1 (1958).

9.6.   Title II, Civil Rights Act, 1964

> In this section of the act, as well as in the other parts of the statute, Congress gave the federal government the power to ensure racial integration in employment, public accommodations, voting, and employment opportunity.

Sec. 201. (a) All persons shall be entitled to the full and equal enjoyment of the goods, services, facilities, privileges, advantages, and accommodations of any place of public accommodation, as defined in this section, without discrimination or segregation on the ground of race, color, religion, or national origin.

(b) Each of the following establishments which serves the public is a place of public accommodation within the meaning of this title if its operations affect commerce, or if discrimination or segregation by it is supported by State action:

(1) any inn, hotel, motel, or other establishment which provides lodging to transient guests, other than an establishment located within a building which contains not more than five rooms for rent or hire and which is actually occupied by the proprietor of such establishment as his residence;

(2) any restaurant, cafeteria, lunchroom, lunch counter, soda fountain, or other facility principally engaged in selling food for consumption on the premises, including, but not limited to, any such facility located on the premises of any retail establishment; or any gasoline station;

(3) any motion picture house, theater, concert hall, sports arena, stadium or other place of exhibition or entertainment; and

(4) any establishment (A)(i) which is physically located within the premises of any establishment otherwise covered by this subsection, or (ii) within the premises of which is physically located any such covered establishment, and (B) which holds itself out as serving patrons of such covered establishment.

(c) The operations of an establishment affect commerce within the meaning of this title if (1) it is one of the establishments described in paragraph (1) of subsection (b); (2) in the case of an establishment described in paragraph (2) of subsection (b), it serves or offers to serve interstate travelers or a substantial portion of the food which it serves, or gasoline or other products which it sells, has moved in commerce; (3) in the case of an establishment described in paragraph (3) of subsection (b), it customarily presents films, performances, athletic teams, exhibitions, or other sources of entertainment which move in commerce; and (4) in the case of an establishment described in paragraph (4) of subsection (b), it is physically located within the premises of, or there is physically located within its premises, an establishment the operations of which affect commerce within the meaning of this subsection. For purposes of this section, "commerce" means travel, trade, traffic, commerce, transportation, or communication among the several States, or between the District of Columbia and any State, or between any foreign country or any territory or possession and any State or the District of Columbia, or between points in the same State but through any other State or the District of Columbia or a foreign country.

(d) Discrimination or segregation by an establishment is supported by State action within the meaning of this title if such discrimination or segregation (1) is carried on under color of any law, statute, ordinance, or regulation; or (2) is carried on under color of any custom or usage required or enforced by officials of the State or political subdivision thereof; or (3) is required by action of the State or political subdivision thereof. . . .

(e) The provisions of this title shall not apply to a private club or other establishment not in fact open to the public, except to the extent that the facilities of such establishment are made available to the customers or patrons of an establishment within the scope of subsection (b).

Sec. 202. All persons shall be entitled to be free at any establishment or place, from discrimination or segregation of any kind on the ground of race, color, religion, or national origin, if such discrimination or segregation is or purports to be required by any law, statute, ordinance, regulation, rule, or order of a State or any agency or political subdivision thereof.

Sec. 203. No person shall (a) withhold, deny, or attempt to withhold or deny, or deprive or attempt to deprive, any person of any right or privilege secured by section 201 or 202, or (b) intimidate, threaten, or coerce, or attempt to intimidate, threaten, or coerce any person with the purpose of interfering with any right or privilege secured by section 201 or 202, or (c) punish or attempt to punish any person for exercising or attempting to exercise any right or privilege secured by section 201 or 202.

Source: U.S. Statutes at Large 78 (1964) 241.

ANNOTATED RESEARCH GUIDE

Books

Branch, Taylor. *Parting the Waters: America in the King Years, 1954–63.* New York: Simon and Schuster, 1988; and *Pillar of Fire: America in the King Years, 1963–1965.* New York: Simon and Schuster, 1998. A finely researched narrative of the civil rights movement in the South as it was organized by the Reverend Martin Luther King, Jr.

Chafe, William H. *Civilities and Civil Rights: Greensboro, North Carolina, and the Black Struggle for Equality.* New York: Oxford University Press, 1981. Focuses on the city of Greensboro between 1945 and 1975 and examines the complex "etiquette of civility" that permeated the struggle for racial justice, black protest movements, and ordinary interaction between blacks and whites in the community.

Chappell, David L. *Inside Agitators: White Southerners in the Civil Rights Movement.* Baltimore: Johns Hopkins University Press, 1994. The best analysis of white support for the movement for racial justice.

Kluger, Richard. *Simple Justice: The History of Brown v. Board of Education and Black America's Struggle for Equality.* New York: Alfred A. Knopf, 1976. The most comprehensive history of the desegregation struggle in the United States from the Jim Crow era through the Supreme Court's landmark decision.

Morris, Aldon D. *The Origins of the Civil Rights Movement: Black Communities Organizing for Change.* New York: Free Press, 1979. A significant examination that uses historical records and social theory to emphasize the ways ordinary black people, acting through church organizations, moved toward the cause of civil rights before 1960.

Patterson, James T. *Brown v. Board of Education.* New York: Oxford University Press, 2000. Summarizes the criticism of the *Brown* decision that has developed since 1954. These detractors include African Americans who found *Brown* racist and agree with Justice Clarence Thomas's contention that it reflected "an assumption of black inferiority." Others criticize *Brown*'s vagueness or complain that the decision's immediate impact was to halt the mellowing of race relations in the South and encourage white supremacists.

Raines, Howell. *My Soul Is Rested: Movement Days in the Deep South Remembered.* New York: Penguin Books, 1983. Perhaps the most reliable oral history of the civil rights movement by one who participated in it as a journalist and interviewed a diverse group of participants.

Robinson, Jo Ann Gibson. *The Montgomery Bus Boycott and the Women Who Started It.* Knoxville: University of Tennessee Press, 1987. Edited by David J. Garrow as a memoir by one of the key figures in organizing the Montgomery bus boycott. Focuses on the role of both working-class and middle-class black women.

Sitkoff, Harvard. *The Struggle for Black Equality, 1954–1980.* Rev. ed. New York: Hill and Wang, 1981. Provides one of the best and most succinct narrative interpretations of the civil rights movement. Includes an excellent biographical essay on sources up to 1975.

Tushnet, Mark V. *The NAACP's Legal Strategy Against Segregated Education.* Chapel Hill: University of North Carolina Press, 1987. A detailed history of the important role Thurgood Marshall played in leading the fight against educational segregation in state and federal courts.

Weisbrot, Robert. *Freedom Bound: A History of America's Civil Rights Movement.* New York: W. W. Norton, 1990. A penetrating one-volume history of the movement that emphasizes the strained relationships between blacks and white liberals. Ties the movement into the overall history of reform in America.

Nonprint Sources

Web Sites

http://foioa.fbi.gov/marshall.htm. FBI Freedom of Information Act page has documents on Thurgood Marshall: 1,394 pages of records relating to Marshall's activities with the National Association for the Advancement of Colored People.

http://www.nps.gov/brvb. Homepage for the *Brown v. Board of Education* National Historic Site.

http://www.sjbc.org/lr.htm. "1957 Desegregation at Little Rock, Arkansas" is a history and timeline of the desegregation of Little Rock's public schools.

http://usinfo.state.gov/usa/infousa/facts/democrac/37.htm. An introduction to the Supreme Court's opinion in *Cooper v. Aaron.*

Videos

The American Experience: George Wallace—Settin' the Woods on Fire. PBS Video, 180 minutes, Code A3917.

The Ground Beneath Our Feet: Virginia's History Since the Civil War—Massive Resistance. Central Virginia Public Television; George H. Gilliam, 2000.

Thurgood Marshall: Portrait of an American Hero. PBS Series. 30 minutes on one tape, Code MARDX0. Columbia Video Productions.

10

The Supreme Court, Women's Rights, and Abortion

Roe v. Wade was one of the most divisive opinions of the Supreme Court after *Brown* involving the significant extension of federal power into areas formerly under local control. In the 1973 decision, the Court struck down forty-six state laws regulating a woman's right to terminate her pregnancy. This judicial extension of federal authority did not come out of the blue, for it was in many ways the result of the movement for women's rights and equality that began in the 1960s. It also was in some ways a spin-off of the black civil rights movement, which focused on the power of federal courts and Congress to rectify the inequities of racism. And like those who led other social movements in the "rights revolution" of the 1960s and after, women's rights advocates looked to the federal government to provide relief from discrimination in the workplace, education, and public life and to create and enforce uniform national standards of equality and justice.

One of the earliest signs of the federal government's entrance into the area of women's rights appeared in 1961 when President John F. Kennedy created the Commission on the Status of Women, which, in 1963, published *American Women*, a study that recommended that all obstacles be removed to women's full participation in education, employment, and the "legal treatment of women in respect to civil and political rights." Within four years every state had its own commission studying, and sometimes pursuing, the same goals.

In 1964 the Civil Rights Act outlawed discrimination on the basis of sex and established the Equal Employment Opportunity Commission to eliminate job discrimination because of sex or race. But little progress resulted from either *American Women* or enforcement of the Civil Rights Act. Consequently, in 1966 the National Organization for Women (NOW) began to lobby for federal laws guaranteeing women equal rights with men and to pursue gender equality in the federal courts.

Their cause got a boost in the 1960s with the rise of a new generation of feminists sparked by the publication of Betty Friedan's *The Feminine Mystique* (1963). Writing about the suburban housewife, Friedan identified a "problem with no name," the prevailing mystique of the happy middle-class homemaker. Friedan exploded the myth that "she had everything that women ever dreamed of" and the glorification of her occupation as a housewife. Radical feminists such as Charlotte Bunch pursued "personal politics" and argued that every personal issue was a political one. She and others condemned the treatment of women as second-class citizens and protested that the Miss America pageant in Atlantic City was an insult to womanhood. In 1970 prominent feminist Gloria Steinem testified before the Senate Judiciary Committee for an equal rights amendment to the Constitution. Most women, she said, "both wage-earners and housewives, routinely suffer . . . humiliation and injustice." She believed that they suffered "second class treatment from the moment they are born." "The law makes much more sense," she testified, "when it treats individuals, not groups bundled together by some condition of birth." In 1972 Congress, in the Educational Amendments to the 1965 Higher Education Act, Title IX, required that all women athletes in state colleges and universities receive the same financial aid as male athletes.

In that same session Congress sent to the states the Equal Rights Amendment (ERA), which forbade the denial of "equality of rights under the law" because of sex. But the amendment failed the required three-fourths majority when only thirty-five states ratified it. Part of the reason for the amendment's failure was the steady rise of vocal opposition against it, some from women themselves. Phyllis Schlafly, for example, stated categorically that the ERA "will not give women anything which they do not already have, or have a way of getting, but it will take away from women some of their most important legal rights, benefits and exemptions." The amendment, she wrote in *Trial Magazine* in 1973, "is like trying to kill a fly with a sledgehammer; you probably won't kill the fly, but you surely will break up some of the furniture." The Reverend Jerry Falwell of the Moral Majority, a conservative, states' rights organization committed to the election of God-fearing candidates to political office who stood for values important to Christians, saw the amendment both as a delusion and as a threat to "the foundation of our entire social structure." Despite the amendment's defeat, eighteen states adopted their own Equal Rights Amendments and gave their courts a higher standard with which to fight gender discrimination than that used in the Fourteenth Amendment. And in 1975 a Washington State court vacated laws that prohibited qualified girls from engaging in interscholastic high school athletics.

In 1965 the Supreme Court, in *Griswold v. Connecticut*, handed down a landmark decision in the history of judicial extension of federal power into areas controlled by the states. It was an opinion that not only expanded federalism but also discovered a new constitutional right and placed the federal courts in the vanguard of protecting women from state intrusion on this right. In a 7 to 2 vote, it handed down what legal historian Kermit L. Hall describes as "one of the most important [decisions] of the twentieth century," one that "in its argument and effect . . . revealed much about the way in which the Court was attempting to adapt the Constitution to new realities."[1] Here the Court struck down an 1879 Connecticut law that made it a crime to use, or to provide information on, birth control because the statute violated the right to privacy in marriage.

Justice William O. Douglas, in the majority opinion, argued that the "zones of privacy" emanating from the Bill of Rights, specifically the First, Third, Fourth, Fifth, and Ninth Amendments, "created several fundamental constitutional guarantees," among which was the right of married people to privacy. This right was "older than the Bill of Rights—older than our political parties, older than our school system." "Marriage," he wrote, "is a coming together for better or for worse, hopefully enduring, and intimate to the degree of being sacred," into which this state law could not intrude. Justice Arthur Goldberg, in a concurring opinion, emphasized the importance of the Ninth Amendment in establishing the constitutional right of marital privacy. He wrote that it revealed that "the Framers of the Constitution believed that there are additional fundamental rights, protected from governmental infringement, which exist alongside those fundamental rights specifically mentioned in the first eight constitutional amendments." "To hold that a right so basic and fundamental and so deep-rooted in our society as the right of privacy in marriage may be infringed because that right is not guaranteed in so many words by the first eight amendments," he stated, "is to ignore the Ninth Amendment and to give it no effect whatsoever."

The next decision by the Supreme Court extending federal jurisdiction to women's rights over and against that of the states, *Roe v. Wade*, was one of the century's most controversial. Handed down in 1973 by a 7 to 2 vote, it raised serious questions not just about women's constitutional rights but about the authority of the states to deal with strongly held social and religious values. The case was initiated as a class action suit brought by Norma McCorvey, an unmarried, pregnant woman who used a pseudonym, Jane Roe, to challenge Texas laws that criminalized abortion except when the life of the mother was at risk. Her attorneys argued that the statutes were a denial of the Fourteenth Amendment's due process guarantees and that the rights of the state must be balanced against the "right of privacy" of the mother. Justice Harry Blackmun's majority opinion faced squarely the issues raised by *Griswold*, where the justices had affirmed a right to privacy in marriage but had disagreed on its sources and reach. His thirty-one-page opinion used both history and case law to vacate state laws on abortion and expand the right of privacy beyond married couples, as established in *Griswold*.

Blackmun's historical sketch of abortion law showed that in common law during the colonial period an "abortion performed *before* 'quickening'—the first recognizable movement of the fetus *in utero*, appearing usually from the 16th to the 18th week of pregnancy—was not an indictable offense." He further claimed that "the law in effect in all but a few States until mid-19th century was the pre-existing English common law." After the Civil War, states prohibited abortion after quickening "but were lenient with it before quickening." Over time, though, the distinction between abortion before and after quickening disappeared, and by the 1950s "a large majority of the jurisdictions banned abortion . . . unless done to save or preserve the life of the mother." This statutory intervention was justified to discourage sexual misconduct and to assure safe medical abortion procedures. But, Blackmun reasoned, these considerations were no longer viable; no one in 1973 took the sexual misconduct factor seriously, and modern medical techniques had made abortion "now relatively safe."

The third historic reason for the state's interest in abortion was to protect prenatal life. On this sensitive moral question, Blackmun wrote carefully, asserting that "a legitimate state interest in this area need not stand or fall on acceptance of the belief that life begins at conception or at some other point prior to live birth." "In assessing the State's interest," he affirmed, "recognition may be given to the less rigid claim that as long as at least *potential* life is involved, the State may assert interests beyond the protection of the pregnant woman alone." Still, since state anti-abortion laws had adopted the quickening distinction, these statutes "tacitly" recognize "the greater health hazards inherent in late abortion and impliedly [repudiate] the theory that life begins at conception."

Referring to *Griswold*, he wrote that the right of privacy included "activities relating to marriage, procreation, contraception, family relationships, and child rearing and education." But, he argued, the right to privacy was "broad enough to encompass a woman's decision whether or not to terminate her pregnancy." This right was not absolute because "a State may regulate the abortion procedure to the extent that the regulation reasonably relates to the preservation and protection of maternal health." During the first trimester the decision to have an abortion "may be effectuated by an abortion free of interference by the State." During the second trimester pregnancy was a greater risk to the mother's health, and states could regulate abortion to protect it. Only during the third trimester could the state impose severe restrictions on abortion, but even then the reason had to be to safeguard the woman's life.

Justice William H. Rehnquist's dissent provided arguments that opponents of *Roe* would use for the next three decades. "I have difficulty in concluding, as the Court does," he wrote, "that the right of 'privacy' is involved in this case. . . . A transaction resulting in an operation such as this is not 'private' in the ordinary usage of that word." The Court, he stated, had completely misunderstood the history of the due process clause of the Fourteenth Amendment, and "the Court's opinion will accomplish the seemingly impossible feat of leaving this area of the law more confused than it found it." Moreover, the "decision here to break pregnancy into three distinct terms and to outline the permissible restrictions the State may impose in each one, for example, partakes more of judicial legislation than it does of a determination of the intent of the drafters of the Fourteenth Amendment."

At the same time that the Court was dealing with state intrusion into a woman's right of privacy, it ruled in two key cases involving state laws that created sexual discrimination. In a unanimous 1971 ruling in *Reed v. Reed*, it held for the first time that statutory gender discrimination violated the Fourteenth Amendment's equal protection clause. An Idaho law had established preferential categories based on sex in selecting administrators for individuals who died without a will. Chief Justice Warren Burger held that "giving a mandatory preference to members of either sex over members of the other . . . constitutes an arbitrary legislative choice forbidden by the equal protection clause." All such legislation, to be constitutional, "must be reasonable, not arbitrary." Two years later, in *Frontiero v. Richardson*, the justices further prohibited sex discrimination in federal law. The case struck down a statute that gave an extra salary supplement, a housing allowance, and extra medical benefits to married males in the armed services. By a vote of 8 to 1, it held that all job-related classifications based on sex were "inherently suspect" and "unconstitutional."

A conservative backlash soon began to build against these Supreme Court decisions and the intrusion of federal law into state and local "rights." *Roe v. Wade* and abortion were targeted for attack. Illinois congressman Henry Hyde, in every session between 1976 and 1979, introduced resolutions to end Medicaid funds for abortions "except where the life of the mother would be endangered." In 1982 the Senate supported three proposed amendments to the Constitution against abortion. This same Senate also passed Senate Bill 158, the Human Life Statute. It proclaimed that "Congress finds that present day scientific evidence in-

dicates a significant likelihood that actual human life exists from conception." And some states, among them South Dakota, enacted
resolutions calling for a constitutional convention to propose human
rights amendments.

Under the leadership of President Ronald Reagan and a new Chief
Justice, William H. Rehnquist, the conservative assault on abortion and
the right of privacy intensified. Reagan issued an executive order with-
holding money from clinics that practiced or counseled abortion. In 1989
the Rehnquist Court, by a vote of 5 to 4, watered down *Roe v. Wade* in
Webster v. Reproductive Health Services. The case, a suit between William
L. Webster, the attorney general of Missouri, and Reproductive Health
Services (supported by a friend-of-the court brief by the American Civil
Liberties Union), essentially reversed anti–states' rights rulings of the
Warren-Burger Courts by upholding a state law that imposed restrictions
on abortion. The preamble to the Missouri law said that life began at
conception and that this "human being" could be protected by state law.
Another section forbade the use of public facilities to perform abortions
that were not essential "to save the life of the mother." A third part of
the law stopped the use of public funds for "encouraging or counselling"
a woman to have an unnecessary abortion. The fourth provision of the
state statute, the most controversial, imposed medical examinations on
a pregnant woman seeking an abortion during the second trimester.

The Court, in the majority opinion written by Chief Justice Rehnquist,
held that the preamble, with its statement that life began at conception,
was not a legal issue. It was not applied "to restrict the activities of the
appellees in some concrete way." Until it was, the Court was "not empowered to decide . . . abstract propositions." On the provision barring
the use of state facilities for abortions, Rehnquist stated that this was
consistent with a ban on public funding of abortions decided in a 1980
Supreme Court case, *Harris v. McRae*, where it sustained a congressional
law that withheld from states federal Medicaid funds to reimburse the
costs of abortions. On the fourth provision, Rehnquist admitted that it
amounted to the state promoting its "interest in potential human life
rather than in maternal health." It also violated the "rigid trimester analysis of the course of a pregnancy enunciated in *Roe.*" But he went on to
criticize the "rigid *Roe* framework" as inconsistent with the "Constitution
cast in general terms, as ours is." He saw no reason why the state's
"interest in protecting potential human life should come into existence
only at the point of viability," or the third trimester. Missouri had chosen
an earlier period for the physician to "determine viability," and "the
State's interest in protecting potential human life . . . we therefore believe
to be constitutional." Even though the majority ruling did not overturn
Roe, it sanctioned state regulations at any point in the pregnancy to promote its interest in protecting potential life, even by criminal statutes.

Justice Harry Blackmun, who wrote the *Roe* opinion, crafted a scathing dissent. "Today," he began, "*Roe v. Wade*, and the fundamental constitutional right of women to decide whether to terminate a pregnancy, survive but are not secure." He branded the Rehnquist opinion "deceptive" and criticized the Chief Justice for trying to conceal "the real meaning" of the Missouri law—namely, "its intended evisceration" of *Roe v. Wade*. It was an opinion, he wrote, "filled with winks, and nods, and knowing glances to those who would do away with *Roe* explicitly." "I fear for the future," he lamented. "I fear for the liberty and equality of the millions of women who have lived and come of age in the 16 years since *Roe* was decided." "I fear," he concluded, "for the integrity of, and public esteem for, this Court."

Some states, encouraged by the Rehnquist Court, moved against abortion. For example, Pennsylvania enacted an abortion control act that restricted abortions in two ways. First, it required women under the age of eighteen seeking an abortion to have parental consent or a special court order. Second, it mandated that all women must have pre-abortion counseling with a physician and postpone the abortion for twenty-four hours. Most disturbing, physical attacks on abortion clinics and physicians increased.

However, in the 1990s signs appeared of a liberal defense of a woman's right to abortion as defined in *Roe*. In 1993 President William J. Clinton rescinded Reagan's anti-abortion order. And in 1997 the Wisconsin Supreme Court, in *State of Wisconsin v. Kruzicki* (the case of "Ms. M. W."), held that the fetus was not a person under the law and that the state had no jurisdiction over it. The case dealt with William Kruzicki, the sheriff of Waukesha County, and a pregnant woman carrying a viable fetus who was using drugs. In July 1995, the woman's obstetrician had suspected that she was using cocaine and performed blood tests. In September, acting on the physician's information, the Waukesha County Department of Health and Human Services went to the juvenile court and obtained an order to have the sheriff confine the woman in the Waukesha Memorial Hospital in Milwaukee in order to place the unborn child in protective custody. This detention, the court said, "will by necessity result in the detention of the unborn child's mother."

Faced with these circumstances, Ms. M. W. voluntarily entered a drug treatment center. The juvenile court responded by stating that if she left the treatment center she would be taken back to the hospital. It further determined that the fetus was a child and needed the protection of the law. Ms. M. W.'s lawyers appealed the juvenile court's position, maintaining that the fetus was not a person and that the juvenile court had no jurisdiction. When the appeals court upheld the lower court's ruling, the case went to the state supreme court.

The American Civil Liberties Union's Women's Rights Project lawyer argued on behalf of Ms. M. W. and claimed that the juvenile court had trampled on the woman's constitutional rights. The Wisconsin Supreme Court ruled that a fetus is not a child under the state's child welfare laws. It further added, "[W]e find a compelling basis for concluding that the legislature intended a 'child' to mean a human being born alive." It held that the state's argument "that interpreting 'child' to not include a fetus is to work an absurd result, 'by rendering the state's power to protect a child dependent upon whether the child is inside or outside of the womb,'" was a "circular method of reasoning." It was as if "the legislature intended the term 'child' to include a viable fetus because the State must have the power to protect children." "We decline to consider an argument that assumes the result," the court concluded. As the new millennium began, there was no indication that the conflicting positions on the right to privacy and abortion were capable of reconciliation, nor that the federal-state relation to it was any clearer.

NOTE

1. Kermit L. Hall, *The Magic Mirror: Law in American History* (New York: Oxford University Press, 1989), p. 319.

DOCUMENTS

10.1.   *Griswold et al. v. Connecticut* **(1965) and the Right to Privacy in Marriage**

> In 1965 the Warren Court decided one of the most important federalism cases of the twentieth century. It found, in a 7 to 2 vote, in the words of Justice William O. Douglas, the right to privacy in marriage in the "penumbra" of the Bill of Rights. Therefore, a Connecticut law that made the use of contraceptives a crime was invalid as an unconstitutional invasion of this right. Associate Justice Arthur J. Goldberg, joined by Chief Justice Earl Warren and Justice William Joseph Brennan, Jr., concurred. Goldberg, writing the concurrence, emphasized the importance of the Ninth Amendment in establishing this right of privacy.

OPINION: MR. JUSTICE DOUGLAS delivered the opinion of the Court.

* * *

Coming to the merits, we are met with a wide range of questions that implicate the Due Process Clause of the Fourteenth Amendment. Overtones of some arguments suggest that *Lochner* v. *New York* . . . should be our guide. But we decline that invitation as we did in *West Coast Hotel Co.* v. *Parrish.* . . . We do not sit as a super-legislature to determine the wisdom, need, and propriety of laws that touch economic problems, business affairs, or social conditions. This law, however, operates directly on an intimate relation of husband and wife and their physician's role in one aspect of that relation.

The association of people is not mentioned in the Constitution nor in the Bill of Rights. The right to educate a child in a school of the parents' choice—whether public or private or parochial—is also not mentioned. Nor is the right to study any particular subject or any foreign language. Yet the First Amendment has been construed to include certain of those rights.

By *Pierce* v. *Society of Sisters, supra,* the right to educate one's children as one chooses is made applicable to the States by the force of the First and Fourteenth Amendments. By *Meyer* v. *Nebraska, supra,* the same dignity is given the right to study the German language in a private school.

In other words, the State may not, consistently with the spirit of the First Amendment, contract the spectrum of available knowledge. The right of freedom of speech and press includes not only the right to utter or to print, but the right to distribute, the right to receive, the right to read and freedom of inquiry, freedom of thought, and freedom to teach— indeed the freedom of the entire university community. Without those peripheral rights the specific rights would be less secure. And so we reaffirm the principle of the *Pierce* and the *Meyer* cases.

* * *

The foregoing cases suggest that specific guarantees in the Bill of Rights have penumbras, formed by emanations from those guarantees that help give them life and substance. Various guarantees create zones of privacy. The right of association contained in the penumbra of the First Amendment is one, as we have seen. The Third Amendment in its prohibition against the quartering of soldiers "in any house" in time of peace without the consent of the owner is another facet of that privacy. The Fourth Amendment explicitly affirms the "right of the people to be secure in their persons, houses, papers, and effects, against unreasonable searches and seizures." The Fifth Amendment in its Self-Incrimination Clause enables the citizen to create a zone of privacy which government may not force him to surrender to his detriment. The Ninth Amendment provides: "The enumeration in the Constitution, of certain rights, shall not be construed to deny or disparage others retained by the people."

The present case, then, concerns a relationship lying within the zone of privacy created by several fundamental constitutional guarantees. And it concerns a law which, in forbidding the *use* of contraceptives rather than regulating their manufacture or sale, seeks to achieve its goals by means having a maximum destructive impact upon that relationship. Such a law cannot stand in light of the familiar principle, so often applied by this Court, that a "governmental purpose to control or prevent activities constitutionally subject to state regulation may not be achieved by means which sweep unnecessarily broadly and thereby invade the area of protected freedoms." Would we allow the police to search the sacred precincts of marital bedrooms for telltale signs of the use of contraceptives? The very idea is repulsive to the notions of privacy surrounding the marriage relationship.

We deal with a right of privacy older than the Bill of Rights—older than our political parties, older than our school system. Marriage is a coming together for better or for worse, hopefully enduring, and intimate to the degree of being sacred. It is an association that promotes a way of life, not causes; a harmony in living, not political faiths; a bilateral loyalty, not commercial or social projects. Yet it is an association for as noble a purpose as any involved in our prior decisions.

Reversed.

CONCUR: MR. JUSTICE GOLDBERG, whom THE CHIEF JUSTICE and MR. JUSTICE BRENNAN join, concurring.

I agree with the Court that Connecticut's birth-control law unconstitutionally intrudes upon the right of marital privacy, and I join in its opinion and judgment. Although I have not accepted the view that "due process" as used in the Fourteenth Amendment incorporates all of the first eight Amendments . . . I do agree that the concept of liberty protects those personal rights that are fundamental, and is not confined to the specific terms of the Bill of Rights. My conclusion that the concept of liberty is not so restricted and that it embraces the right of marital privacy though that right is not mentioned explicitly in the Constitution[1] is supported both by numerous decisions of this Court, referred to in the Court's opinion, and by the language and history of the Ninth Amendment. In reaching the conclusion that the right of marital privacy is protected, as being within the protected penumbra of specific guarantees of the Bill of Rights, the Court refers to the Ninth Amendment. I add these words to emphasize the relevance of that Amendment to the Court's holding.

* * *

This Court, in a series of decisions, has held that the Fourteenth Amendment absorbs and applies to the States those specifics of the first eight amendments which express fundamental personal rights. The language and history of the Ninth Amendment reveal that the Framers of the Constitution believed that there are additional fundamental rights, protected from governmental infringement, which exist alongside those fundamental rights specifically mentioned in the first eight constitutional amendments.

The Ninth Amendment reads, "The enumeration in the Constitution, of certain rights, shall not be construed to deny or disparage others retained by the people." The Amendment is almost entirely the work of James Madison. It was introduced in Congress by him and passed the House and Senate with little or no debate and virtually no change in language. It was proffered to quiet expressed fears that a bill of specifically enumerated rights could not be sufficiently broad to cover all essential rights and that the specific mention of certain rights would be interpreted as a denial that others were protected.

Although the Constitution does not speak in so many words of the right of privacy in marriage, I cannot believe that it offers these fundamental rights no protection. The fact that no particular provision of the Constitution explicitly forbids the State from disrupting the traditional relation of the family—a relation as old and as fundamental as our entire civilization—surely does not show that the Government was meant to have the power to do so. Rather, as the Ninth Amendment expressly recognizes, there are fundamental personal rights such as this one, which are protected from abridgment by the Government though not specifically mentioned in the Constitution.

NOTE

1. My Brother STEWART dissents on the ground that he "can find no . . . general right of privacy in the Bill of Rights, in any other part of the Constitution, or in any case ever before decided by this Court." *Post*, at 530. He would require a more explicit guarantee than the one which the Court derives from several constitutional amendments. This Court, however, has never held that the Bill of Rights or the Fourteenth Amendment protects only those rights that the Constitution specifically mentions by name. See, *e.g.*, *Bolling* v. *Sharpe*, 347 U.S. 497; *Aptheker* v. *Secretary of State*, 378 U.S. 500; *Kent* v. *Dulles*, 357 U.S. 116; *Carrington* v. *Rash*, 380 U.S. 89, 96; *Schware* v. *Board of Bar Examiners*, 353 U.S. 232; *NAACP* v. *Alabama*, 360 U.S. 240; *Pierce* v. *Society of Sisters*, 268 U.S. 510; *Meyer* v. *Nebraska*, 262 U.S. 390. To the contrary, this Court, for example, in *Bolling* v. *Sharpe, supra*, while recognizing that the Fifth Amendment does not contain the "explicit safeguard" of an equal protection clause, *id.*, at 499, nevertheless derived an equal protection principle from that Amendment's Due Process Clause. And in *Schware* v. *Board of Bar Examiners, supra*, the Court held that the Fourteenth Amendment protects from arbitrary state action the right to pursue an occupation, such as the practice of law.

Source: 381 U.S. 479 (1965).

10.2.   *Roe et al. v. Wade* (1973) and Abortion Rights

In 1973 the Supreme Court expanded the right of privacy as found in the *Griswold* case to include a woman's constitutional right to have an abortion. Texas and many states had a law making it a crime to procure an abortion except to save the mother's life. By a vote of 7 to 2, the Court declared that privacy included the right to autonomy over a woman's body. Justice Rehnquist's dissent set the issues that would mark a public debate on the *Roe* decision into the twenty-first century.

OPINION: MR. JUSTICE BLACKMUN delivered the opinion of the Court.

* * *

We forthwith acknowledge our awareness of the sensitive and emotional nature of the abortion controversy, of the vigorous opposing views, even among physicians, and of the deep and seemingly absolute convictions that the subject inspires. One's philosophy, one's experiences, one's exposure to the raw edges of human existence, one's religious training, one's attitudes toward life and family and their values, and the moral standards one establishes and seeks to observe, are all likely to influence and to color one's thinking and conclusions about abortion.

In addition, population growth, pollution, poverty, and racial overtones tend to complicate and not to simplify the problem.

Our task, of course, is to resolve the issue by constitutional measurement, free of emotion and of predilection. We seek earnestly to do this, and, because we do, we have inquired into, and in this opinion place some emphasis upon, medical and medical-legal history and what that history reveals about man's attitudes toward the abortion procedure over the centuries. We bear in mind, too, Mr. Justice Holmes' admonition in his now-vindicated dissent in *Lochner* v. *New York*, 198 U.S. 45, 76 (1905):

> [The Constitution] is made for people of fundamentally differing views, and the accident of our finding certain opinions natural and familiar or novel and even shocking ought not to conclude our judgment upon the question whether statutes embodying them conflict with the Constitution of the United States.

* * *

The principal thrust of appellant's attack on the Texas statutes is that they improperly invade a right, said to be possessed by the pregnant woman, to choose to terminate her pregnancy. Appellant would discover this right in the concept of personal "liberty" embodied in the Fourteenth Amendment's Due Process Clause; or in personal, marital, familial, and sexual privacy said to be protected by the Bill of Rights or its penumbras, see *Griswold* v. *Connecticut*, 381 U.S. 479 (1965); *Eisenstadt* v. *Baird*, 405 U.S. 438 (1972); *id.*, at 460 (WHITE, J., concurring in result); or among those rights reserved to the people by the Ninth Amendment, *Griswold* v. *Connecticut*, 381 U.S., at 486 (Goldberg, J., concurring). Before addressing this claim, we feel it desirable briefly to survey, in several aspects, the history of abortion, for such insight as that history may afford us, and then to examine the state purposes and interests behind the criminal abortion laws.

It perhaps is not generally appreciated that the restrictive criminal abortion laws in effect in a majority of States today are of relatively recent vintage. Those laws, generally proscribing abortion or its attempt at any time during pregnancy except when necessary to preserve the pregnant woman's life, are not of ancient or even of common-law origin. Instead, they derive from statutory changes effected, for the most part, in the latter half of the 19th century.

* * *

3. *The common law*. It is undisputed that at common law, abortion performed *before* "quickening"—the first recognizable movement of the fetus *in utero*, appearing usually from the 16th to the 18th week of pregnancy—was not an indictable offense. The absence of a common-law crime for pre-quickening abortion appears to have developed from a confluence of earlier philosophical, theological, and civil and canon law concepts of when life begins. These disciplines variously approached the question in terms of the point at which the embryo or fetus became "formed" or recognizably human, or in terms of when a "person" came into being, that is, infused with a "soul" or "animated." A loose consensus evolved in early English law that these events occurred at some point between conception and live birth. This was "mediate animation." Although Christian theology and the canon law came to fix the point of animation at 40 days for a male and 80 days for a female, a view that persisted until the 19th century, there was otherwise little agreement about the precise time of formation or animation. There was agreement, however, that prior to this point the fetus was to be regarded as part of the mother, and its destruction, therefore, was not homicide. Due to continued uncertainty about the precise time when animation occurred, to the lack of any empirical basis for the 40–80-day view, and perhaps to Aquinas' definition of movement as one of the two first principles of life, Bracton focused upon quickening as the critical point. The significance of quickening was echoed by later common-law scholars and found its way into the received common law in this country.

* * *

5. *The American law*. In this country, the law in effect in all but a few States until mid-19th century was the pre-existing English common law. Connecticut, the first State to enact abortion legislation, adopted in 1821 that part of Lord Ellenborough's Act that related to a woman "quick with child." The death penalty was not imposed. Abortion before quickening was made a crime in that State only in 1860. In 1828, New York enacted legislation that, in two respects, was to serve as a model for early anti-abortion statutes. First, while barring destruction of an unquickened fetus as well as a quick fetus, it made the former only a misdemeanor, but the latter second-degree manslaughter. Second, it incorporated a concept of therapeutic abortion by providing that an abortion was excused if it "shall have been necessary to preserve the life of such mother, or shall have been advised by two physicians to be necessary for such purpose." By 1840, when Texas had received the common law, only eight American States had statutes dealing with abortion. It was not until after the War Between the States that legislation began generally to replace

the common law. Most of these initial statutes dealt severely with abortion after quickening but were lenient with it before quickening. Most punished attempts equally with completed abortions. While many statutes included the exception for an abortion thought by one or more physicians to be necessary to save the mother's life, that provision soon disappeared and the typical law required that the procedure actually be necessary for that purpose.

Gradually, in the middle and late 19th century the quickening distinction disappeared from the statutory law of most States and the degree of the offense and the penalties were increased. By the end of the 1950's, a large majority of the jurisdictions banned abortion, however and whenever performed, unless done to save or preserve the life of the mother. The exceptions, Alabama and the District of Columbia, permitted abortion to preserve the mother's health. Three States permitted abortions that were not "unlawfully" performed or that were not "without lawful justification," leaving interpretation of those standards to the courts. In the past several years, however, a trend toward liberalization of abortion statutes has resulted in adoption, by about one-third of the States, of less stringent laws. . . .

It is thus apparent that at common law, at the time of the adoption of our Constitution, and throughout the major portion of the 19th century, abortion was viewed with less disfavor than under most American statutes currently in effect. Phrasing it another way, a woman enjoyed a substantially broader right to terminate a pregnancy than she does in most States today. At least with respect to the early stage of pregnancy, and very possibly without such a limitation, the opportunity to make this choice was present in this country well into the 19th century. Even later, the law continued for some time to treat less punitively an abortion procured in early pregnancy.

* * *

Three reasons have been advanced to explain historically the enactment of criminal abortion laws in the 19th century and to justify their continued existence.

It has been argued occasionally that these laws were the product of a Victorian social concern to discourage illicit sexual conduct. Texas, however, does not advance this justification in the present case, and it appears that no court or commentator has taken the argument seriously. The appellants and *amici* contend, moreover, that this is not a proper state purpose at all and suggest that, if it were, the Texas statutes are overbroad in protecting it since the law fails to distinguish between married and unwed mothers.

A second reason is concerned with abortion as a medical procedure. When most criminal abortion laws were first enacted, the procedure was a hazardous one for the woman. This was particularly true prior to the development of antisepsis. Antiseptic techniques, of course, were based on discoveries by Lister, Pasteur, and others first announced in 1867, but were not generally accepted and employed until about the turn of the century. Abortion mortality was high. Even after 1900, and perhaps until as late as the development of antibiotics in the 1940's, standard modern techniques such as dilation and curettage were not nearly so safe as they are today. Thus, it has been argued that a State's real concern in enacting a criminal abortion law was to protect the pregnant woman, that is, to restrain her from submitting to a procedure that placed her life in serious jeopardy.

Modern medical techniques have altered this situation. Appellants and various *amici* refer to medical data indicating that abortion in early pregnancy, that is, prior to the end of the first trimester, although not without its risk, is now relatively safe. Mortality rates for women undergoing early abortions, where the procedure is legal, appear to be as low as or lower than the rates for normal childbirth. Consequently, any interest of the State in protecting the woman from an inherently hazardous procedure, except when it would be equally dangerous for her to forgo it, has largely disappeared. Of course, important state interests in the areas of health and medical standards do remain. The State has a legitimate interest in seeing to it that abortion, like any other medical procedure, is performed under circumstances that insure maximum safety for the patient. This interest obviously extends at least to the performing physician and his staff, to the facilities involved, to the availability of after-care, and to adequate provision for any complication or emergency that might arise. The prevalence of high mortality rates at illegal "abortion mills" strengthens, rather than weakens, the State's interest in regulating the conditions under which abortions are performed. Moreover, the risk to the woman increases as her pregnancy continues. Thus, the State retains a definite interest in protecting the woman's own health and safety when an abortion is proposed at a late stage of pregnancy.

The third reason is the State's interest—some phrase it in terms of duty—in protecting prenatal life. Some of the argument for this justification rests on the theory that a new human life is present from the moment of conception. The State's interest and general obligation to protect life then extends, it is argued, to prenatal life. Only when the life of the pregnant mother herself is at stake, balanced against the life she carries within her, should the interest of the embryo or fetus not prevail. Logically, of course, a legitimate state interest in this area need not stand or fall on acceptance of the belief that life begins at conception or at some other point prior to live birth. In assessing the State's interest, recognition may be given to the less rigid claim that as long as at least *potential* life is involved, the State may assert interests beyond the protection of the pregnant woman alone.

Parties challenging state abortion laws have sharply disputed in some courts the contention that a purpose of these laws, when enacted, was to protect prenatal life. Pointing to the absence of legislative history to support the contention, they claim that most state laws were designed solely to protect the woman. Because medical advances have lessened this concern, at least with respect to abortion in early pregnancy, they argue that with respect to such abortions the laws can no longer be justified by any state interest. There is some scholarly support for this view of original purpose. The few state courts called upon to interpret their laws in the late 19th and early 20th centuries did focus on the State's interest in protecting the woman's health rather than in preserving the embryo and fetus. Proponents of this view point out that in many States, including Texas, by statute or judicial interpretation, the pregnant woman herself could not be prosecuted for self-abortion or for cooperating in an abortion performed upon her by another. They claim that adoption of the "quickening" distinction through received common law and state statutes tacitly recognizes the greater health hazards inherent in late abortion and impliedly repudiates the theory that life begins at conception.

The Constitution does not explicitly mention any right of privacy. In a line of decisions . . . the Court has recognized that a right of personal privacy, or a guarantee of certain areas or zones of privacy, does exist under the Constitution. In varying contexts, the Court or individual Justices have, indeed, found at least the roots of that right in the First Amendment . . . ; in the Fourth and Fifth Amendments . . . ; in the penumbras of the Bill of Rights . . . ; in the Ninth Amendment . . . ; in the concept of liberty guaranteed by the first section of the Fourteenth Amendment. . . . These decisions make it clear that only personal rights that can be deemed "fundamental" or "implicit in the concept of ordered liberty," are included in this guarantee of personal privacy. They also make it clear that the right has some extension to activities relating to marriage . . . ; procreation . . . ; contraception, family relationships, and child rearing and education. . . . This right of privacy, whether it be founded in the Fourteenth Amendment's concept of personal liberty and restrictions upon state action, as we feel it is, or, as the District Court determined, in the Ninth Amendment's reservation of rights to the people, is broad enough to encompass a woman's decision whether or not to terminate her pregnancy. The detriment that the State would impose upon the pregnant woman by denying this choice altogether is apparent. Specific and direct harm medically diagnosable even in early pregnancy may be involved. Maternity, or additional offspring, may force upon the woman a distressful life and future. Psychological harm may be imminent. Mental and physical health may be taxed by child care. There is also the distress, for all concerned, associated with the unwanted child, and there is the problem of bringing a child into a family already unable, psychologically and otherwise, to care for it. In other cases, as in this one, the additional difficulties and continuing stigma of unwed motherhood may be involved. All these are factors the woman and her responsible physician necessarily will consider in consultation.

On the basis of elements such as these, appellant and some *amici* argue that the woman's right is absolute and that she is entitled to terminate her pregnancy at whatever time, in whatever way, and for whatever reason she alone chooses. With this we do not agree. Appellant's arguments that Texas either has no valid interest at all in regulating the abortion decision, or no interest strong enough to support any limitation upon the woman's sole determination, are unpersuasive. The Court's decisions recognizing a right of privacy also acknowledge that some state regulation in areas protected by that right is appropriate. As noted above, a State may properly assert important interests in safeguarding health, in maintaining medical standards, and in protecting potential life. At some point in pregnancy, these respective interests become sufficiently compelling to sustain regulation of the factors that govern the abortion decision. The privacy right involved, therefore, cannot be said to be absolute. In fact, it is not clear to us that the claim asserted by some *amici* that one has an unlimited right to do with one's body as one pleases bears a close relationship to the right of privacy previously articulated in the Court's decisions. The Court has refused to recognize an unlimited right of this kind in the past.

We, therefore, conclude that the right of personal privacy includes the abortion decision, but that this right is not unqualified and must be considered against important state interests in regulation.

* * *

In view of all this, we do not agree that, by adopting one theory of life, Texas may override the rights of the pregnant woman that are at stake. We repeat, however, that the State does have an important and legitimate interest in preserving and protecting the health of the pregnant woman, whether she be a resident of the State or a nonresident who seeks medical consultation and treatment there, and that it has still *another* important and legitimate interest in protecting the potentiality of human life. These interests are separate and distinct. Each grows in substantiality as the woman approaches term and, at a point during pregnancy, each becomes "compelling."

With respect to the State's important and legitimate interest in the health of the mother, the "compelling" point, in the light of present medical knowledge, is at approximately the end of the first trimester. This is so because of the now-established medical fact . . . that until the end of the first trimester mortality in abortion may be less than mortality in normal childbirth. It follows that, from and after this point, a State may regulate the abortion procedure to the extent that the regulation reasonably relates to the preservation and protection of maternal health. Examples of permissible state regulation in this area are requirements as to the qualifications of the person who is to perform the abortion; as to the licensure of that person; as to the facility in which the procedure is to be performed, that is, whether it must be a hospital or may be a clinic or some other place of less-than-hospital status; as to the licensing of the facility; and the like.

This means, on the other hand, that, for the period of pregnancy prior to this "compelling" point, the attending physician, in consultation with his patient, is free to determine, without regulation by the State, that, in his medical judgment, the patient's pregnancy should be terminated. If that decision is reached, the judgment may be effectuated by an abortion free of interference by the State.

With respect to the State's important and legitimate interest in potential life, the "compelling" point is at viability. This is so because the fetus then presumably has the capability of meaningful life outside the mother's womb. State regulation protective of fetal life after viability thus has both logical and biological justifications. If the State is interested in protecting fetal life after viability, it may go so far as to proscribe abortion during that period, except when it is necessary to preserve the life or health of the mother.

Measured against these standards, Art. 1196 of the Texas Penal Code, in restricting legal abortions to those "procured or attempted by medical advice for the purpose of saving the life of the mother," sweeps too broadly. The statute makes no distinction between abortions performed early in pregnancy and those performed later, and it limits to a single reason, "saving" the mother's life, the legal justification for the procedure. The statute, therefore, cannot survive the constitutional attack made upon it here.

* * *

DISSENT: MR. JUSTICE REHNQUIST, dissenting.

The Court's opinion brings to the decision of this troubling question both extensive historical fact and a wealth of legal scholarship. While the opinion thus commands my respect, I find myself nonetheless in fundamental disagreement with those parts of it that invalidate the Texas statute in question, and therefore dissent.

I

The Court's opinion decides that a State may impose virtually no restriction on the performance of abortions during the first trimester of
pregnancy. Our previous decisions indicate that a necessary predicate
for such an opinion is a plaintiff who was in her first trimester of pregnancy at some time during the pendency of her lawsuit. While a party
may vindicate his own constitutional rights, he may not seek vindication
for the rights of others. The Court's statement of facts in this case makes
clear, however, that the record in no way indicates the presence of such
a plaintiff. We know only that plaintiff Roe at the time of filing her
complaint was a pregnant woman; for aught that appears in this record,
she may have been in her *last* trimester of pregnancy as of the date the
complaint was filed.

Nothing in the Court's opinion indicates that Texas might not constitutionally apply its proscription of abortion as written to a woman in
that stage of pregnancy. Nonetheless, the Court uses her complaint
against the Texas statute as a fulcrum for deciding that States may impose virtually no restrictions on medical abortions performed during the
first trimester of pregnancy. In deciding such a hypothetical lawsuit, the
Court departs from the longstanding admonition that it should never
"formulate a rule of constitutional law broader than is required by the
precise facts to which it is to be applied."

II

Even if there were a plaintiff in this case capable of litigating the issue
which the Court decides, I would reach a conclusion opposite to that
reached by the Court. I have difficulty in concluding, as the Court does,
that the right of "privacy" is involved in this case. Texas, by the statute
here challenged, bars the performance of a medical abortion by a licensed
physician on a plaintiff such as Roe. A transaction resulting in an operation such as this is not "private" in the ordinary usage of that word.
Nor is the "privacy" that the Court finds here even a distant relative of
the freedom from searches and seizures protected by the Fourth Amendment to the Constitution, which the Court has referred to as embodying
a right to privacy.

If the Court means by the term "privacy" no more than that the claim
of a person to be free from unwanted state regulation of consensual
transactions may be a form of "liberty" protected by the Fourteenth
Amendment, there is no doubt that similar claims have been upheld in
our earlier decisions on the basis of that liberty. I agree with the statement of MR. JUSTICE STEWART in his concurring opinion that the "liberty," against deprivation of which without due process the Fourteenth

Amendment protects, embraces more than the rights found in the Bill of Rights. But that liberty is not guaranteed absolutely against deprivation, only against deprivation without due process of law. The test traditionally applied in the area of social and economic legislation is whether or not a law such as that challenged has a rational relation to a valid state objective. The Due Process Clause of the Fourteenth Amendment undoubtedly does place a limit, albeit a broad one, on legislative power to enact laws such as this. If the Texas statute were to prohibit an abortion even where the mother's life is in jeopardy, I have little doubt that such a statute would lack a rational relation to a valid state objective under the test stated in *Williamson, supra*. But the Court's sweeping invalidation of any restrictions on abortion during the first trimester is impossible to justify under that standard, and the conscious weighing of competing factors that the Court's opinion apparently substitutes for the established test is far more appropriate to a legislative judgment than to a judicial one.

The Court eschews the history of the Fourteenth Amendment in its reliance on the "compelling state interest" test. But the Court adds a new wrinkle to this test by transposing it from the legal considerations associated with the Equal Protection Clause of the Fourteenth Amendment to this case arising under the Due Process Clause of the Fourteenth Amendment. Unless I misapprehend the consequences of this transplanting of the "compelling state interest test," the Court's opinion will accomplish the seemingly impossible feat of leaving this area of the law more confused than it found it.

While the Court's opinion quotes from the dissent of Mr. Justice Holmes in *Lochner* v. *New York*, the result it reaches is more closely attuned to the majority opinion of Mr. Justice Peckham in that case. As in *Lochner* and similar cases applying substantive due process standards to economic and social welfare legislation, the adoption of the compelling state interest standard will inevitably require this Court to examine the legislative policies and pass on the wisdom of these policies in the very process of deciding whether a particular state interest put forward may or may not be "compelling." The decision here to break pregnancy into three distinct terms and to outline the permissible restrictions the State may impose in each one, for example, partakes more of judicial legislation than it does of a determination of the intent of the drafters of the Fourteenth Amendment.

The fact that a majority of the States reflecting, after all, the majority sentiment in those States, have had restrictions on abortions for at least a century is a strong indication, it seems to me, that the asserted right to an abortion is not "so rooted in the traditions and conscience of our people as to be ranked as fundamental." Even today, when society's views on abortion are changing, the very existence of the debate is evidence that the "right" to an abortion is not so universally accepted as the appellant would have us believe.

To reach its result, the Court necessarily has had to find within the scope of the Fourteenth Amendment a right that was apparently completely unknown to the drafters of the Amendment. As early as 1821, the first state law dealing directly with abortion was enacted by the Connecticut Legislature. By the time of the adoption of the Fourteenth Amendment in 1868, there were at least 36 laws enacted by state or territorial legislatures limiting abortion. While many States have amended or updated their laws, 21 of the laws on the books in 1868 remain in effect today. Indeed, the Texas statute struck down today was, as the majority notes, first enacted in 1857 and "has remained substantially unchanged to the present time."

* * *

Even if one were to agree that the case that the Court decides were here, and that the enunciation of the substantive constitutional law in the Court's opinion were proper, the actual disposition of the case by the Court is still difficult to justify. The Texas statute is struck down *in toto*, even though the Court apparently concedes that at later periods of pregnancy Texas might impose these selfsame statutory limitations on abortion. My understanding of past practice is that a statute found to be invalid as applied to a particular plaintiff, but not unconstitutional as a whole, is not simply "struck down" but is, instead, declared unconstitutional as applied to the fact situation before the Court.

For all of the foregoing reasons, I respectfully dissent.

Source: 410 U.S. 113 (1973).

10.3.   The Hyde Amendments

U.S. Representative Henry Hyde of Illinois introduced the following three separate amendments to restrict the use of public money for abortions in 1976, 1977, and 1979 to appropriation acts for the Department of Health, Education and Welfare. Each time they failed to pass, but the amendments bespoke a "right-to-life" position that gained enough political force by the 1980s to limit state support of abortions, help defeat the Equal Rights Amendment, and make the abortion issue a "litmus test" in the appointment of federal judges.

Hyde Amendment 1976 [90 Stat. 1418, 1434]: None of the funds contained in this Act shall be used to perform abortions except where the life of the mother would be endangered if the fetus were carried to term.

Hyde Amendment 1977 and 1978 [91 Stat. 1460, 92 Stat. 1567, 1586]: [N]one of the funds provided for in this paragraph may be used to perform abortions except where the life of the mother would be endangered if the fetus were carried to term; or except for such medical procedures necessary for the victims of rape or incest, when such rape or incest has been reported promptly to a law enforcement agency or public health service; or except in those instances where severe and long-lasting physical health damage to the mother could result if the pregnancy were carried to term when so determined by two physicians.

Hyde Amendment 1979 [93 Stat. 923, 926]: [N]one of the funds provided in this joint resolution shall be used to perform abortions except where the life of the mother would be endangered if the fetus were carried to term; or except for such medical procedures necessary for the victims of rape or incest when such rape or incest has been reported promptly to a law enforcement agency or public health service.

Source: Robert H. Birkby, *The Court and Public Policy* (Washington, DC: Congressional Quarterly Press, 1983), pp. 436–437.

10.4.   Senate Bill 158, the "Human Life Statute," 1983

This bill expanded on the failed Senate amendment asserting that life begins at the moment of fertilization with a broader statement that the Fourteenth Amendment should be interpreted to mean that the Constitution protects the right of the fetus to live from the moment of conception. The bill failed to pass the House.

Section 1. The Congress finds that present day scientific evidence indicates a significant likelihood that actual human life exists from conception.

The Congress further finds that the fourteenth amendment to the Constitution of the United States was intended to protect all human beings.

Upon the basis of these findings, and in the exercise of the powers of Congress, including its power under section five of the fourteenth amendment to the Constitution of the United States, the Congress hereby declares that for the purpose of enforcing the obligation of the States under the fourteenth amendment not to deprive persons of life without due process of law, human life shall be deemed to exist from conception, without regard to race, sex, age, health, defect, or condition of dependency; and for this purpose "person" shall include all human life as defined herein.

Section 2. Notwithstanding any other provision of law, no inferior Federal court ordained and established by Congress under Article III of the Constitution of the United States shall have jurisdiction to issue any restraining order, temporary or permanent injunction, or declaratory judgment in any case involving or arising from any State law or municipal ordinance that (1) protects the rights of human persons between conception and birth, or (2) prohibits, limits, or regulates (a) the performance of abortions or (b) the provision at public expense of funds, facilities, personnel, or other assistance for the performance of abortions.

Source: Birkby, *Court and Public Policy*, pp. 453–454.

10.5.   Proposed Anti-Abortion Amendments to the Constitution, 1982–1983

Three times opponents of *Roe* and foes of abortion introduced into the Senate amendments that denied the constitutional right to have an abortion and stating that life begins at conception. All three failed to pass.

Senate Joint Resolution 110, 97th Congress, 2nd Session: A right to abortion is not secured by this Constitution. The Congress and the several States shall have the concurrent power to restrict and prohibit abortions: *Provided*, that a law of a State which is more restrictive than a law of Congress shall govern.

Senate Joint Resolution 17, 97th Congress, 2nd Session: Section 1. With respect to the right to life, the word "person," as used in this article and in the fifth and fourteenth articles of amendment to the Constitution of the United States, applies to all human beings, irrespective of age, health, function, or condition of dependency, including their unborn offspring at every stage of their biological development.

Section 2. No unborn person shall be deprived of life by any person; *Provided, however,* that nothing in this article shall prohibit a law permitting only those medical procedures required to prevent the death of the mother.

Senate Joint Resolution 19, 97th Congress, 2nd Session: The paramount right to life is vested in each human being from the moment of fertilization without regard to age, health, or condition of dependency.

Source: Birkby, *Court and Public Policy*, pp. 452–453.

10.6.   ***Webster v. Reproductive Health Services* (1989): The Supreme Court Rules to Restrict Access to Abortion**

The Rehnquist Court's 5 to 4 ruling, in *Webster, Attorney General of Missouri, et al. v. Reproductive Health Services et al.,* was a major reversal from the restrictions that *Roe* had placed on the states regarding abortion. It allowed states to deny a pregnant woman access to state facilities to have an abortion if her life was not in jeopardy. With a preamble that stated that life begins with conception, it further imposed restrictions on a woman's access to counseling about an abortion and sustained Missouri's requirement that a woman pregnant for more than four months must have a medical examination before an abortion could be performed. Justice Harry Blackmun's dissent, which was joined by Justices William Brennan and Thurgood Marshall, reiterated the validity of the right to privacy established in *Roe* and accused his brethren of engaging in a thinly disguised plan to "do away with *Roe* explicitly."

OPINION: CHIEF JUSTICE REHNQUIST announced the judgment of the Court and delivered the opinion of the Court with respect to Parts I, II-A, II-B, and II-C, and an opinion with respect to Parts II-D and III, in which JUSTICE WHITE and JUSTICE KENNEDY join.

This appeal concerns the constitutionality of a Missouri statute regulating the performance of abortions. The United States Court of Appeals for the Eighth Circuit struck down several provisions of the statute on the ground that they violated this Court's decision in *Roe* v. *Wade*, 410 U.S. 113 (1973), and cases following it. . . .

* * *

The United States Supreme Court need not pass on the constitutionality, under the Federal Constitution, of the preamble of a state statute regulating the performance of abortions—which preamble sets forth findings by the state legislature that the life of each human being begins at conception and that unborn children have protectable interests in life, health, and well-being, and mandates that the laws of the state be interpreted to provide unborn children with all the rights, privileges, and immunities available to other persons, citizens, and residents of the state, subject to the Federal Constitution and the precedents of the Supreme Court—because (1) the preamble does not by its terms regulate abortion or any other aspect of the medical practice of health care professionals offering abortion services or pregnancy counseling and can be read simply to express a value judgment favoring childbirth over abortion, which the state is authorized to make since the Supreme Court's decision in Roe v Wade (1973) implies no limitation on such authority, (2) the preamble can be interpreted to do no more than offer protections to unborn children in tort and probate law, and the extent to which the preamble's language might be used to interpret other state statutes or regulations is something that only the state's courts can definitively decide, and (3) it will be time enough for federal courts to address the meaning of the preamble should it be applied in some concrete way to restrict the activities of such health care professionals; such considerations make it equally inappropriate, before the state courts have interpreted the state statute, for a federal court to pass upon the claim that the preamble violates the state's constitution.

ABORTION §3

validity of statute restricting use of public employees and facilities—public funding—

State statutory provisions which make it unlawful for any public employees within the scope of their employment to perform or assist an abortion not necessary to save the life of the mother and which prohibit the use of any public facility for the purpose of performing or assisting an abortion not necessary to save the life of the mother do not contravene the abortion decisions of the United States Supreme Court, because (1) the state's decision to use public facilities and staff to encourage childbirth over abortion places no governmental obstacle in the path of a woman who chooses to terminate her pregnancy and leaves a pregnant woman with the same choices as if the state had chosen not to operate any public hospitals at all, (2) such provisions restrict a woman's ability to obtain an abortion only to the extent that she chooses to use a physician affiliated with a public hospital, which circumstance is more easily remedied, and thus is considerably less burdensome, than indigency, which may make it difficult—and in some cases, perhaps impossible—for some women to have abortions without public funding, (3) if the state may make a value judgment favoring childbirth over abortion and implement such judgment by the allocation of public funds, it likewise may do so through the allocation of other public resources, such as hospitals and medical staff, and (4) nothing in the Federal Constitution requires states to enter or remain in the business of performing abortions, nor do private physicians and their patients have some kind of constitutional right of access to public facilities for the performance of abortions, and a state need not commit any resources to facilitating abortions even if it can turn a profit by doing so. . . .

* * *

ABORTION §6

validity of state statute—physician's standard of care in determining viability—required tests—state's authority to regulate under Supreme Court's precedents—

The United States Supreme Court will uphold the constitutionality of a state statute which provides that, before a physician performs an abortion on a woman he has reason to believe is carrying an unborn child of 20 or more weeks' gestational age, the physician shall first determine if the unborn child is viable by using and exercising the degree of care, skill, and proficiency commonly exercised by the ordinarily skillful, careful, and prudent physician engaged in similar practice under the same or similar conditions, and that in making such determination of viability, the physician shall perform or cause to be performed such medical examinations and tests as are necessary to make a finding of the gestational age, weight, and lung maturity of the unborn child, where (1) three Justices of the Supreme Court are of the view that (a) the trimester-and-viability analysis of state laws regulating abortion, pursuant to the Supreme Court's decision in Roe v Wade (1973) should be abandoned, and (b) although viability tests required by the statute will show in many cases that a fetus is not viable, and although the tests will have been performed for what were in fact second-trimester abortions, the statute's viability-testing requirement is constitutional because it permissibly furthers the state's interest in protecting potential human life, (2) a fourth Justice is of the view that (a) the statute is not inconsistent with any of the Supreme Court's prior precedents concerning state regulation of abortion, where requiring the performance of tests useful in determining whether a fetus is viable, when viability is possible and when it would not be medically imprudent to perform such tests, does not impose an undue burden on a woman's abortion decision, and (b) there will be time enough to re-examine Roe, and to do so carefully, when the constitutional invalidity of a state's abortion statute actually turns on the constitutional validity of Roe, and (3) a fifth Justice is of the view that (a) given that it is an arguable question whether the statute contravenes the Supreme Court's understanding of Roe, the court should examine Roe rather than avoid the question, and (b) the statute should be held valid based upon an explicit overruling of Roe, since it is needless to prolong the Supreme Court's self-awarded sovereignty over a field where it has little proper business.

* * *

The United States Supreme Court is not empowered to decide abstract propositions, or to declare, for the government of future cases, principles or rules of law which cannot affect the result as to the thing in issue in the case before it.

* * *

The due process clauses of the Federal Constitution's Fifth and Fourteenth Amendments generally confer no affirmative right to governmental aid, even where such aid may be necessary to secure life, liberty, or property interests of which the government itself may not deprive the individual.

* * *

In *Roe* v. *Wade*, the Court recognized that the State has "important and legitimate" interests in protecting maternal health and in the potentiality of human life. During the second trimester, the State "may, if it chooses, regulate the abortion procedure in ways that are reasonably related to maternal health." After viability, when the State's interest in potential human life was held to become compelling, the State "may, if it chooses, regulate, and even proscribe, abortion except where it is necessary, in appropriate medical judgment, for the preservation of the life or health of the mother."

* * *

We think that the doubt cast upon the Missouri statute by these cases is not so much a flaw in the statute as it is a reflection of the fact that the rigid trimester analysis of the course of a pregnancy enunciated in *Roe* has resulted in subsequent cases like *Colautti* and *Akron* making constitutional law in this area a virtual Procrustean bed. . . .

* * *

In the first place, the rigid *Roe* framework is hardly consistent with the notion of a Constitution cast in general terms, as ours is, and usually speaking in general principles, as ours does. The key elements of the *Roe* framework—trimesters and viability—are not found in the text of the Constitution or in any place else one would expect to find a constitutional principle. Since the bounds of the inquiry are essentially indeterminate, the result has been a web of legal rules that have become increasingly intricate, resembling a code of regulations rather than a body of constitutional doctrine. As Justice White has put it, the trimester framework has left this Court to serve as the country's "*ex officio* medical board with powers to approve or disapprove medical and operative practices and standards throughout the United States."

In the second place, we do not see why the State's interest in protecting potential human life should come into existence only at the point of viability, and that there should therefore be a rigid line allowing state regulation after viability but prohibiting it before viability. The dissenters in *Thornburgh*, writing in the context of the *Roe* trimester analysis, would have recognized this fact by positing against the "fundamental right" recognized in *Roe* the State's "compelling interest" in protecting potential human life throughout pregnancy. "[T]he State's interest, if compelling after viability, is equally compelling before viability." *Thornburgh*, 476 U.S., at 795.

The tests that § 188.029 requires the physician to perform are designed to determine viability. The State here has chosen viability as the point at which its interest in potential human life must be safeguarded. It is true that the tests in question increase the expense of abortion, and regulate the discretion of the physician in determining the viability of the fetus. Since the tests will undoubtedly show in many cases that the fetus is not viable, the tests will have been performed for what were in fact second-trimester abortions. But we are satisfied that the requirement of these tests permissibly furthers the State's interest in protecting potential human life, and we therefore believe § 188.029 to be constitutional.

Justice Blackmun takes us to task for our failure to join in a "great issues" debate as to whether the Constitution includes an "unenumerated" general right to privacy as recognized in cases such as *Griswold* v. *Connecticut*, and *Roe*. But *Griswold* v. *Connecticut*, unlike *Roe*, did not purport to adopt a whole framework, complete with detailed rules and distinctions, to govern the cases in which the asserted liberty interest would apply. As such, it was far different from the opinion, if not the holding, of *Roe v. Wade*, which sought to establish a constitutional framework for judging state regulation of abortion during the entire term of pregnancy. That framework sought to deal with areas of medical practice traditionally subject to state regulation, and it sought to balance once and for all by reference only to the calendar the claims of the State to protect the fetus as a form of human life against the claims of a woman to decide for herself whether or not to abort a fetus she was carrying. The experience of the Court in applying *Roe* v. *Wade* in later cases suggests to us that there is wisdom in not unnecessarily attempting to elaborate the abstract differences between a "fundamental right" to abortion, as the Court described it in *Akron*, a "limited fundamental constitutional right," which Justice Blackmun today treats *Roe* as having established, or a liberty interest protected by the Due Process Clause, which we believe it to be. The Missouri testing requirement here is reasonably designed to ensure that abortions are not performed where the fetus is viable—an end which all concede is legitimate—and that is sufficient to sustain its constitutionality.

Justice Blackmun also accuses us, *inter alia*, of cowardice and illegitimacy in dealing with "the most politically divisive domestic legal issue of our time." There is no doubt that our holding today will allow some governmental regulation of abortion that would have been prohibited under the language of cases such as *Colautti* v. *Franklin*, and *Akron* v. *Akron Center for Reproductive Health, Inc.* But the goal of constitutional adjudication is surely not to remove inexorably "politically divisive" issues from the ambit of the legislative process, whereby the people through their elected representatives deal with matters of concern to them. The goal of constitutional adjudication is to hold true the balance between that which the Constitution puts beyond the reach of the democratic process and that which it does not. We think we have done that today. Justice Blackmun's suggestion, that legislative bodies, in a Nation where more than half of our population is women, will treat our decision today as an invitation to enact abortion regulation reminiscent of the Dark Ages not only misreads our views but does scant justice to those who serve in such bodies and the people who elect them.

Both appellants and the United States as *amicus curiae* have urged that we overrule our decision in *Roe* v. *Wade*. The facts of the present case, however, differ from those at issue in *Roe*. Here, Missouri has determined that viability is the point at which its interest in potential human life must be safeguarded. In *Roe*, on the other hand, the Texas statute criminalized the performance of *all* abortions, except when the mother's life was at stake. This case therefore affords us no occasion to revisit the holding of *Roe*, which was that the Texas statute unconstitutionally infringed the right to an abortion derived from the Due Process Clause, and we leave it undisturbed. To the extent indicated in our opinion, we would modify and narrow *Roe* and succeeding cases.

Because none of the challenged provisions of the Missouri Act properly before us conflict with the Constitution, the judgment of the Court of Appeals is
Reversed.

DISSENT: JUSTICE BLACKMUN, with whom JUSTICE BRENNAN and JUSTICE MARSHALL join, concurring in part and dissenting in part.

Today, *Roe* v. *Wade*, and the fundamental constitutional right of women to decide whether to terminate a pregnancy, survive but are not secure. Although the Court extricates itself from this case without making a single, even incremental, change in the law of abortion, the plurality and Justice Scalia would overrule *Roe* (the first silently, the other explicitly) and would return to the States virtually unfettered authority to control the quintessentially intimate, personal, and life-directing decision whether to carry a fetus to term. Although today, no less than yesterday, the Constitution and the decisions of this Court prohibit a State from enacting laws that inhibit women from the meaningful exercise of that right, a plurality of this Court implicitly invites every state legislature to enact more and more restrictive abortion regulations in order to provoke more and more test cases, in the hope that sometime down the line the Court will return the law of procreative freedom to the severe limitations that generally prevailed in this country before January 22, 1973. Never in my memory has a plurality announced a judgment of this Court that so foments disregard for the law and for our standing decisions.

Nor in my memory has a plurality gone about its business in such a deceptive fashion. At every level of its review, from its effort to read the real meaning out of the Missouri statute, to its intended evisceration of precedents and its deafening silence about the constitutional protections that it would jettison, the plurality obscures the portent of its analysis. With feigned restraint, the plurality announces that its analysis leaves *Roe* "undisturbed," albeit "modif[ied] and narrow[ed]." But this disclaimer is totally meaningless. The plurality opinion is filled with winks, and nods, and knowing glances to those who would do away with *Roe* explicitly, but turns a stone face to anyone in search of what the plurality conceives as the scope of a woman's right under the Due Process Clause to terminate a pregnancy free from the coercive and brooding influence of the State. The simple truth is that *Roe* would not survive the plurality's analysis, and that the plurality provides no substitute for *Roe*'s protective umbrella.

I fear for the future. I fear for the liberty and equality of the millions of women who have lived and come of age in the 16 years since *Roe* was decided. I fear for the integrity of, and public esteem for, this Court.

* * *

How ironic it is, then, and disingenuous, that the plurality scolds the Court of Appeals for adopting a construction of the statute that fails to avoid constitutional difficulties. By distorting the statute, the plurality manages to avoid invalidating the testing provision on what should have been noncontroversial constitutional grounds; having done so, however, the plurality rushes headlong into a much deeper constitutional thicket . . . in search of a pretext for scuttling the trimester framework. . . .

B

Having set up the conflict between § 188.029 and the *Roe* trimester framework, the plurality summarily discards *Roe*'s analytic core as "unsound in principle and unworkable in practice." This is so, the plurality claims, because the key elements of the framework do not appear in the text of the Constitution, because the framework more closely resembles a regulatory code than a body of constitutional doctrine, and because under the framework the State's interest in potential human life is considered compelling only after viability, when, in fact, that interest is equally compelling throughout pregnancy. The plurality does not bother to explain these alleged flaws in *Roe*. Bald assertion masquerades as reasoning. The object, quite clearly, is not to persuade, but to prevail.

The plurality opinion is far more remarkable for the arguments that it does not advance than for those that it does. The plurality does not even mention, much less join, the true jurisprudential debate underlying this case: whether the Constitution includes an "unenumerated" general right to privacy as recognized in many of our decisions, most notably *Griswold* v. *Connecticut* (1965), and *Roe*, and, more specifically, whether, and to what extent, such a right to privacy extends to matters of childbearing and family life, including abortion. . . . contraception . . . marriage . . . procreation . . . childrearing. These are questions of unsurpassed significance in this Court's interpretation of the Constitution, and mark the battleground upon which this case was fought, by the parties, by the United States as *amicus* on behalf of petitioners, and by an unprecedented number of *amici*. On these grounds, abandoned by the plurality, the Court should decide this case.

But rather than arguing that the text of the Constitution makes no mention of the right to privacy, the plurality complains that the critical elements of the *Roe* framework—trimesters and viability—do not appear in the Constitution and are, therefore, somehow inconsistent with a Constitution cast in general terms. Were this a true concern, we would have to abandon most of our constitutional jurisprudence. As the plurality well knows, or should know, the "critical elements" of countless constitutional doctrines nowhere appear in the Constitution's text. The Constitution makes no mention, for example, of the First Amendment's "actual malice" standard for proving certain libels or of the standard for determining when speech is obscene. Similarly, the Constitution makes no mention of the rational-basis test, or the specific verbal formulations of intermediate and strict scrutiny by which this Court evaluates claims under the Equal Protection Clause. The reason is simple. Like the *Roe* framework, these tests or standards are not, and do not purport to be, rights protected by the Constitution. Rather, they are judge-made methods for evaluating and measuring the strength and scope of constitutional rights or for balancing the constitutional rights of individuals against the competing interests of government.

With respect to the *Roe* framework, the general constitutional principle, indeed the fundamental constitutional right, for which it was developed is the right to privacy, a species of "liberty" protected by the Due Process Clause, which under our past decisions safeguards the right of women to exercise some control over their own role in procreation. . . . Fashioning such accommodations between individual rights and the legitimate interests of government, establishing benchmarks and standards with which to evaluate the competing claims of individuals and government, lies at the very heart of constitutional adjudication. To the extent that the trimester framework is useful in this enterprise, it is not only consistent with constitutional interpretation, but necessary to the wise and just exercise of this Court's paramount authority to define the scope of constitutional rights.

* * *

Finally, the plurality asserts that the trimester framework cannot stand because the State's interest in potential life is compelling throughout pregnancy, not merely after viability. The opinion contains not one word of rationale for its view of the State's interest. This "it-is-so-because-we-say-so" jurisprudence constitutes nothing other than an attempted exercise of brute force; reason, much less persuasion, has no place.

* * *

Thus, "not with a bang, but a whimper," the plurality discards a landmark case of the last generation, and casts into darkness the hopes and visions of every woman in this country who had come to believe that the Constitution guaranteed her the right to exercise some control over her unique ability to bear children. The plurality does so either oblivious or insensitive to the fact that millions of women, and their families, have ordered their lives around the right to reproductive choice, and that this right has become vital to the full participation of women in the economic and political walks of American life. The plurality would clear the way once again for government to force upon women the physical labor and specific and direct medical and psychological harms that may accompany carrying a fetus to term. The plurality would clear the way again for the State to conscript a woman's body and to force upon her a "distressful life and future."

The result, as we know from experience, would be that every year hundreds of thousands of women, in desperation, would defy the law, and place their health and safety in the unclean and unsympathetic hands of back-alley abortionists, or they would attempt to perform abortions upon themselves, with disastrous results. Every year, many women, especially poor and minority women, would die or suffer debilitating physical trauma, all in the name of enforced morality or religious dictates or lack of compassion, as it may be.

Of the aspirations and settled understandings of American women, of the inevitable and brutal consequences of what it is doing, the tough-approach plurality utters not a word. This silence is callous. It is also profoundly destructive of this Court as an institution. To overturn a constitutional decision is a rare and grave undertaking. To overturn a constitutional decision that secured a fundamental personal liberty to millions of persons would be unprecedented in our 200 years of constitutional history. . . .

* * *

For today, at least, the law of abortion stands undisturbed. For today, the women of this Nation still retain the liberty to control their destinies. But the signs are evident and very ominous, and a chill wind blows.

Source: 192 U.S. 490 (1989).

10.7.   State Courts Challenge *Webster* (1997)

> The Supreme Court of Wisconsin in *State of Wisconsin v. Kruzicki* ruled that there was no basis in state law for the contention that human life began at conception. The case reflected the problem of defining the boundaries of state authority for an issue so contested as abortion. Throughout the 1980s and 1990s various states drafted laws regarding the rights of a woman to have access to abortion facilities and the rights of opponents of abortion to protest the practice of abortion and the presence of abortion clinics. State definitions sometimes collided with federal ones, bringing on challenges in state and federal courts as to the proper meaning of the laws and the extent of government power, and which government(s)—state and/or federal—had the authority to define and enforces law regarding abortion.

OPINION BY: ANN WALSH BRADLEY

ANN WALSH BRADLEY, J. The petitioner, Angela M.W., seeks review of a court of appeals' decision denying her request for either a writ of habeas corpus or a supervisory writ to prohibit the Waukesha County Circuit Court, Kathryn W. Foster, Judge, from continuing to exercise jurisdiction in a CHIPS (child alleged to be in need of protection or services) proceeding. She maintains that the CHIPS statute does not confer jurisdiction over her or her viable fetus. In the alternative, if the CHIPS statute does confer such jurisdiction, the petitioner contends that as applied to her, it violates her equal protection and due process rights. Because we determine that the legislature did not intend to include a fetus within the Children's Code definition of "child," we reverse the decision of the court of appeals.

* * *

Case law reveals that different courts have given different meanings to the terms "person" and "child." This court has previously held that a viable fetus is a "person" for purposes of Wisconsin's wrongful death statute. On the other hand, the United States Supreme Court has concluded that a fetus is not a "person" under the Fourteenth Amendment to the United States Constitution. Perhaps most compelling, courts in other states have arrived at different interpretations of statutory language nearly identical to that in *State v. Gray*, 62 (Ohio, 1993) . . . (holding that a third trimester fetus is not "a child under eighteen years of age," as provided in Ohio's child endangerment statute). Against this backdrop of conflicting authority, we conclude that the term "child" is ambiguous.

* * *

By reading the definition of "child" in context with other relevant sections of Chapter 48, we find a compelling basis for concluding that the legislature intended a "child" to mean a human being born alive. Code provisions dealing with taking a child into custody, providing parental notification, and releasing a child from custody would require absurd results if the definition of "child" included a fetus. Each of the provisions addresses a critical juncture in a CHIPS proceeding. Yet, each also anticipates that the "child" can at some point be removed from the presence of the parent. It is manifest that the separation envisioned by the statute cannot be achieved in the context of a pregnant woman and her fetus.[1]

NOTE

1. The dissent asserts that interpreting "child" to not include a fetus is to work an absurd result, "by rendering the state's power to protect a child dependent upon whether the child is inside or outside of the womb." This argument employs a circular method of reasoning, which may be summarized as follows: the legislature intended the term "child" to include a viable fetus because the State must have the power to protect children. We decline to consider an argument that assumes the result.

Source: 209 Wis. 2d 112; 561 N.W. 2d 729; 1997.

ANNOTATED RESEARCH GUIDE

Books

Berry, Mary Frances. *Why ERA Failed: Politics, Women's Rights, and the Amending Process of the Constitution.* Bloomington: Indiana University Press, 1986.

The standard treatment of why the amendment failed to win state approval.

Chafe, William H. *The American Woman: Her Changing Social, Economic, and Political Roles, 1920–1970.* New York: Oxford University Press, 1972. An important work for laying the groundwork for other studies of women in the second half of the twentieth century.

Cott, Nancy F. *The Grounding of Modern Feminism.* New Haven, CT: Yale University Press, 1987. Chronicles the first wave of women's rights activism in the twentieth century.

Davis, Flora. *Moving the Mountain: The Women's Movement in America Since 1960.* New York: Simon and Schuster, 1991. Provides a detailed narrative of the connection between feminism and legislation.

Evans, Sara. *Personal Politics: The Roots of Women's Liberation in the Civil Rights Movement and the New Left.* New York: Vintage, 1980. Deals with the second wave of feminism and its connection with the black civil rights crusade.

Faux, Marian. *Roe v. Wade: The Untold Story of the Landmark Supreme Court Decision that Made Abortion Legal.* New York: New American Library, 1988. Remains the standard historical work on this controversial decision.

Friedan, Betty. *Life So Far.* New York: Simon and Schuster, 2000. An important memoir by this key figure of the movement that offers an insider's view of events.

Hess, Beth B. *Controversy and Coalition: The New Feminist Movement.* Boston: Twayne, 1985. Approaches the movement from a sociological perspective and stresses social movement theory.

Rhode, Deborah. *Justice and Gender.* Cambridge, MA: Harvard University Press, 1989. Perhaps the best work dealing with the women's movement and the courts.

Stevens, Leonard A. *The Case of Roe v. Wade.* New York: G. P. Putnam's Sons, 1996. Examines the people, events, and legal questions connected to the Court's decision. Especially valuable in investigating the trials and litigation from 1947 that preceded the landmark ruling.

Wandersee, Winifred D. *On the Move: American Women in the 1970s.* Boston: Twayne, 1988. A readable summary of the changes in American society that brought women into political life. Includes a detailed treatment of the National Organization for Women.

Women's Research and Education Institute. *The American Woman.* New York: W. W. Norton, 1987. Has the most recent descriptions of women's status in America. This series has been updated biannually since it was first published in 1987.

Nonprint Media

Web Sites

http://web.lexis-nexis.com/univers. Contains the full opinions of the Supreme Court cases discussed in this chapter.

http://www.lib.umich.edu/govdocs/jfkeo/eo/10980.html. Executive Order 10980 establishing the President's Commission on the Status of Women.

http://www.eeoc.gov/welcome.html. Homepage of the Equal Employment Opportunity Commission.

http://www.eeoc.gov/laws/vii.html. Title VII of the Civil Rights Act of 1964.

http://www.now.org. National Organization for Women information on women's issues for women activists.

Selected Bibliography

Abbott, Richard H. *The Republican Party and the South, 1855–1877*. Chapel Hill: University of North Carolina Press, 1986.

Abraham, Henry J., and Barbara A. Perry. *Freedom and the Court*. 6th ed. New York: Oxford University Press, 1994.

Ambrose, Stephen E. *Eisenhower: Soldier and President*. New York: Simon and Schuster, 1991.

Anderson, Thornton. *Creating the Constitution: The Convention of 1787 and the First Congress*. University Park: Pennsylvania State University Press, 1993.

Baere, Judith A. *Women in American Law: The Struggle Toward Equality from the New Deal to the Present*. New York: Holmes and Meier, 1991.

Banning, Lance. *The Sacred Fire of Liberty: James Madison and the Founding of the Republic*. Ithaca, NY: Cornell University Press, 1995.

Belz, Herman Julius. *A New Birth of Freedom: The Republican Party and Freedmen's Rights, 1861–1866*. Westport, CT: Greenwood Press, 1976.

Benson, Paul R., Jr. *The Supreme Court and the Commerce Clause, 1937–1970*. New York: Dunellen, 1970.

Bentley, George R. *A History of the Freedmen's Bureau*. New York: Octagon Books, 1974.

Berman, William C. *The Politics of Civil Rights in the Truman Administration*. Columbus: Ohio State University Press, 1970.

Bernstein, Michael A. *The Great Depression: Delayed Recovery and Economic Change in America, 1929–1939*. New York: Cambridge University Press, 1988.

Bloom, Jack M. *Class, Race, and the Civil Rights Movement*. Bloomington: Indiana University Press, 1987.

Blum, John M. *Woodrow Wilson and the Politics of Morality*. Boston: Little, Brown, 1956.

Brinkley, Alan. *The End of Reform: New Deal Liberalism in Recession and War*. New York: Alfred A. Knopf, 1995.

Brown, Roger H. *Redeeming the Republic: Federalists, Taxation, and the Origins of the Constitution*. Baltimore: Johns Hopkins University Press, 1993.

Burk, Robert F. *The Eisenhower Administration and Black Civil Rights*. Knoxville: University of Tennessee Press, 1985.

Burnett, Edmund Cody. *The Continental Congress*. New York: W. W. Norton, 1941.

Campbell, Stanley W. *The Slave Catchers*. New York: W. W. Norton, 1972.

Chambers, William Nisbet. *Political Parties in a New Nation: The American Experience, 1776–1809*. New York: Oxford University Press, 1963.

Choper, Jessie H. *Judicial Review and the National Political Process*. Chicago: University of Chicago Press, 1980.

Clements, Kendrick A. *The Presidency of Woodrow Wilson*. Lawrence: University Press of Kansas, 1992.

Clinton, Lowry. *Marbury v. Madison and Judicial Review*. Lawrence: University Press of Kansas, 1989.

Coletta, Paolo E. *The Presidency of William Howard Taft*. Lawrence: University Press of Kansas, 1973.

Conkin, Paul K. *The New Deal*. 2nd ed. New York: Alfred A. Knopf, 1975.

Cooper, John M., Jr. *The Warrior and the Priest: Woodrow Wilson and Theodore Roosevelt*. Cambridge, MA: Belknap Press of Harvard University Press, 1983.

Cornell, Saul. *The Other Founders: Anti-Federalism and the Dissenting Tradition in America, 1788–1828*. Chapel Hill: University of North Carolina Press, 1999.

Cortner, R. C. *The Jones and Laughlin Case*. New York: Alfred A. Knopf, 1970.

Cunningham, Noble E. *The Jeffersonian Republicans: The Formation of Party Organization, 1789–1801*. Chapel Hill: University of North Carolina Press, 1965.

———. *Jefferson vs. Hamilton: Confrontations that Shaped a Nation*. Boston and New York: Bedford/St. Martin's, 2000.

Davis, Abraham, and Barbara Luck Graham. *The Supreme Court, Race, and Civil Rights*. Thousand Oaks, CA: Sage Publications, 1995.

Donald, David. *The Politics of Reconstruction, 1863–1867*. New York: Harper, 1962.

Dumond, Dwight L. *Antislavery: The Crusade for Freedom in America*. Ann Arbor: University of Michigan Press, 1961.

Duncan, Christopher M. *The Anti-Federalists and Early American Political Thought*. DeKalb: Northern Illinois University Press, 1995.

Elkins, Stanley, and Eric McKitrick. *The Age of Federalism*. New York: Oxford University Press, 1963.

Ellis, Richard E. *The Union at Risk: Jacksonian Democracy, States' Rights, and the Nullification Crisis*. New York: Oxford University Press, 1987.

Ely, John H. *Democracy and Distrust: A Theory of Judicial Review*. Cambridge, MA: Harvard University Press, 1980.

Epstein, Lee, and Joseph Kobylka. *The Supreme Court and Legal Change: Abortion and the Death Penalty*. Chapel Hill: University of North Carolina Press, 1992.

Faludi, Susan. *Backlash: The Undeclared War Against American Women*. New York: Anchor Books, 1992.

Fausold, Martin L. *The Presidency of Herbert C. Hoover*. Lawrence: University Press of Kansas, 1985.

Fehrenbacher, Don E. *Slavery, Law, and Politics: The Dred Scott Case in Historical Perspective*. New York: Oxford University Press, 1981.

Foner, Eric. *Reconstruction: America's Unfinished Revolution, 1863–1877*. New York: Harper and Row, 1988.

Freehling, William W. *Prelude to Civil War: The Nullification Movement in South Carolina, 1816–1832*. New York: Harper and Row, 1966.

Garraty, John A. *The Great Depression*. San Diego: Harcourt Brace Jovanovich, 1986.

———. *Woodrow Wilson*. Westport, CT: Greenwood Press, 1977.

Garrow, David J. *Bearing the Cross: Martin Luther King, Jr., and the Southern Christian Leadership Conference*. New York: William Morrow, 1986.

———. *Liberty and Sexuality: The Right to Privacy and the Making of Roe v. Wade*. New York: Macmillan, 1994.

Gorney, Cynthia. *Articles of Faith: A Frontline History of the Abortion Wars*. New York: Simon and Schuster, 1998.

Gould, Lewis L. *The Presidency of Theodore Roosevelt*. Lawrence: University Press of Kansas, 1991.

Graham, Hugh Davis. *The Civil Rights Era*. University Park: Pennsylvania State University Press, 1994.

Greenwalt, Kent. *Discrimination and Reverse Discrimination*. New York: Alfred A. Knopf, 1983.

Hair, William Ivy. *The Kingfish and His Realm: The Life and Times of Huey P. Long*. Baton Rouge: Louisiana State University Press, 1992.

Hamilton, Holman. *Prologue to Conflict: The Crisis and Compromise of 1850*. Lexington: University Press of Kentucky, 1964.

Hampton, Henry, and Steve Fayer. *Voices of Freedom: An Oral History of the Civil Rights Movement*. New York: Bantam Books, 1990.

Harbaugh, William H. *Power and Responsibility: The Life and Times of Theodore Roosevelt*. New York: Oxford University Press, 1975.

Heilbrun, Carolyn G. *The Education of a Woman: A Life of Gloria Steinem*. New York: Dial Press, 1995.

Hofstadter, Richard. *The Idea of a Party System: The Rise of Legitimate Opposition in the United States, 1780–1840*. Berkeley: University of California Press, 1969.

James, Joseph B. *The Framing of the Fourteenth Amendment*. Urbana: University of Illinois Press, 1956.

———. *The Ratification of the Fourteenth Amendment*. Macon, GA: Mercer University Press, 1984.

Klatch, Rebecca. *Women of the New Right*. Philadelphia: Temple University Press, 1987.

Kluger, Richard. *Simple Justice: The History of Brown v. Board of Education and Black America's Struggle for Equality*. New York: Alfred A. Knopf, 1975.

Kutler, Stanley I. *The Dred Scott Decision: Law or Politics*. Boston: Houghton Mifflin, 1967.

Leuchtenburg, William E. *The Supreme Court Reborn: The Constitutional Revolutions in the Age of Roosevelt*. New York: Oxford University Press, 1995.

Levinson, Sanford. *Constitutional Faith*. Princeton, NJ: Princeton University Press, 1988.

Levy, Leonard W. *Legacy of Suppression: Freedom of Speech and Press in Early American History*. Cambridge, MA: Harvard University Press, 1960.

Link, Arthur, and Robert L. McCormick. *Progressivism*. Arlington Heights, IL: Harlan Davidson, 1983.

Lofgren, Charles A. *The Plessy Case: A Legal-Historical Interpretation*. New York: Oxford University Press, 1987.

Luce, W. Ray. *Cohens v. Virginia (1821): The Supreme Court and States' Rights. A Reevaluation of Influences and Impacts*. New York: Garland, 1990.

Luker, Kristin. *Abortion and the Politics of Motherhood*. Berkeley: University of California Press, 1985.

Magrath, C. P. *Yazoo: Land and Politics in the New Republic. The Case of Fletcher v. Peck*. Providence, RI: Brown University Press, 1966.

Main, Jackson Turner. *The Anti-Federalists: Critics of the Constitution, 1781–1788*. Chapel Hill: University of North Carolina Press, 1961.

McDonald, Forrest. *Confederation and Constitution, 1781–1789*. Columbia: University of South Carolina Press, 1968.

McPherson, James M. *Battle Cry of Freedom: The Civil War Era*. New York: Oxford University Press, 1988.

Miller, William Lee. *Arguing About Slavery: The Great Battle in the United States Congress*. New York: Alfred A. Knopf, 1996.

Mills, Nicolaus. *The Great School Bus Controversy*. New York: Teachers College Press, Columbia University, 1973.

Morrison, Chaplin. *Democratic Politics and Sectionalism: The Wilmot Proviso Controversy*. Chapel Hill: University of North Carolina Press, 1967.

Neeley, Richard. *How Courts Govern America*. New Haven, CT: Yale University Press, 1981.

Nelson, William E. *The Fourteenth Amendment: From Political Principle to Judicial Doctrine*. Cambridge, MA: Harvard University Press, 1988.

Oates, Stephen B. *Let the Trumpet Sound: The Life of Martin Luther King, Jr.* New York: Harper and Row, 1982.

O'Neil, T. J. *Bakke and the Politics of Equality*. New York: Harper and Row, 1985.

Patterson, James T. *Congressional Conservatism and the New Deal*. Lexington: University Press of Kentucky, 1983.

Peterson, Merrill D. *Olive Branch and the Sword? The Compromise of 1833*. Baton Rouge: Louisiana State University Press, 1982.

Potter, David M. *The Impending Crisis, 1848–1861*. New York: Harper and Row, 1976.

Reid, John Phillip. *The Constitutional History of the American Revolution*. Madison: University of Wisconsin Press, 1995.

Rossum, Ralph A. *Reverse Discrimination: The Constitutional Debate*. New York: Marcel Dekker, 1980.

Rutland, Robert A. *The Ordeal of the Constitution: The Antifederalists and the Ratification Struggle of 1787–88*. Norman: University of Oklahoma Press, 1966.

Saloutos, Theodore M. *The American Farmer and the New Deal*. Ames: Iowa State University Press, 1982.

Savage, David G. *Turning Right: The Making of the Rehnquist Supreme Court*. New York: Wiley, 1992.

Schwartz, Bernard. *Decision: How the Supreme Court Decides Cases*. New York: Oxford University Press, 1996.

———. *Inside the Warren Court*. Garden City, NY: Doubleday, 1983.

———. *The NAACP's Legal Strategy Against Segregated Education*. Chapel Hill: University of North Carolina Press, 1987.

———. *Swann's Way: The School Busing Case and the Supreme Court*. New York: Oxford University Press, 1986.

Schwarz, Jordan A. *Interregnum of Despair: Hoover, Congress, and the Depression*. New York: Free Press, 1970.

Sefton, James. *Andrew Johnson and the Uses of Constitutional Power*. Boston: Little, Brown, 1980.

Shevory, Thomas C. *John Marshall's Law: Interpretation, Ideology, and Interest*. Westport, CT: Greenwood Press, 1994.

Silver, James W. *Mississippi: The Closed Society*. New York: Harcourt, Brace and World, 1966.

Spann, Giradeau A. *Race Against the Court: The Supreme Court and Minorities in Contemporary America*. New York: New York University Press, 1993.

Staggenborg, Suzanne. *The Pro-Choice Movement: Organization and Activism in the Abortion Conflict*. New York: Oxford University Press, 1991.

Stern, Mark. *Calculating Visions: Kennedy, Johnson, and Civil Rights*. New Brunswick, NJ: Rutgers University Press, 1992.

Terkel, Studs. *Hard Times: An Oral History of the Great Depression*. New York: Pantheon Books, 1970.

Thernstrom, Stephen. *America in Black and White*. New York: Simon and Schuster, 1997.

Tushnet, Mark V. *Making Civil Rights Law: Thurgood Marshall and the Supreme Court, 1936–1961*. New York: Oxford University Press, 1994.

Urofsky, Melvin I. *Louis D. Brandeis and the Progressive Tradition*. Boston: Little, Brown, 1981.

Warren, Donald. *Radio Priest: Charles Coughlin, the Father of Hate Radio*. New York: Free Press, 1996.

Wilkinson, J. Harvie. *From Brown to Bakke: The Supreme Court and School Integration, 1954–1978*. New York: Oxford University Press, 1979.

Wilson, Theodore B. *The Black Codes of the South*. Tuscaloosa: University of Alabama Press, 1965.

Index

About the Author

ROBERT P. SUTTON is Professor of History at Western Illinois University where he has taught since 1970. His fields of expertise include American legal history, communal utopias, and Illinois history. From 1990 to 1998, he was on the Board of Directors of the National Communal Studies Association, and in 1999 he was presented with that organization's "Donald E. Pitzer Distinguished Service Award."

320.473   Sutton, Robert P.
Sut
          Federalism.